Preface

The Indian Springs Treaty of 1821 ceded the lands which are now DeKalb County to the State of Georgia in 1821. After that, all of the ceded lands were surveyed and numbered according to Districts and Land Lots. The lands were then parcelled out by the State of Georgia via the fourth land lottery.

The original DeKalb County was created December 9, 1822 with land from Fayette, Gwinnett, and Henry Counties (mostly Henry). Many persons drew in the land in DeKalb County from the lottery. Some conveyances of land which are now located in DeKalb can be found in the Henry County courthouse records.

In 1853, the original DeKalb County was divided almost in half, with the western half becoming part of Fulton County.

Jeannette Holland Austin

DeKalb County, Georgia

Probate Records

Will Book A: 1841-1869
Will Book B: 1870-1889
Will Book C: 1890-1919

Sales and Appraisements, Book B: 1852-1858

Jeannette Holland Austin

HERITAGE BOOKS
2008

HERITAGE BOOKS
AN IMPRINT OF HERITAGE BOOKS, INC.

Books, CDs, and more—Worldwide

For our listing of thousands of titles see our website at
www.HeritageBooks.com

Published 2008 by
HERITAGE BOOKS, INC.
Publishing Division
100 Railroad Ave. #104
Westminster, Maryland 21157

Copyright © 1996 Jeannette Holland Austin

Other books by the author:
Alabama Bible Records
Virginia Bible Records
North Carolina -- South Carolina Bible Records
1860 Paulding County, Georgia, Census
The Georgians Database, Genealogical Notes
Fayette County, Georgia Probate Records: Volume II, Annual Returns, Inventories, Sales, Bonds, 1845-1897
Georgia Obituaries, 1905-1910
Jackson County, Georgia Tombstones
Georgia Bible Records, Supplement, 1772-1940
Georgia Obituaries, 1740-1935
Masters of the Low Country, A History of the Georgia Colony

All rights reserved. No part of this book may be reproduced or transmitted in any form or by any means, electronic or mechanical, including photocopying, recording or by any information storage and retrieval system without written permission from the author, except for the inclusion of brief quotations in a review.

International Standard Book Numbers
Paperbound: 978-1-58549-676-1
Clothbound: 978-0-7884-7119-3

DeKalb County, Georgia
Will Book A (1841-1869)

William Scarfe
Page 1-3

Daus: Elizabeth Foote, Sarah Hancock
Sons: Heirs of William Jr. (decd), heirs of Jesse (decd), Cherne?,
Ferdaman? Jemerson.
To:_____Humphries.
Wife: Elizabeth.
Exrs; W. and Joel F. Scarfe

/s/William Scarfe
Date: 3 Aug 1839
Wit: C. Murphey, S. Furmer and Thomas Atkins
Recorded: Mar 1841

John C. Parker
Page 4-5

Sons: David, James, Robert and Joseph Gresham Parker
Daus: Elizabeth Gresham Parker, Sarah Graham Parker, Mary Jane Graham Parker.
Wife: Mary

/s/John C. Parker
Date: 8 Jan 1842
Wit: Fanning Brown, James Nickels and Robert Harris
Recorded: 4 Jul 1842

Charles Lively
Page 6-9

Wife: Mary
Daus: Jane T. McGrady, Nancy Jones, Milly G. Gober, Polly M. Lovely, Lucinda Dobbs,
Elizabeth Ann, Judith Matilda

/s/Charles Lively
Date: 23 Sept 1840
Wit: Spencer P. Wright, Thomas C. Gober, Thomas T. Akin
Recorded: 4 Jan 1841

Isaac Awterry
Page 10

Wife: Armenty
Exr: James W. Stewart

/s/Isaac Awterry
Date: 6 Mar 1841
Wit: Joseph D. McEver, William Thomas, William McEver and William C. Williams, J. P.
Recorded: 16 ---- 1842

William Reeve
Page 11-12

Wife: Nuttey.
Children: George W., Thomas W., Nuttey Hughes, heirs of daughter, Elizabeth Naswoord,
decd, heirs of dau., Jane Mitchell, decd, heirs of dau., Lucy Mitchell, decd, heirs of dau., Nancy
Nusom, decd.

Sons and Exrs: Noah R., William D., Joshua S.

/s/William Reeve
Date: 4 Feb 1838

John Morris
Page 13-14

To: Children of my son, William F. Morris, decd, i.e.....John W., Polly, Ann, William L.

To: Oliver Hubbard, son of Elisha.

Children: Elizabeth Ann, wife of Thomas Turner, James B. Morris, Garrett T. Morris, John B.
Morris, George Washington Morris, Elijah Morris, Joseph Morris and Benjamin Morris.

Exrs: James B. and Garrett L. Morris (sons).

/s/John Morris
Date: 29 Apr 1842
Wit: Lachlin Johnson, John H. Jones and David Roper
Recorded: 11 Jan 1845

James M. C. Montgomery
Page 15-16

Eldest son: Tarleman Farlow Montgomery
Dau-in-law: Harriet M. Montgomery (wife of son, Rhadamanthus).
Son: James Floyd Montgomery
Exrs: James Floyd Montgomery (son), Joseph Fennel Monroe, Hugh Brown Troup.
Grandsons: James Samuel Franklin
To: Levin Hartson, Mrs. Betty Hartson - their eldest daughter, Sally Allen, wife of Beverly Allen.

/s/James C. Montgomery
Date: 24 Sept 1842
Wit: Elias Campbell, Nathaniel Sweat, Reuben Higgins

Samuel B. Hill
Page 17

Son: Benjamin B.
Grandson: Samuel B. Hill

/s/Samuel B. Hill
Date: 1 Mar 1838
Wit: Carter Mehaffey, William Couey and R. C. Anderson, J. P.

Daniel Ferguson
Page 18-19

Nuncupative LWT.
Wife: Elizabeth.
"To my girls."
Grandson: William Ferguson
Daus: Elizabeth, Nancy, Flora Jane.

/s/Daniel Ferguson
Date: 23 Mar 1842
Wit: John M. Smith, John B. Holbrooks, Daniel B. Wooten

Benjamin Plaster
Page 20-21

Wife: Sally
Son-in-law: John Williamson

Daus: Dorey Daniel, Elizabeth Gober, Piety Plaster
Sons: Edwin, Benjamin.
Granddau: Sally Williamson

/s/Benjamin Plaster
Date: 8 Nov 1836
Wit: Samuel Walker, Sarah and John N. Balinger

Robert Lemon
Page 22-23

Wife: Mary

Living children: James, Anna Pitts, Jane Davis, John, Robert, Mary Harris.
To: Martha Hamilton
To: Robert Robuck, son of dau., Elizabeth Robuck, decd.
To: Willis Robuck
To: Daniel Johnson
Exr: James Lemon (son)

/s/Robert Lemon
Date: 19 Dec 1843
Wit: John Johnson, Edwin Plaster and Patrick Porter
Recorded: Jan 1844

Robert Joyce, farmer
Page 24

Wife: Nancy
Children: Thomas A., James M., Sarah
Exrs: John Roberts of Rockingham Co., N. C. and John Raines.

/s/Robert Joyce
Date: 18 Oct 1844
Wit: Samuel House, Charles Horne and John E. Jefferies
Recorded: 15 Jan 1845

Robert W. Holcombe
Page 25-26

Wife: Sarah
Children: James Richison Holcombe, Elizabeth Ann, Mary Jane, Sarah Caroline, Susan.
/s/Robert W. Holcombe

Date: 5 Nov 1845
Wit: John Holcombe, Sr., Reuben B. Perkins and James Eschew
Recorded: 2 Mar 1846

Thomas Gober
Page 27-28

Children: John Akins, George W. Gober, J. H. Gober, Martha M. Akins, Thomas C. Gober
Exrs: Thomas C. and J. H. Gober
/s/Thomas Gober
Date: 6 May 1846
Wit: John Rainey, Jabez M. Lord and John M. Ridling, J. P.
Recorded: Dec 1846

Benjamin Chapman
Page 29-32

Wife: Theba
Children: Eli T., Benjamin F. (youngest), James H.
Exrs: Wife, Pheba and James H. Chapman, John Stephenson and son, Eli T. Chapman
/s/Benjamin Chapman
Date: 16 Jan 1841
Wit: James R. George, Andrew Boyd and John Veal
Recorded: 10 Mar 1841

William Anderson
Page 33
Wife: Sarah.
/s/William Anderson
Date: 8 Dec 1829
Wit: Vincent Sanford, Thomas W. Farmer and Francis H. Cone
Recorded: 19 Mar 1847

Thomas Grogan
Page 34-36

Children; Richard, Henry, Nelly House (wife of William House), Mary Baker, Sarah Austin (wife
of Green Austin), Lucy.
Granddau: Rachel Austin
Exrs: Henry and William Grogan (sons)

/s/Thomas Grogan
Date: 26 Apr 1847
Wit: James S. Hackett, Samuel Fee and Aubrey Martin
Recorded: Jul 1847

William Mitchell
Page 37-40

Sons: John Allison, Daniel Jackson, George Washington, Ava Marian, James Wesley, Leangle Hershel, William Jasper.

Sons of J. A. Doss: George W., Asa M., James M., William Jasper, L. H.

Daus: Rebecca, Winaford, Louisa, Synthia, Irene, Elizabeth, Dolly Ann and little son, Green Cleveland.

To: Green Cleveland
Exr: Daniel Jackson Mitchell (son)

/s/William Mitchell
Date: 21 Apr 1847
Wit: Nathan Center, William Miller and Kenley S. Morris
Recorded: Jan 1848

Joseph Stone
Page 41-42

Wife: Flora, extrx.
"All her children".

/s/Joseph Stone
Date: 16 Oct 1847
Wit: J. M. Smith, John E. Screvell and Wiley Suttles
Recorded: 10 Jan 1848

Henry Henry
Page 43-44

Children: Lucinda Little, etc.
Grandchildren: Mary Ann and Harvey Little.

/s/Henry Henry
Date: 5 Jun 1846
Wit: Edward Jones, Lodawick Tuggle, C. W. McGinnis and John Henry
Recorded: Jul 1848

Benjamin Sprayberry
Page 45-46

Wife: Amy.
"My children".
Exr: James W. McLain

/s/Benjamin Sprayberry
Date: 24 Jul 1848
Wit: Levi Betterton, Hardy Cornett, Robert C. Goff and Alfred S. Fowler
Recorded: 4 Sept 1848

James Morris
Page 47-50

Wife: Nancy, Extrx.

/s/James Morris
Date: 24 Feb 1848
Wit: George Lyon of DeKalb Co., Thomas J. Lyon and John H. Morris of DeKalb Co.
Recorded: Nov 1848

Sarah Waits
Page 51-53

Grandchildren: James W., Samuel P., William J., Madison, Franklin, Samantha, Clegan, Julian,
Elizabeth, Caroline, Mary, Abner -- all children of my son, Absalom Waits (Exr).

/s/Sarah Waits
Date: 21 Feb 1863
Wit: William C. Austin, William E. Sprewell and John W. Mitchell
Recorded: Mar 1849

William Mangum
Page 54-55

Wife: Mary, Extrx.

Son: William S.
"My children"

/s/William Mangum
Date: 12 Mar 1848
Wit: A. B. Knight and John L. Evans
Recorded: 2 Jul 1849

Mason Shumate
Page 56-63

To my children now living.
To: Children of Sarah Farrar, decd.

Children: Benjamin Franklin Shumate, Joseph D. Shumate, Lucinda Cone, Harriet Cory, Cynthia Stone, Elizabeth Adams, Elizabeth Glen

Grandchildren: Children of decd dau., Sarah Farrar....Catherine Curier, Laura Farrar, Abner Farrar, Sarah Farrar.

/s/Mason Shumate
Date: 29 Jun 1848
Wit: G. Akins, James A. Reeves, William H. Dabney

Codicil dated 9 Jun 1848. Wit: Joseph A. Reeves and William H. Dabney
Recorded: Jul 1849

David Franklin
Page 64-65

Wife: Tabitha
Five grandchildren
Exrs: Levi Betterton, Davis E. Grisham

/s/David Franklin
Date: 14 Aug 1838
Wit: J. D. McEver, J. P., John B. Austin and William J. Chandler
Recorded: Sept 1846

Solomon Goodwin, Sr.
Page 66-68

Children: Solomon, Jr., Harris, Starling, Sarah E., Catharine Cheshire (wife of Hezekiah Cheshire), Isabella A. Evans (wife of George W. Evans).

/s/Solomon Goodwin, Sr.
Date: 12 May 1847
Wit: Robert H. Smith, Francis Langford and Burch Jett
Recorded: Jan 1850

Mary Lemon
Page 69-71

Children: Ann Pitts, Mary Harris, Robert, children of decd son, John, Jane Davis, Martha Hamilton, children of decd son, James.

Grandchildren: Robert Roberts
Exr: Robert Lemon (son)

/s/Mary Lemon
Date: 3 Dec 1849
Wit: George D. Rice, Anderson Cook and William Garber.

Codicil dated Dec 1840, Recorded 25 Jan 1850 (same witnesses)

Henry G. Collier
Page 72-73

Wife and children.

Exrs: William Ezzard, John Collier, friends and relatives.

/s/Henry G. Collier
Date: 23 Jan 1850
Wit: Reuben Cone, Samuel Walker and Edwin Payne
Recorded: Mar 1850

Philip McDaniel of Henry Co.
Page 74

Children: Ira O., Henry L., Philip E., Mary A. Mitchel, Nancy B. Adamson, Martha J. Cheek, Caroline A. McDaniel, Sarah J. Key.

Exrs: Ira O. and Henry McDaniel (sons)

/s/Philip McDaniel
Date: 28 Dec 1849
Wit: William Dodson, William H. Gilbert and Charles A. McDaniel
Recorded: Mar 1850

John Reid
Page 76-80

Children: Permelia A. Ford, wife of Zachariah Ford, William J., John Marion, Elizabeth J., Newton M., Mary A., Arminda, Eleanor A. and Zachariah.

Wife: Mary A., Extrx, and son, William J. Reid, and friend, James R. George

/s/John Reid
Date: 26 Dec 1849
Wit: William Goldsberg, W. T. Meador and Nelson Anderson
Recorded: May 1850

Jennings Hulsey
Page 81-87

Wife: Dicy
Three minor children: Susan A., M. C., Sarah E.
Other children: Elizabeth Hambrick, widow of John Hambrick, decd, of Alabama and her children.
Sons: William M., Eli, Aaron G.
Daus: Anna K. Swan and her children (wife of John Swan), Susan A. and her children, Sarah E. and her children.
Son: Jenning M. C. Jennings
Grandchildren: Elizabeth Rebecca, Kizza and Caroline Barr
Exrs: Eli J. and Aaron G. Hulsey.

/s/Jennings Hulsey
Date: 4 Feb 1847
Wit: A. F. Stephenson, John Stephenson, J. M. Philips

Codicil dated 26 Mar 1847. Recorded: Jan 1857 (same witnesses)

Joseph S. Knox
Page 88-90

-Wife: Frances J.
Only child: Allen
Exr and trustee: friend, Moses W. Formwalt

/s/Joseph S. Knox
Date: 1 Feb 1851
Wit: Marcus A. Bell, Joseph J. Martin, Elizabeth Formwalt and M. W. Formwalt
Recorded: Mar 1851

Littleton Haws
Page 91-92

Sons: Layton W., William L.

/s/Littleton Haws
Date: 22 Jul 1850
Wit: John Boyd and Mural Magee
Recorded: May 1851

Isaac Towers
Page 93-96

Children: Frances N. Towers, Parthenia A. Williams (wife of Hiram D. Williams), Martha A. Anderson (wife of Harvey Anderson).

8 Grandchildren: Children of decd dau., Lavinia F. Hairston -- Albert M., Matilda C., Arminda A., William R., Lucinda, Martha A. E., Toliver Little and Amanda C. Hairston

Wife: Elizabeth
Son-in-law: Hiram D. Williams
/s/Isaac Towers
Date: 20 May 1851
Wit: C. Murphy, L. S. Morgan and G. Akins
Recorded: 13 Jun 1851

Garland Dabney
Page 97-98

Granddau: Mary M. Humphries, wife of Isaac Humphries, wife of Isaac, only child of my decd
dau., Ann H. Hays, wife of John.

Children: Anderson B., William G., Narcissa J. Goody (wife of William G. Goody), Hilda M. Cochran (wife of William Cochran).
Exrs: Anderson B. Dabney (son) and friends, James W. Kirkpatrick and John B. Adams

/s/Garland Dabney
Date: 22 Apr 1851
Wit: James W. Kirkpatrick, John B. Johns, D. C. Jackson and John C. Evins
Recorded: Jul 1851

William Terrell
Page 99-102

To: Seleta Hinson, wife of James Hinson of Alabama
To: Mary Ford, wife of my grandson, William Ford.
Grandson: Colman Ford.
Friend: William Ezzard, in trust for grandson, William Terrell, alias William Terrell Ford.
Exr: Grandson, Colman Ford.

/s/William Terrell
Date: 19 Feb 1851
Wit: William Carlisle, James Head and Robert Jones
Recorded: Jul 1851

Francis Griffin
Page 103

Heirs: James Yancy, Robert Yancy, Elizabeth Hargers, Stella Cavins, Hezekiah Griffin, Zepheniah Griffin.
Wife: Susana.

/s/Francis Griffin
Date: 10 Mar 1851
Wit: Martha Defoor, Killis Brown and Leroy Crawford
Recorded: Jul 1851

John Armstrong
Page 104-105

Son: Jonathan

/s/John Armstrong
Date: 8 Jul 1851
Wit: J. M. Smith, William Bryant and Alfred G. Suttles
Recorded: Sept 1851

Bartholomew Still
Page 105-108

"My children".

/s/Bartholomew Still
Date: 9 May 1851
Wit: William Goldberry, John M. Born and Edmond J. Bailey
Recorded: Nov 1851

William Annesley of Botetourt Co., Virginia
Page 109-111

Mother: Sarah Annesley
To: John Reforcey, John Shirkey, Charles Beale, John Snider, John Smith, Clerk, James Davis of Belfast, solicitor, John Charles White, Clerk, and John Wade of Belfast.

/s/William Annesley
Date: 6 Nov 1838
Recorded: Nov 1851

Thomas Austin
Page 112

Wife: Susan
Five children: John C., Nancy Atwood, William A., Mary Atkins, Nathaniel R. and their children.
Exrs: Wife, Susan, and Joel Adkins.

/s/Thomas Austin
Date: 11 Mar 1851
Wit: Joseph Walker, William R. Ayers and Daniel J. Ayers
Recorded: Feb 1852

Richard C. Todd
Page 113

Wife: Martha
Children: James H., Richard F., John C., Elizabeth T. Armsted.

/s/Richard C. Todd
Date: Nov 1851
Wit: John W. Medlock and H. Cheshire
Recorded: Mar 1852

Patrick Connally
Page 114

Children: Mary Ann Daughterty.

Exrs: Geneva Doonan, Daniel McShaffeny.

/s/Patrick Connally
Date: 27 May 1851
Wit: John Lynch, Joseph Gatens and Patrick Lynch
Recorded: Mar 1852

James Crowley
Page 115-117

Wife: Darcus.
Children: Washington (youngest), Josiah, Nancy, Allen, Sealey, James, Benjamin, Seaborn, Susan and Harris

/s/James Crowley
Date: 9 Feb 1828
Recorded: Jun 1852

James W. Reeves
Page 118-121

Wife: Sarah
Daus: Henrietta Childress (decd), Gabriel Cone (wife of John H. Cone), Nuty L. Donalson (wife of William J. Donalson), Mahala J.

Sons: Ausbery W., Strawberry R., William J. C., James M.
To: Children of Polly M. Wilson, dau., wife of L. S. Wilson

Exrs: Wife, Salley, and friend, John Y. Flowers, and brother-in-law, William J. Donalson.

/s/James W. Reeves
Date: 29 Apr 1853

Wit: E. Worthington, Joseph Steward, Spencer T. Wright, John L. Evans, George W. Humphries and William C. Wilson
Recorded: Jun 1853

Benjamin Simons Anderson of Macon Co., Ga.
Page 122-123

Wife: Susan Harper Anderson, Extrx.
/s/Benjamin Simons Anderson
Date: 15 Feb 1851
Wit: J. B. Clayton and Joseph M. Scott
Recorded: 10 Jun 1853

Thomas Thweatt
Page 124-125

Wife: Catharine A.
Children: John T. Thweatt, Susan F. Birdsong, Mary E. Clarke, Sarah W. Mitchell
Exrs: Wife and son, Uriah J. Thweatt

/s/Thomas Thweatt
Date: 22 Jun 1852
Wit: J. D. Wells, R. S. Baker and W. H. Jones
Recorded: Aug 1853

Martha Ogilly of Atlanta, Ga.
Page 126-129

To be buried in Town of Fayetteville, Ga.
Grandchildren: Exa Marie Beall, Margaret Ann H. Meadows.
Heirs: Judith Ann Haynes (daughter) and children; children of decd son, Frank Ogilly, William E. Ogilly, Margaret Ann Holland.

Mother: Ann Ogilly
Exrs: Philip J. Echols and Samuel B. Hoyt of Atlanta

/s/Martha Ogilly
Date: 7 Jun 1853
Wit: B. F. Bonner, W. H. Roberts and Ira O. McDaniel
Recorded: Sept 1853

John N. Bellinger
Page 130-133

Wife: Sarah Ann
Children: Laura Jane, Martha Florence, James Knox Polk, John Meredith Smith, William Clinton and Nelson Tallulah Bellinger.

Bro: Joseph T. Bellinger, Exr, and wife.

/s/John N. Bellinger
Date: 24 Jun 1853
Wit: Andrew J. Rea, Richard Rea and J. M. Smith
Recorded: Sept 1853

William J. Kilpatrick
Page 134-135

Wife: Mary Jane.
Exr: friend, Rozin Lyon
/s/William J. Kilpatrick
Date: 14 Aug 1853
Wit: William H. Steavins, Thomas Bell, William Ireland and N. L. Angers, J. P.
Recorded: Sept 1853

John McDonald
Page 134-135

5 youngest children: Martha Jane, Henry J., Sary Elizabeth, William Jackson, Nancy Elsnetta.
Dau: Mary Ann Magee.
Exr: son, Premason McDonald

/s/John McDonald
Date: 1 Feb 1853
Wit: Marat Megee, John S. Wilson, Alex. Cochran
Recorded: Sept 1853

Francis Gideonof of Atlanta, Ga.
Page 138-140

To: Pres. and Director of American Colonization Society, his slaves, to send them to Liberia, Africa.
Children: Louisiana O. Gartree..
Exrs: Nathan Holbrook, Albon Chase of Athens.

/s/Francis Gideon
Date: 25 Jun 1853
Wit: J. A. Hazden, Rezin Lyon and B. H. Overby
Recorded: Sept 1853

James H. Kirkpatrick
Page 141-145

Wife: Ann
Grandchildren: Mary Ann Shaw, Margaret Ann Hoyle
Children: Mrs. Jane Morgan, Hugh P., Thomas M., John L., William N., and James W. Kirkpatrick
To: Children of Joseph Morgan
To: James H., son of James W. Kirkpatrick
To: Thomas S., son of James W. Wallis
To: son of Thomas M. Kirkpatrick

Exrs: James W. Kirkpatrick, Levi Willard and James M. Calhoun

/s/James H. Kirkpatrick
Date: 19 Feb 1851
Wit: William Tedder and Levi Willard
Recorded: 18 Nov 1853

Margaret Davis
Page 146-147

Grandchildren: John Wilson Davis, Sarah Jane Davis, Jonathan D. Smith, Leroy Davis, Eli A. Davis
Exr: Eli A. Davis

/s/Margaret Davis
Date: 29 May 1853
Wut: G. Johnson, Alfred S. Fowler and C. W. McGinnis
Recorded: 29 Nov 1853

James Russell
Page 148-149

Wife: Susannah, and friend, Azariah Mims, Exrs.

/s/James Russell
Date: 23 May 1853
Wit: John T. Smith, John Lee and Samuel T. Lee
Recorded: 3 Aug 1853

Nancy Camron
Page 150-151

Children : Elvira Ann Barrett - land in Lexington, S. C.
Exr: William Ezzard

/s/Nancy Camron
Date: 24 Jun 1853
Wit: Francis Lindsey, N. R. Bloodworth and J. M. Holley
Recorded: Feb 1854

Joel Fowler
Page 152-155

Wife: Sarah of 40 years.
Children: Drury, Thomas, Eliza, William J., Joel M., Alfred M.
Grandchildren: William and Joel, children of son, John, decd.
Grand daus: Lorena S. and Sarah M., in right of my daughter, Sarah A. (decd), wife of William F.
Connelly.
Grandchildren: Elizabeth Emma, Gapen?, and Joel, in right of my dau., Charlotte (decd),
wife of Solomon Johnson.

Daus: Mary A., wife of David Boring, and Amana M., wife of George Franks.
Son: Alfred M. made gdn of property of three grandchildren, minor heirs of my dau., Sarah A.

Son, Hilliard J., gdn of property of grandchildren, minor heirs of my dau., Permelia.

Five children.
Exrs: sons, Hilliard J. and Alfred M. Fowler.
/s/Joel Fowler
Date: 22 Dec 1853
Wits: W. L. Williams, Nathan Lumer and Lachlin Johnson
Recorded: 6 Feb 1854

John Blake
Page 156

Wife: Mary

Nephew: William Palmer

To: John D. Stell, James Castleberry, Mary Stewart, Shastley Gilmer, my sisters (after the death of my wife)

To: John Carroll and at his death to Charles J. Carroll, son of James M., the grandson of Charles Railey.

To: John Carroll and Rhoda Carroll.

To: Louisiana Mathew and Jane Burns, orphans raised by me from a small size.

Children: Thomas, William, Allen and Henry W. Blake

Exrs: John Carroll, Allen and Henry W. Blake

/s/John Blake
Date: 1 Feb 1854
Wit: S. P. Wright, James S. Elliott and John Y. Flowers
Recorded: Jul 1854

Archibald Johnson
Page 157-161

Wife: Elizabeth

Children: Rachel, wife of James McCurdy, Eleanor, wife of John Gordon, Mary, Ruth, Daniel, John, Angus Alexander and Archibald.

Grandson: Archibald McCurdy, the son of James McCurdy

/s/Archibald Johnson
Date: 3 Dec 1831
Wit: Lachlin Johnson, Jonathan Lather and John Kile
Recorded: 1854

William Johnston
Page 162-165

Wife: Naomi
Afflicted dau., Dority Andrews Johnston (wife to be Gdn)

Children: Nancy Elliott Evins wife of William H. C. Evins, Jackson F. Johnston and Washington P. Johnston
Exrs: sons, Jackson F. and Washington P. Johnston
/s/William Johnston
Date: 6 Jun 1855

Wit: James S. Elliott, John Adams, C. Murphey
Recorded: Jul 1855

Merrill Collier
Page 166-168

Children: Martha W. Loky, Malinda Collier, Charlotte Hulsey, Jane B. Lofton, Margaret E. Brantley, Nancy W. Cook

Grandchildren: William C. and John Collier, sons of son, Henry G. Collier (decd)

Wife: Elizabeth

Exrs: wife, and William Ezzard

/s/Merrill Collier
Date: 29 Nov 1854
Wit: Lachlin Johnson, D. S. M. Boring and Nathan Lamar
Recorded: Jul 1855

Joseph Wooton
Page 169-171

Wife: Avis
Sister: Nancy Bishop's children
Exrs: Wife and friend, Samuel Potts

/s/Joseph Wooton
Date: 27 Oct 1854
Wit: Kendly N. Morris, James B. Robertson, Nathan Center and Asa W. Howard
Recorded: 25 Oct 1855

Augustus E. Ellis of Abbeville, South Carolina
Page 172-173

Wife: Polly Ann
Children: John Calvin, James Lucian, Mahala, Elizabeth, Permelia, Paratine
Exrs: Wife, and friend, John McElroy

/s/Augustus E. Ellis
Date: 8 Oct 1855
Wits: W. P. Ellis and R. M. Ellis
Recorded: 5 Nov 1855

Kezia Boyd
Page 174-175

Children: Margaret, Nancy, Hugh M.
Exr: son, Hugh M. Boyd

/s/Kezia Boyd
Date: 17 Mar 1856
Wit: Thomas L. Thomas, James Davis.
Recorded: 8 Jun 1856

Luke Johnson
Page 176-177

Children: Mary Amanda Mason, Rebecca M. Phillips
Exrs: wife, Ava Ann, and son, George W.

/s/Luke Johnson
Date: 29 Jun 1856
Wit: Jacob Chupp, Daniel R. Chupp, Michael Marbut and David Chupp
Recorded: 22 Jul 1856

Charles Rainey
Page 178-180

Wife: Rebecca
Grandchildren: Charles J. and Mary M. Carroll
Bro: Bennett Rainey
Exrs: friends, John Jett, Alexander Chesnut and Spencer P. Wright

/s/Charles Rainey
Date: 19 Sept 1854
Wit: James Elliott, Bennett Rainey and John Y. Flowers
Recorded: Apr 1857

J. J. P. White
Page 181-182

Wife: Sarah.
Four children.
Exrs: Stephen T. Beggers and John White (father)

/s/J. J. P. White
Date: 27 Jul 1857
Wit: Samuel McWilliams, Malachi S. Carter and William C. White
Recorded: Sept 1857

Richard H. Eskins
Page 183-185

To: Henry Gentry who lives with me.
Wife: Jinney
My children.
Exrs: Thomas J. Eskins, William R. Brandon and Jincy Eskew

/s/Richard H. Eskins
Date: 11 Aug 1857
Wit: John W. Fowler, W. Moseley and Sarah J. Anderson
Recorded: May 1858

James Brown
Page 186-187

Wife: Lydia
Children: William D., James W. and Jackson Brown, Harriet McWilliams, wife of Alexander McWilliams, Jane Wilkins, wife of Thomas Wilkins

/s/James Brown
Date: 10 Mar 1855
Wit: James C. Thompson, Amherst W. Stone and James M. Calhoun
Recorded: Jun 1858

Moses Liddell of Gwinnett Co.
Page 188-193

Wife: Mary

Children: Freeman Hardy (oldest), Elizabeth Haney (decd), Moses Franklin, Harriet Susan
(Mrs. Shotwell), Newton Stiles (son), Andrew Rutherford (son), Sarah Ann Demaras (Mrs. Garmany), Mary Isabella Jane, Nancy Johnston, Laura Amanda.

Children of decd dau., Elizabeth Haney, viz.....James Freeman, Moses Liddell, Mary Ann and Gertrude Elizabeth Haney.

Exrs: wife, Mary, and sons, Moses Franklin and Newton Stiles Liddell

/s/Moses Liddell
Date: 5 Jul 1855
Wit: Grant Taylor, Ira Vaughan and James H. Thompson
Recorded: 30 Jun 1858

Edward Jones
Page 194-195

Children: Elizabeth Brown, Eliza Stokes, Martin, Robert, John, Richard W.
To: Milly Berry and her children.
Exr: Robert Jones

/s/Edward Jones
Date: 1852
Wit: John Hawkins, W. W. Davis, C. W. McGinnis and Benjamin Crowley
Recorded: Aug 1858

William Johnson
Page 196-198

Wife: Jane

Children: Polly Meador, Sarah Ford, Lucretia Goldsmith
Grandchildren: William, Thomas and George W. Johnson, John L. Hamilton.
Exrs: Grandsons, Thomas Johnson and Benjamin F. Veal.

/s/William Johnson
Date: 7 Aug 1858
Wit: W. W. Diamond, James Veal, George K. Hamilton and W. W. Veal
Recorded: 22 Oct 1858

Thomas H. Chivers
Page 199-201

Wife: Harriet.
First wife: Frandces E. Chivers and her dau., Frances
Children: Emma, Isodore, Thomas Holly and Fannie Isabelle
Exr: bro., Joel R. Chivers

/s/Thomas H. Chivers
Date: 18 Dec 1858
Wit: P. F. Hoyle, G. E. Wilson, T. R. Hoyle and John N. Pate
Recorded: 7 Feb 1859

James H. Ragan
Page 202-203

Sister: Jane, wife of George F. Smith of Walton Co.
Sister: Sarah H., wife of Stephen S. Smith of Walton Co.
Nephew: William England
Bro: Josiah H. Ragan, Exr.

/s/James H. Ragan
Date: 14 Jul 1859
Wit: A. McWilliams, Edward Jones, Augustus L. Pitts and Robert W. Cobbs
Recorded: 1 Aug 1859

Larkin W. Mitchell
Page 204-205

Wife: Louisa E., Extrx.

/s/Larkin W. Mitchell
Date: 5 Aug 1859
Wit: Ezekiel Reeves, John Cochran and M. C. Maddox
Recorded: 7 Nov 1859

Mary Blake
Page 206-207

To be buried beside my husband, John B. Blake

Children: Suzaney Mathes, wife of George Mathews and her children;
Thomas Blake,
Sisero Blake, Dashey Blake and Jane Bunnes.

Exr: William Misbet

/s/Mary Blake
Date: 4 Nov 1859

Wit: Spencer P. Wright, Greenville Henderson and William J. Palmer
Recorded: 7 May 1860

Thomas F. Hall
Page 208

Wife: Nancy B., and friend, Daniel McNeill, Exrs.
Children mentioned.

/s/Thomas F. Hall
Wit: William Ezzard, David U. Sheppard and William W. Wells
Recorded: 13 Jul 1860

Benjamin Woodson
Page 209-212

Wife: Mary, Extrx.
Son: William
Five daus.

/s/Benjamin Woodson
Date: 9 Sept 1860
Wit: Moses Richardson, James McLain and E. A. Davis
Recorded: 9 Oct 1860

John McCullock
Page 213-216

Daus: Sophiah, Margaret; Susan Davis, wife of Eli Davis.
Sons: David H., James W.
Other children.
Exr: son, James W. McCullock

/s/John McCullock
Date: 4 Feb 1860
Wit: C. Murphey, R. M. Brown and T. B. George
Recorded: Jun 1861

Isaiah P. Parker
Page 217-219

Dau: Martha Beauchamp
Niece of present wife (living with me): Nancy A. Parker
To: Littleton G. Jackson, son of William J. Thomas J. Dean, my friend, to be Gdn

Wife: Celia
Exr: Thomas J. Dean

/s/Isaiah P. Parker
Date: 13 Oct 1859
Wit: Samuel F. Alexander, John L. Hamilton, George K. Hamilton and John W. Scruggs
Recorded: 11 May 1861

James S. Elliott
Page 220-223

Wife: Nancy

Sons: James Monroe, Franklin Pierce, Andrew Adell, Cicero C., John C., William P., Joseph E.
Daus: Parthenia Graves, Mary C. Graves, Sarah A. Montgomery, Maraway Braswell

Exrs: wife and friend, John Y. Flowers

/s/James S. Elliott
Date: 14 Sept 1860
Wit: Bennett Rainey, Richard M.Wilson and G. N. Flowers
Recorded: 1 Jul 1861

Lachlin Johnson
Page 224-227

Daus: Elizabeth Ann Kiddoo and children; Nancy P. Farrar and children; Catharine M. Winn; Jane
E. L. Robinson, wife of James; Sarah Ann W. Fendall; Margaret M. P. Lichtinstadt and
children, wife of W. L.

Son: David J. Johnson
Granddau: Mary Richie and children
Exrs: son, James A. W. Johnson and grandson, Lachlin J. Winn

/s/Lachlin Johnson
Date: 29 Nov 1860
Wit: Reuben Nash, John N. Tate, James N. Tate and Arabella M. Nash
Recorded: 5 Aug 1861

James P. George
Page 228-230

Children: Margaret Hudson, Ann, Sarah Born, John R. (four oldest), James R., Vashti P., William H., Mercer M., Thomas T.
Exrs: wife, Elizabeth and son, James R. George

/s/James P. George
Date: 31 Mar 1862
Wit: W. H. Brassell, John M. Born, Jr. and John N. Swift
Recorded: May 1862

Eli W. Hoyle
Page 231-233

To: Eli Hoyle, son of George S.; Eli Hoyle Nesbit, son of John W.

Bros: T. R., A. H.
Sis: Elizabeth H. Nesbit, wife of John W.

/s/Eli W. Hogle
Date: 27 May 1861
Wit: John W. Scruggs, T. M. Allen and G. P. Bradley
Recorded: Aug 1862

James Evans
Page 234-236

Wife: Dicy
Sons: James F., Reuben D., John F., William A.
Dau: Mary J.
Exr: son, Reuben D. Evans

/s/James Evans
Date: 17 Oct 1862
Wit: Ansel Willingham, William S. Johnson, Abraham Martin and William W. Mitchell
Recorded: Dec 1862

A. J. H. Pool of Chatham Co., Ga., now DeKalb Co.
Page 237-238

Wife: J.M.
Bro: Wesley H. Pool, Exr.
To: Sarah M. McGrady, M. C. Lively, W. T. Canuth's children.

/s/A. J. H. Pool
Date: 2 Apr 1862
Wit: John Y. Flowers, Edmund T. Harris, John B. Baxter, James A. Flowers, W. A. C. Pool, James A. and John W. Miller, C. W. Wallis, James S. Jett and J. M. Loyd
Recorded: Dec 1862

Solomon Goodwin
Page 239

Dau: Sarah Elizabeth S. Rea
Wife: Mary
Son: William T., Exr.

/s/Solomon Goodwin
Wit: A. A. McKee, Harris Goodwin and Richard Rea
Recorded: Mar 1863

Nathan Turner
Page 240-243

"If I am killed in service of my country....."

Wife: Arminda and her children.

Daus: Frances Ann, Sarah Eliza (youngest)

Exrs: Bro., Edward F. Turner and James L. Philips

/s/Nathan Turner
Date: 14 Mar 1862
Wit: J. C. Avary, John J. Whitlow and W. L. Williams
Recorded: Mar 1863

Spencer P. Wright
Page 244-246

Wife: Elizabeth L.
Sons: Zaceny T., James M.
Daus: Mary J.
Exrs: James Carroll, Burdine Rainey and Samuel McWilliams

/s/Spencer P. Wright
Date: 26 Jan 1863
Wit: John Y. Flowers, T. W. Miller, James F. Akins, M. A. Henderson and
Greenville Henderson
Recorded: Apr 1863

Judah McLindon
Page 247-253

Grandchildren: Children of Clark McLindon, son.
Grandsons: George Crockett, Andrew J. Crockett, children of decd,
daus., Lucinda Crockett and
Melissa Crockett, Joel McLendon, decd son's children.
Grandsons: Clark and George Crockett
Granddau: Meriam Davis, wife of Thomas J. Davis
Son-in-law: James W. Crockett, exr.
/s/Judah McLindon
Date: 9 May 1857
Wit: James W. Crockett, Amey W. Watts, Harriet E. McNair
Codicil dated Henry Co., Ga. dated 22 Sept 1859 states that Robert P.
Crockett (son of Lucinda), his portion to go to his wife, Mary Ann. (page 250-254)
Recorded: 28 Jan 1863

James H. Young
Page 254

Dau: Margaret S.
Sons: James C., G. T.
/s/James H. Young
Date: 7 Apr 1862
Wit: William T. Cobb, J. H. Wiggins, R. McWilliams
Recorded: Apr 1863

Jesse Jordan
Page 255-257

Son: William I. or J.
To: Sarah A. C. Hollingsworth, wife of Robert; Solomon E. Jordan; Mary
Ann E. Pritchard, wife of Silas; Nancy A. Hannada, wife of N. A.,; Sarah
Ann Crockett, wife of Joel J.

To: Elijah B. Jordan's children (decd), said decd being married 2nd time,
and Sarah Ann Crockett receiving no part of her father's estate in
Florida.
Son-in-law: Robert Hollingsworth, Exr.

/s/ Jesse Jordan
Date: 14 Jan 1860
Wit: James W. Crockett, Alfred S. Fowler and Paschal H. Hightower
Recorded: 23 Sept 1863
John Collier
Page 258-259

Wife and minor children.

Children: George W., Nancy, Mary Ann Turner, William F., J. E. J., Joseph M., Sarah Elizabeth Spain, Martha F. Cox, Lucinda Caroline, James J. W., B. F. and G. W.

Exrs: Wife and son, Joseph H. Collier

/s/ John Collier
Date: 6 Sept 1861
Wit: James M. Huey, John Parker and R. McWilliams
Recorded: 1 Jan 1864

John W. Crockett
Page 260-262

To be buried at Wesley Chapel Cemetery beside wife, Mary.

Daus: Marietta Green, Nancy Walker, Margaret P. Hightower and Lucinda Hartsfield

Sons: Joel J., William, Wilks W., James P.

Heirs of dau., Lucinda Hartsfield, viz: James, Melissa, Martha.
Exrs: sons, Joel and J. P. Crockett

/s/ John W. Crockett
Date: 31 May 1864
Wit: James C. Avary, Edward Watts, John Clark and John J. Harper
Recorded: 11 Jul 1864

James Paden
Page 263-266

Wife: Lettice

Children: John, Jane, Thomas N., Elizabeth (wife of W. B. Chandler), Lettice Caroline
(wife of James Strange), James.

-30-

To: William Ezzard and Thomas N. Paden, int rust.

Exrs: William Ezzard and son, Thomas M. Paden

/s/James Paden
Date: 29 Nov 1859
Wit: James C. Powers, Richard Gittens, Andrew Rodgers and Andrew McCrary
Recorded: 27 Dec 1864

William Veal
Page 267

Three minor children: Asa, Millard, Larrice Ann

Dau: Sarah O.

Son: Francis.

To: William J. Veal, J. M. Hambrick, G. W. Miner
Exr: friend, James M. Smith

/s/William Veal
Date: 1 Oct 1862
Wit: Leander Biffle, William Gibson, Albert M. Hairston and Alfred S. Fowler
Recorded: 2 Jan 1865

Leonard Sims
Page 270-271

Wife: Elizabeth Mirandon, Extrx.
Children: Marietta, Julius Fayette, John Lawrence, Orpha Jane, Joseph, Trull Marth, Alice, Sallie.

/s/Leonard Sims
Date: 20 Aug 1863
Wit: E. Burnham, G. M. Hendon and J. T. Lambert
Recorded: 2 Jan 1865

Patrick Warick of Pike Co., Ga.
Page 272-273

Wife: Elizabeth
Our children

/s/Patrick Warick
Date: 5 Aug 1864
Wit: H. Green, D. T. White and William R. Nash
Recorded: Jun 1865

James A. Robertson of Fulton Co.
Page 274-275

Wife: Harriett
Children.
Exr: father, James B. Robertson

/s/James A. Robertson
Date: 12 Dec 1862
Wit: N. L. Anger, M. A. Huson and John Collier
Proved: 20 Dec 1865

Gideon Morris
Page 276-277

Wife: Mary
Children: Joseph G., Mary J., Laura A., Newton S.
Exr: Joel E. Morris of Cobb Co.

/s/Gideon Morris
Date: 17 Aug 1863
Wit: J. W. Buchanon, S. M. Harmn and James T. M. Dade
Recorded: 1 Jan 1866

Eli T. Chapman
Page 278

Wife: Narcissa, Extrx. with William F. Chapman
My children

/s/Eli T. Chapman
Date: 14 Sept 1863
Wit: William L. Born, Thomas L. and John N. Swift
Recorded: 19 Feb 1866

George W. Bagley
Page 279-280

Wife: Winney, Extrx.

/s/George W. Bagley
Date: 12 Sept 1863
Wit: W. R. Venable, R. B. Hicks and Jethro W. Manning
Recorded: 4 Jun 1866

Andrew Gordon
Page 281-282

Wife: Martha
My youngest children
Exr: E. Tilly

/s/Andrew Gordon
Date: 9 Aug 1863
Wit: James Gardner, M. J. Trimble and John Y. Flowers
Recorded: Apr 1866

Stephen Martin
Page 283-284

Wife of 24 years: Sarah
Children: Mary J., Martha, Benjamin S., Neomy, Sopha C., Margaret, Nancy T., William S., Semanthey
Exr: James Polk
/s/Stephen Martin
Date: 21 Mar 1866
Wit: William M. Cox, Nicholas A. Moss and James H. Polk
Recorded: Oct 1866

Avis Potts, wife of Samuel Potts
Page 285-287

Property inherited from decd husband, Joseph Wooten, to his heirs: Children of Nancy Bishop, his sister; Susan Spinks, wife of John, and daughter of Nancy Bishop; Joshua, J. James and Luke Bishop (sons of Nancy); John T., Elijah and Edmond Bishop (sons of Nancy); Avis Braswell, wife f William H. and dau. of Nancy Bishop; Margaret, now wife of ed New and dau. of Nancy Bishop.
Exr: Husband, Samuel Potts

/s/ Avis Potts
Date: 4 Mar 1859
Wit: C. Murphy, N. M. Reid and A. H. Howard
Recorded: 7 Jan 1867

John McWilliams
Page 288-290

Sons: John G., Alexander, Robert, Samuel, David
Dau: Mary N. Brown, wife of William D.
To: Jackson G. Brown, husband of dau., Susan; James W. Brown, husband of dau., Martha; Francis L. Wright, husband of dau., Nancy.
Exrs: sons, John G., Robert

/s/John McWilliams
Wit: J. E. George and C. Murphey
Recorded: Feb 1867

William Crowell
Page 291-292

To: Mrs. Ann Lacuent who attended to me during my afflictions
Exr: H. H. Veal

/s/William Crowell
Date: 6 Oct 1861
Wit: J. L. Hamilton, Samuel F. Alexander, James H. Weed, George K. Hamilton and
Berry Hollingsworth
Recorded: 23 Apr 1866

Elizabeth Gresham
Page 293-294

Bro: Robert G. Parker, Exr.
Sis: Mary Jane Parker and her dau., Margaret Ann

/s/Elizabeth Gresham
Date: 4 Sept 1868
Wit: R. A. Alston, J. C. Avary and A. C. Hamby
Recorded: Oct 1868

Sarah Fowler
Page 295-297

Children: Joel M., Alfred M., Amanda M. (now wife of George Franks), Elias, William N., Hilliard J., Mary M. (wife of David S. Boring)

Exrs: sons, Alfred M. and Hilliard J. Fowler

/s/Sarah Fowler
Date: 1 Apr 1854
Wit: Nathan Turner, W. L. Williams, Robert W. Cobb and Alfred S. Fowler
Recorded: Nov 1868

Tunstall B. George
Page 298-299

Children: Mary A., Benjamin F., Martha A.
Exr: Benjamin F. George

/s/Tunstall B. George
Date: 31 Jan 1868
Wit: W. L. Goldsmith, John George and John N. Swift
Recorded: Mar 1869

Abner B. Donahoo
Page 300-302

Son: David H.
Wife.
Dau: Martha G. Robeson
Grdandau: Virginia Jane Elizabeth by son, David H. Donahoo

/s/Abner B. Donahoo
Date: 22 Jan 1869
Wit: John McElroy, Thomas A. Panel and John Y. Flowers
Recorded: 9 Jun 1869

Aaron Goza
Page 303-306

Wife: Elizabeth
Single daus: Leannah and M. E.
Other dau: Sarah Emiline Lane

Son: R. D. Ferdinand.
Decd son's children of Alabama.
Decd son, John's children.
Exrs: friend, David Chestnut

/s/ Aaron Goza
Date: 2 Jun 1869
Wit: J. M. Carroll, R. A. Chewning and C. S. Chestnut
Recorded: 2 Aug 1869

Greenville Henderson
Page 307-311

Wife: Nancy
Sons: John B., Rufus, William G., Major A., Exrs.
Daus: Irena Harris, Martha Conn

/s/Greenville Henderson
Date: 14 Nov 1868
Wit: Ezekiel Reeve, John Baxter, J. L. Wright and Noah Dilda
Recorded: 20 Aug 1869

Daniel E. Jackson
Page 312-313

Wife: Ann
Dau: Mary A. Webb
Exr: son, Thomas J. Jackson

/s/Daniel E. Jackson
Date: 8 Jul 1869
Wit: Leroy Hudgins and W. N. Webb
Recorded: 27 Aug 1869

Josiah Graham
Page 314-316

Wife: Rebecca, Extrx.
Grsons: Josiah Thomas and John Austin (sons of William)
Grdau: Amanda Graham, dau. of son, James.

/s/Josiah Graham

Date: 29 Jul 1869
Wit: William Owens, Jr., Wesley Braswell and W. J. Turner
Recorded: Nov 1869

Joseph T. Bond
Page 317

Wife: Smitha E.
Bro: Elam J. Bond, Exr.
Four children: James e., Daniel E., Leetson, David.

/s/Joseph T. Bond
Date: 30 Apr 1869
Wit: John C. Ragsdale, Abraham Martin and Newton M. Reid
Recorded: 24 Nov 1869

END OF WILL BOOK A

DeKalb County, Georgia Wills
Book B (1870-1889)

John Parker
Page 1-3

To wife: Sarah F. Parker - 107 acres of land being the E half of Land Lot 149 in 15th District.
Children: John H., Robert L. and Anna Eliza and Billings Washington Parker

/s/John Parker (x, his mark)
Wit: William H. Webb, John D. Wills, James Clay (x, his mark)
Dated: 9 Sept 1869. Probated: 3 Feb 1870

James B. Lofton
Page 3-5

Wife: Hannah R. - the house and lot in which I now reside in the town of Decatur, all the real estate I own in City of Atlanta, houses, lots and tenements. And all the rest, balance and residue of my real estate, lands and tenements wheresoever the same may be situated, my bank notes, entire stock, buggy, etc.

Executrix: Wife, Hannah R. Lofton
/s/James B. Lofton
Dated: 8 Aug 1870
Wit: George T. F.Mitchell, John N. Pate, W. W. Durham, R. W. Brown, J. C. Avary

Reuben B. Perkins
Page 5-7

Wife: Martha Ann all property, lands, negroes, stock, plantation tols, etc. Then at her demise to divide equally between my children, viz: Valera Ann Hawkins, Mary Caroline Jones and Martha Elizabeth Perkins and my son, Berry C. Perkins' two children, William T. and James A. Perkins. (my two grandsons)

Dated: 5 Oct 1862
/s/Reuben B. Perkins
Wit: Joseph Walker, Francis F. Shumate, Daniel McNeill
Probated: 11 Nov 1870

John Fanin
Page 7-8

Wife: Isalinda - all the property, real and personal to be sold and divided equally among all my wife's children - Sarah Ann Dabo, decd, her children in Texas one share to be paid to them.

Daughters: Elizabeth Lucinda and Isalinda Cunningham, apptd Executrixes

Date: 2 Aug 1870
/s/John Fanin
Wit: Watson Kittridge of DeKalb Co., M. A. Steele of DeKalb Co.,and Ed M. Kittridge of DeKalb Co.
Probated: 28 Nov 1870

John White of DeKalb Co.
Page 9-10

Wife: Nancy M. -all of my property during her natural life...cnsisting of lands, stock, household, etc., and at her death to be divided equally between all my legal heirs.

Exrs: sons, James J.and J.W. White

/s/John White
Date: 7 Aug 1856
Wit: James C. Avary, William S. McClain (x, his mark), and Nathan Turner
Probated: 2 May 1871

Anna M. Brunt of DeKalb Co.
Page 11-12

Children: Annie M. Brunt, the said Annie M. Brunt to be in charge of my daughter, Carrie D. Brunt until she becomes of age or marries.

The plantation in DeKalb Co. to remain in the hands of my Exr, Bradford B. Brunt, in the best interests of my children, viz: Carrie D. Brunt, Joseph F. Wilson, Sarah V. Wilson, John W. Wilson, Annie M. Brunt.

Bequest to Very Johnson, bed and bedstead as long as she lives with my children.

/s/ Annie M. Brunt (x, her mark)
Dated: 9 Jul 1871
Wit: L. H. Jones, W.T. Dawson, Willis B. Harris, W. S. Heronton
Probated: 2 Sept 1871

William C. Anderson of DeKalb Co.
Page 13-15

Wife: Rosetta F. - Land Lots No. 160 and 161 in DeKalb Co., the place whereon my family now lives, being parts of two lots containing 202 1/2 acres, my cattle, etc., to be the property of my wife during her natural life or widowhood for the support, maintenace and education of my living children under the control of my Exr.

Children: Martha C. H., Joseph B., Edgar M.

/s/William C. Anderson
Dated: 9 Aug 1871
Wit: C. A. C. Dorsey, Peyton S. Dorsey, Mary K. Dorsey, John M. Dorsey
Probated: 11 Dec 1871

William H. Clark of DeKalb Co.
Page 16-18

Wife: Julia A. - my homeplace in Decatur on which I now live, consisting of about 220 acres, being parts of Lots Nos. 233, 234, 216, 201. At her death to be equally divided between my three children, viz: Elijah H., Alice E. and Albert A. Clark

To son Elijah H. Clark I give Lot No. 25 known as the Meador lot, the half lot No. 26 known as the Chandler Lot , 50 ares of the same lot number 26, SW corner of said lot, and 50 acres of lot number 8 known as the Badger land, containing in all about 400 acres of land in the 16th District of DeKalb Co. My said son, Elijah H. has received of my estate property to the value of $1700 of which I make no charge that he may be made equal with my other two children, Alice E. and Albert A. Clark.

To daughter, Alice Eugenia Clark, the following lands - Lot No. 106, E half of Lot No. 159 and 150 acres of Lot No. 7 known as the Betterton and Maulding Lands, containing inall about 450 acres.

To son, Albert A. Clark, the following lands - Lot No. 12, 150 acres of Lot 8 and known as the Badger Land and 50 ares of Lot No. 7, it being the S half of Drewry Mauldin lot, the whole containing abut 400 acres in DeKalb Co. Also, furniture, etc.

Extrx: Wife, Julia A. Clark

/s/William H. Clark
Dated: 29 Mar 1872
Wit: I. N.Wilson, James E. Avary, C. J. Ragan
Probated: 1 July 1872

James Phillips of DeKalb Co.
Page 19-21

Wife: Sarah, the lot of Land No. 90 in 16th District of DeKalb Co. Also 42 1/2 acres on SS of No. 91, and also No. 103, all in said district. At her death, estate to be divided between my lawful heirs.

Children: James (deceased), daughter (not named)

/s/James Philips
Date: 10 Jun 1868
Wit: D. T. Smith, J. S. Fincher, John W. Weekes
Probated: 16 Aug 1872

James J. Ragan of DeKalb Co.
Page 22-23

Wife: Talitha C. Ragan (Executrix) - Lot of Land where I now live known as Lot No. 140 in 16th District of DeKalb Co., and 50 ares off of N side of Lot No. 141, etc.

/s/James J. Ragan
Dated: 18 Aug 1869
Wit: Thomas J. Richardson, John A. W. Fleming, Asa W. Howard
Probated: 21 Apr 1873

Zachariah Eidson
Page 24-25

I have given my two oldest sons, Newton E. and Robert W., $130 each.

I want my two oldest daughters, Julia Almeda and Margaret C. to have $130 each in cash as they become 21 years of age. My son, Newton E., to act as their guardian.

I want my four youngest children to have the land that I live on 8 years, to-it: Mary Jane,
Marcellus Douglas, John Galveston, and Charles, and my son, Robert W. to be their guardian.

/s/Zachariah Eidson
Dated: 12 Apr 1873
Wit: J. H. Roberts, W. J. Donalson, James Spruell
Probated: 5May 1873

Thomas J. Akins of DeKalb Co.
Page 26-27

Wife: Sarah S. - the N. 1/2 of Lot No. 207 whereon I now residein 18th District of DeKalb Co., etc. After her death - John M. and Daniel W. Akins to have the above-named property to be equally divided between myelder children - James F., William G., Eliza L., Thomas B., Lewis L., Allen R., Henry M., Jefferson P.M .and Harriet E.

/s/Thomas J. Akins
Date: 13 Sept 1872
Wit: Dicy Jackson (x, her mark), E. S.Walker, Joseph Walker
Probated: 2 Jun 1873

Boyce Eidson of DeKalb Co.
Page 28-30

Wife: Catharine with whom I have lived for some 50 years - my home lot whereon I now life known as Lot No. 307, lying and being in originally Gwinnett Co., now DeKalb Co. At her death, to go to my two daughters - Sarah Ann and Jane.

Children: Elizabeth Woodall, wife of James Woodall, Nancy Roberts, wife of James Roberts, J. G. Eidson, Zachariah Eidson, Mary Smith, wife of Sanford Smith, Martha Gardner, wife of A. Gardner, Sarah Ann Eidson, Jane Eidson, William Eidson and Robert Eidson.

Exr: son, J. G. Eidson.

/s/Boyce Eidson (x, his mark)
Dated: 29 Aug 1861
Wit: John R. Humphries, G. N. Flowers, A. P. Flowers, John Y. Flowers
Probated: 6 Oct 1873

Joseph Pitts of DeKalb Co.
Page 30-32

Wife: Ann A. - one servant girl named Etta of dark complexionand one boy named Mathew of yellow complexion, etc.

Children: Rebecca M. Wilson, Augustus L. Pitts, Frances M. Pitts, Mary Ann Byrd, Eliza
Jane Rickel, John R. Pitts.
Exrs: Sons, Augustus L.Pitts and John R. Pitts.
/s/Joseph Pitts
Dated: 4 Dec 1860
Wit: R. M. Brown, Robert McWilliams, Daniel Johnson
Probated: 6 Oct 1873

Thomas White of DeKalb Co.
Page 33-35

Wife: Sarah with whom I have lived for about 50 years.
"All my children"

Wife's sister: Cana Coulman (an equal share with my children)

Exr: son, William C. White

/s/Thomas White
Date: 23 Aug 1872
Wit: Wilkan McKee, Levi Simpson, Samuel C. Martin
Probated: 2 Jun 1873

David M. Sheppard of DeKalb Co.
Page 35-39

Wife: Huldah F. - all estate and at her death to be divided among all my children.

Sons: James A. - 50 acres in Browning's District
    David C. - 68 acres in S part of portion of Lot No. 222....

George W. - 68 acres off N part, parallel to Lot No. 222, including 32 acres bought of Mrs. Anderson

Henry J. - 88 acres inluding homeplae of Lot 222, the line to be N and S between said place and land given to Nancy Ann S. E. M. Moore.

Andrew J. - 1/3rd of my Aycock land, being part of Lot No. 225

Daughters: S. F. A. Benefield - 53 acres, being part 13 of the middle of the Aycock provision of the Aycock place, lines running EW with except of 1/2 acre including Davis Spring and part of Lot 225

Nancy Ann S.E.. M.Moore - 68 acres adjhomeplace on the e lands given t George W. Sheppard on the N and to David C. Sheppard on the S, and being part of Lot 222

Martha C. Moore - 50 acres of land on G. R. R., No. 95 in 1813 Dist.

Huldah J. Davice - 1/3rd of my Aycock lands, being part of Lot No. 225.

Grandchildren: Liser A.Jones, daughter of Mary Ann Jones and George T. Aycock, Sarah E. Aycock, Franklin T. Aycock.

Exrs: sons, James A. and David C. Sheppard.

/s/David M. Sheppard
Date: 8 Jan 1872
Wit: J. M. Smith, James J. Lee, Angus M. McLeod, J. P.
Probated: 17 Oct 1873

Samuel House of DeKalb Co.
Page 40-43

Wife: Elizabeth - with whom I lived for 48 years. Lot No. 305 in 18th District of DeKalb Co., 100 acres. Sons: Thomas J. and Bazel - Lot No. 305, 18t District DeKalb Co., 180 acres.
Exrs: son, Jacob G. House, Philip House and Thomas J. House

/s/Samuel House
Dated: 31 Aug 1857
Wit: James Polk, Henry H. Walker, John B. Davidson
Probated: 4 Nov 1873

Ann Beck of DeKalb Co.
Page 44-46

Sons: Charles J. Beck, W. Gilman Beck
Granddaughter: Roberta Beck
Daughters: Harriet B. Winn, Mary Jane Wood
Exrs: L. J. Winn and Charles J. Beck

/s/ Ann Beck
Dated: 2 Apr 1874
Wit: James Hunter, Hiram J. Williams, H. C. Jones
Probated: 1 Jun 1874

Wesley C. White of DeKalb Co.
Page 47-49

Wife mentioned but unnamed.
I desire that my property shall be distributed when the youngest child is 21 years old...Each of my children shall receive a good English education.....

Exr: friend, Wilton A. Candler

/s/W. C. White
Dated: 11 May 1874
Wit: J. E. George U. F. George, John W. Weeks
Probated: 2 Nov 1874

Richard Gregory Taylor of DeKalb Co.
Page 49-51

Wife: Florence Williamson Taylor to distribute property 1 Jan 1880 among heirs
Children: Katie G. Taylor, Georgia W. Taylor, Florinda Taylor and Toulinin Taylor $7000
each. Extrx: wife, Florence Williamson Taylor

/s/R. G. Taylor
Dated: 23 Jun 1873
Wit: John L. Hamilton, Jr., R. M. Thompson, W. H. Hamilton and W. S. Herrinton
Probated: 2 Nov 1874

Robert H. Smith of DeKalb Co.
Page 51-53

Wife: Elizabeth with whom I have lived for 43 years, part of Land Lot No. 185, part of Land Lot

No. 184 in 6th District of Gwinnett Co. containing 275 acres known as the John Shambly old place. Exrs: sons-in-law, Robert Medlock and Michael A. Steel
/s/Robert H. Smith
Dated: 22 Apr 1875
Wit: J. W. Tilley, D. Y. Hicks, James Polk and W. R. Peavy
Probated: 7 Jun 1875

Dempsey Perkerson
Page 54-56

I will and desire that all my personal property be sold.....the proceeds to....be divided among my children and their descendants. [Children not named]
Son: Thomas J. Perkerson, Exr

/s/Dempsey Perkerson
Dated: 15 Oct 1866
Wit: W.L. Williams, Jennings J. Hulsey and Addie S. Hulsey
Probated: 6 Sept 1875

Jacob Chupp of DeKalb Co.
Page 57-60

Being of advanced age.
Wife: Elizabeth - homeplace containing 175acres, etc.

Children: Daniel R. Chupp, David B. Chupp, James C. Chupp, Elijah Braswell (my son-in-
law), Josiah L. Chupp, Mary M. Chupp and Emer S. Chupp - 202 1/2 acres on Rockibridge Road,
lying
on Mill Creek, known as Henry Place, below the little mountain.
Exrs: sons, Daniel R.Chupp and David B. Chupp

/s/Jacob Chupp (x, his mark)
Dated: 21 Apr 1875
Wit: John C. Ragsdale, J. L. Johnson and Wesley Mitchell
Probated: 13 Aug 1875

Brice M. Sprayberry of DeKalb Co. of advanced age
Page 61-65

Wife: Permelia Elizabeth - W half of Land Lot 6 in 15th District of DeKalb Co., 101 1/4 acres. Sons: William H. Sprayberry - E half of Lot 6, 15th District, 101 1/4 acres, DeKalb Co., Brice M. Sprayberry, and Harvey J. Sprayberry (minor), William H. Sprayberry (Gdn of minor daughter,

Sarah V. L. E. and minor son, Harvey J.)
Daughters: Amanda C. Bowden, wife of Walter T. Bowden, Sarah V. L. E. Sprayberry (minor) Grandsons: John G. Sprayberry, Francis C. South (minor)

/s/B. M.Sprayberry
Dated: 27 Jan 1876
Wit: Samuel C. Masters, John B. Morris, W. W. Sprayberry
Probated: 13 Apr 1876

G. J. Pearce of DeKalb Co.
Page 66-69

Wife: Eliza Ann
Son: John W. Pearce

/s/G. J. Pearce
Dated: 21 Apr 1875
Wit: Julind Brown, W. F. Pattillo, William S. Thomson, Milton A. Candler
Probated: 30 May 1876

John Hollingsworth of DeKalb Co.
Page 69-71

Sons: James M. Hollingsworth, John N. Hollingsworth
Daughters: Emily, Sally, Charotn, Alisey, Martha Wight, Rebecca J., Rebecca Jane
Trustee: John Stowers, trustee for Sarah and Thomas Hollingsworth, children of John A. Hollingsworth, decd.

/s/John Hollingsworth
Dated: 4 Dec 1870
Wit: D. M. Parker, William W. Walcott, J. M. Leftwich, J. H. Hollingsworth
Probated: 5 Jun 1876

John W. Fowler of DeKalb Co.
Page 72-75

Grandchildren: Royal J., John F. and Lou A. Moseley, heirs of James and Emma Moseley.
Wife: Harriett
Son-in-law: John Mayes
Son: A. C. Fowler, John W. Fowler
Exrs: wife, Harriett, and son, John W. Fowler
/s/John W. Fowler
Wit: B. S. Spivey, John P. Ray and E. A. Davis

Codicil dated 26 Sept 1876 appoints A. C. Fowler, son, in addition to two already appointed. Wit: D. Elener Fowler, John L. Tuggle and E. A. Davis
Probated: 4 Dec 1876

Elizabeth Dean of DeKalb Co.
Page 76-78

Daughter: Amelia Carter
Exr: friend, Alexander Potts

/s/Elizabeth Dean (x, her mark)
Dated: 8 Apr 1872
Wit: John C. Harris, William W. Griffin, Edward Turner (x, his mark), and Henry Glen (x, his mark)

Probated: 4 Dec 1876

James M. Leftwich of DeKalb Co.
Page 78-80

To wife, Sarah J., Land Lot 78 and 83 in 16th District of DeKalb Co.

Children: R. M. Leftwich and M. P. Leftwich and R. S. Leftwich, Mary E. Hollingsworth, M. T. Rogers, J. M. Leftwich, Sarah Jane Leftwich.

Exrs: J. M. Leftwich and R. M. Leftwich

/s/J. M. Leftwich
Dated: 23 Oct 1872
Wit: John I. Patillo, W. L. Cummings, William G. Staple, J. P.
Probated: 5 Feb 1877

William Wright of DeKalb Co.
Page 81-82

Wife: Lucy
Daughters: Martha C. and Harriet E.

Grandaughter: Martha V. V. and Mary Jane (daughter of Martha C.)
Exr: friend, George B. Hudson
/s/William Wright (x, his mark)
Dated: 21 Dec 1872
Wit: A. H. Tucker, W. N. Henderson and George B. Henderson all of DeKalb Co.
Probated: 5 Feb 1877

John C. Ragsdale of DeKalb Co.
Page 83-85

Wife: Nancy - part of Lot No. 192 in 16th District of DeKalb Co.

Daughters: Eugenia Ragsdale, Ara Bell
Son: Bartow D. Ragsdale

Exrs: Sylvester Powers, R. H. Connor and James J. Phillips

/s/John C. Ragsdale
Dated: 20 Mar 1877
Wit: Esom J. Bond, John T. Alford and J. E. McGuire
Probated: 7 Apr 1877

Thomas Rigney of DeKalb Co. of advanced age
Page 86-88

Nephews: Washington Rigney of New York, James A. Rigney, Joanna Hanlen, Mary C. Hamilton and John L. Hamilton, trustee. Cornelus Hanlen apptd trustee for the use of his daughter, Joanna Hanlen. Mentions some lots deeded to him by Thomas T. Wright (26,250 ft.) on Decatur Street.

Bequest to Father Reelly, pastor of Immaculate Conception, and Father Joseph residing in Augugsta, Ga.
Exrs: friends, James Purcell and E. O. Donnell

/s/Thomas Rigney
Dated: 15 Mar 1877
Wit: Allen J. Veal, Miles M. Mann and William S. Herronton
Codicil dated: 15 Mar 1877 witnessed by Allen J. Veal, Miles Mason and William S. Herronton....bequeaths all remaining money to friend, Cornelus Haulen for his kind attention to me during my last illness.
Recorded: 7 May 1877

Cornelius Hanlon of DeKalb Co.
Page 89-91

Wife: Julia, Extrx.
Children: Hanorah, Johannah M., Mary Ann, Owen and John Jeremiah Hanlon
/s/Cornelius Hanlon (x, his mark)
Dated: 25 Jun 1878
Wit: Thomas P. Wells, Shelton H. Campbell and Edwin L. Phillips
Probated: 7 Oct 1878

Mary P. Tufts of DeKalb Co.
Page 92-96

I desire to be buried in the family grave yard in Jones Co. by the side of that of my beloved husband.
Daughters: Jane E. Wilson, Lou Tufts
Son: Orry Tufts, Joseph F. A. Tufts (in trust for his brother, Orry Tufts)

/s/Mary P. Tufts
Dated: 25 Jan 1873
Wit: P. Pelham, W. D. Robinson, W. A. McAuley, E. F. Pelham

Codicil makes son, Joseph F. S. Tufts in trust for the sole use of my daughter, Lou.
Wit: P. Pelham, W. S. Neel, E. F. Pelham
Date: 4 Oct 1878
Probated: 4 Oct 1878

James B. Robertson of DeKalb Co.
Page 97-99

Daughter: Minerva Ragsdale - 100 acres on S half of Lot No. 84 in 16th Dist. of DeKalb Co.
Other children: Martha A. Lyons, Nancy Bailey
Children of my decd son, James A. Robertson
Grandsons: James D. Robertson, Josiah James
Son-in-law: John J. Bailey, Exr

/s/James B. Robertson
Dated: 30 Dec 1878
Wit: Bennett Robertson, Thomas L. Robertson and A. P. Robertson
Probated: 30 Mar 1874

Joseph Stewart of DeKalb Co.
Page 100-102

Wife: Elizabeth
Children and grandchildren (unnamed)

/s/Joseph Stewart
Dated: 30 Mar 1874
Wit: Charles J. Carroll, D. H. Dunbar, J. W. Keheley, James Polk
Probated: 4 Apr 1879

Joseph Dunbar of DeKalb Co.
Page 103-105

Wife: Marcena

Children: James Dunbar, John H. Dunbar
Exrs: son, John H. Dunbar and Henry H. Walker

/s/Joseph Dunbar
Dated: 24 Aug 1878
Wit: Charles J. Carrol, W. F. Gay, W. J. Flowers
Probated: 5 May 1879

Robert S. Argoe of DeKalb Co.
Page 106-108

I devise and hereby direct that my Exr shall sell all my right and interest in the lands of the real estate of my father and mother.

Sisters: Martha A. Argoe, Margaret A. Argoe and Sarah F. Argoe

Brother: Samuel L. Argoe of DeKalb Co., Exr

/s/R. S. Argoe
Dated: 1 Feb 1879
Wit: J. W. Clay, R. S. Parker, E. B. Huey
Probated: 3 Mar 1879

William Hairston of DeKalb Co.
Page 108-109

Children: Miles Hairston, Arminda Armon Anderson, wife of William Anderson, Martha Elizabeth Akin, wife of James Akin and Amanda Clemantine Rutledge, wife of Joseph Rutledge.
Exr: son, Albert M. Hairston

/s/William Hairston (x, his mark)
Dated: 10 May 1875
Wit: James M. Smith, J. W. Ozmer and S. B. Langford
Probated: 5 Aug 1879

Robert H. Hart of DeKalb Co.
Page 110-111

To be buried in the graveyard near Orange Church in Cherokee Co.
My dear children have pre-deceased me.
Dau: Nancy
Son: William Riley Hart (first born son), Jesse Burtz Hart (third son).
Wife.

/s/Robert H. Hart
Date: 28 Mar 1871
Wit: Mattie Bankston, Thomas Ivey, J. M. Burtz
Probated: 24 Jul 1879 by Mattie Stovall

Samuel Potts of DeKalb Co.
Page 112-115

Of advanced age.
Wife: Mary A. Potts who whom I have lived for years - Land Lots 74 and 86, includes my dwelling home and other houses, DeKalb Co., being on the waters of Pole Bridge Creek, containing 405 acres, etc.

Sons: Martin E. Potts, John H. Potts, Samuel J. Potts
Daus: Nancy E. Miller, wife of Robert Miller and Frances R. Park, wife of Russell Park and S. E. A. Deal, wife of J. S. Deal.
Granddau: Susan Elizabeth Potts, a minor dau. of William C. Potts
To: Mary A. Miller's five children, former wife of John W. Miller.
To: James D. Robertson, a son of my present wife when he becomes of age.
Exrs: friends, David A. Clotfelter and Russell Park

/s/Samuel Potts
Dated: 25 May 1878
Wit: C. G. Keys, R. C. Shed, J. M. Fleming, P. W. Clotfelter, A. W. Howard
Probated: 4 Aug 1879

George W. Cash of DeKalb Co. of advanced age
Page 115-118

Wife: Lucinda with whom I have lived for 55 years, 50 acres off the SW corner of Lot 317 in the 18th District of DeKalb Co.
To: Betsey Ann Jolly, my daughter
To: James E. Cash, my son

To: Nancy Belinda, my daughter, 1/2 of undivided 50 acres in lot above named, it being in the SE corner of said lot and 1/3rd of the live stock, etc.
To: Amanda Jane Cash, wife of Oliver P. Cash, my daughter.
To: Mary Frances, daughter, 1/2 of undivided 50 acres in lot afore written, it being the SE corner of said lot.

Grandson: John Moses Cash - 50 acres, Lot 146, 18th Dist. of DeKalb Co., it being the N
50 acres of the S half of said lot except 10 acres in the NE corner now owned by Oliver P. Cash.

/s/George M. Cash (x, his mark)
Dated: 27 Sept 1878
Wit: T. E. Chewning, John B. Jones, John J. McDaniel
Recorded: 6 Jul 1880

Ann B. Jones
Page 118-123

State of Georgia
Richmond County

WHEREAS, by virtue of the marriage settlement made and entered into on the 8th day of May 1851 and recorded in the clerk's office of the Superior Court of Richmond County, Book 33, folio 354 and on the 5th day of Jan 1859 and recorded in the Clerk's office of the Superior Court of Morgan County in Book L, folio 322 and 323, full power was given to Ann B. Jones, formerly Ann B. Vinson and Ann B. Anderson notwithstanding coveture to grant, sell, assign, transfer and devise said property therein described and in the increase in income and profits thereof in the same way and manner and all intents and purposes as if she continued sole and unmarried.

And Whereas, the said Ann B. Jones is now a widow and desirous to disposing of all the property remaining to her which consist of $4000 bonds of the City Council of Augusta in the hands of Frank H. Miller, my lot and improvements in Decatur, Georgia besides other property. Now therefore I, Ann B. Jones, the widow of Dr. John W. Jones and now of DeKalb County and State aforesaid mindful of the uncertainties of life and by virtue of the authority contained in said marriage settlements and by authority of law do make, publish and declare this my Last Will and Testament, revoking all wills heretofore made by me.
To bro: Dr. Young B. Olive
Nephew: Frank H.Miller
Son of my husband, Dr. John W. Jones - Henry C. Jones
To: Mary Jones
To: Burt O. Miller
To: Annie C.Miller

Niece: Harriet A. Clemence
Sister: Martha B.Miller, widow of Andrew J. Miller (if dead, to her children)
Exrs: Young B. Olive (brother) and John T.Miller (nephew)

/s/Ann B. Jones
Date: 13 Jun 1877
Wit: Andrew J. Smith, Oliver M. Harris, John D. Baker
Probated: 6 Jun 1880

Joseph M. Huey
Page 124-125

Wife: Sarah G. Huey (appointed Extrx) - 100 acres, part of Lot 149 and part of Lot 144 in 15th District of DeKalb Co. All my children..

/s/Joseph M. Huey
Date: 7 Mar 1863
Wit: William H. Beaty, James W. Beaty and J. W. White
Probated: 4 Apr 1881

John P. Marbut of advanced age
Page 126-130

Wife: Susan - all my estate

Dau: Mary I. Marbut - 50 acres in 16th Dist. of DeKalb Co., on E side of Ga Railroad between Gibson F. Blalock and John P. Marbut to the S of the lane near G. H. Weaver, thence S to corner between John P. Marbut, Burrell B. Braswell and Ellen Bosin, thence W to the NW corner of Burrel B. Braswell and W to a stake on line of Ga. Railroad right-of-way.

Dau: Susan C. Bailey - 40 acres off of Lot 273

Sons: Job J. Marbut and Robert H. Hollingsworth, Exrs. and trustees for Susan C. Bailey and Mary I. Marbut. I hereby order and direct that my Exrs lay off 1/4th of an acre off of Lot No. 134 where the graveyard now is to be bound on the S by the original line and on the W by the right-of-way-of-the Ga. Railroad for a graveyard.

/s/John P. Marbut
Date: 25 Aug 1880
Wit: F.M. Wellborn, I. M. Smith, H. C. Almand, W. L. B. Crossley
Probated: 25 Apr 1881

Archibald McElroy
Page 131-132

Dau: Emeline Poss - 40 acres, SW corner of Lot No. 61 in DeKalb Co.
Dau: Caroline Kers - 40 acres, SE corner of Lot No. 61 in DeKalb Co.
Dau: Viola Palmer - 43 acres, being the east side of Lot No. 36 and 7 acres, being the NW corner of Lot 61 on which my dwelling house is situated, which 10 acres of the last named land my son-in-law, Thomas I. Palmer, who agrees to take care of me and dwelling (during) my natural life.

Son: A. J. McElroy

/s/ Archibald McElroy
Date: 26 Nov 1878
Wit: James M. Smith, Williamson Hollingsworth, L. J. Hughes and I. N. McElroy (x, his mark)
Probated: 4 Jul 1881

Vincent R. Tommey
Page 133-135

Wife: Elizabeth
Son: Albert P.
Daus: Sarah Mary, Lizzie, Carrie (Lewis H. Beck to be Gdn of Carrie)
Wife, Elizabeth (Extrx) and friend, Lewis H. Beck (Exr)

/s/ V. R. Tommey
Date: 31 Aug 1869
Wit: R. M. Brown, Samuel A. Echols and Hiram J. Williams
Probated: 2 Jan 1882

Martin C. McKee of advanced age
Page 136-138

Wife: Mary Ann, with whom I have lived...for more than 40 years - land on east side of the public road leading from S. C. Martins to Hulseys Mills commencing at the Creek on Lot No. 253 in the 12th Dist. and running t the Atlanta Road on Lot No. 4 in the 15th Dist., together with 3 acres on the W side ...in front of the house...being the present omestead...

Dau: Mary R. McKee

To: child of my daughter, Amanda M. Simpson, namely, William R. Simpson.
Sons: Madison C. McKee and Z. T. McKee, Exrs.

/s/Martin C. McKee
Date: 22 Nov 1881
Wit: Samuel C. Masters, George W. Mathews and Ebenezer P. Ellis
Probated: 13 Mar 1882

James M. Carroll
Page 138-140

I direct that all my property be kept together by my Exrs for the support, maintenance and education of my minor children....and my wife...until the youngest child becomes 21 years of age. To be paid $100 or have given them a horse, etc....to make them equal with their older brothers.

Sons: Lorenze F.D., James E. and Robert T. (not of age)

Daus: Julia A., Ida J. and Sarah M. (not of age)

Dau: Mary M. Bolton

Exrs: Sons, Charles J. and William D. Carroll and sons-in-law, L. H. Jones and John Pound

/s/James M. Carroll
Date: 28 Apr 1882
Wit: Sylvester Pound, Thomas P. Grant and William S. Johnson
Probated: (not given)

Cyrus Twilley
Page 141

Wife to be Executrix.
400 acres in DeKalb Co. upon which I and my family now reside to wife.

/s/Cyrus Twilley
Date: 27 May 1879
Wit: T. J. Flake, J. W. Mitchel, Benjamin Owens
No probate date given

James M. Ball
Page 142-147

Adopted Dau: Georgia Hendree Ball - $25,000 in notes.

Dau. of my sister, Sarah C. Edwards - Eva Edwards

Son of my sister, Sarah C. Edwards - Jackson Edwards - and her grandson, Barnard.

Youngest sister: Sarah C. Edwards, widow of Andrew Edwards

Sister: Mary P. Edwards, wife of George M. Edwards and her children - Fannie Owens, Cornelius
Allen, Lilly Griver and Samuel Edwards.

To: Mary P. Edwards in trust for her son, Sumner.

To: Fannie Owens
To: Cornelius Allen

To: The children of my sister, Eliza P. Edwards - Malissa Miller, Ursula Roberts, Ophelia Peacock, Milton Edwards and Theodore Edwards.
Sister: Joann F.Thompson and her children and grandchildren. To the children of her daughter, :Laura Hart. To Oveana DeLoach, James Thompson, and sister, Joann F. Thompson in trust for her daughter, Ida.
To: Z. D. Harrison in trust for my grandniece, Laura Hendree Harrison
To: Virginia Foster, daughter of my sister, Eliza P. Edwards and her husband, Dr. S. A. Foster
Exrs: Z. D. Harrison, E. Payson Miller and Lewis William Burton

/s/James M. Ball
Date: 14 Jan 1883

Georgia, DeKalb Co. - Personally appeared. D. Harrison and on oath says that he was requested by James M. Ball, who departed this life on 18th day of Jan 1883 to write his Will.... as deponent now remembers on the wth day of Jan 1883 deceased instructed to deponent to request W. F. Patillo, Mrs. C. P. Hendree and the wife of deponent to come his room to witness the signing of his Will....

Probated: 5 Feb 1883

George Key
Page 147-
then continues on Page 155-158

Wife: Mary J. J. - parts of lots 83 and 84 containing about 50 acres, known as the place on which I now live, on E side of Atlanta and McDonough Road on the line between me and Mrs. Mary Young, etc.

Land in City of Atlanta to be sold and divided between my two children - William B. Key and Thomas T. Key.

/s/George Key
Date: 1 Mar 1882
Wit: F. P. H. A. Kees, Thomas F. Scully and Robert McWilliams
Probated: 1 Oct 1883

G. A. Rice
Page 148-149

Children: Charley P. Rice, Sarah Elizabeth Rice and Minnie Lee Rice
Wife: Mary Jane Rice (resides in Atlanta) - 95 acres of Lot No. 210 in 18th Dist. of DeKalb Co.

/s/G. A. Rice (x, his mark)
Date: 27 Nov 1882
Wit: John W. McCurdy, E. J. Carroll, J. A. Sheppard, John R. Maddox
Probated: 5 Mar 1883

Harris Crowey
Page 151-152

Dau: Darcus Jane Petaway and her two children
Wife: Mary Jane, Extrx.

At my wife's death or marriage my will is that all my property, both real and personal, be sold and equally divided between my children then living, and in case any of my children depart this life leaving children, that they drew his or her pro-rata part as I direct. That my daughter, Susan Wright's children be entitled to her pro-rata part as same as she would be in case she was alive.

/s/Harris Crowey
Date: Apr 1874
Wit: A. L. Pitts, J. G. McWilliams and R. M. McWilliams
Probated: 1 Jun 1883

B. F. Kimbro
Page 153-154

Wife: Mary F., apptd Extrx.
Sons: John R., Joseph M. - 100 acres, being part of Lot No. 344, being my homestead
Dau: A. Z. Burnham and her husband, J. W. Burnham - 50 acres, in N part of my Land Lot No. 345 in 18th Dist. of DeKalb Co.

/s/B. F. Kimbro
Date: 11 Mar 1883
Wit: J. Y. Flowers, T. J. House and A. J. Morris
Probated: 4 Jun 1883

Aid McNight
Page 159

State of Georgia
DeKalb County

This request of Aid McNight made before James Lyons in regards to property, both personal and real, ...James Lyons says he was present at the time of his death and he as in his right mind andknew what he was talking about and his desire was that Isaac and Nancy McNight should take his property, both real and personal estate, and settle his debts in full and the balance to be used by them for their own special use and benefit. /s/James Lyons (x, his mark)
/s/Aid McNight
Wit: W. M. Rowdup
Dated: 11 Jun 1883

Leanna McNeil
Page 160-162

Daus: Louisa Keyer, Jane Fannin and Viola Burdett - land in Decatur, town lot number 121, containing one acre, the same being on the W side of McDonough St. and near the jail lot and being the same conveyed to me by G. A. and T. R. Ramspeck by deed dated 23 Feb. 1880 and recorded in the clerk's office of the Superior Court of DeKalb County in Book V, Record of Deeds, page 443.
Exrs: friend, William Fannin and James Hunter

/s/Leanna McNeil
Date: 3 Aug 1882
Wit: James Hunter, R. M. Brown and N. C. Jones
Probated: 4 Feb 1884

John Cochran of advanced age
Page 162-165

Wife: Julia with whom I have lived for 55 or 60 years
After wife's death, property to be equally divided between children.
Daus: Parthena E. Gunter, Helen M. Gunter, Emeliza S. Baxter, Sarah B. Cochran, Julia A.Cochran

Son: Samuel W. Cochran, Exr

/s/John Cochran
Date: 23 Oct 1879
Wit: John Kilgore, David Chestnut, Andrew Haynes, and E. A. Turner
Probated: 7 Dec 1883

Jarrett C. Purcell, Sr.
Page 165-167

Wife: Mary - 50 acres, Lot No. 246 in 18th District, DeKalb Co.
After death of wife, above property to be property of Laura M. Purcell
Children: L. J. Norton, Sarah E. Echols, Laura M. Purcell, Martha A. Holland, L. C. Timley, H. M. Elliott, E. S. Purcell, R. R. Purcell, Jarrett C. Purcell and the heirs of C. W. Purcell and M. H.Hooper.

/s/Jarrett C. Purcell, Sr.
Date: 28 Oct 1883
Wit: J. C. Purcell, T. J. Christian, J. W. F. Tally, J. A. Holbrook
Probated: 16 Jan 1884

George B. Hudson
Page 167-169

Wife: Sarah Evaline - my hmeplace, being Lot No. 163, and 50 acres off of Lot No. 191, in 18th Dist., DeKalb County.

Children: Octavia M. Wright, William T. Hudson, George G. Hudson, Charles M. Hudson, Ludocia Johnson, Etta C. Shumate, Forrest P. Hudson, James D. Hudson, Pliny E. Hudson, Sarah E. Hudson and John L. Hudson.

/s/George B. Hudson
Date: 18 Jul 1884
Wit: J. J. McDaniel, James M. Livesay and R. T. Livesay
Probated: 2 Sept 1884

END OF BOOK WILL BOOK B

DeKalb County, Georgia
Will Book C
(1890-1919)

Note: No pages 1 and 2
Joseph Walker
Page 4

To: The children of Henry B. Morgan by my daughter, Juliann, decd - 50 acres in SW corner of Lot No. 229 in 15th District of DeKalb Co., containing my family mansion as their part of the estate.

To: The heirs of my son, Jabez B. Walker, decd - James W. Walker, Eliza Jane Corley, the children of Sarah Elizabeth Corley, decd, and the children of Joseph H. Walker.

/s/Joseph Walker
Date: 21 Apr 1879
Wit: William H. Carter, Charles B. Carter and George W. Weems
Recorded: 23 Jan 1890

John N. Swift of Lithonia
Page 5

Daus: Elizabeth Griffin and Annie Ray Swift - my lot on which I live in town of Lithonia Other children: Thomas Latimer Swift, John N. Swifrt, Jr., Dean T. Swift, Mary J. Goldsmith, Lucy Reese, Harriet E. Brogdon.

Exr: Thomas L. Swift (son)

/s/John N. Swift
Date: 19 Jan 1890
Wit: H. W. Gibbs, J. L. Johnson and W. H. Hollingsworth
Recorded: 7 Mar 1890

Stephen Hightower
Page 6

Wife: Debby
Dau: Florine Evans
Property to be sold and divided among my children.

Wit: Isaac N. Wilson, J. R. McAlister and B. F. Swanton
Recorded: 23 May 1890

Jesse Boring
Page 7

Wife: Harriet C.

Children: Sallie J., Addie H. and Isaac A. Boring - real estate in City of Atlanta on NW corner of
Frazier and Jones Streets.

Children: Mrs. Ella C. Stewart, Mrs. Jesse B. DuBose and John K.Boring - N half of property,
fronting 51 1/2 feet on W side of Jones Street in City of Atlanta

/s/Jesse Boring
Date: 24 Dec 1885
Wit: William S. Thompson, C. M. Candler and Thomas Pullum
Recorded: 24 May 1890

Isalinda C. Craig
Page 8-9

Sisters: Mrs. Ava A.Wright, Elizabeth L. Walker

To: Children of my step-daughter, Mrs. Mary Jane Clark, decd.

Niece: Mrs. Indiana M. Madison.

To: Decatur Female Seminary which is under the control of the Decatur Presbyterian Church of which I have been a member for more than 40 years.
To: Children of my decd sister, Mary E. Rainey
To: Children of my decd sister, Mrs. Jane M. Britt
Exr: friend, Milton A. Candler

/s/I. C. Craig
Date: 26 May 1890
Wit: J. W. Kirkpatrick, W. J. Houston and George A. Ramspeck
Recorded: 17 Jul 1890

Jabez M. Loyd
Page 9-10

Wife: J. M. C. Loyd
Son: Charles M. Loyd - Lot 204 and 25 acres of land, Lot No. 235, being the mill place, all in the 18th Dist. of DeKalb Co.

Son: Samuel P. Loyd - 60 acres, being part of Lot No. 234 in 18th Dist. of DeKalb Co.

Dau: Mary A. House and her children - 50 acres, being part of Lot No. 235 in 18th Dist., DeKalb Co.

Son: Joseph A Loyd and to his children and to his wife, Mary Loyd - 140 acres, being part of Lot No. 234 in 18th Dist. of DeKalb Co., the place where he now resides.

Son: James E. B. Loyd and his heirs - 50 acres, part of Lot No. 235 and 15 acres of Lot No. 236 in 18th Dist. of DeKalb Co

Dau: Susan A. Loyd.

/s/Jabez M. Loyd
Date: 23 Nov 1882
Wit: A. M. Hairston, J. R. Russell and John B. Stewart
Recorded: 25 Jul 1890. Probate of Will recorded in Minutes of Ordinary, Book F page 480

R. C. Word
Page 11-12

"I have my medical book marked book C solvent accts amount to $860 more or less. (Lists accts owed him)

Five children: J. P. Word, A. M. Word Mary E. Hanes, Ida Ramspeck and Frank H. Word

Exr: Theodore R. Ramspeck

/s/R. C. Word
Date: 1 Jun 1890
Wit: J. A. Mason, John B. Steward and W. M. Ragsdale
Recorded: 21 Aug 1890
Record of Probate in Minutes of Court of Ordinary Book F, page 494

Caroline E. Hambrick
Page 13

Son: Isaac E. Hambrick (Exr)

/s/C. E. Hambrick
Date: 21 Aug 1890
Wit: John J. Albert, J. D. Gordon and W. M. Hairston
Recorded: 9 Oct 1890
Record of Probate in Minutes of Court of Ordinary, Book F, page 513

Thompson A. Browning
Page 13

Wife: Caroline all my property consisting of 101 1/4 acres of land, being the homestead on which I now reside. Appointed Extrx.

/s/Thompson A. Browning
Date: 18 May 1889
Wit: G. F. Hopkins, G. M. England and F. M. Bryson

Seaborn Crowley
Page 14

Wife: Fannie E. Crowley
Nephew: James Johnson

/s/Seaborn Crowley
Date: 10 Jan 1890
Wit: J. C. Cobb, E. Webb (x, his mark) and Alexander C. Tuggle

Recorded: 15 Dec 1890
Probate of Will recorded on Minutes of Court of Ordinary, Book F, page 534-536

George R. Quillian's Nuncupative LWT
Page 15-16

William F. Quillian, Harwell P. Quillian and Daniel E. Bond were present on 17 Oct 1890 at the home of George R. Quillian in Lithonia, Georgia, where he died.

Bro: William F. Quillian

He willed that Fletcher A. Quillian of Atlanta, Ga. should attend to the legal part of winding up his business

/s/George R. Quillian
Date: 10 Nov 1890
Wit: William F. Quillian, Harwell P. Quillian and Daniel E. Bond

William F. Quillian swore on 11 Nov 1890 in Floyd Co. to above LWT
Harwell P. Quillian swore on 11 Nov 1890 in Banks Co. to above LWT
Recorded: 22 Jan 1891

Probate of Will recorded in Minutes Court of Ordinary, Book F, page 549-552

Paschal C. Philips
Page 17

It is my will and desire that the portion of my estate that falls to the children of my daughters deceased, shall be retained in the hands of my executors until they shall become of age.

Sons: James L. Philips, Pierce R. Philips and Crawford Philips (Exrs)

/s/Paschal C. Philips
Date: 5 Sept 1888
Wit: A. M. Calaway, W. J. Bishop and Benjamin F. George
Recorded: 26 Feb 1891

Probate of Will and oath recorded in Minutes of Court of Ordinary, Book F, page 560-561

James C. Vaughan
Page 18

Wife: Julia, all my property

/s/James C. Vaughan
Date: 12 Mar 1889
Wit: W. D. Varner, L. W. Talton and W. C. Moore
Recorded: 6 Mar 1891

Probate of Will recorded in Minutes of Court of Ordinary, Book F, page 572-573

S. H. Campbell
Page 19-20

To: Wife, Sarah J., and 3 youngest children: Charley, Dock and Mattie - 50 acres of Lot No. 93 in 18th Dist. of DeKalb Co., the same being the land deeded to S. H. Campbell by J. P. Maddox, Admr of F. Maddox on 5 Nov 1889, and 112 acres of Lot 70 in 18th Dist. of
DeKalb Co., said land being the same as was deeded to S. H. Campbell by J. P. Maddox, Admr of F. Maddox on 15 Nov 1890, and 50 acres, Lot No. 93 deeded to S. H. Campbell by George W. Maddox on 10 Dec1889.

Sons: Charley Campbell and Dock Campbell apptd Exrs.

/s/S. H. Campbell (x, his mark)
Date: 4 Feb 1891
Wit: T.J. Campbell, Charles L. Simmey and James M. Thomason
Recorded: 5 May 1891. Probate of Will recorded in Minutes of Court of Ordinary, Book G, page
5-6

A. M. Mitchell
20-21

Bros: William J. Mitchell, B. G. Mitchell
Nephew: Wesley Mitchell

Above heirs to receive mill property situated on Snapfinger Creek, known as the Mitchell and Miller Mill property.
To: Rebecca Mitchell - 3 acres of land which includes my homeplace, part of Lot No. 10 in 16th Dist. Sister: Elizabeth Ozmer - 40 acres, part of Lot No. 10 in 16th Dist. of DeKalb Co.
Sister: Reany Fowler
Exr: Brother, William J. Mitchell

A. M. Mitchell contd.....

/s/A. M. Mitchell
Date: 10 Mar 1891
Wit: Russell Park, J. S. Deal and D. C. Thompson
Recorded: 10 Apr 1891
Probate of Will recorded in Minutes of Court of Ordinary, Book G, page
7-8

George M. Everhart
Page 22-24

Wife: Cornelia Adelaide
Sons: Edgar and Henry
Dau: Mary Sue
Our six children: Edgar, Henry, Mary Sue, Adelaide, Loy Hampton and Laurena.

I leave my family uncertainly located that I can but mentin persons and two of whom according as it may seem to my wife most expedient, I desire to act as my Executors except that only one of them shall be a member of my family.

I ask that the court requires no security. The following are the names: George H. Hammond and E.E. Bates of Decatur, Ga., John L. Cowan of Opela Alabama, my son, Lay Hampton, my daughter, Adelaide, and my wife, Cornelia Adelaide.

/s/George M. Everhart
Date: 2 Apr 1891
Wit: Daniel Fraser, Mary Cornelia Hall and Eugenie Herbert Hall
Recorded: 2 Jun 1891
Probate of Will and oath recorded in Minutes of Court of Ordinary, Book G, page 18

Elizabeth Pierce
Page 24

I desire my body to be buried ....in the family burying ground at my brothers, J. O. Alford.
Daus: Mary Mitchell, Ellen Cain and Louisa Nesbit
Bro: J. T. Alford, Extrx.

/s/Elizabeth Pierce (x, her mark)
Date: 15 Dec 1890
Wit: T. A. Floyd, N. M. Reid and Crawford Philips
Probate of Will recorded in Minutes of Court of Ordinary, Book G, page 26-27

Jesse Baubb
Page 25

Wife: Sopha - 3 3/4 acres
Son: Robert Lucas Baubb - 1 3/4 acres

/s/Jesse Baubb (x, his mark)
Date: 3 Jul 1891
Wit: J. A. Dahlgren, Robert Lucust Baugg (his son) and Sopha Baubb (his wife)
Recorded: 7 Oct 1891
Probate of Will recorded in Minutes of Court of Ordinary, Book G, pages 39-40

James H. Baxter
26-27

Wife: Fannie
Daus: Annie, Birdie and Lois
Son: Hubert

Extrx: wife, Fannie, and to be Gdn of Annie, Birdie, Hubert and Lois.

/s/James H. Baxter
Date: 6 Sept 1891
Wit: I. N. Wilson, H. H. Burgess and John B. Stewaard
Recorded: 7 Oct 1891
Probate of Will recorded in Minutes of Court of Ordinary, Book G, pages 47-48

Hilliard Fowler
Page 28-30

Wife: Amanda - 500 acres in 15th Dist.of DeKalb Co.

Daus: Permelia C. Chandler and Mary F. Francis

Exrs: sons, David P. Chandler and William M. Francis

/s/Hilliard J. Fowler
Date: 14 Sept 1889
Wit: J. S. Fowler, A. S. Fowler, J. T. Cobb and T. J. Jackson, all of DeKalb Co., Ga.
Recorded: 14 Dec 1891
Probate of Will recorded in Minutes of Court of Ordinary, Book G, page 75

Robert M. Clark of Edgewood, County of Fulton
Page 31-32

Property to be divided equally between my children and wife and guardians appointed for the minors
Wife: Fannie P. Clark, Extrx.

/s/ Robert M. Clark
Date: 23 Jan 1884
Wit: J. R. Cook, Thomas J. Wesley and John I. Whitlow
Recorded: 20 Jan 1892
Probate of Will recorded in Minutes of Court of Ordinary, Book G, page 82

Martha Eliza Grant of Decatur, Ga.
Page 32

Dau: Susan Eliza Grant - the home in which I now reside situated in Decatur, Ga., containing ¾ acre

Sons: Walter Grant, John Grant, Edgar Grant and Irby Grant

/s/ Martha E. Grant
Date: 10 Dec 1885
Wit: Ella G. Grant, Ed L. Grant and Irby H. Grant
Recorded: 25 Jan 1892
Probate of Will recorded in Minutes of Court of Ordinary, Book G, page 87

Polly McWilliams
Page 33

Nephew: James N. Clay - Lot No. 78 in 18th Dist. of DeKalb Co. on which I now reside
Niece: Anna Eliza McWilliams

I give and bequeath all the remainder....to be divided into two equal parts, one part to the legal heirs of my decd husband, Robert McWilliams, and the other part to my legal heirs.

Exr: nephew, James N. Clay

/s/ Polly McWilliams (x, her mark)
Date: 27 Jan 1891
Wit: J. A. Wright, L. E. Hatcher and James R. Quillian
Recorded: 27 Jun 1892
Probate of Will recorded in Minutes of Court of Ordinary, Book G, page 140

William Sheppard
Page 34-35

Wife: Sarah A.

Son: John T. (Lot No. 39 in 18th Dist. of DeKalb Co., 202 1/2 acres) except one equal acre known as the family grave yard lot of my first wife's grave to be the center of said reserve.

Children and Grandchildren: Nancy Pritchett, William M. Sheppard, Elizabeth Hadden's children now living and John T. Sheppard.

Daus: Talitha Lock, Nancy Pritchett, Elizabeth Hadden

/s/William Sheppard
Date: 10 Dec 1890
Wit: Jesse I. Robinson, W. G. Lanford, T. T. Jnes
Recorded: 20 Jun 1892
Probate of Will recorded in Minutes of the Court of Ordinary, Book G, page 142-144

George W. Matthews' Nuncupative LWT
Page 36

Declared on 11 May 1892 on his deathbed. Wife.
Son: (little) Johnny.

After speaking these words and giving these directions he was satisfied as to the disposition made and died on the 16th of May 1892 never having gotten up from his bed anymore.

Wit: W. J. Clark, E. P. Ellis, M. C. McKee
Date: 9 Jun 1892
Recorded: 14 Jul 1892
Probate of Will in Minutes of Court of Ordinary, Book G, page 151

George A. Thomas
Page 37

I give to my cousins, Joseph E. Wiggins and M. W. Wiggins all of my property...and all the property or interest of whatsoever nature I may have now, or may come to me from the estate of my father and my mother.

Exr: friend, James R. Morris

/s/George A. Thomas (x, his mark)
Date: 9 Aug 1890
Wit: R. D. Evans, Jr., A. M. Callaway, A. W. Howard, Jr.
Recorded: 4 Nov 1892
Probate of Will in Minutes of Court of Ordinary, Book G, page 21-25
(Final Order and Oath,
page 169)

Mahala Seay
Page 38

To be buried on my lot in the cemetery in the Town of Decatur, Ga.
Nephew: Isaac E. Hambrick - all my property, and for the support of my brother, John J. Seay
(because of mental weakness).

Exr: nephew, Isaac E. Hambrick

/s/ Mahala Seay
Date: 9 Jan 1891
Wit: J. M. Hawkins, J. L. Born and Milton A. Candler
Recorded: 18 Oct 1892
Probate of Will recorded in Minutes of Court of Ordinary, Book G, page 177

Elijah W. Green
Page 39-40

Estate to be divided between wife and children.
Exr: brother John W. Green
/s/Elijah W. Green
Date: 22 Sept 1892
Wit: W. Lively, T. R. Burnside and J. R. Jackson
Recorded: 20 Dec 1892
Probate of Will recorded in Minutes of Court of Ordinary, Book G page 187

Toliver Dillard
Page 41

Dau: Carrie C. Carter - Lot No. 4 and Lot No. 5, fronting on Indian Creek Avenue.
My 3 children: Mary Lou Butler of Atlanta, Annie Vawters of Nashville, Tenn. and John T. Dillard, present location unknown.

Exr: Julius Augustus Scott
/s/Toliver Dillard
Date: 11 Feb 1893
Wit: William P. Girardeau, William J. Robbins and Frank P. Singleton
Recorded: 8 May 1893
Probate of Will and oath of Executor in Minutes of Court of Ordinary, Book G, pages 242-243

Robert Cagle
Page 42

Wife: Aley
Legal Heirs: Parthenia J.Martin, Sarah F. Anderson, Elizabeth H. Argo, James K. Cagle, Mary M. Crawford, Agatha S. Henderson and David D. Cagle.
Exr: son, James K. Cagle

/s/Robert Cagle
Date: 8 Mar 1887
Wit: R. H. Randall, J.C. Chupp and M. L. Underwood
Recorded: 8 May 1893
Probate of Will in Minutes of Court of Ordinary, Book G, page 247

James Brown
Page 43-44

5 children: George P. Brown, Elizabeth Jane McKee, Josephine Margaret McWilliams, Zipporah Lanora Clay and James F. Brown.
Exrs: J. W. McWilliams and James F. Brown

/s/James Brown
Date: 25 Jun 1890
Wit: Thomas R. Guess, D. B. Sullivan and C. J. Simmons
Recorded: 1 May 1893
Probate of Will recorded in Minutes of Court of Ordinary, Book G, page 250

John F. Haynie
Page 45

Wife: Sarah - about 65 acres of land, the place whereon I reside, etc.
Wife apptd Extrx.

/s/John F. Haynie
Date: 21 Jun 1892
Wit: J. M. Bagwell, W. A. Varner and S. S. Carter
Recorded: 20 Jun 1893
Probate of Will and oath in Minutes of Court of Ordinary, Book G, pages 257-258

T. L. Lallerstedt
Page 46

To: Martha A. Lallerstedt

/s/T. L. Lallerstedt
Date: 6 Apr 1893
Wit: M.D. Wiggins, J. P., J. W. Pattillo and S. M. Prather
(No probate dates)

Easom J. Bond
Page 46-47

Wife: Mollie E. - 190 acres of Lot No. 190, and 120 acres of Lot No. 195, 1/2 interest in 75 acres, being part of Lot No. 189, all in 16th Dist. of DeKalb Co. 1/2 interests include a partnership with his brother, J. T. Bond's estate.
5 children: Atticus Y., George R., Ira A., William A. D. and Joseph B. Bond.
Exrs: sons, Atticus Y. and Joseph B. Bond.'

/s/Easom J. Bond (x, his mark)
Date: 13 Apr 1892
Wit: Irwin L. Peat, L. M. Mitchell and L. A. Ragsdale
Recorded: 21 Aug 1893
Probate of Will and oath of Executors recorded in Minutes of Court of Ordinary Book G, pages
276-277

John U. Ridling
Page 48-49

Wife: Sarah
Children: Georgia Maloney, now the widow of Joseph Maloney, decd, Loula Spinks, wife of J. W. Spinks, and Omie Ridling and Adaline Ridling, and Catharine, wife of Charles O'Shields., and Adaline.

Exr: friend and son-in-law, J. W. Spinks. Also apptd trustee for daughter, Adaline and her estate.

/s/John U. Ridling
Date: 17 Oct 1892
Wit: C. J. Carroll, A. J. Rudicile and H. J. Mattox (x, his mark)
Recorded: 10 Oct 1893
Probate of Will in Minutes of Court of Ordinary, Book G pages 298-299

Eliza J. Baker
 Page 49
Husband: Joel C. Baker
Sons: Robert T. and Samuel W. Baker

/s/E. J. Baker
Date: 7 Oct 1893
Wit: J. W. Watson, J.T. Holliingsworth and W. M. Plunket
Recorded: 15 Feb 1894
Probate and oath in Minutes Book G, page 313

Marcellus B. Hallman of County of Fulton
Page 50-51

Wife: Addie F. Son: John F.

My children.
The children of deceased bros. and sisters to take share which such brother or sister would if in life receive.

Bro: John C. Hallman, Exr.

/s/M. B. Hallman
Date: 11 Jul 1887
Wit: W. D. Ellis, J. Henley Smithand J. R. Gray
Recorded: 10 May 1894
Probate of Will in Common form in the Minutes Court of Ordinary, Book G, page 324. In Solemn form, pages 329-331

Samuel L. Argo of Fulton Co.
Page 52

Son: Robert T. Argo
Sister: Fannie E. Argo
Exr: friend, James T. W. Green, Sr.

/s/S. L. Argo

Date: 13 Jun 1893
Wit: E. H. Mason, J. L. Powell and B. F. Burgess
Recorded: 15 May 1894
Probate of Will and oath of Executor in Minutes of Court of Ordinary, Book G, pages 334-335

Johnanna E. Rowland
Page 53

Dau: Mary Leona Weeks - Lot No. 21 in town of Clarkston, containing one acre, the same which was conveyed to me by the Georgia Railroad and Banking Company by deed executed 28 Aug 1878 and recorded in Deed Book EE, page 180, and it is also described in a deed to me dated 6 Jan 1880 made by William H. Rowland, Admr of the Estate of John W. Fowler, Jr. and recorded in Book EE, page 181.

/s/Johnanna E. Rowland
Date: 12 May 1893
Wit: C. L. Weeks, P. L. Weekes and E.M. Bugg
Recorded: 15 May 1894

Probate of Will and oath in Minutes of Court of Ordinary, Book G, pages 335-336

Andrew Camp
Page 54

Wife: Catherine - 20 acres being part of Lot No. 75 in the 18th Dist. of DeKalb Co. adj. land of Venable Bros. and Nancy Martin.

Exr: I. N.Nash

/s/Andrew Camp (x, his mark)
Date: 10 Jan 1894
Wit: F. C. Wilkie, I. W. Hambrick and W. G. Lanford
Recorded: 18 May 1894
Probate of Will in Minutes of Court of Ordinary, Book G, pages 336-337

George Pressley Elliott
Page 55-57

Exrs to sell my house in City of Conyers, Rockdale Co.
Wife: Nancy C. - lots in Lithonia
Sons: Jesse Mercer Elliott and Levi Septimus Elliott (not of age), and Charles S. Elliott
Daus: Nancy V. Elliott and Toder Jane Elliott (not of age), Mary E. Bellah and Georgia
V. Stewart

/s/George P. Elliott
Date: 11 Jul 1894
Wit: John T. Brand, Charles A. Rankin and A. J. Almand
Recorded: 13 Aug 1894
Probate of Will recorded in Minutes of Court of Ordinary Book G, page 355

George M. Carpenter
Page 58

Wife: Susannah - 165 acres, being all my property.

Exr: nephew, John S. Carpenter

/s/George M. Carpenter (x, his mark)
Date: 20 Jul 1888
Wit: Ambrey Martin, Andrew J. Ball and William S. Power
Recorded: 10 Sept 1894
Probate of Will in Minutes of Court of Ordinary, Book G, page 366

Martha N. Akin
Page 59-60

Dau: Nancy Dora Ann W. Akin - land in Doraville, Ga.
Husband: James F. Akin, Exr.

/s/Martha N.Akin   Date: 8 Feb 1888
Wit: John A. Wimpey, D. A. Chesnut and D. G. Miller
Recorded: 14 Sept 1894
Probate of Will in Minutes G, pages 369-370

Caroline Larendon Gay, widow of G. Larendon of Atlanta, County of Fulton
Page 60-61
Sons: Walter S., Charles A.
Dau: Leila L. Sisson of Kirkwood, Atlanta, Ga.
I desire a wall to be built around our cemetery lot.

My children to date are: Dr. Josh Larendon of Houston, Texas, Col. Charles A. Larendon of New Orleans, La., W. M. Larendon of New York, Leila L. Sisson of Kirkwood and Walter S Larendon of Atlanta, Ga.

/s/Caroline Larendon Gay
Date: 9 Mar 1894

Wit: H. Morrow, H. Mozley and D. Morrison
Recorded: 3 Oct 1894

John Bryce
Page 62-63

Granddau: Anna Elizabeth Corley, formerly Anna Elizabeth Johnson - the S half of Lot No. 9 in 18th District, except Ga Railroad right-a-way, and S half of Lot No. 47 in 18th Dist. Of DeKalb Co., containing in all about 320 acres.

Dau: Parthenia A. Collier, decd.
Son: George W. Bryce
Extrx: granddau., Anna Elizabeth Corley
/s/John Bryce
Date: 15 Jun 1887
Wit: J. R. Russell, John B. Steward and J. W. Kirkpatrick
Recorded: 1 Nov 1894
Probate of Will in Minutes, Court of Ordinary, Book G, page 379

Randolph Payton
Page 63
To my living children and my two grandchildren, viz: Thomas C. Payton, Louvenia C. Brockston, Serena E. Payton, Elmina A. Payton, William F. Payton, Leonard C. Payton, Maritn N. Payton, Melvin C. Payton and Sarry J. Johnson, the two children of my daughter, Nancy Ann Permeathea Johnson (decd).

/s/Randolph Payton
Date: 5 Sept 1894
Wit: H. F. Talton, H.G. Harris and J. S. Atkinson
(no further dates)

Jasper H. Miller
Page 64

Wife: Rebecca A.Miller - 106 acres of land off of Lot No. 337, 18th Dist. of DeKalb Co., etc., and then said property to become the property of Luther D.and Aaron B. Miller, heirs of A. B. Miller and Roxie D. Miller.

Exr: Ebenezer Miller, son of N. R.Miller
/s/Jasper H. Miller
Date: 8 Jun 1888
Wit: H. H. Corley, John R. Reese and William H. Mitchell
Recorded: 8 Nov 1894

Henry Matthews
Page 65

Wife: Francis C. Mathews

I further desire that all the remainder of my estate...be equally divided between my surviving heirs and grandchildren whose parents have died (for as uncle I now have one, Howe P. Lankford).

Exr: son, Henry J. Matthews

/s/Henry Matthews
Date: 28 Aug 1886
Wit: William B. Braswell, John C. Liddell and James W. Andrews
Recorded: 15 Feb 1895
Probate recorded in Minutes G, Court of Ordinary, page 418

John M. Farrar
Page 66

To wife: Three houses and lots in Fulton C. in Forest Park, and lots in Fulton Co. on corner of Maple St., Atlanta, one vacant lot in Decatur, also two cavant lots in Atlanta on Buena Vista Ave.
Wife: Essie Tamora Farrar, sole Extrx

/s/John M. Farrar
Date: 15 Apr 1895
Wit: J. H. Meacham, J. H. Dabney, D. C. Hardage and E. J.Barnes
Recorded: 10 May 1895
Probate of Will in Minutes of Court of Ordinary, Book G, page 435

Mrs. M. F. Slater of Warrenton, Ga., formerly of Atlanta, Ga.
Page 67

Cousin: Jesse W. Stanley
Dau: Mrs. Ida Harbert, wife of High Harbert

/s/M. F. Slater
Date: 14 Jul 1894
Wit: J. A. Allen and I. H. Brinson
Recorded: 15 Jun 1895
Probate of Will recorded in Minutes of Court of Ordinary, Book G, page 449

John W. Clark
Page 68

Wife: Sarah A.
Exrs: wife, Sarah A. Clark, and James Edward Clark

I desire that all my property .... remain just as it is until the minor children are raised and
educated...

/s/ J. W. Clark
Date: 10 Nov 1894
Wit: M. O. Wiggins, J. P., W. P. House and W. H. Burgess
Recorded: 15 Jun 1895
Probate recorded in Minutes G, page 450
Thomas L. Swift of City of Atlanta, County of Fulton
Page 68

Sister: Elizabeth Griffin Swift, Extrx

/s/Thomas L. Swift
Date: 2 Feb 1895

Wit: A. F. Flemming, A. J. Maysfield and C. J. Sheehan
No further dates

Daniel C. Kilgore
Page 69-70

Father: James L. Kilgore (To pay off and fully discharge all debts owing to my father, except the claim of alimony due from my father to Mrs. P. A. Kilgore and the debt of Frank M. Stanley. To my father and his wife, Savannah Kilgore, all of 160 acres, 100 acres being in S half of Lot No. 63 in 16th Dist. of DeKalb Co. and 50 acres which is in the NE corner of said lt, and 10 acres, which is part of Lot No. 66 in said district.

Sister: Mary J. Holcombe

To: Mrs. L. A. Pritchett
To: Samuel Holcombe, son of my sister, Eva
Exr: father, James L. Kilgore

/s/Daniel C. Kilgore
Date: 20 Nov 1894

Wit: William H. Holcombe, John A. Wimpy and J.M. Holt (x, his mark)
Recorded: 15 Jun 1895

Hayden C. Gay
Page 70

Wife: Mittie P.

All my children
Exrs: brother, John F. Gay, and Rebecca E. Gay
/s/Hayden C. Gay

Date: 4 Oct 1890
Wit: John T. Brand, James B. Whatley and Joshua N. Glenn
Probate of Will in Minutes G, pages 457-458

Eugenia A. Mitchell
Page 71

Son: Norman Parker Mitchell

Husband: Joseph Mitchell (land owned by him at the time of his death, which is land known as the Daniel Mitchell place homeplace, bounded W by John T. Alford, S 0by Brown, E by L. T. Y. Nash, N by Nancy Mitchell, the same being a part of Land Lot Nos. 129 and 130 in the 16th Dist. of DeKalb Co., containing 170 acres - willed to my son.

Mother-in-law: Mrs. Margaret Jane Mitchell
Exr: Dr. Joel A. Farmer

/s/Eugenia A. Mitchell (x, her mark)
Date: 20 May 1895
Wit: R. C. Ozmer, N. P., A. S. Johnson and R. W. Milner
Probate of Will recorded in Minutes, Court of Ordinary, Book G, page 458

Brakston Drake
Page 72

Wife: Aney with whom I have lived for many years -all my property

Son: I. R. Drake, Exr

/s/B. Drake (x, his mark)

Date: 29 Jun 1887
Wit: J. T. Brand, H. C. Gay, Thomas Whaley and H. J. Brice
Recorded: 12 Feb 1896
Probate of Will and oath of Executor recorded in Minutes G, page (blank)

John W. Miller
Page 73

Wife: all possessions

Dau: Margaret M. Garrett -W half of Lot 246, and 15 acres of land in NW corner of Lot 233.

Dau: Sarah A. Henderson - E half of Lot No. 233.
/s/J. W. Miller
Date: 1 May 1895
Wit: F. B. Morgan, W. H. Brooks and W. S. Carroll
Recorded: 20 Feb 1896
Probate of Will in Minutes, Court of Ordinary, Book G, page 527

John F. Morgan
Page 74-75

Wife: Eliza Catharine Morgan

My children

To: Alice Eugenia Stephenson, wife of R. S. Stehenson, who is my step-daughter, being the daughter of my present wife.
Exr: R. S. Stephenson of City of Atlanta, Fulton Co.

/s/John F. Morgan
Date: 15 Jan 1896
Wit: L. A. Johnson, M. J. Johnson and Robert Robert C. Alston
Recorded: 9 Mar 1896
Probate of Will in Minutes of Court of Ordinary, Book G, page 36

Virginia F. Bessart
Page 76-77

Granddau: Jessie Carroll, only child of Jessie F. and Annie Bessant Carroll, both decd.
Brother, Dr. J. P. Mell and m nephews, B. J.Mell and W. O. Foot and my sisters, Mrs. F. J. Mayson and V. E. McFail, my Exrs.

/s/V. G. Bessant
Date: 17 Jul 1894
Wit: A. C. Perry, G. O. Perry and C. H. Robinsn
Recorded: 18 May 1896
Probate of Will in Minutes, Court of Ordinary, Book G, page 559

Allen J. Veal
Page 78-79

Wife: Cynthia
To my six children - William J. Veal, John W. Veal, Mrs. Roan Venable, Mrs.; A.B. Russell, Mrs. L. A. King wife of M. P. King and Mrs. Minnie Veal, wife of Allen B. F. Veal, said daughter-in-law, Minnie Veal, being the beneficiary under the will in lieu of A. B. F. Veal.

Granddaus: Mrs. Angeline Paxon and Mrs. Anna Pagett.

My exrs. to erect a suitable monument, being something on othe order of my first wife's monument, and the amount given to my present wife.

/s/A. J. Veal
Date: 29 Jan 1897
Wit: I. N. Nash, J.S. McCurdy and J. C. Pounds
Recorded: 2 Mar 1897
Probate of Will in Minutes, Court of Ordinary, Book H, pages 53-54

Charles Ackerman of Fulton County
Page 80
Wife: Lena, all property. Also apptd Extrx.

/s/Charles Ackerman
Date: 16 Sept 1895
Wit: Aaron Haas, Lounds Calhun and G. A. Howell

Recorded: 8 Mar 1897
Probate of Will in Minutes Book H, page 57
Gideon T. Norman of Greene County
Page 81-82

Sons: James M. and John G. Norman in trust for my daughter, Mary P. Norman during her life.

Son: Alvea P. Norman in trust for his eldest daughter, Louise Norman, during her life.

Should any of my other children during the life of daughter, Mary P. Norman, from affliction or otherwise, be likely to come to want, I desire that my Exr give such assistance as in his judgment is needed out of my estate

Exr: son, James M. Norman

/s/Gideon T. Norman
Date: 11 Oct 1894
Wit: James M. Griffin, J. H. McCommons and James Davison
Recorded: 14 Jun 1897
Probate of Will recorded in Minutes, Court of Ordinary, Book H, pages 90-91

Everett C. Bidwell
Page 83

Wife: Caroline Bucher Bidwell, all my estate, to care for all our children. Apptd Extx.
/s/Everett C. Bidwell
Date: 20 May 1897
Wit: H.I.Ansley, J. C.Bucher and George C. Scott
Recorded: 12 Jul 1897
Probate of Will in Minutes, Court of Ordinary, Book H, pages 109-110

John B. Swanton
Page 84-85

Dau: Eleanor Miles Swanton

Sons: Joe Wallace Swanton, Scott K. Swanton
Wife: Josephine F., Extrx. and trustee of three children (above)

/s/John B. Swanton
Date: 3 Jul 1897
Wit: John E. Miles, T. L. Galloway, E. E. Johnson
Recorded: 10 Aug 1897
Probate of Will in Minutes, Book H, paage 117

J. J. Cowan
Page 85-86

Wife: Mary O. - all property.
/s/J. J. Cowan
Date: 10 Jan 1894

Wit: H. D. Moore, J. D. Moore and E. W. Tanner
Recorded: 12 Feb 1898
Probate of Will in Minutes, Court of Ordinary, Book H, pages 186-187

F. W. Jones
Page 87-89

Wife: all property for herself and benefit of children

/s/T. W. Jones
Date: 2 Mar 1898
Wit: W. H Payne, D. W. Jones and M. W. Murphy
Recrded: 10 May 1898
Probate of Will in Minutes, Court of Ordinary, Book H, page 212-214

Walter S. Alford
Page 90

Wife: Syrena

Children; Luther, Ruth and Foster (minors)

/s/W. S. Alford
Date: 5 Aug 1898

Wit: J. O. Alford, D. A. Alford, Newton M. Reid and M.A. Wellborn, N. P.
Recorded: 6 Sept 1898
Probate of Will in Minutes, Book H, page (blank)

Clary Ann Harper
Page 91

Husband: J. J. Harper, 50 acres, being part of Lots No. 95 and 96 in 15th Dist. of DeKalb Co.

/s/Clary Ann Harper
Date: 21 Jan 1896
Wit: E. E. Watts, James D. Morris and M. O. Wiggins, J. P.
Recorded: 10 Sept 1898
Probate of Will in Minutes, Court of Ordinary Book H, page (blank)

W. D. Adams
Page 92

All my property to my son, J. J. Adams and my son, G. T. Adams, and my daughter, Arminda Davis, to be divided equally.

/s/W. D. Adams
Date: 1 May 1896
Wit: W.R. Warnock, S. H. Wade and W. S. Power
Recorded: 16 Nov 1898
Probate of Will in Minutes H, page 262

William B. Haygood
Page 93

Day: Martha T.
Wife: Sallie M.

/s/William B. Haywood
Date: 22 Feb 1896
Wit: Carlos Know, Thomas L. Sims and J. A. Earl
Recorded: 14 Mar 1899

Madison C. McKee
Page 94

Wife: Sarah E.
Sons: Samuel, George M. and William W.

/s/Madison C. McKee
Date: 12 Apr 1899
Wit: William H. Clark, W. H.Sprayberry and B. M. Sprayberry
Recorded: 5 Jun 1899
Probate of Will in Minutes H, page 331

Samuel C. Masters
Page 95-96

Wife: Mary Jane
Children with my present wife: Samuel W., Mary Jane, William G. and John G. Masters

To: Children of my daughter, Mary Ann, namely, William Stevens and Lucy Stevens. Children of my present wife and all my children by my former wife, namely: Anna Lizar Dorkes. Emily the children of Amanda Ellen, Henry T. Masters, Samuel, Washington, Mary Jane, William Griffin and John Gordon.

Exrs: wife, Mary Jane Masters, and Henry T. Masters and John W. White and William E. Burns

/s/Samuel C. Masters
Date: 17 Sept 1888
Wit: W. J. Clark, T. J. Matthews and William H. Clark
Recorded: 5 Jun 1899
Probate of Will in Minutes f Court of Ordinary, Book H, page 333

Martin McMasters of Fulton County
Page 97-98

Wife: Martha
Daus: Margaret Elizabeth McMasters, Julia M. Lyd and Ida T. Honour.

Extrx: wife, Martha

/s/Martin McMasters
Date: 13 Dec 1893
Wit: M. Taylor, W. M. Middlebrooks and E. B. Rosser
Recorded: 2 Jan 1894
Filed in office and proven in common form 27 Dec 1893

Robert Booth of Oconee County
Page 99

To the children of my decd sister, Louisa Ashford, their share of all of my property.

Exrs: nephews, W. T. Ashford and C. H. Ashford

/s/Robert Booth
Date: Dec 1895
Wit: John W. Johnson, John C. Johnson and R. M. Jackson
Recorded: 8 Nov 1899
Probate of Will in Minutes H, page 380

William H. Ellis
Page 100

Dower to be set aside for wife and minor children
Wife: Minnie L.

/s/W. H. Ellis
Date: 19Dec 1899
Wit: William H.Clark, William H. Boyd and John Ross McKee
Recorded: 5 Jan 1900
Probate of Will and oath of Executr recorded in Minutes H, pages 394-395

J. N. McElroy
Page 101

Dau: Margaret McDaniel apptd Extrx.

/s/J. N. McElroy
Date: 6 May 1899
Wit: John W. McCurdy, W. D. Maddox and James C. Pounds
Recorded: 8 May 1900
Probate of Will in Minutes, Court of Ordinary, Book H page 427

Sarah Ann Caroline Hollingsworth
Page 102-103

Nieces: Mrs. Jnnins Kelley and Mrs. Lula Harper, daus of Mrs. Sarah Ann Caroline Crockett.
Exr: Milton Alexander

/s/Sarah Ann Caroline Hollingsworth
Date: 12 Jan 1899
Wit: J. W. Maysn, C. H. Talley and E. H. Mason
Recorded: 12 May 1900

Probate of Will in Minutes H, page 450

Thomas Jackson
Page 104

Wife: Amanda
Should wife predecease him, estate to be divided between nephews and nieces, except the heirs of deceased brother John Jackson, except Mrs. Lenard by dau of Jhn Jackson. My

bro. and Mrs. M. A. Webb, my sister, share with my nephews and nieces should they inherit.

Son: Thomas C. Jackson

/s/Thomas J. Jackson (x, his mark)
Date: 10 Aug 1900
Wit: H. V. Payne, R. L. Clay and R. A. Kelly
Recorded: 10 Aug 1900
Probate of Will in Minutes Book H, page487

James W. Kirkpatrick
Page 105-106

Daus: Elizabeth Anna Kirkpatrick and Mrs. Mary Parks Fraser (house and lot in Decatur, fronting Atlanta Street, where I now live.

To: Thomas Parks Kirkpatrick, the only child of my decd son, Thomas S. Kirkpatrick, the farm known as the Ragsdale Place on Flat Shoals Road, 3 miles SE of Decatur, about 50 acres.

To: Mrs. Mattie Flowers Kirkpatrick and Thomas Parks Kirkpatrick, the widow and only son of my decd son, Thomas S. Kirkpatrick, 10 acres W of McDonough Road, about a mile from Decatur.

Children: John C. Kirkpatrick, Mrs. Emma G. Stone, James H. Kirkpatrick, Elizabeth Anna Kirkpatrick, Mrs. Mary Parks Fraser and Wallace M. Kirkpatrick.

Exrs: sons, John C. and Wallace M. Kirkpatrick

/s/James W. Kirkpatrick
Date: 7 Mar 1899
Wit: Benjamin F. George, W. J. Houston and Milton A. Candler
(no further dates)

Frank W. Hall
Page 107-117

Widowed mother: Mrs. L. C. Hall
That mother's body be buried in the family burial grounds at Jericho Centre, Vermont. Exrs to select a suitable burial ground for testator.

Estate to be divided between all the brothers and sisters of my decd father, and to all the children of any decd brother or sister of half brother or sister of my father.

To: All the children of Melvin Church, decd, of Randolph, Vermont, who was the only brother of my mother and who had no sister.

To: Mrs. W. W. Gifford of Hardwick, Vermont, the only sister of my decd wife and to all her children.

To: Orville H. Hall of Dahlonega, Ga., a son, and to Mrs. Jesse M. Almand of Conyers, Ga., a dau. of Harmon Hall, decd.

Exrs: Orville H. Hall of Dahlonega, Ga. and Jesse M. Almand of Conyers, Ga.

/sFrank W. Hall
Date: 16 Nov 1896
Wit: P. Roman, H.M. Milam and J. W. Pound

Codicil dated 28 Dec 1898 names William A. Charters of Dahlonega Ga. as Exr instead of Orville H. Hall. Wit: P. Roman, J. W. Pound and H.M. Milam

Codicil dated 4 Jan 1899 withdraws instructions in LWT dated 16 Nov 1896 as to the removal of the remains of my father and mother to Jericho Centre Cemetery. I now suggest to my Exrs that same cemetery in or near Atlanta or Decatur or some other growing place be used.
Nominates wife, Esther C. Hall
of Dahlonega, Ga. as Extrx instead of William A. Charter of Dahlonega. Wit: P. Roman, J. W. Pound and H. M. Milam

Codicil dated 17 Dec 1900 replacing LWT dated 16 Nov 1898 and the Codicils thereto executed on 28 Dec 1898 and 4 Jan 1900. Since the execution of the last Codicil to my LWT, a child has been born to me. Share provided for child and subsequently born children. Wit: C. E. Currier, J. W. Pound and H. M. Milam.

(No further dates)

Mrs. Annie Thrower
Page 118

Husband: James G. Thrower

/s/Mrs. Annie Thrower (x, her mark)
Date: 30 Jan 1897
Wit: Charles W. Smith, Maria C. Harrison and Ellen Dowman
Recorded: 23 Jan 1902

H. M. Thomas
Page 119

Wife: Mrs. S. M. Thomas - 150 acres of Lot No. 12, and 50 acres of Lot N. 21.
Exr: W. P. Staples

/s/H. M. Thomas (x, his mark)
Date: 23 Jan 1902
Wit: W.R. Parks, M. W. Bishop and J. O. McWilliams

George M. Howell
Page 120-121

Father: James Howell
Nephews: Elton Richardson, Oby Howell and Hudie Maulding - the land which was conveyed by deed from James Howell to G. M. Howell.

/s/G. M. Howell
Date: 11 Dec 1896
Wit: John W. McCurdy, J. H. Cantrell and Joseph Gibson
Probate of Will in Minutes I, page 165-166

James T. Cobb
Page 121

Wife: Cordelia E. Cobb
Estate to be divided equally between my children.
To: Susan A. Williams, formerly Susan A. Cobb, part to be divided between her children.
Exrs: sons, James R. and Samuel H. Cobb
/s/James T. Cobb
Date: 27 Dec 1889
Wit: Charles O. Barnes, Edgar F. Barnes and Edward T. Weaver (x, his mark)
Probate of Will in Minutes I, page (blank)

Mrs. Elizabeth J. Veal
Page 122-123

Dau: Annie R. Torrey
Son: Benjamin H. Veal
Granddau: Louise Ragsdale
Children: Mary E. Cloud, Benjamin H. Veal, Bartie C. Ragsdale, Ada I. Hamilton, Lucy G. Wells and Annie R. Torrey.
Grandson: Robert B. Cloud

To be buried in the cemetery at Stne Mountain beside my husband, B. F. Veal.

/s/Mrs. E. J. Veal
Date: 10 Jan 1896
Wit: George R. Wells, J. T. Hamilton and A. J. Goldsmith
Recorded: 20 Jun 1902
Probate of Will before John R. Wilkinson Ordinary, Fulton County, June Term 1902.
See Minutes I, pages 193-194

Nancy E. Brown
Page 124

Great grandchild: Louis Anderson

/s/Nancy E. Brwn (x, her mark)
Date: 31 Jan 1896
Wit: J. J. Hulsey, W. B. DeLoach and T. A. White, J. P.
(no further dates)

Archibald G. Johnson of Acworth, Ga.
Page 124

Wife: I. J. Johnson
Dau: Lizzie Cotton
Grandson: W. W. Johnsn, son of Rev. J. J. Johnson

/s/Archibald G. Johnson
Date: 3 Sept 1892
Wit: W. T. Bate, M. J. Abbott and R. L. McMillan
(no further dates)

Jeff Tate
Page 125

Wife: Ann
Step-granddau: Frances Tate

Exr: W.E. McCalla
/s/Jeff Tate (x, his mark)
Date: 22 Aug 1902
Wit: W. E. McCalla, James R. George and H. C. Austin
Recorded: 14 Oct 1902
Will Probated 6 Oct 1902, Minutes I, page 222

Mary Green Virgin of Bibb County
Page 126

I want to be buried at Riverside Cemetery, with a granite slab. Also, over the graves of my father, Jonathan A. Virgin, my mother, Judiah S. Virgin, and my brother, Frederick B. Virgin.

Brothers: William H. and Jonathan A. Virgin
Sis: Mrs. Loretta J. Hayes

/s/Mary Green Virgin
Date: 17 Mar 1902
Wit: W. D. Barkey, W. E. Britt, N. B. Ousley, J. P.
Recorded: 8 Nov 1902
Probate of Will in Minutes I, pages 240-241

William J. Donaldson
Page 127-128

Wife: Milla A. all land in 18th Dist. of DeKalb Co., Lot No. 361, 54 acres, and 37 acres of Lot No. 352, and Lot No. 353.

Dau: N. L. Turley, wife of Nathan Turley - an equal share with rest of my children.
Dau: Flora L. Wade, wife of Stephen H. Wade.
Son: Thomas M. Donaldson
Son: J. G. Donaldson
Son: A. H. Donaldson
Dau: M. V. Cobb, wife of J. F. Cobb
Dau: Cordelia Donaldson
Son: William A. Dnaldson

William J. Donaldson contd....
Dau: Amanda A. Donaldson

Extrx: wife, Milla A.

/s/W. J. Donaldson
Date: 23 Sept 1899
Wit: W. R. Warnock, J. W. Burnham and W. S. Power
Recorded: 10Nov 1902
Probate of Will, Minutes I, pages 242-243

Garet L. Morris
Page 128-129

Dau: Sarah A. Dollor, formerly Sarah H. Mrris
To: Heirs of my daughter, Nancy E. Jones, formerly Nancy E. Morris.
Son: John A. Morris
Son: Benjamin F. Morris
Dau: Octave V. Moore, formerly Octave V. Morris
Exr: son, Benjamin F. Morris

/s/Garet L. Morris
Date: 11 Jun 1902
Wit:Ira A. Estes, J. D. Moore and H. D. Moore
Recorded: 6 Dec1902
Probate of Will, Minutes I, pages 256-257

Isaac T. Tichenor
Page 130

Children: Mrs. Mary B. Barnes, Mrs. Kate Tichenor Dill, Mrs. Emma Lou Whitner and W. R. Tichenor
Exr: son, W. R. Tichenor

/s/I. T. Tichenor
Date: Jan 1902
Wit: F. A. Kerfrot, Anna Rogers and M. M. Welch
Recorded: 14 Jan 1903
Probate of Will in Minutes I, and Oath of Exr recorded on pages 267-268

Samuel C. Hitchcock
Page 131

To: The 6 daus. of my nephew, Willie Cook of Baldwin Co., Ga. and to Albert Troup Cox of DeKalb Co., son of m dear friends, Albert H.Cox and his wife.

Sis-in-law: Anna E. Cook of Baldwin Co., Ga.
Exr: friend and neighbor, George W. Webb

/s/S. C. Hitchcock
Date: 5 Aug 1901
Wit: L. J. Steele, B. F. Burgess and J. L. Johnson
(no further dates)
James S. McLendon of Fulton County
Page 133

Wife: Martha E. nominated Extrx.

/s/James S. McLendn
Date: 5 Mar 1903
Wit: William S. Thomson, Robert Zachner and Milton A. Candler
Recorded: 5 Mar 1903
(no further dates)

Mrs. Louisa Francis Benson
Page 134

Niece: Mrs. Lottie Treadwell - sole heir

/s/Mrs.L. F. Benson
Date: 5 Aug 1901
Wit: Louie J. Cassells, J. C. Hamilton and J. E. Coffee
Recorded: 5 Mar 1903
Probate of Will in Minutes I, page 284

Mrs. Elizabeth Frances Stowers
Page 135

Sister: Nancy C. Christian
Niece: Katie Christian
Husband: T. J. Stowers
Brothers: Leander Hutchison and Leroy A. Hutchison
To: Harriett Simms

Niece: Mattie T. Newman
To: Mrs. Emma C. Christian

/s/Elizabeth Frances Stowers (x, her mark)
Date: 8 May 1902
Wit: Jeff Glenn, A. J. Coakley and J. C. A. Branon
Recorded: 19 Mar 1903
(No further dates)

Henry H. Burgess
Page 136

To be buried with the rites of the Baptist Church
Wife: Mary E.

/s/H. H. Burgess
Date: 20 Feb 1895
Wit: W. J. Huston, J. L. Powell and Milton A. Candler
Recorded: 8 May 1903
Probate of Will in Minute Book I, page 330

Milly M. Conn of Molino, Escambia Co., Florida
Page 137

Husband: Adna C. Conn - the entire estate.

/s/Milly M. Conn
Date: 4 Jun 1899
Wit: Edward E. Bates, Amanda Daws and Dossey Coleman, all of Molino, Florida
Recorded: 8 May 1903
Probate of Will in Minute Bok I, page 332

J. J. Bishop
Page 138-139

Wife: Elizabeth - 101 1/4 acres in W half of Land Lot 20 of 16th District, DeKalb Co.

Sons: William J., Reubin, Thomas, Marion, Benjamin, Barters, Martin, Bailey and Joseph.
Daus: Nancy Bolton, Missouri Miller and surviving children of my decd daughters, Martha Evans, and daughter, Mary.

/s/J. J. Bishop (x, his mark)
Date: 27 Mar 1899

Wit: R. W. Milner, J. M. Elliott and J. A. Morris
Recorded: 7 Sept 1903
Probate of Will in Minute Book I, page 354

Mrs. S. D. Possey
Page 140

Being at the home of G. W. Possey in Decatur.
Sis: Emma D. Possey.
"After speaking to us, she died on 11 Jul 1903."
Wit: George W. Possey, Mildred Possey and Camote Possey
Recorded: 16 Sept 1903
Probate of Will in Minute Book I, page 363

Annie Matthews
Page 140-141

Bro: Virgil C. Matthews, Exr
Sis: Julia Jane Matthews - lands of the late George W. Mathews, being in Land Lot 3, 5th District, DeKalb Co., 182 acres.

/s/ Annie Matthews
Date: 24 Jun 1902
Wit: T. J. Flake, W. W. McKee and C. E. Smith of Flake, DeKalb Co., Ga.
Recorded: 7 Oct 1903
Will in Minute Book I, page 378-379

George W. Scott
Page 142-144

Children: George D. Scott, Annie Irvin Cooper, Mary H. Candler, Nellie B. Candler and Bessie N. Harman

To: Agnes Scott Institute, to be kept as the Rebecca Scott Memorial Fund

3 sisters of my wife (now decd) - Miss Annie C. Bucker, Hannah C. Bucker and Clara M. Cassels
Niece: Carrie Irvin Scott, dau. of decd brother, Alfred W. Scott

Nieces: Mary S. Bucker, Susan B. Phillips and Carrie B. Billwell, daus. of my decd sister, Susan Bucker

Niece: Ellen Scott of Tyson, Pa., dau. of my decd 1/2 brother, Allen G. Scott

Niece: Rebecca S. Gregory of Alexandria, Pa., dau. of my 1/2 sister, Nancy S. Gregory.
Son: George B. Scott, in trust for my grandson, George W. Scott who is my namesake

Son-in-law: C. M. Candler, in trust for my grandson and namesake, George Scott Candler.

Exrs: son, George B. Scott and sons-in-law, Thomas L. Cooper, Charles Murphy Candler and
Charles E. Harman.

/s/George W. Scott
Date: 19 Aug 1903

Wit: Hiram M. J. Williams, B. J. Crane and B. F. Burgess
Recorded: 7 Nov 1903
Will in Minute Book I, pages 384-386

George H. Dunwody
Page 144-146

To wife and children, land in Fulton Co., being Lots 22 and 23 in 17th District, and known as the Peter Ball property

Dau: Ellen C. Dunwod

/s/George H. Dunwody
Date: 14 Oct 1902

Wit: Joseph S. Power, W. P. T. Tapp, T. N. Sullivan and J. W. Puckett, M. D.
Codicil dated 31 Jul 1903. Wit: J. W. Puckett, M. D., G. W. Copeland and J. P. Nash

Recorded: Nov 1903
Will in Minute Book I, pages 386-187

Mary A. Lide of Stewart Co., but temporarily of DeKalb Co.
Page 147-148

4 daus: Maggie A., Mary A. and Sarah Jane Lide (unmarried), and Annie Ethridge (married).
4 sons: Samuel W., David R., J. W. and B. A. Lide
40 acres in Decatur on E side of Fayetteville Public Road

/s/Mary Allston Lide
Date: 12 Feb 1898

Wit: John T. Harrison, Frank Kirksey and E. T. Hickey
Recorded: 19 Dec 1903
Will in Minute Book I, pages 415-416

Elizabeth Miller
Page 149

To: H. G. H. Miller - 20 acres, being Lot No. 24 in 16th District of DeKalb Co., and 25 acres on S half of Lot 24, 16th District, Lot 9 in 16th District, and 16 1/2 acres in Lot 40, 16th District.

To: Delila McKinsey, G. S. F. Miller, Mrs. M. J. Roberson, J. W. Miller, J. M. Miller and J. L. Miller

Exr: H. G. H. Miller

/s/Elizabeth Miller (x, her mark)
Date: 30 Sept 1903
Wit: J. W. Park, T. Y .Nash and W. E. Thompson
Recorded; 14 Jan 1904
Will in Minute Book I, page 433-434

Nancy Jane Miller
Page 150-151

To: H. G. Miller - my interest in the mill property of my brother, W. A. Miller, locate on the NE corner of Lot 24 in 16rh District of DeKalb Co.

To: Delila McKinsey, G. S. F. Miller, Mrs. M. J. Roberson, J. W. Miller and J. M. Miller and J. L. Miller and Mary Rose and George E. Miller, and Edner L. Miller

Exr: H. G. H. Miller

/s/Nancy Jane Miller (x, her mark)
Date: 30 Sept 1903
Wit: W. E. Thompson, J. W. Park and T. Y. Nash, J. P.
Recorded: 14 Jan 1904
Will in Minute Book I, page 434-436

John Cunningham, late of Savannah, Georgia, now of DeKalb Co.
Page 151-153

Wife.

Mentions a connection with Col. Cleghorn, as well as a partnership with ?
Children: Anney G. Law, Susan Wickham, Shelvy John Cunningham and Thomas Gould Cunningham
/s/John Cunningham, at Decatur, Ga.
Date: 6 Aug 1898
Wit: J. J. Morrison, Charles J. Kamisey, J. L. Johns and J. W. Kirkpatrick, J. P.
Recorded: 14 Jan 1904
Will in Minute Book I, pages 423-424
Margaret Caroline Holtzclaw
Page 153-154

Daus: Ida Bell Holtzclaw and Eutoka Holtzclaw, heirs and Extrx.

/s/Margaret Caroline Holtzclaw
Date: 12 Feb 1904
Wit: Hubert Baxter, H. J. Ausley and W. O. Steele
Will in Minute Book I, pages 445-446

John B. Gordon
Page 154-160

Previously deeded to my wife, Fannie H. Gordon, the homeplace at Kirkland and the McKellar Plantation in Taylor Co., Ga. (1500 acres) and 7 acres in Fulton Co. on Peachtree Road (suburbs), etc., bequeathed to her by her late brother, Hugh A. Haralson.

Sons: Hugh H. and Frank Gordon - my interest in Flint River lands and Forrest Ave. land at Kirkwood, and land in Orange Lake, Fla.

Daus: Fanny and Carrie Lewis.
Exrs: sons, Frank and Hugh H. Gordon and daughters, Fanny and Carrie Lewis, and friend, Albert H. Cox.
/s/John B. Gordon

Date: 8 Aug 1903
Wit: H. L. Perry, A. T. Cox and Robert F. DeBelle
Recorded: 15 Jun 1904
Will in Minute Book I, pages 448-449

John W. Wilkes
Page 161

Wife: C. J.
Dau: Clara
Son: L. Potter Wilkes
Exrs: W. H. and P. L. and C. L. Wilkes

/s/John W. Wilkes
Date: 30 Oct 1903
Wit: James Hunter, E. H. Mason and C. Q. Huney
Recorded: 7 Mar 1904
Will in Minute Book I, pages 473-474

John Hitmelburger
Page 162

Wife: Minnie
Stepson: E. L. Holes

/s/John Hitmelburger
Date: 5 Apr 1898
Wit: J. G. Brown, J. W. Kirkpatrick and J. H. Wilson
Recorded: 5 Sept 1904

Catherine Dougherty of Fulton Co.
Page 163-166

Only child - Nellie Buchanon

/s/Catherine Dougherty
Date: 16 Aug 1892
Wit: Mrs. S. C. Strickland, Mrs. L. Glynn and E. N. Broyles
Codicil dated 13 Aug 1900 names granddaus. of decd dau., Nellie Buchanon - Hattie Camp nee Buchanan and Lucy Buchanan. Wit: J. N. T. Thompson, W. B. Weaver and I. M. Simpson

A. H. Benning of Fulton Co.
Page 166-167

Wife: Margaret R.
To: Elizabeth L. Benning, Theodore K. Benning, Thomas Cobb Benning, Broughton Benning,

Augustus H. Benning, Jr., the children of my present wife.

/s/ A. H. Benning
Date: 21 Sept 1901
Wit: W. T. Conner, S. C. Owens and T. B. Dailey
Will in Minute Book I, page 628

George A. Rampseck of City of Decatur
Page 168

Wife: Margaret M., Extrx - all my property

/s/George A. Ramspeck
Date: 2 May 1902
Wit: H. H.Burgess, I. N.Nash and B. F. Burgess

C. A. Dunwody
Page 169-170

To be buried in Roswell Presbyterian Cemetery next to wife

Grandchild: Ellen C. Dunwody, dau. of my son, George H. Dunwody, decd.
To: Lessie Dunwody, wife of my son, W. G. Dunwody
Nephew: Jefferson Davis Dunwody, Exr

/s/C. A. Dunwody
Date: 23 Dec 1904
Wit: S. H. Spruill, D. Lemmond and C. A. Spruill

John C. Kirkpatrick
Page 170-171

Wife: Mary A.

/s/John C. Kirkpatrick
Date: 29 Apr 1893
Wit: William S. Thompson, Milton A. Candler and Robert Zachner

Edward Rogers
Page 172

Wife: Jennie N., Extrx
Children: Charles, Edna and Rollin

/s/Edward Rogers
Date: 27 Apr 1905
Wit: William A. Bomar, Mrs. Lora Ella Holmes and E. H. Frazer
Will in Minute Book I, page 690

Abe Lankford
Page 173

Wife: Savanah
Exr: Will Lankford, my son
5,634 acres in Lot 253, Savannah, Ga.

/s/Abe Lankford (x, his mark)
Date: 3 May 1905
Wit: W. A. Clark, W. H. Boyd and W. H. E. Sprayberry
Will in Minute Book I, page 695

Hepsey Bell
Page 174

Nieces Dau: Lucy Belle Brooks
To: Fort Sumpter Brooks (niece), Extrx.
Husband: Jefferson Bell

/s/Hepsey Bell (x, her mark)
Wit: Joe Cureington (x, his mark), J. W. Rodgers and A. M. Weir
No dates

Adna Chapin Conn of Decatur
Page 174-175

Son: Charles Francis Conn, Exr
Grdau: Mary Linn Bates
Dau: Lina Conn Bates

/s/Adna Chapin Conn
Date: 23 May 1893

Wit: Homer F. George, W. J. Houston, Jr. and M. H. George of Decatur
Recorded: 7 Aug 1905
J. F. Jones
Page 176

Wife: Catherine E.
10 children: M. E. Carroll, S. L. Jones, L. V. Jones, F. M. Jones, J. R. Jones, P. E. Jones, M. T. Jones, A. K. Jones, J. C. Jones and J. Q. Jones

Exrs: sons, S. L. and J. A. Jones

/s/J. F. Jones
Date: 16 Jan 1896
Wit: William Hairston, J. N. McElroy (x, his mark) and J. B. Mitchell
Proved 4 Sept 1905 by S. L. Jones

Mrs. E. G. Shumate
Page 177

Husband: Charles F. Shumate, Exr.

/s/Mrs. C. F. Shumate
(E. G. Shumate)
Date: 15 Jan 1904
Wit: B. G. Burgess, G. A. Ramspeck and H. C. Jones
Proved by C. F. Shumate 4 Sept 1905

Charles Dowman and Anna W. Dowman, wife (Joint LWT)
Page 178-179

To all our children. Wife and husband inherit from spouse who first succumbs

/s/Charles Dowman
/s/Anna W. Dowman
Date: 14 Apr 1893
Wit: M. L. Baker, J. M. Baker and George B. Scott
Proved by Charles E. Dowman 2 Oct 1905

Augustus L. Pitts
Page 180-181

Wife: Mary

Property to be distributed between wife and my three grandchildren.
Exr: Mark J. McCord

/s/A. L. Pitts
Date: 11 Apr 1905
Wit: E. H. Thornton, W. F. Manry and Will Mauldin

William A. Bomar
Page 181-182

Wife: Emma Elford Bomar, Exr. and Gdn of my children - Jarman Elfora Bomar and Louise Blassingame Bomar

/s/William A. Bomar
Date: 3 Jul 1905
Wit: Mrs. Lora Ella Holmes, Mrs. Jennie N. Rogers and John C. Hamilton

G. W. Parker
Page 182

Children: H. C., A. C., W. F.and J. A. Parker

/s/G. W. Parker (x, his mark)
Date: 9 Sept 1905
Wit: T. A. White, W. B. Owens and R. J. Kelly

Isaac Henry Winfrey
Page 183-184

To be buried near my boyhood home at Shady Dale, Ga.

Nephew: Birt Winfrey, son of my bro., John W. Winfrey
To: J. T. Wyatt, Sr., my cousin (sole Exr, also heir)

/s/Isaac Henry Winfrey
Date: 28 Aug 1905
Wit: John W.Moore, M. E. Underwood and J. C. Underwood

Dr. Charles L. Summey
Page 184-185

Son: Harry H. Summey- all stock in Stone Mountain Milling Co. in Stone Mountain, Ga.

Sisters: Hattie E. Summey and Lula G. Summey
Wife: Emma V. Summey

/s/Dr. Charles L. Summey
Date: 22 Nov 1904
Wit: W. W. Speer, John C. Rankinand Milton A. Candler

Daniel Hess residing at Kirkwood
Page 186

Bro: Philemon Hess of Cincinnati, Ohio
Wife: Kate, Extrx.

/s/Daniel Hess
Date: 21 Nov 1903
Wit: B. M. Zettler, H. M. Hill and Louie J. Cassels

Addie Shelverton of Fulton Co.
Page 187-188

To: Mrs. Minnie May Shelverton, wife of my son, William Shelverton
To: George Barron Shelverton, son of Minnie May and William Shelverton

Children of W. E. and C. J. Shelverton

/s/Mrs. G. W. Shelverton
Date: 23 Jan 1903
Wit: James W. Austin, Ernest C. Kurtz and George B. Rush

Lou M. Warwick of Fulton Co.
Page 189

Husband: C. A. Warwick
Heirs: E. A. Warick, Jr., A. A. Warwick and Mrs. W. E. Fitzpatrick

/s/Lou M. Warwick
Date: 7 Dec 1905
Wit: W. T. Brown, J. M. T. Gaston and William D. Owens

John Barfield
Page 190

Wife: Sarah
To: Edith Pearl Trevor
Children: Frank R. Barfield and Annie M. Bosard
Tools to Malcom Barfield
/s/John Barfield
Date: 25 Feb 1906
Wit: John J. McGirth, W. R. Daby and C. T. Adams

Mrs. Lenna Conn Bates
Page 191-192

Bro: Charles F. Bates, sole Exr
Dau: Mary Bates

/s/Mrs. Lenna Conn Bates
Date: 18 Aug 1905
Wit: Susy E. Cunningham, Mrs. Ruth Pattillo and Marianne McClellan

Will T. Landrum
Page 193

All estate in DeKalb and Fulton counties to my wife, Mary P. Landrum
I am a member of the firm of Will L. Landrum & Sons - all my interest to go to my mother, M.
B. Landrum

/s/Will T. Landrum
Date: 6 Jan 1906
Wit: John W. Landrum, James M. Quinn, R. O. Hester

Thomas B. Wells of Stone Mountain
Page 194

I give to my sons family of children a town lot that I bought of the estate of T. J. Dean,
and nominate Carl T. Wells to sell said lot and divide the proceeds.

Wife: Maggie E. and her 3 children: Willie, Talmon and May Bell.

/s/Thomas B. Wells
Date: 26 Feb 1906
Wit: E. M. Kittridge, G. R. Wells and William Ragsdale

Miss Casander Meador
Page 195
To: Marshal H. George, son of my nephew, James R. George, all my property.

/s/Miss Cansander Meador
Date: 18 Jan 1906
Wit: B. F. Burgess, C. B. McGinnis and M. D. Googer

John P. Tuggle
Page 196-197

Wife: Mary E.
4 children: W. E. Tuggle, H. C. Tuggle and Mrs. Marie P. McCurdy

/s/John P. Tuggle
Date: 26 Jul 1906
Wit: Irwin L. Teat, G. L. Johnson and John W. McCurdy

John H. Chupp
Page 198

Wife: Mary Lucinda - all property

/s/John W. Chupp
Date: 21 Feb 1901
Wit: E. W. Goddard (x, his mark), B. T. Bishop, John W. McGehee and J. T. Pate, J. P.

E. G. Mitchell
Page 199-200

Wife: Henry, and all my children. My wife to support my sister, A. D. Mitchell

/s/E. G. Mitchell (x, his mark)
Date: 15 Oct 1906
Wit: L. J. Stelle, J. F. Brown and James R. George

Thomas J. Phillips of Fulton Co.
Page 200-203

Son: Frank P. Phillips
Kinsman: James Teetwiler

To: Elizabeth Flanders, granddau. of my sister, Laura G. Flanders, money from the estate
of my mother, Mrs. Mary S. Phillips, yet to be divided.

Niece: Mrs. Laura Clayton

Extrx: sister, Mrs. Laura G. Flanders

/s/Thomas J. Phillips
Date: 27 Oct 1906
Wit: Gordon F. Mitchell, W. T. Justin and Eugene M.Mitchell
Codici; dated 22 Nov 1906. Wit: W. T. Justin, W. B. Sharp and Gordon F. Mitchell

Ann Tate
Page 203

Granddau: Frances Tate, all my property

/s/ Ann Tate (x, her mark)
Date: 22 Aug 1902
Wit: W. E. McCalla, H. C. Austinand James R. George

Warren J. Clark
Page 204

Wife: Mary Ann, house and Land Lot 27 (except 5 acres), and one acre of Lot No. 26, etc.

/s/W. J. Clark
Date: 21 Feb 1902
Wit: B. M. Sprayberry, J. A. Wright and J. S. Freeman
Filed in Office: 1 Apr 1907
Mary J. Hampton
Page 205

Cousin and friend - Mrs. Emma F. Pelham with whom I have lived a number of years, my house and lot in Decatur, on SW corner of Railroad Ave. and Candler Street, fronting on Railroad Ave.

/s/Mary Jane Hampton
Date: 29 Nov 1894
Wit: C. A. Cowers, C. M. Candler and Milton A. Candler
Recorded: 6 aug 1907

Mary F. Anderson
Page 206-208

Lot No. 286 in Newton C. to be sold and proceeds given to the children of J. Bliss Anderson.
Four Nieces: Gertrude T. Henry, Mary Lacy Henry, Clara D. Henry and Eleanor Henry

/s/M. F. Anderson
Date: 19 Feb 1880
Wit: Milton A. Candler, Thomas F. Smith and W. F. Pattillo

"Owing to changed circumstances, I desire to make the following changes in my Will.
$100 to go to Mary F. Johnstone
$400 to Sallie Harris Anderson for the business education of her daughter, Brownie, or if said Brownie is provided for, let this sum be used for the education of the baby girl, Susan Dora
Admr - George H. Hammond of Decatur

/s/Mary F. Anderson
Date: 14 Nov 1891
Wit: I. N. Wilson, Arch Avary and Ida A. Young

Codicil, Georgia, Fulton County appoints nephew, Hugh T. Henry of El Paso, Texas, as Exr.
Date: 22 Dec 1906
Wit: Daisy Davies, M. M. Davies and Ulysses Lewis
Filed in Office: 5 Jun 1907
Recorded: 10 Aug 1907

James L. Born
Page 209-211

Wife: Martha A.
Children: James T., John S. and Katie E. Born

/s/James L. Born
Date: 18 Dec 1906
Wit: E. O. Reagin, E. N. Mason and James R. George

Alexander C. Fowler
Page 212-215

Wife: Juliett
Children: D. Elmer, Frances E., Labonah A., William A., John L., Maletos A. and Marcellus R. Fowler.
/s/Alexander C. Fowler
Date: 15 Dec 1877

Codicil....."the name Maletos A. appears. This was the original name of the son who is now called Thomas A. by custom and common consent Thomas A. has become his accepted name." $112.20 to be taken from portion of my estate coming to Laborah A. Hudson Fowler and be given to Thomas A. My wife, Juliette, who was made the original Extrx, has since departed. I nominate in her place my two sons, William A. and Marcellus Royal as the Exrs.
/s/A. C. Fowler
Date: 15 Jul 1905
Wit: J. B. Brown, H. R. Lee, A. K. Jones, N. P. and Ex. of J. P., DeKalb Co., Ga.

Codicil dated 6 Sept 1906. I revoke the appointment of Marcellus Royal as one of the Exrs and instead appoint in his place, my son, John L. Fowler. Wit: H. R. Lee, J. B. Brown, and A. K. Jones

Codicil directs daughter, Frances E. Fowler receive $300. Date: Nov 1907. Wit: James R. George, J. C. Mason, and E. H. Mason.
Recorded: 8 Jan 1908

Martha Goodwin
Page 216

Dau: Mary Irene Walthour, all my property

/s/Martha Goodwin
Date: 8 Jun 1907
Wit: Mrs. A. H. Goodwin, Mrs. A. M. Luck and Paul E. Johnson
Recorded: 3 Mar 1908

V. P. Sisson of DeKalb Co., dated at Fulton Co.
Page 217

Wife: Leila L., sole extrx

/s/V. P. Sisson
Date: 15 Jun 1895

Wit: W. L. Calhoun, A. P. Stewart and P. H. Calhoun
Probate of Will Minutes, Book J, page 472
Recorded: 27 Mar 1908

Mrs. Mary Butler Floyd of Decatur
Page 218

Dau: Mrs. Florida Floyd Hammond of Decatur
/s/Mrs. Mary Butler Floyd   Date: 3 Sept 1904
Wit: L. E. Floyd, Ruth W. White and S. C. Goodman
Probate of Will in Minutes Book J, page 471
Tandy Y. Nash
Page 219

Wife: Mary K.

Children: Leonidas Theodore Young Nash, Lila Pate and Lois Nash

To heirs of daughters, Mrs. Lavonia Minor and Lucy Allen, decd.

/s/Tandy Y. Nash
Date: 29 Aug 1905
Wit: L. B. Norton, A. J. McGahee and J. T. Goose
Recorded: 30 Apr 1908

Mary Veal
Page 220-221

Grandson: Milledge Lee Hadaway, oldest son of W. P. Hadaway
Sons: William W. Veal and P. Veal

/s/Mary Veal
Date: 17 Jan 1901
Wit: J. W. McCurdy, W. S. McCurdy and C. H. Wales
Recorded: 30 Apr 1908

Mrs. Sophie W. Daves
Page 222

Husband: Joel T. Daves, trustee of my children

/s/Mrs. Sophie W. Daves
Date: 4 Jan 1908
Wit: Charles M. Riphern, Charles Whitefoord Smith and Mrs. Fannie W. Smith
Probated in solemn form Feb. Term 1913

Mrs. Virginia A. Douglas
Page 223-226

Children: Peyton Douglas and Mrs. Roberta Douglas Prosser
Sons: Douglas Prosser and Robert O. Prosser
Mother: Mrs. Virginia A. Kimbro
Sis: Mrs. Ella Kimbro Fanley

/s/Mrs. V. A. Douglas
Date: 21 Apr 1908
Wit: D. C. Patterson, Elizabeth Rhodes and Lillie F. Owe4ns
Recorded: 17 Aug 1908

Amanda K. Houston
Page 227-229

Children: Eliza Katherine Sams, Laura Leila Gibbs, Washingon J. Huston, Alice Farr Billups, Sarah Amanda Ripley, Appolonius Bahon Houston, Annie L. Johnson, Robert W. Billups, children of my decd dau., Anna Louisa E., Charles W. Houston, John Chapman Houston, Tyler Peeples Houston, children of decd son, John C. Houston

In the event of the death of Annie L. Johnson, her share to go to her husband, Edward Johnson, to be divided equally and paid to Robert W. Billups and Lanier R. Billups.

In the event of the death of Robert W. Billups, his share to be divided among Annie L. Johnson and Lanier R. Billups

In the event of the death of Appolonius B. Houston, his share to go to his wife, Anna.

The cemetery lots at Oakland Cemetery in Atlanta to be maintained.

Exrs: husband, W. J. Houston and sons, Washington J. Houston and Appolonius B. Houston

/s/Amanda K. Houston
Date: 10 Nov 1906
Wit: Benjamin J. Simpkins, G. W. Pinnell and J. H. Morris
Recorded: 5 Jan 1909

Emma Hendrix
Page 230

Children: Clarence and Emma Hendrix - the house in Decatur, Mary Hendrix

/s/Emma Hendrix (x, her mark)
Date: 5 Oct 1907
Wit: L. F. McClelland, R. W. Ranspess, J. C. Mason
Recorded: 22 Mar 1909

W. R. Warnock
Page 231

Wife: Martha Arminda

/s/W. R. Warnock
Date: 3 Aug 1903
Wit: P. S. Moss, W. R. Nash and W. S. Power, J. P.
Recorded: 20 Mar 1909

Louis O. Stadel, aged 37 years
Page 232

Sis: Lena Stadel Elberta
Exr: J. Ed Balenheimer of Atlanta

/s/Louis O. Stadel
Date: 13 Jan 1909
Wit: Edgar D. Tearing, Nura M. Tearing and Joseph W. Lane, residents of Toledo, Ohio
Recorded: 6 May 1909

James L. Hight
Page 233

Son: Emmett Hight

/s/James L. Hight
Date: 28 Apr 1909
Wit: J. H. Goss, M. D., W. H. Wilkes and D. C. Thompson
Filed in Office: 10 Jun 1909
Recorded: 6 Jul 1909

Ida A. Gillespie of Decatur
Page 234

Husband: David Gillespie

/s/Ida A. Gillespie
Date: 3 Dec 1909
Wit: Daisy West Segar, Hiram Jackson and John Gilfillan
Filed in Office: 10 Jun 1909
Recorded: 7 Jul 1909

William Eugene Perkins of Fulton County
Page 234

Wife: Eva Allen Perkins

/s/W. E. Perkins
Date: May 1909
Wit: W. H. Davidson, J. R. Hardin and M. E. O. Baker
Filed in Office: 1 Jul 1909

George W. Johnson
Page 235

Dau: Florence
Wife: Vashtin P. Johnson

/s/G. W. Johnson
Date: 7 Feb 1889
Wit: T. E. Anderson, J. N. Johnson and J. W. Albert

Milton A. Candler
Page 236

Wife: Eliza A., previously Eliza A. Murphy (before marriage)

/s/Milton A. Candler
Date: 27 Dec 1902
Wit: H. H. Burgess, J. L. Johnson and W. T. Buchanan

Avy Braswell
Page 236-237

Children: J. W. Braswell, Susie Mitchell and Jennie Auchenactie
Exr: John W. Braswell

/s/Avy Braswell (x, his mark)
Date: 10 Jun 1909
Wit: J. K. Marbut, D. P. Philips and L. B. Norton

James D. King
Page 237-238

To be buried decide my decd wife, Rebecca Ann, at Oak Grove Cemetery
To: Oak Grove Methodist Church
To: Carl Nudgins
Present wife: Mary Jane King
Friend: L. T. Wright, Exr

/s/James D. King
Date: 1909
Wit: W. W. Lively, M. C. Akin and H. C. Jones

Isabel Chivers Brown
Page 239-240

To be buried in Decatur Cemetery
Niece: Bernice Chivers for support of her brother, Miller Chivers, a minor, now living with me.
Exrs: friends, Milton A. Candler and W. J. Houston

/s/Isabel Chivers Brown
Date: 8 Dec 1904
Wit: E. A. Northen, T. G. Cunningham and R. W. Trotter

O. P. Ford
Page 240

Wife: Virginia M., sole Executrix
Youngest children: Charlie, Jesse Fernando and Claud P. Ford

/s/O. P. Ford
Date: 17 Mar 1909
Wit: E. H. Mason, B. F. Burgess and R. W. Ramspeck

Belle S. Covington
Page 242-243

Dau: Varina Adolph Covington

son: Henry Clay Covington
Husband: M. L. Covington

/s/ Bell S. Covington
Date: 12 Jan 1909
Wit: George F. Bell, Fred G. Hodgson and C. J. Sheehan
Recorded: 5 Apr 1910

J. R. Long
Page 243

Wife: Lora Jane, Executrix

/s/J. R. Long
Date: 16 Oct 1909
Wit: J. H. Hudgins, W. T. Hudgins and H. P. Tilly

J. D. Miller, Jr.
Page 244-246

Father: J. D. Miller
Sisters: Ella C. Miller and Mabel C. Miller and Nancy E. Miller
Bros: James A. Miller, William A. Miller and George H. Miller
Mother: Mrs. Nancy A. Miller

/s/J. D. Miller, Jr.
Date: 27 Nov 1909
Wit: George N. Croft, Alain T. Richards and Waverly Farmer

Lacie L. Luckie
Page 247

Son: Lane L. Luckie, Exr
Dau: D. I. Pounds
To: Lula L. Nesbit, D. I. Pounds and Emmer L. Nash

/s/Lacie L. Luckie
Date: 2 Mar 1906
Wit: H. C. Jordan, C. W. Phillips and W. P. Lankford

Sadie J. Donaldson
Page 248-249

Son: Donald Donaldson

Dau: Jessie Grinnell Parry
Son (in-law), Harvey L. Parry

/s/Sadie J. Donaldson
Date: 30 Jul 1901
Recorded: 27 Sept 1911, page 290
W. M. Rowden
Page 250

Wife: Martha A.
Exr: George W. Bond

/s/W. M. Rowden
Date: 1 Sept 1906
Wit: Z. J. Almand, J. T. Pate and T. J. Nash

Rebecca J. Phillips
Page 251

Husband: Joseph J. Phillips, Exr

/s/Rebecca J. Phillips (x, her mark)
Date: 3 Mar 1910
Wit: W. P. Huse, J. W. Clay and Fannie E. Prater

John R. George
Page 252

Wife: Mary E. George
Sons: John H., George and William R. George

/s/John R. George
Date: 24 Jul 1908
Wit: G. L. Johnson, J. H. Bailey and Benjamin F. George

William H. Turpin
Page 253-254

Sons: O. B. Turpin (and his children) and J. J. Turpin. Wife: Ruth E.

/s/William H. Turpin
Date: 19 Jan 1904
Wit: S. K. Austin, W. M. Austin and E. M. Smith
Recorded: 23 Sept 1910

Jane E. Cleborne
Page 255-257

Grandson: Christopher Clifford Cleborne - the oil painting of grandfather Christopher James Claiborne and William Claiborne, Colonial Secretary of Virginia; also the miniature of Thomas Claiborne Hall of Westmoreland, England.

Grandson: Edward Bryce DuVal Cleborne - the oil painting of Thomas Claiborne of Claiborne Hall, Westmoreland, England, brother of Secretary, and his progenitor.

Son: Arthur Cleborne, the father of Christopher Clifford Cleborne and Edward Bryce DuVal Cleborne

Sons: Ronayne Cleborne, Cuthbert Cleborne and Alan Cleborne
Dau: Edith Cleborne
Mother: Lucy Parker
Dau-in-law: Cornelia DuVal Cleborne

Children: Ronayne K. Cleborne, Cuthbert J. Cleborne, Alan B. Cleborne, Lucy Cleborne Glover,
Alice Cleborne Rowland, Arthur Cleborne (decd) and children, viz.
Christoher C. and Edward
Bryce DuVal Cleborne, both of Washington, District of Columbia

Exr: Son-in-law, Henry W. B. Glover, and son, Cuthbert J. Cleborne, Paymaster, US Navy

/s/Jane E. Cleborne
Date: 28 Dec 1909
Wit: W. J. Tilson, Fred A. McReynolds and V. V. Tilson
Recorded: 4 Oct 1910

James H. Seavy
Page 258

Wife: Mrs. N. R. Seavy

/s/James H. Seavy
Date: 3 Oct 1908
Wit: Benjamin J. Simpkins, R. W. Ramspeck and L. A. O'Brien

Fannie E. Argo
Page 259-260

Nephew: Robert T. Argo
To: Mrs. Sarah Ann Jackson
To: William Hall, who is a son of my cousin, Martha Hall, living in Atlanta
Decd Bro: Samuel Argo

Mentions an interest in the property Willed to Robert T. Argo

/s/Fannie E. Argo (x, her mark)
Date: 5 Jul 1894
Wit: H. C. Jones, J. L. Powell and B. F. Burgess
Recorded: 14 Nov 1910

Mrs. S. J. Toon of Mell Ave., Edgewood, Ga.
Page 261

Exr: O. R. Lane
Bro: Owen Randolf Lane and his wife, Maria Louisa Lane

/s/Mrs. S. J. Toon
Date: 3 Dec 1907
Wit: A. C. Bruce, E. S. Chipley and S. Schumler

J. D. Smith
Page 261-263

To: Beulah Josephine and Rebecca Smith, my three minor children of wife, Beulah Richardson Smith
Daus: Miss Rosalie Smith and Miss Gladys Smith

/s/J. D. Smith
Date: 5 Nov 1910
Wit: M. L. Covington, Henry S. Wright, M. D. and C. J. Shehan

Missouri N. Stoker
Page 264-265

To: Mrs. Mary Jeffie Foster of Macon
To: Executive Committee of Home Mission of Presbyterian Church of USA
Exr: friend, C. M. Candler

/s/Missouri N. Stoker
Date: 26 Aug 1910
Wit: V. A. Galloway, L. E. Futral and Charles D. McKimey
Recorded: Dec 1910

F. M. Ewing of Richmond Co., dated at Rockdale Co.
Page 266-267

Dau: Nancy H. Ewing, Extrx.
Wife: Nancy

/s/F. M. Ewing
Date: 8 Aug 1904
Wit: David C. Langford, T. T. Hopkins and J. R. Irwin
Recorded: 2 Jan 1910

William O. VanVorst of Savannah, Georgia
Page 268

Wife: Sarah H.
Brother: Christian E. VanVorst
To: Julian P. VanVorst, Garnett Henry VanVorst and Martha Kipp Parramore, children of my brother, Christian E. VanVorst
Mentions real estate in Waresboro

/s/William O. VanVorst
Date: 16 Apr 1897
Wit: J. E. Constantine, H. D. Stevens, and Harring Russell, J. P.
Recorded: 6 Feb 1917

E. H. Guess
Page 270-272

Sons: Robert E. Lee Guess and Andrew White Guess
Daus: Ladonia Texas Shuter and Harriett Eliza Goddard

/s/E. H. Guess
Date: 13 Jan 1906
Wit: T. E. Anderson, J. W. Talley and H. S. Rogers
Recorded: 10 Feb 1911

William C. Gill
Page 273-274

Dau: Grace E. Perry
Grandson: William G. Perry
Wife: Ida M. Gill

/s/William C. Gill
Date: 9 Nov 1910
Wit: Stewart D. Jones, J. W. White and E. T. Stanley

W. H. E. Sprayberry
Page 374-275

Wife: Adella
Exrs: wife, Adella and J. E. Sprayberry
/s/W. H. E. Sprayberry
Date: 31 Jan 1911
Wit: J. G. Sprayberry, B. M. Sprayberry and W. H. Clark

Carl T. Wells
Page 275-280

To: J. S. McCurdy and Dr. W. T. McCurdy and J. I. Nash, in trust for my wife, Bertha Ellen and two children born of wedlock with her, viz. Carl T. Wells, nearing 2 years of age, and Mary Elizabeth Wells, about 3 months of age.

My children: John Dean Wells, Robert Fletcher Wells, Bonnie Jackson Wells, Emily Winfred Wells, Steve Acres Wells and Myrtie Ida Lou Wells, all minors, except John Dean Wells.
/s/Carl T. Wells
Date: 24 Sept 1910
Wit: J. M. Floyd, J. D. Wade and H. H. Suber

B. B. Braswell
Page 281-282

To: Mrs. W. M. Rodgers for looking after Grace Eakes
Exrs: B. B. Braswell, Jr. and W. P. Evans
Heirs: N. P. Evans by N. A. Braswell, and N. A. Braswell
/s/B. B. Braswell
Date: 28 Jan 1911
Wit: E. W. Reagin, J. K. Davidsonand L. B. Norton

Sarah H. Cain of advanced age
Page 282-283

Nephews: Bennett Wiley Jeffares and John N. W. Jeffares, Exrs
To surviving sisters and brothers: Mrs. P. E. Gunter, Mrs. M. A. Gunter,
Mrs. E. S. Baxter, Mrs. P. E. N. Baxter and S. W. Cochran
Mrs. E. S. Baxter is now dead

/s/Sarah H. Cain
Date: 21 Dec 1895
Wit: R. S. Chesnut, Mayfield Nash and G. M. Britt
Recorded: 5 Jul 1911

Mary Jane Carter
Page 284

Children: Eugene Brooks and Fannie Brooks
Bro: Charley Glenn, Exr
/s/Mary Jane Carter (x, her mark)
Date: 21 Mar 1911
Wit: Mary E. Holmes, Ed Brireo and Sam Holmes

Mollie Lewis
Page 285-286

To father, brothers and sisters, Lot No. 9, on E side of Whiteford Ave. in Atlanta
Father: Eugene Carlton, Exr

/s/Mollie Lewis
Date: 13 Mar 1911
Wit: Lee Roberson, Jack Denham and Charles W. Smith

Mrs. Clara G. White
Page 287

Dau: Mrs. Ora Wall, Extrx
To: Mrs. Mary Gazaway, Riff Strickland and Daisy White

/s/Mrs. Clara G. White
Date: 26 Jun 1911
Wit: A. S. Allen, R. H. Ledford and E. H.Mason
Recorded: 7 Aug 1911

Ada Pence
Page 288

See homestead, Record Book B, page 60
Furniture and personal property belonging to John Pence...which claimed under Code of Ga
1882....a family consisting of said wife and his children, to-wit: Ada Pence, age 24 years, Josephine, age 4, Nellie Lee, age 10 months.

/s/Ada Pence (x, her mark)
Filed in Office: 28 Aug 1911
John S. Fowler
Page 289

Wife: Nancy E.

/s/John S. Fowler
Date: 8 Jun 1908
Wit: Charles E. Gibbs, Robert W. Ramspeck and E. H. Mason

Sadie J. Donaldson
Page 290-291

Sons: Donald Donaldson and Harvey L. Parry
Dau: Jessie Grinnell Parry

/s/Sadie J. Donaldson
Date: 30 Jul 1901
Wit: J. W. Moore, J. D. Kilpatrick, Fitzhugh Lee
Recorded: 27 Sept 1904
See Page 148

James Irby
Page 292

Sis: Bular Ledbetter and her son, my namesake, James Britt

5 bros: J. W. Dickerson, M. H. Dickerson

Sisters: Carrie McManors and Bular Ledbetter

/s/James Irby (x, his mark)
Date: 21 Jul 1911
Wit: J. Steve McCurdy, W. G. Miller and C. J. Britt

B. B. Braswell
Page 293-294

Wife: D. C.
To: Mrs. W. M. Rodgers

Mentions N. A. Braswell's share

To: W. P. Evans

/s/B. B. Braswell
Date: 28 Jan 1911
Wit: E. W. Reagin, J. K. Davidson and L. B. Norton

Mary C. Upshaw
Page 295-296

To: Sarah E. Goolsley, Mary J. Harper, late of Cullman Co., Alabama, decd, Lenorah M. Reed, Ida P. Upshaw, late of Carroll Co., decd, and Georgia E. Furlow

Exrs: Ruban D. Read and C. W. Furlow

/s/Mary C. Upshaw
Date: 5 Nov 1903
Wit: E. L. Jones, High Jones and D. M. Boatright

Codicil names daughter, Georgia Ella Furlow, dated 5 Nov 1903

John D. Moore of City of St. Louis
Page 297-298

Children: Clara M. Jones, Arthur E. Moore, Gertrude P. Deering (wife of John R. Deering)

Wife: Sarah Ann

/s/John D. Moore
Date: 19 Feb 1904
Wit: Louis A. Bosso, George W. Jenkins and Herbert Haid

Charles H. Weld of Cobb Co.
Page 298-300

Dau: Mrs. Imogene Murray, Extrx, and trustee for her children. Her husband, George C. Murray
Grandsons: Cecil R. Murray and George F. W. Murray
Granddau: Mabel Davis Murray
Grandson: Archie G. Murray
Daus: Mrs. Imogene Murray, wife of George C. Murray of Cobb Co.
Granddau: Marjorie M. Murray
Land in Lot No. 588, 18th Dist., 2d Section of Cobb Co.

/s/Charles H. Weld
Date: 22 Sept 1903
Wit: Harvey Hatcher, Eugene M. Mitchell and Gordon F. Mitchell

William Henry Green
Page 300

Wife: Sarah Frances, Extrx

/s/William Henry Green
Date: 16 Apr 1911
Wit: J. E. Van Valkenberg, O. O. Williams and J. B. Wheat

Margaret C. Keys
Page 301

Husband: Lewis A. Keys
Dau: Cynthia Keys
/s/Margaret C. Keys

Date: 21 Feb 1896
Wit: B. F. Burgess, E. H. Mason and M. D. Googer

J. B. Ragsdale of East Atlanta
Page 302

Dau: D. D.
To: J. T. Ragsdale, O. L. Ragsdale, M. C. Ragsdale, Mrs. Parker, Mrs. Keen, Mrs. Owens, Mrs. Simmons, Mrs. Crumby

/s/J. B. Ragsdale
Date: 14 Jan 1911
Wit: C. C. Cravill, Wayne Pattillo and J. G. Lietch

Cobbie Hoad Ridley
Page 303

Husband: R. B. Ridley
Children: Carl Hood Ridley, Mrs. Sarah Claire Hunnicutt, Marie Hood ridley, Nellie Hood Ridley

/s/Cobbie Hoad Ridley
Date: 13 Sept 1912
Wit: J. Howell Green, B. F. Burgess and R. B. Ridley, Jr.
Recorded: 7 Oct 1912

Thomas I. Loudon Walker
Page 304

Dau: Mattie Walker Davis
Granddau: Beulah Parlee Walker, dau. of Lillie Walker, now of Fulton Co., Ga.
Exr: J. J. Davis

/s/Loudon Walker (x, his mark)
Wit: E. L. Stowers, H. Tyler and H. T. Brown
Recorded: 3 Feb 1913

R. C. Shumate
Page 305

Dau: Mrs. Elizabeth Hawkins
Son: Henry C. Shumate

/s/R. C. Shumate
Date: 23 Oct 1912
Wit: Charles E. Gibbs, W. G. Hudson and Alfred Bouliguy

C. H. Visby
Page 306

Wife: Betty Marie Visby, born Jenson. We were married 12 Sept 1903 at Woodward Avenue Baptist Church. The witnesses were Mrs. Kate Clark and Mr. Hafley, 18th and Spring Street.
Dau: Emma Eliza Visby
Exr: Valdeman Gude

/s/C. H. Visby
Date: 12 Sept 1912
Wit: Eugene Hardaman, Sr., M. I. Mable and Mrs. Elizabeth Mable
Recorded: 4 Mar 1913

William Green Middleton
Page 307

Wife: Ida B. Haig Middleton

/s/William Green Middleton (x, his mark)
Date: 11 Jan 1913
Wit: C. C. Goode, J. W. Green and W. C. Jones
Recorded: 8 Apr 1913

James S. Bryan of Newton Co.
Page 308

Wife: Ella B., Extrx.

/s/James S. Bryan
Date: 30 Jun 1897
Wit: James M. Belcher, John F. Henderson and J. M. Pace
Recorded: 8 Apr 1913

Fannie L. Pratt of Decatur, dated Atlanta
Page 309

Sis: Julia Pratt Kennedy
Exr: Nathaniel P. Pratt

/s/Fannie L. Pratt
Date: 10 Jun 1910
Wit: C. H. Paine, Linna Brown and Mary Fulbright
Recorded: 5 May 1913

Josephine Davis
Page 310

Niece: Annie Stephenson, house at #22 Foster Street
/s/Josephine Davis
Date: 15 Aug 1912
Wit: Sol Worthorp, M. Worthern, Moses Pritchett (x, his mark)
Recorded: 12 Jun 1913
Mrs. F. E. Crittenden of Fulton Co.
Page 311

Daus: Mrs. Susie R. Wicks and Mrs. Mary E. Wilkins

Grandson: Joe Julin McGrann

/s/Mrs. F. E. Crittenden
Wit: Frances Junckel, R. C. Harris and Paul S. Etheridge
Recorded: 8 Jul 1913

Mary E. Bryan
Page 312

Daus: Mrs. Pearl Byrd - house and lot in Lloyds, Florida, and Mrs. Ada Wilcox

Exr: Walter McElreath

Son: Fred Bryan - house and lot where I now reside in Clarkston, Ga.

Son: John E. Bryan

/s/Marty E. Bryan
Date: 16 May 1913
Wit: Mrs. L. E. Bloodworth, Mrs. Addie L. Lindsey and E. R. Clarkston
Recorded: 9 Jul 1913

Paul F. Long
Page 313

To be buried at Corinth Baptist Church in Chamblee beside my beloved wife's grave
Sons: F. C., P.M., C. D. and M. B. Long

Real estate to go to Mollie Long, wife of my son, W. B. Long and her son, D. L. Long, heir of W. B. Long
Exr: W. D. Wallace of Chamblee

/s/Paul F. Long
Date: 2 Dec 1911
Wit: J. R. Burriss, C. M. Lancaster and H. C. Holbrook
Recorded: 9 Jul 1913

Joseph E. Munday of Doraville
Page 314

Wife: Eunice B.

/s/Joseph E. Munday
Date: 2 Dec 1911
Wit: W. T. Stewart, W. R. McCurdy and J. L. Beaty
Recorded: 11 Sept 1913

Amos A. Kittridge
Page 315

Bro: Edward M. Kittridge
Sis: Susan Metlock

/s/Amos A. Kittridge
Date: 24 Apr 1913
Wit: Syrena E. Snead, H. L. Hardman and James J. Moore
Recorded: 8 Oct 1913

Thomas Terrell
Page 315

To: Thomas Weldon Beasley, all my property, and to be my Exr

/s/Thomas Terrell (x, his mark)
Date: 9 Jan 1911

Wit: N. P. Pruitt, Palmer Pruitt and Julia E. Pruitt
Recorded: 8 Oct 1913

Martha Jane Johnson
Page 316

Nephews: William P. Bailey and Edmond T. Bailey

/s/ Martha Jane Johnson (x, her mark)
Date: 2 Nov 1912
Wit: J. T. King and J. E. Chupp
Recorded: 4 Nov 1913

Moses R. Stephenson
Page 317-318

To be buried in cemetery at Conyers
Wife: Mary

/s/ Moses R. Stephenson
Date: 24 Oct 1907
Wit: L. G. Evans, J. T. Pate and T. Y. Nash, J. P.
Recorded: 8 Jan 1914

Alonzo M. Callaway
Page 319-321

4 children: Thomas G., Sarah L., John L. and Ernest e.
Wife: Sarah A., Extrx.

I have made provision in the year 1895 by a settlement out of my property for a girl child of Blanche Callaway nee Blanche Chupp, the daughter of J. C. Chupp.
/s/ Alonzo M. Callaway
Date: 11 Dec 1896
Wit: A. J. Almand, W. N. George and T. P. George
Recorded: 8 Jan 1914
I. N. Nash
Page 322

Wife: Indiana
To: Douglas Nash McCurdy
Dau: Marietta McCurdy and her children

Exrs: wife and J. DeWit McCurdy

/s/I. N.Nash
Date: 12 Nov 1913
Wit: E. A. Graham, R. W. Evans and G. L. Johnson, J. P.
Recorded: 2 Feb 1914

Mrs. Annie Lee Gower
Page 323

Father: John J. Albert as trustee for my mother and my six children: Harry, age 19, Mary Bell, age 17, George W., age 15, Sarah Frances, age 13, and Luther J., age 11, and Robert Lee, age 9.

/s/Mrs. Annie Lee Gower
Date: 19 Jun 1913
Wit: Piromis N. Bell, J. J. Hudson and T. A. White
Recorded: 9 Feb 1914

Harriett Humphries
Page 324

Husband: David
Grandchildren: Luther, Arthur, Willie and Nay George
Grandson: Luther George, exr
Son: Israel George

/s/Harriet Humphriex (x, her mark)
Date: 13 Aug 1902
Wit: W. D. Broadnax, A. A. Warwick and E. A. Warwick
Recorded: 11 Mar 1914

Rebecca T. Vaughan
Page 325

I own Lot 519, Sec. 9, Westview Cemetery, Atlanta. I am to be buried in grave No. 3. Paul E. Vaughan being buried in Grave No. 1 and Kate E. Vaughan in grave No. 2

A monument to be placed over my aunt's grave, Sarah E. Pittard, at Winterville, Ga. And my sweet mother.

To: Myrick B. Pittard, Katie Sue Ferbey, Ella Denson and Egthel Torbey

Mother's cousin: J. T. Pittard, Exr.
/s/ Rebecca T. Vaughan
Date: 11 Jul 1912
Wit: L. T. McDowell, Dameron Black, and Lillian C. Cresthurst
Recorded: 6 Apr 1914
Anna Lou Ella Stallings of Atlanta
Page 327

Son: Luther Kennedy Stallings

/s/ Anna Lou Ella Stallings
Date: 6 Mar 1914

Wit: Virginia Avera, N. Pittman and Texie Ann Hatcheson
Will recorded in Minutes Book M, page 479

Samuel H. Braswell
Page 328-329

To be buried in family graveyard at Prospect Church near Doraville.
Also, Georgia A. Braswell.
Children: George P. and Loutie E. Braswell, N. Dora Tapp, Bessie A. Ross and P. Pearl Hannah
Son: George P. Braswell, Exr

/s/Samuel H. Braswell
Date: 10 Sept 1913
Wit: David G. Miller, M. T. Ellis and J. E. Flowers
Recorded: 17 Apr 1914
Recorded Minute Book M, page 473

Thomas H. Fincher
Page 330-331

Children: Alonzo Fincher, Thomas N. J. Fincher, Edgar F., Lizzie E. Simpson, Allison M. Fincher
and Hassie M. Matthews

/s/Thomas H. Fincher
Date: 18 Mar 1910
Codicil: 15 Jul 1910. Wit: Jake Hall, B. M. E. Elliott, Jr. and C. C. Crabill
Recorded: 5 Jun 1914

Elizabeth Frances Nash
Page 332-333

Son: J. A. Austin
Grandchildren: Ida May and Maggie Austin
To: W. F. Nash
Exrs: J. A. Austin and W. F. Nash

/s/Elizabeth Frances Nash
Date: 21 Dec 1900
Wit: J. W. Mitchell, W. C. Horton and G. B. Walker
Recorded: 10 Jun 1918
Recorded in Minutes Book M, page 552

Walter G. Bothwell
Page 334

Wife: Nannie Bell Thornton Bothwell
To: Charles Lovejoy Bothwell, furniture

/s/Walter G. Bothwell
Date: 2 Jun 1914
Wit: D. King Summers, Pauline Rose and Mary E. Cook
Recorded: 6 Jul 1914

Mrs. Alice W. Perry
Page 335-336

Sis: Cecilia A. Mayhew
Husband: John James P. Perry
Son: Charles Henry Mayhew Perry
Cousin: Charles Hayes
Daus: Helen Frances Perry and Alice Patrick Perry
Exrs and Gdns of my minor childeren - Ren Troy Beatty, and my husband

/s/Mrs. Alice W. Perry
Date: 2 Aug 1910
Wit: R. P. Shapard, E. G. Black and M. G. Couch
Recorded: 6 Jul 1914

James Kelly
Page 336

Wife: Janette, Extrx

/s/James Kelly
Date: 6 Jun 1912
Wit: S. B. Norton, Dr. George W. Carrell and D. T. Phillips
Recorded: 5 Aug 1914

George S. May
Page 337-342

To: Pauline J. Handsman of Munich, Vavaria, Germany
To: Marion, dau. of my wife, M. Florence May, lately decd
To: Mari Taege, my housekeeper
To: James R. Nutting and Wharton O. Wilson of Fulton Co.
To: Ethel, sister of M. Florence May

Dau: Edith K. May

To the children of my decd daughter, Margaret E., former wife of Anderson Henshaw Ward of Milton, Massachusetts

Exrs: friends, Marcus W. Beck and Henry C. Peeples of Fulton Co.

/s/George S. May
Date: 17 Feb 1913

Wits: Walker Denson, J. T. Moore and J. V. Dunlap

Codicil dated: 17 Feb 1913 names Mrs. Ethel Adamson, wife of Robert, and Marie Taege, housekeeper. Also, William Howard White of Boston, Massachusetts, in trust for my daughter, Edith K. May. Wit: C. G. Parish, Mrs. C. C. Cliett and Charles C. Cliett

Codicil dated: 1 Aug 1914, names Marion McClintock, dau. of my wife, M. Florence May. To: Mrs. Ethel Adamson. Revoke bequest to Marion McClintock, dau. of my decd wife, M. Florence May. Wit: Wilbur S. Powell, Ruth Blackman and Mary E. Cook. Recorded: 8 Sept 1918. Probated in common form 7 Sept 1914. Minute Book N, page (blank)

John A. W. Fleming
Page 343

Wife: Mary N., Extrx

/s/John A. W. Fleming
Date: 31 Aug 1909

Wit: R. T. Gilliam, R. C. W. Ramspeck and E. H.Mason
Recorded: 9 Sept 1914
Probated in solemn form 7 Sept 1914. See Minute Book N, page (blank)

Alexander Hamilton Kent, Sr.
Page 344-346

Sons: Alexander Hamilton Kent, Jr., Edgar Ross Kent, Thomas S. Kent, Clement F. Kent and
Harry W. Kent.

Dau: Mrs. Annie Kent Russell

To be buried in Thomas T. Freeman's lot at Episcopal Cemetery at Marietta adjoining my decd wife.

Exr: Trust Company of Georgia

/s/ Alexander Hamilton Kent, Sr.
Date: 20 Apr 1912
Wit: Alfred M. Battey, Edward R. Rowlin and C. C. Williams
Probate in Minutes Book N, page 68, 244

Mary Elizabeth Leverett
Page 347

Nephew: Simeon E. Leverett, Exr

/s/ Mary Elizabeth Leverett (x, her mark)
Date: 12 Mar 1896
Wit: James R. Smith, William J. Veal and T. T. Nash, J. P.
Recorded: 7 Oct 1914
Recorded Minutes Book N, page (blank)

Marthy Frances Leverett
Page 348

Nephew: Simeon E. Leverett, Exr.

/s/ Marthy Frances Leverett (x, her mark)
Date: 12 Mar 1896
Wit: James R. Smith, William J. Veal and T. T. Nash, J. P.
Recorded: 10 Oct 1914
Recorded in Minutes Book N, page (blank)

Kate Robson
Page 349-352

To: Corrie Robson Dunwody, daughter

Granddaus: Kate, Elizabeth, Cornelia, Mabel, Roberta, Julia and Norwood Dunwody
My namesake, Kate Hester Dunwody

I sold to B. M. Bishop the old homeplace described in a deed from Peter Pelham to my decd husband dated 25 Jan 1873 and recorded in Book K, page 528, DeKalb Co. Record.

Son: Henry Robson

/s/Kate Robson
Date: 23 Feb 1912
Wit: William A. Fleming, C. H. House and John J. Armstrong

Codicil dated 22 Oct 1912 names son-in-law, Jefferson Davis Dunwody, now decd.
Appoints sons, Henry and Paul Robson and dau., Cornelia Robson Dunwody, Exrs. Wit: J. H. Lowery C. H. House and John J. Armstrong

Codicil dated 28 Feb 1913, Kirkwood. A stone wall to be built around the family cemetery

3rd Codicil dated 21 Mar 1914. Henry Robson having died on 28 Aug 1913, I appoint my grandson, Robson Dunwody, Exr. Wit: Robert S. Wynn, Jr. and J. M. Hartley.
Will probated 2 Nov 1914. See Minutes Book N, page 110

Alfred L. Britt
Page 352-353

Wife: Minnie, Extrx
Bro: George W. Britt to be Exr in case my wife dies
Children

/s/Alfred L. Britt
Date: 22 Sept 1914
Wit: C. N. Britt, W. E. Hughes and Thomas A. Maney

Amandy Smith of Fulton Co.
Page 353

Adopted dau: Mary Nesbet
To: William Smith

Granddau: Lizzie Walker
My only son - John A. Smith

/s/ Amandy Smith
Date: 13 Nov 1913
Wit: John Gibson, O. M. Adams, M. D., and A. E. Kay
Will probated :7 Dec 1914

Oliver Winningham
Page 354-357

Daus: Laura Ann Humphreys, wife of Nat Humphreys, Bella Reid, wife of Ira Reid, Katie Miller, wife of William Miller, Nattie Sheppard, wife of Samuel Sheppard.

To: Minnie Veal, wife of A. B. F. Veal

Son: Frank R. Winningham

Grandchildren: Ione, Josephine and Nattie Sam, children of my son, Mike Winningham, decd

Exrs: Sam S. Sheppard, William W.Miller (sons-in-law), and son, Frank R. Winningham

/s/Oliver Winningham
Date: 16 Jun 1910
Wit: W. O. Woods, W. N. Maddox and James R. Wells

Fannie R. Lamb of Atlanta
Page 358

Niece: Mattie Manceley
To: George E. Lewis of Tallahassee Florida
Brother's wife: Mary Hicks
Nephew's wife: Nannie Bolton and to children of David E.. Bolton after her date
Niece: Sara Ann Golitle
To: G. E. Lewis intrust for Mattie Manceley and at her death to be paid to Fannie May Bennett, Raymond Manceley and Hazel Saunders
To: Pat and Albert Lamb

To be buried deside husband in Tallahassee

Residue of estate to: Mary Hicks, Napoleon Hicks, Nannie Bolton, Mattie Manceley, Ada Loder, Sarah Ann Golitle, Fannie May Bennett, Raymond Manceley and Hazel Saunders

Exr: George C. Lewis

/s/Fannie R. Lamb
Date: 25 Mar 1912
Wit: George Lewis, A. Bernard Byrd and W. S. Quarterman

Robert C. Wilson
Page 359

Wife: Henrietta

/s/Robert C. Wilson
Date: 22 Feb 1912
Wit: R. W. McElroy, B. B. Check and J. M. Check
Recorded: 19 Jan 1915

William J. Campbell
Page 360

Wife: Nattie Erwin Campbell

/s/William J. Campbell
Date: 9 May 1900
Wit: J. L. Harrison, John H. Ewing and Charles D. Meador
Will probated 1 Feb 1915

W. J. Wiggins
Page 361

Wife: Mrs. Anna Wiggins

/s/W. J. Wiggins (x, his mark)
Date: 28 Nov 1913
Wit: O. G. McConnell, J. M. Farmer ande E. T. White
Will probated 2 Feb 1915
++++

Mrs. Virginia M. Ford
Page 361

6 sons: Albert Ford, Vivian Ford, P. P. Ford, Charlie Ford, Fernanda Ford and Claud Ford.

/s/Mrs. Virginia M. Ford
Date: 23 Oct 1914
Wit: Alfred Bouliguy, J. A. McCurdy and B. F. Burgess
Will probated: 8 Feb 1915

J. F. Harris
Page 362

Wife:Mary F.
Son: L. W. Harris

/s/J. F. Harris
Date: 26 Sept 1910
Wit: J. F. Harris, C. A. Morris and D. C. Thompson
Will probated Feb 1915

Mrs. Mary Taylor Jones
Page 363

Dau: Virginia Stuart Jones

Exr: L. M. Jones

Bro: John Ross Taylor

/s/Mrs. Mary Taylor Jones
Date: 23 Oct 1914
Wit: Weyman Patillo, B. H. Burgess and Alfred Bouliguy
Will probated Feb 1915 Term

Walter S. Larendon
Page 364

Wife: Mary Elizabeth, Extrx

Daus: Caroline Morgan and Phillis Margaret

Mother-in-law: Mrs. Laura G. Flanders

Sis: Mrs. Leila L. Sissons

Nephew: Charles A. Sissons, Exr

/s/Walter S. Larendon
Date: 7 Oct 1905
Wit: John W. Collier, E. M. Holland and W. E. Armistead
Probated in solemn form March Term 1915
Recorded: 2 Mar 1915

C. S. Reid
Page 365-368

Sis: Florence is allowed to live in the old home at Blairsville during her lifetime.

Sis: Laura, Florence, Emily

Bro: Normy and Harry

Wife: Nettie Handley Reid
Daus: Katherine, Ethel and Grave

/s/C. S. Reid
Date: 23 Mar 1915
Wit: J. A. McCurdy, E. H. Mason and B. F. Burgess
Recorded: 7 Jul 1915
Will probated Jul Term 1915 in solemn form

Elijah Braswell
Page 369-370

Dau: Flonnie

Children: Samuel, Quillian

Children of dau., Arci (decd)

/s/Elijah Braswell
Date: 9 Feb1915
Wit: J. L. Chupp, H. B. Jenkinsand J. T. Brooks
Recorded: 7 Jul 1915
Recorded in common form Jul Term 1915

James Selkirk Burney
Page 371

Uncle: James Melrose Selkirk, sole Exr and heir

/s/James Selkirk Burney
Date: 27 Apr 1915
Wit: Belle Berman, W. H. Roach and O. R. Moore
Recorded: 7 Jul 1915
Will probated in solemn form Jul 1915

W. J. Reagen
Page 372

We, the undersigned, on the night of 8 Feb 1915, at the home of W. J. Reagen,,,who was then in life and himself knwing that he was dying....he died 7 Feb 1915, named his wife and children as heirs.
Wit: Mrs. M. E. Carroll, J. A. Jenkins, E. H. Reagin, Byron White and T. H. Reagin
Date: 12 Feb 1915

W. S. Johnson
Page 373-374

Wife: Sarah E. - homeplace on Rowlin St. in Clarkston, Ga.

Son: Robert W. Johnson
/s/W. S. Johnson
Date: Mar 1915
Wit: J. C. Estes, C. Stephenson and W. P. Brown

William Jackson
Page 374

Sis: Martha Jackson Marion
Exr: G. M. Britt
/s/William Jackson
Date: 3 Aug 1915
Wit:L. H. Letson, J. H. Brooks and W. N. Henderson
Probated Oct Term 1915

George W. Warren
Page 375-377

Wife: Ann Hollingsworth Warren

Nephew: Lee Hollingsworth of Rockdale Co., son of James

Niece: Beulah G. Knapp (my wife's niece)

Nephew: J. W. Warren of Gordon Co.

/s/George W. Warren
Date: 17 Jun 1915
Wit: H. T. Thompson, B. B. Patterson and Alfred Bouliguy

J. W. Ozuier
Page 377-379

Son: R. C. Ozuier.
My children

Exrs: sons, John N. and William A. Ozuier

/s/J. W. Ozuier
Date: 29 Jul 1911
Wit: John F. Bates, W. P. House and E. P. Hamilton
Probated Oct Term 1915

George W. Webb
Page 380-382

To be buried beside my mother in Ousley Chapel Cemetery.
To: Trustees of Ousley Chapel Church - C. C. Childress, J. B. Loyd, D. R. Barfield and J. W. Scott
Wife: Mary

If I had three brothers and one sister living
Exrs: nephews, Guy Webb and Thomas C. Jackson

/s/George W. Webb
Date: 23 Jun 1914
Wit: C. C. Childress, M. P. Scott and T. A. White
Will probated Oct Term 1915

Codicil dated May 1915. Niece: Mary Webb. To: Bernard and Roy Burnham and William A. Jackson. Wit: Lee H. Jackson, D. R. Barfield, Nelson Snow.
Will Probated Oct Term 1915

Stewart Jackson
Page 384-385

Dau: Martha Jackson Scruggs, Extrx
Wife: Queen Terrell Jackson
Son: Efford Jackson

/s/Stewart Jackson
Date: 21 Jul 1915
Wit: R. J. Holt, W. T. Buchanan and William F. Buchanan
Will Probated Oct Term 1915

L. G. Carroll
Page 386

Wife: Martha, Extrx

To: Candler W. Bennett and his wife, Sallie A. Bennett

/s/L. G. Carroll
Date: 21 Jun 1915
Wit: V. S. Morgan, R. E. Carroll and B. F. Burgess
Will probated in solemn form 6 Dec 1915

Lizzie Parker
Page 387

To: Mrs. Ella Collier, wife of Charles Collier of Decatur, half-sister, sole heir and Extrx.

/s/Lizzie Parker
Date: 19 Jan 1915
Wit: Mrs. Gracia George, G. L. Loder and L. J. Steele
Will probated in solemn form 6 Dec 1915

J. F. Hatcher
Page 388

Wife: Leo E., Extrx
To all my children

/s/ J. F. Hatcher
Date: 5 May 1915
Wit: H.N. Tilly, S. M. Clark and D. M. McKee
Will probated in solemn form 13 Jan 1916
See Minutes Book N, page 576

William H. Davidson
Page 390-391

City of Atlanta property
Dau: Jewell W. Haskett
Granddau: Adeline Davidson, the share she is to receive in place of her father, J. B. Davidson, decd.

Son: Leonard B. Davidson
Dau: Pearl M. Davidson

son and dau., Exrs

/s/William H. Davidson
Date: 23 Sept 1915
Wit: R. G. Head, R. B. Fortress and Scott Candler
Recorded: 3 Sept 1915
Will probated in solemn form Sept Term 1916

Ophelia T. Erwin
Page 392-393

Sns: Frank, Hugh Milton and Howell C., Jr.
Husband: Howell C. Erwin
Grdau: Runa Patterson Erwin

/s/Ophelia T. Erwin
Date: 17 Jan 1913
Wit: J. Howell Green, H. R. Alinson and W. C. McLain
Will probated in solemn form Apr Term 1916

Edward M. Kittredge
Page 394

Wife: Eliza.
Youngest child: S. Emma
Children: Minnie L. Bugg, Mattie M. Hudgins

/s/Edward M. Kittredge
Date: 18 Sept 1913
Wit: J. L. Johnston, L. M. Johns and J. A. Leavell
Will probated in common form Apr Term 1916

Mrs. Sallie E. Chesnut
Page 395

Daus: Dora, Susie and Ruth
Son: Wilbert Chestnut, Exr

/s/Mrs. Sallie E. Chesnut
Date: 21 Dec 1915
Wit: J. K. Coman, G. C. Roberts and Roy E. Patterson

Thomas J. Hightower
Page 396-400

Wife: Georgia H.

Sons: Milton H., Allen R., Harrison H., Thomas Jefferson, John Bedney, Mary and Albert Sidney Hightower

Dau: Ida Ruth Sisson

Exrs: T. J. and J. B. Hightower, sons

/s/Thomas J. Hightower
Date: 29 Oct 1913
Wit: W. V. Crowley, J. C. Overstreet and Samuel A. Swanson
Codicil dated 29 Oct 1913
Codicil dated 1 Nov 1913 names Trust Co. of Ga. as trustee at death of son, Albert Sidney Hightower

Codicil dated 16 Nov 1915

Mary Jane Parker
Page 401

To be buried at High Point Cemetery, Newton Co., beside my husband 8 children.

Son: John G. Park, Exr

/s/Mary Jane Parker
Date: 20 Jul 1915
Wit: B. F. Burgess, L. A. McCurdy and Alfred Bouliguy
Will probated: 7 Aug 1916

Fred Kach
Page 402

Wife: Marguerite
Children: Tillie, Ada, Fred, Kate, Mamie, Bessie and Maggie

/s/Fred Kach
Date: Dec 1912
Wit: John W. Zuber, N. W. Cameron and F. E. Redenslen
Probated: 8 Aug 1916

Joseph Lane Richardson
Page 403-408

Son-in-law: Presley D. yates, Exr and Gdn of the property of my minor children

Wife:Mary

Daus: Julia Richardson Yates and her son, Charles Richardson Yates; Gertrude Ely Richardson; Katharine Richardson Reeves and Louise Bradsley Richardson

Son: Alan

Wife's Mother: Julia A. Jones

"Mammy Grace", Alan's colored nurse

/s/Joseph Lane
Wit: W. H. Howard, C. D. Wayne and R. C. Rose

Fernando S. Irby of Fulton Co.
Page 409

Wife: Laura G., Extrx and sole heir

/s/Fernando S. Irby
Date: 19Aug 1910
Wit: R. E. Collings, R. P. Cheshire and Grover C. Middlebrooks

Mrs. Mary A. Covington
Page 410

Dau: Ellen Levuona C., my Gordon Co. property

Youngest son - F. V. Covington, Exr.

/s/Mrs. Mary A. Covington
Date: 17 Feb 1915
Wit: J. L. Acres, N. J. Hardinand M. T. Wooten

John L. David
Page 411

Wife: Sara Jane

/s/John L. David
Date: Jun 1915
Wit: W. L. Hauley, P. A. Eddleman and J. C. Wallace
Will probated in common form 2 Oct 1916

C. A. Everhart of Decatur
Page 412-413

Children: Edgar, Susy, Henry, Addia, Lay and Laurence, Adelaid
Grdaus: Elfrida Adelaid and Adelaid Louise
Grson: Laurance Everhart, Jr.

/s/C. A. Everhart
Date: 18 May 1906
Wit: M. T. Eugene, H. Wilson, Miss Isabel C. Footman and Mrs. Lloyd B. Parks
Will probated in solemn form Oct 1916 Term

Sarah C. Venable
Page 414

Daus: Lula, wife of Dr. J. N. Ellis and Elizabeth, wife of Frank Mason, all my property
Son: Samuel H. Venable

/s/Sarah C. Venable
Date: 1 Jan 1907
Wit: T. C. Miller, Austell Thornton and William H. Rice

Mrs. Maggie E. Merritt
Page 415-416

Bro: William J. Bridgewell
Sis: Miss Mary S. Bridewell

My house in Kirkwood

/s/Mrs. Maggie E. Merritt
Date: 10 Aug 1915
Wit: S. L. Owens, Mary Stewart Wannamaker and Lillie Lee Nelms

Eliza C. Candler
Page 416-417

Two daus: Mrs. Claude Candler M. McKinney and Mrs. Ruth Candler Pope
Late husband:MiltonA.Candler
Son: Charles Murphy Candler, Exr

/s/Eliza C. Candler
Date: 13 Jul 1914
Wit: Mary S. Candler, Rebekah S. Candler and Scott Candler

Martha E. Prater
Page 418

Son: Guy S. Prater
Dau: Nellie C. Thompson

/s/Martha E. Prate
Date: 28 Jun 1916
Wit: J. B. Sargent, G. C. Lindsey and R. F. Helms
Eugene Carlton
Page 419-421

Wife: Lula

Son: Tom Carlton

Daus: Fleta Travit, Annie Ranson, Jennie Weldon and Mary Lizzie McNeal

Grch: Fleta Annie McNeal and Mollie May McNeal

Exr: friend, Charles W. Smith

/s/Eugene Carlton (x, his mark)
Date: 1 Apr 1916
Wit: William F. Buchanan, C. A. Stokes and J. J. Barge

Joseph S. Owens
Page 421-422

Wife: Mrs. M. T. Owens

Son: W. B. Owens, Exr

/s/Joseph S. Owens
Date: 8 Aug 1907
Wit: R. F. Burgess, E. H. Mason and E. O. Reagin

Andrew Haynes
Page 422-423

Wife: J. N.

4 acres in Gwinnett Co., Berkshire District. After the death of my wife, to go to Minnie L. Cofer, Martha Irene Miller and Sarah Veda Miller

/s/Andrew Haynes
Date: 24 Sept 1914
Wit: E. D. Jordan, H. H. Holley, J. D. McCurdy and G. L. Johnson

Lula Larendon Sisson of Kirkwood, Relict of Vardy Pritchard Sisson
Page 424-425

Children: Charles Amos, Caroline, Louise and Gustave Beauregard Sisson.

/s/Lula Larendon
Date: 26 Jul 1909
Wit: Rufus W. Andrews, J. H. Apperson, Jr. and John M. D. Sanssue

Martha A. L. Compton, now of Clarke Co.
Page 426-428

Cousin: Mattie Lumpkin Smith

Nephew: David C. Barrow
Friend: Miss Lucy Bishop
Friend and kinsman: George M. Napier
To: Miss AnnieL. Bernard, dau. of Mr. and Mrs. Hugh Bernard
To: Emma Foster, colored, dau. of my servant who died in service
Exr to give $10 to by Susie Payne and Wilson Lampkin, children of Caroline Holt and of Elder Field

A trunk of my handiwork to be sent to George W. Smith, Smith Basin, Washington Co.,
NewYork

Friend: George Napier

To: young Dave Barrow, son of Pope Barrow
To: William L. Peel

The portriat of my father when he was Governor of Georgia to be hung on the walls at the State Capitol.

The bust of my father to go to E. K. Lumpkin

To: Mrs. L. Q. Young, E. Dan Smith

Exr: George M. Napier of Monroe, Ga., a friend of the family for many years

/s/Martha A. L. Compton
Date: 16 Apr 1908
Wit: Algernon Martin, Jesse M. Wood and Sam A. Boorston

L. A. Johnson
Page 429

Wife: Mary, Extrx
2 children: Alder Holcomb and Zelma Snow

/s/L. A. Johnson
Date: 14 Mar 1912
Wit: C. O. Carroll, H. W. Ward and Alonzo Field

Mary Melissa Austin
Page 430

Children: Mary Melissa Austin and Arch Avery Austin
Sis: Inez Alexander, Exgtrx and trustee for children

/s/Mary Melissa Austin
Date: 15 Jun 1914
Wit: Sue V. Coates, Harry M. Paschal and Charles S. McKinney

A. J. Sheppard
Page 431

Wife: Ollie D.

/s/A. J. Sheppard
Date: 25 Jun 1898
Wit: D. P. Philips, A. M. Brand and R. W. Milnett

David Moury of Atlanta
Page 432-434

Nephew: William Hanks

Grandsons: Burtin Craigg of Atlanta, Collin Craigg of Atlanta

Baby friend: Juanita Lucile McVey of Kenton, Harding Co., Ohio, dau. of Bruce and Gladys McVey

Wife: Leota M.

To: Old Peoples Home of Methodist Episcopal Church of Ohio, College Hill, Cincinnati, Ohio and Logan County Infirmary known as "Poor House"

Admr: W. E. Harris of DeGraff, Ohio

Having served the public schools of DeGraff, Ohio, during 6 years as superintendent, I desire that the pallbearers shall be selecgted from my then pupils, I remeber Thomas Rairdon, BenjaminPhineger, J. L. Longfellow of Belle Fontaine, O. Alfred Butler of Belle Fontaine, Charles Strayer, Evy Strayer, etc.

/s/ David Moury
Date: 28 Oct 1914
Wit: Alfred Butler, J. L. Longfellow and Harry S. Travis

Codicil dated: 8 Aug 1916. Should my wife refuse to accept the East Lake home, then W. E. Floding shall sell it and 1/2 to go to niece, Mayme Mourny of DeGraff, Ohio. Half-sister, Kesiah Parker of Columbus, Ohio

Mrs. Elizabeth W. Jackson
Page 437-438

Children: Carl Sherwood Jackson and Helen Ruth Jackson
Husband: Charles M. Jackson

/s/Mrs. Elizabeth W. Jackson Date: 3 Sept 1913
Wit: Oscar Ragland of Kings Highway, Decatur, Gordon Mitchell, 318 N. Boulevard, Atlanta, and Eugene Mitchell of 449 Peachtree Street, Atlanta

Mrs. Lula N. Harris of Fulton Co.
Page 439-440

Sons: Benton Neal Harris and Robert H. Harris
Children: Lucins L., Robert H., Benton Neal and Henry R. Harris and Mrs. Louise Harris Moore

The River Plantation in Meriwether Co.

/s/Mrs. Lula N. Harris
Date: 29 Sept 1915
Wit: L.M. Christian, 680 Piedmont Ave, Atlanta, Gordon F. Mitchell, 343 N. Boulevard, and Eugene M. Mitchell of 1149 Peachtree Street, Atlanta.

Elbert Askew
Page 441-442

To: Mamie Tuggle who was the wife of my son, James A. Askew who died leaving no heirs

Wife: Mary A.

Exrs and Trustees: Mrs. Mae Anderson, Mrs. Clifton E. Lane and Mrs. Kate Jarrell

/s/Elbert Askew
Date: Feb 1817
Wit: W. J. Langley, Clem Jolly and E. A. Warwick

Charles P. Beddingfield
Page 443-444

Nephew: Charles Young McMullen, heir and Exr

/s/Charles P. Beddingfield
Date: 3 Sept 1917
Wit: James L. Key, W. L. Champion and Fred B. Law

W. P. Lankford
Page 444

Wife: Mary, Extrx

/s/W. P. Lankford
Date: 23 Feb 1917
Wit: Ben W. Burgess, J. Augustus McCurdy and Marcus D. Googer

Mrs. Nannie Johnson of Atlanta
Page 445

3 sisters: Mrs. Sam Knox of Atlanta, Mrs. Mary Gibson of Rome, Ga. and Mrs. Ed Holder of
Rome, Ga.

To: Hazel Harris

/s/Mrs. Nannie Johnson
Date: 20 Jun 1917
Wit: L. C. Dean, Ina Butterfield and Mrs. Lee F. Lewis
Francis Jones
Page 446

Son: Francis Andrew Jones
Wife: Mary A. R.

/s/Francis Jones
Date: 6 Sept 1916
Wit: D. P. Phillips, F. M. Starr and M. E. Sappington

Thomas H. Gibson
Page 447-448

Dau: Mrs. Mary Julia Brooks of Agricola of Glascock Co.
Wife: Alma Bayne Gibson

Son: W. Bayne Gibson, Exr

/s/Thomas H. Gibson
Date: 29 Aug 1917
Wit: Oscar Davis, B. B. Mann and Harriet G. Henry

Martha A. Chupp
Page 448-449

Husband: Edward T.
Sons: Daniel T. and James W. D.

/s/Martha A. Chupp
Date: 14 Jan 1913
Wit: Josiah Brooks, J. T. Brooks and E. A. Braswell

George N. Flowers
Page 449-450

Wife: Sarah A., the homestead at Doraville and the Peachtree Creek farm, known as "The
Plantation"
Daus: Lula B., Daisy.

5 children: John E., Lula B., Daisy, Arthur P. and Lamar
/s/George N. Flowers
Date: 27 Sept 1912
Wit: J. W. Munday, Sylvester Pounds and G. E. Miller

Mrs. Cicily Smith
Page 451-452

Widow of James R. Smith and daughter of Watson Kittridge
Afflicted son: Edward P. Smith
Daus: Mrs. Lena Pearce, wife of W. D. Pearce; Mrs. Minnie Wallace, wife of Clifford Wallace.
Decd dau's children: Said A. Garner (decd), wife of A. A. Garner, her children: Henr and Irene Garner and Mrs. Ellen Garner Askew
Son: Dr. Donald F. Smith, Exr

/s/Mrs. Cicily Smith
Date: 31 May 1915
Wit: J. J. Mooney, H. L. Hardman and J. D. Goddard

Hiram J. Williams of Decatur
Page 453-454

Trustee for Ida, Isabel, Jane and Adelaide Hamilton - Arthur H. Stewart
To be buried in Decatur Cemetery where my mother and sisters are buried

/s/Hiram J. Williams
Date: 14 Jul 1913
Wit: G. B. Scott,C. E. Wisner and M. C. Farrar

W. S. Kendrick
Page 455-460

Wife: Lula Groves Kendrick

Niece: Clara Kendrick

Sisters: Mrs. Mary Rudisail, Miss C. A. Kendrick, Mrs.N. S. Dodson, and Mrs. Martha J. Bailey
Bros: John F., James M.and George F. Kendrick

To: Miss Lula Mallett

Nieces and nephews: Frank L. Jones,Martha Jones Wright and Arthur Jones.

Brothers and sisters of Edward G. Jones

Niece: Mary Jones Campbell, sister of Edward G. Jones
To: Henry Scroggins, my former hand

To: Edward G. Jones, Jr., son of Edward G. Jones

/s/W. S. Kendrick
Date: 25 May 1917 Wit: Charles E. Waits, Eugene DeGraffenried and William Lee

John W. Pierce
Page 461-463

Son: John Watkins Pierce, Jr.
Dau: Marie Elizabeth
Wife: Josie Williams Pierce, Gdn for children

/s/John W. Pierce
Date: Mar 1917
Wit: E. H. Mason, T. J. Steele and W. S. McCurdy

W. L. Cline
Page 464

Bro: R. A. Cline, Exr

/s/W. L. Cline
Date: 13 Feb 1918
Wit: W. J. Tilson, R. J. Ward and Charles D. McKinney
August Denk of Fulton Co.
Page 465-466

To be buried in Oakland Cemetery, Atlanta

Children of first wife: Christian Denk, Rosa Frech, Augusta Muench, Josie Belschig and Annie Weitnauer

Present wife: Anna

/s/August Denk
Date: 8 Feb 1918
Wit: E. C. Crouheim, W. P. Vaughn and W. T. Henry

William Jardine
Page 467-468

To: Gordon T. Jardine

Friend: William Leslie of Lithonia

To: Lillie and Ruth Jardine, daus. of Gordon F. Jardine of Lithona

/s/William Jardine (x his mark)
Date: 16 May 1915
Wit: J. H. Patterson, E. P. White and D. P. Phillips

Julia Howard Walker
Page 469-470

To be buried in Westview Cemetery, Atlanta.

Husband: Thomas Edward Walker

Cousin: Susan Isabel Reagan

Exr: Central Bank and Trust Corp.

/s/Julia Howard Walker
Date: 17 Oct 1917

Page 471 blank

Francis Coldwell
Page 472-473

Should my sister be in life (Mollie Lula Duness) at the death of Mary Coldwell, then Mary's share
to go to her.

To: Mary Coldwell - home place in Stone Mountain
Exr: Carl N. Guess
/s/Francis Coldwell
Date: 30 Mar 1918
Wit: E. A. Graham, Ernest Cathron and M. D. Maddox

Eugenia Fulton Avary of Fulton Co., 475 Springdale Road
Page 474-475

Husband: Dr. Arch Avary and cousin, Hamilton Phinizy of Augusta, Exrs.

Only son: Arch Avary, Jr.

Sis: Mrs. M. T. Peed of Oxford, Ga. and her two daus., Virginia and Eugenia

/s/Eugenia Fulton Avary
Date: 19 Oct 1917
Wit: Mrs. W. L. Champion, Charles B. Shelton and Stewart R. Roberts

Julius C. Johnson
Page 475-476

Wife: Martha A.,
sole heir and extrx

/s/Julius C. Johnson
Date: 14 Aug 1909
Wit: A. M. Brand, J. H. Bailey and Paul E. Johnson

Miss Lizzie A. Kirkpatrick
Page 476-477

Bro: Wallace W. Kirkpatrick of Atlanta

Sis: Mrs. Mamie Fraser of Decatur

/s/Miss Lizzie A. Kirkpatrick
Date: 29 Jan 1916
Wit: Mrs. Mary H. Fraser, Mrs. H. F. Bellingrath and Charles D. McKinney

Delia A. McCurdy of Gwinnett Co., dated Carroll Co.
Page 477

Bro: L. A. Weaver, Exr

Nephew: Harry Mobley, and Ruby Mobley

Sister; Nannie Nuchels' children

/s/Delia A. McCurdy
Date: 11 Nov 1901
Wit: M. A. Boyd, A. H. Hinesly and J. E. Harper

Martha Emily Hunnicutt
Page 478-479

Brothers and sisters:

George F. Hunnicutt
Thomas P. Hunnicutt
Wilbur L. Hunnicutt
Lydia J. Hunnicutt
Mrs. Lula Hunnicutt Drake
Mrs. Georgia Hunnicutt Dempsey
B. Harris Hunnicutt

/s/Martha Emily Hunnicutt
Date: 6 Jan 1913
Wit: T. C. Sheve, C. M. Yates and John D. Humphries

Thomas Humes Williams of Fulton Co.
Page 479

Wife: Annie Rhea Williams

Son: Copeland R. Williams, Exr

/s/Thomas Humes Williams
Date: 4 Feb 1915
Wit: J. T. Smith, B. L. Daniel and W. H. Smith

James A. Simpson
Page 479-480

Wife: Louise E.

Children:

Mary S. Clark
Martha A. Ninson
Lula V. Sprayberry

Thomas L. Simpson
Joe P. Simpson

/s/James A. Simpson
Date: 14 Jan 1911
Wit: J. M. White, O. C. Waldrop and W. R. Whitaker

END OF WILL BOOK C

DeKalb County Sales and Appraisements
Book B (1852-1858)

Inventory and Appraisement of Estate of Bynom Alford, Sr.
Page 1-2

Appraisers: James J. Deaman E. A. Gumer, J. B. Luckey, John T. Henry sworn 8 Sept 1852
Sale Bill sold to Nancy Alford for cash 7 Dec 1852

Includes 125 acres of land

Inventory and Appraisement of the Estate of John M. Corley, decd
Page 2-3

Appraisers sworn 12 Sept 1852 - Jacob Chupp, Thomas Johnson, Wesley Braswell and Lewis Davis

Sale Bill of the Estate of B. F. Hardman, decd, sold on 1st Tues in Dec 1852
Page 4

Lot 451 sold to Martha P. Hardman
Lot 111 sold to Martha P. Hardman
Rena I. Hardman, Admr

Recorded: 13 Dec 1852

Inventory and Appraisement of the Estate of Reubin Cone, decd
Page 4-6

Negroes - Jack, Felix, Peter, Lucy, Betsey, Emiline, Mary
City Lots Nos. 61 & 62, 25, 28, 29, N 1/2 of No. 41, N 1/2 of No. 40, part of Lot No. 131,129,136, 137,119, 91, 94, 95, 98, 168, 169, 170, 171, 172, 147, 148, 162, 163, 164, 165,166, 167,151, 152, 153, 154, 88, 89, 103, 104, 109, 110, 111and 112

All of the above lots are composed out of and a part of Land Lot No. 78 in the 14th Dist. of formerly Henry, now DeKalb Co., City of Atlanta 47, a part of Land Lot No. 84 in the 14th District....supposed to be about 100 acres.

Lot 69, 11th Dist.,Lot 139, 11th Dist., Lot 229, 11th Dist., Lot 1032, 12th Dist., Lot 13, 13th Dist., Lot 805, 14th Dist., Lot 246, 16th Dist., Lot 224, 16th Dist., Lot 226, 18th Dist., Lot 1103, 2nd Dist., Lot 1152, 2nd Dist., Lot 1154, 2nd Dist., Lot 185, 9th Dist.Dist., Lot 306, 10th Dist., Lot 185, 15th Dist., Lot 355, 15th Dist., Lot 714, 15th Dist., Lot 697,17th Dist Lot 134, 24th Dist.,Lot 274, 26th Dist., Lot 1192, 4th Dist., Lot 212, 10th Dist., Lot 82, 11th Dist., Lot 310 ,11th Dist., Lot 315, 13th Dist., Lot 25, 14th Dist., Lot 1190, 18th Dist., Lot 1216, 18th Dist., Lot 1043, 18th Dist., Lot 815, 19th Dist., No. 819, 19th Dist., No. 509, 19th Dist., No. 65, 19th Dist., No. 380, 19th Dist., No. 390, 18th Dist., Lot 145, 20th Dist., Lot 474, 20th Dist., Lot 618, 1st Dist., No. 204, 1st Dist., No. 203, 2nd Dist., No. 1172, 2nd Dist., No.329, 2nd Dist., No. 529,2nd Dist., No. 2453, 14thDist., No. 185, 2nd Dist. of Carroll Co., No. 53, 4th Dist. of Carroll Co., No. 117, 4th Dist. of Lee Co., No. 79, 15th Dist. of Lee Co., No. 27, 4th Dist. of Bibb Co., No. 206, 2nd Dist. of Pike Co., and No. 743 17th Dist. of Pike Co.
3/4 of City Lot No. 81 in Atlanta

Appraisers: Stephen Terry, William M. McAffee, Edwin Payne, sworn 10 Nov 1852

J. A. Hayden, Admr
Inventory and Appraisement of Estate of James Daniel, late of said county, decd
Page 7

Appraisers: Cardmer Adams, W. A. Powell, John N. Swift, J. R. McAlister and E. Rosser
Sworn: 11 Jan 1853

Josiah Greer, Admr

Inventory and Sale of Perishable Property of Estate of James Crowley, decd, late of DeKalb Co., this 23 Oct 1852 on 12 months' credit
Page 7-8

Purchasers: G. W. Crowley, S. Crowley, B. Crowley, H. Crowley, C.M.McGinnis, M. M. Brown
Appraisers: Stephen Terry, William M. McAffee, Edwin Payne, sworn 10 Nov 1852
J. A. Hayden, Admr

Inventory and Appraisement of Estate of James Daniel, late of said county, decd
Page 9

Appraisers: Cardman Adams, W. A. Powell, John N. Swift, J. R. McAlister, and E. Rosser, sworn 19 Jan 1853
One sorrel horse and saddle

Sale of a Part of the Real Estate of John Dobson, late of Alabama, decd, Sold on 1st Tues. in Feb 1857
Page 9

Josiah Greer, Admr
Sold on a credit of 12 months for $441.00 (nothing listed)

Inventory and Sale of the Perishable Property of the Estate of James Crowley, decd, late of DeKalb Co., this 23rd Oct 1852 on a 12 months' credit
Page 9-10

Purchasers: G. W. Crowley, S. Crowley, B. Crowley, H. Crowley, C. M. McGinnis, M. M. Brown, James Thurman.

Sale of Negroes, sold first Tues. in Dec 1852 on a credit until 23 Dec 1853

woman, Eda sold to G. W. Crowley
woman, Cynthia and child sold to J. J. Jones
boy, Isaac to F. G. Ross
boy, Simon to James F. Alexander
boy, Exekiel to David Boning
boy, Green to George W. Crowley

Seaborn Crowley, Admr

Sale of Negroes Belonging to Estate of James F. Montgomery, decd, sold on Tues, 4th day of Jan 1853 before Court House door of DeKalb County on a Credit until 25 Dec 1853
Page 11-13

Includes Notes and accounts
Appraisers: Willis Carlisle W. J. Houston and J. B. Lofton, sworn 15 Jan 1853
Dec. 1, 1852 Sale of Perishable Property of John M. Corley, decd
Page 13-14
C. J. Bailey Admr
Purchasers: L. J. Robinson, Wesley Braswell, J. W. Braswell, E. J. Bailey, J. M. Born, Lucy Corley, J. Chupp, S. J. Robinson, B. Drake, Samuel Davis, Cardin Corley, L. P. Robinson, G. K.Hamilton

Inventory of the Property of William Goldsmith, decd, by the Appraisers 1852
Page 15-20

girl, Charlotte
girl, Sarah
boy, Lewis

Appraisers: L. Lowers, William Beauchamp, James Veal, L. Dean, Thomas Johnson, sworn 9
Nov 1852

Sale of Perishable Property of Wilson Woods, decd, Sold on 31 Jan 1853
Page 20

1 black mare purchased by A. Doolin
Joseph Thompson, Admr

Sale of Real Estate of Thomas W. Mappin, decd, sold on 1st Tues. in Nov. 1852, 1/2 for cash and the other half on a credit of 12 months
Page 20

One house and lot in City of Atlanta, it being the livery stable sold to James M. Cathman
James W. Mappin, Admr
Recorded: 14 Feb 1853

A Sale Bill of the Personal Property of James Daniel, decd, Sold on 1st Tues. in Feb 1853 before the Court House Door in Decatur for Cash
Page 21

R. M. Brown, Admr
Horses sold to James Ragan and N. Swift

Mar. 1, 1853 Sale at Auction by Elijah Steward, Admr of Estate of B. Alford, decd, Sold on a Credit until 25 Dec thereafter
Page 21-48

Among purchasers: John Evans, M. Winningham, G. K. Smith, J. M.Hambrick, G. B.Hutson, Joseph Roberts, Lewis Wiggins, J. Cain, Abner Wells, William Camp, Seaborn Cochran, Thomas Alexander, William Mason, Absalom Stoddard, J. W. Beauchamp, Sanford Killey, G. K. Smith, J. M. Evans, James Veal, , Robert Ross, B. F. Veal, Joseph Hambrick, J. R. Mahaffee, etc.

Appraisers: Benjamin Crowley, John M. Hawkins, Seaborn Crowley, sworn 11 Feb 1853

Inventory and Appraisement of Estate of John Austin, decd
Page 49-50

Appraisers: W. W. Sentell, W. B. Butwell and John Abernathy, sworn 23 Feb 1853

Inventory and Appraisement of Estate of Fannan Brown, decd
Page 50-51

Appraisers: William Akers, John Huey, James Nichols and John Collum, sworn 18 Feb 1853

An Account of the Personal Estate of Fanning Brown, decd, Sold on 18th day of Mar 1853 on a credit until 25 Dec next

Page 52-53

Purchasers: Rhody Brown, John Cllier, W. Collier J. A. Lankford, Ezekiel Farris, N.W. Brown, Isham Brown W. Akers, Emanuel Brown and A. Nelson.

19th Mar 1853. Rhody Brown, Admx

A Sale of Rachel, an old Negro Woman Belonging to the Estate of Joseph Walker late of Wilkes Co., decd.

Page 53

Joseph Walker, Admr
Sold to lower bidder on first Tues. in Jul 1852 before court house door in Decatur and was bid off by Richard T. Burdett.

An Inventory of the Personal Property of John Austin, decd Sold at Public Sale on 1st Feb 1853 sold on a Credit until 25 Dec next
Page 53-55

Purchasers: Elizabeth Austin, E. Austin, W. E. Sprewell, Franklin Waters, H. C. Austin, James Abernathy, Shelton Johnson, James Power, A. Austin, John W. Mitchel, William G. Head, Jane Spruell, W. C. Austin, Alex Austin, John Henry, Calvin Garman, John Power, Absalom Waits, Benjamin Foote, Madison Waits, John Heard, Samuel Power, Russell A. Fenn, Asa Morgan, D.Green, W. Deaken and B. Front.

T. F. Austin, Admr
Recorded: 23 Mar 1853

7 Mar 1853. Inventory and Appraisement of Estate of William Beauchamp, decd
Page 55-58

Includes numerous book accounts
Appraisers: L. Dean, J. W. Goldsmith, Thomas Johnson, sworn 10 Mar 1853
Registered: 23 Mar 1853

Sale of Perishable Property of William Goldsmith, decd, Sold on 25th Jan 1853 on a Creidt until 25 Dec 1853
Page 59-87

Among purchasers: G. W. T. Goldsmith, Drewry Lee, James Parker, R. R. Bagwell, D. N. Pittman, William Loveless, Mrs. C. H. McCurdy, Thomas Walker, W.M. Pounds, Paschal House, Milton Brown Lee, James A. Reeves, William Sheppard, etc.

A. J. Goldsmith, Admr

An Account of the Sale of 10 acres Belonging to the Estate of Mary Doyal, decd, Sold on 1st Tues in Jan to F. T. McAlpin for cash.
Page 87

F. T. McAlpin Admr
Recorded: 28 Mar 1853

H. B. Latimer, Gdn, in Account with William E. Wilson
Page 88

Received for hire of boy, Levi, for 1852
Received for hire of girl, Harriet, for 1852
Aug 3rd, by cash paid Ordinary for Marriage License
Oct. 20th, by cash for expenses to New York to attend lectures

Filed: 10 Jan 1853

Estate of Garland Dabney in Account Current with A. B. Dabney, Exr for 1852
Page 89

10 vouchers (not included) . To cash paid - Kirkpatrick & Calhoun, E. N. Calhoun, S. P. Wright, J. C. Evins Harris, John C. Evins, Campbell & Hamilton, W. T. Dabney and Alexander Johnson, Ordinary

John C. Cannon, Gdn of Minor Heirs of Washington Cash, decd in Account Current for year 1852

Page 89

To cash recd of M. E. Cannon, Admr
3 vouchers (not included). To cash paid - T. B. McCrary, J. G. Worley and Alexander Johnson

The Estate of Miles Patey in Account Current with John N. Bellinger, Exr, from 1 May 1852 to 3 Dec inclusive, to-wit:

Page 89

Voucher No. 39 and No. 40 (not included), paid ordinary cost and 1852 tax.
Sworn in open Court 10 Jan 1853. J. N. Bellinger, Exr

Nancy J. Gholston in Account Current with Gilbert C. Gholston, Gdn, from 1 Mar 1852 to 31 Dec 1852
Page 90

6 vouchers (not included) for schooling, ordinary, etc.,and to Admr of Z. Gholston.
Sworn 15 Jan 1853. G. C. Gholston, Gdn

Zachariah Gholston in Account Current with Gilbert C. Gholston, Gdn, from 1st day of Mar 1852
up to 31 Dec 1852
Page 90

Cash paid for schooling, boarding, etc. (6 vouchers, not included)
Sworn 15 Jan 1853. G. C. Gholston, Gdn

Gilbert C. Gholston's Vouchers
Page 91

Recd of G. C. Gholston, Gdn of Elizabeth Gholston, minor of Z. Gholston, $1.25 for letter of guardianship, 1 Mar 1852. Abr. Johnson, Ordinary

Elizabeth A. Gholston in Account Current with G. C. Gholston, Gdn from 1 Mar 1852 to 31 Dec 1852
Page 91

6 vouchers (not included). Cash paid to Admr of G. Gholston, schooling, etc.
Sworn 15 Jan 1853. G. C. Gholston, Gdn

Annual Return of Thomas Farr, Trustee for Estate of Nancy Bruce of DeKalb Co., decd, for year 1852
Page 91

6 vouchers (not included). Ordinary, taxes, etc.
Sworn 1 Jan 1853. Thomas Farr Trustee

E. C. Harris, Admrs' Return of Estate of James F. Montgomery for year 1852
Page 92

Vouchers numbered 35-47 (not included). To cash paid - Alexander Johnson, C. W.McGinnis, James M. Cook, agent for E. B., tax, Milton Turk, C. N. Wooddall, William H. Hunt, L. S. Morgan, Alexander Johnson and H. G. Dean

Sworn 7 Mar 1853. E. C. Harris Admr

Estate of Mason Shumate, late decd, in Account Current with John Glen and B. D. Shumate, Exrs of said Estate for year 1852
Page 92-93

Vouchers numbered 43-70 (not included) - to cash paid - Cynthia Stone, John Glen, Harriet Corn, Laura E. White, E. Mason, Sarah Farrer, Eliza Glen, Elizabeth Adams, J. D. Shumate, A. M. Farrar C. A. Carnes, B. D. Shumante, L. E. White, J. S. Baker, B. F. Shumate, Sarah Farrar, Abner Farrar, Lucinda Cone, Harriet Corry.

Sworn 27 Jan 1853. John Glen and B. D. Shumate, Exrs

Estate of Isaac Towers, decd, in Account Current for the year 1852 with H. D. Williams Exr
Page 93

9 vouchers (not included). To cash paid - W. R. Hairston, M. M. Kemp, J. Akins P. F. Hugh, J. Walker J. Crockett, William Hairston, L. Tuggle.

Includes traveling expense, two trips from Harris Co.

Estate of Zachariah Gholston, decd, in Account Current with Joseph Walker and J. R. McAlister, Admrs, from 2 Feb 1852 to 31 Dec inclusive
Page 94

20 vouchers (not included). To cash paid - Birdwell & Ruggles, Joseph A. Reeves, J. M. Holley,

Alexander Johnson, Allen Woodall Moses Howard, W. A. Powell, W. R. Ruggles, L. Tuffle, W. F. Liddell, E. N. Calhoun L. Williams, J. L. Williams J. L. S. Morgan and J. R. McAllister

Received from J. E. A. Davis for rent of 11 1/2 acres
Received from R. F. Davis for hire of boy, Dan
Received from Joseph Walker for hire of boy, Lewis
Received from W. Wells for hire of boy, Jim
Received from John M. Hawkins for hire of Nelms
Received from John C. Austin for hire ofr girl Eliza
Received from L. Wiggins for hire of girl, Manda

Sworn 12 Feb 1853. James R. McAllister, Admr

Estate of Jimmers Hulsey to A. G. Hulsey, Exr
Page 95

Vouchers numbered 13-24 (not included).

To cash paid Legatees as follows:

Elizabeth Hambrick
John Swan
James A. Barr
Hayden Coe
J. M. Philips
E. J. Hulsey
Dicey Hulsey, Gdn

Joel Herring, Gdn of M. M. M. Wells, minor of Thomas Wells in Account Current for the year
1852
Page 95

4 vouchers (not included) includes schooling, clothing, etc.

Joel Herring, Gdn of Margaret M. E. Wells, minor of Thomas Wells in Account Current for the year 1852
Page 95

4 vouchers (not included) includes schooling, clothing etc.
Sworn 8 Mar 1853. Joel Herring, Gdn

Sworn 31 Mar 1853 F. T. McAlpin, Admr

Remick I. Hardman, Admr of Estate of B. F. Hardman decd, in Account Current for the year1852
Page 98

13 vouchers (not included). To cash paid - W. A. Powell, A. Johnson, Ordinary, C. W. McGinnis, W. Stephens, C. Powell, John Blake, Charles Whitlock, E. Mason and Martha P. Hardman.

Sworn 16 Feb 1853 R. I. Hardman, Admr

W. D. Gholston to Joseph Walker, Gdn, 1852
Page 99

To cash paid - W. A. Powell, Rosser & Adams, J. E. George, I. A. Reeves, J. W. Kirkpatrick, A. Johnson, Seaborn Crowley (for house) Reuben B. Perkins (for pork), and money advanced for tuition.

Sworn 1 Feb 1853. Joseph Walker, Gdn

Estate of R. C. Todd to Martha Todd, Admx
Page 100

14 vouchers (not included). To cash paid - A. W. Woodin, Thomas Kile, A. B. Forsyth, Levi Willard, A. B. Forsyth, H.M. Boyd, R. H. Carmichael, E. W. Mondy Willis Carlisle, William L. Ivy, Erban Powell.

Sworn 28 Mar 1853 Martha Todd, Admx

J. T. and Avy Peacock, Admrs of Estate of Lewis Peacock in Account for year 1852
Page 100-101

To cash paid - John Foster Avey Peacock, D. M. Peacock, R. M. Lin (no note), Thomas Rusk, W. B. Chapman, recd as gdn of L. P. Peacock, James H. Kirkpatrick (on note), John N. Bellinger, J. Norcross, R. M. Brown, etc. Rent for Mills 1853
Sworn 4 Apr 1853 James T. Peacock, Admr

Edward Howard, Admr on Estate of Edward Howard, decd, in Account Current from 1 Jan 1852 to 31 Dec inclusive
Page 101

3 vouchers.
Sworn 6 Jan 1853. Edward Howard, Admr

J. G. Peacock's Return as Gdn for L. P. Peacock, minor, from 1 Jan 1852 to 1 Jan 1853
Page 101

Cash recd for renting dwelling and for negro woman for 1853 (unnamed)

Sworn 4 Apr 1853 J. T. Peacock, Gdn

H. H. Embry, Admr de bonis non of Estate of Jesse Childress, decd, in Account Current for the year 1852 and up to 5 Apr 1853
Page 102

By cash paid W. B. Ruggles and Alexander Johnson, Ordinary (vouchers 1 and 2)

Chames Humphries, Gdn of Chames Cornwell, minor, in Account Current for the year 1852
Page 102

3 vouchers (not included)

Joseph A. Reeves, Gdn, in Account with John A. O. Mann for the year 1852
Page 102

2 vouchers (not included)

John Bryce, Gdn of C. G. Butler, minor, in Account Current from 1 Jan 1852 to 31 Dec 1852
Page 102

2 vouchers (not included)
John Richardson, Gdn of Alexander Richardson in Account Current from 1 Jan 1851 to 31 Dec 1852
Page 103

Legatees paid - W. R. Richardson, Isaac Richardson, Drury Sparks, Gracy Waldrup, Thomas Richardson, and John W. Richardson.

Sworn 6 Dec 1852

Mary Parker, Executrix of John W. Parker, decd, in Account Current for the year 1852
Page 103

2 vouchers (not included)
Mary Parker, Extrx (x, her mark)

William Clark, Admr of Thomas Clark, decd, in Account Current for the year 1852
Page 103

3 vouchers (not included)
Sworn 12 Feb 1853

Sale of Perishable Property of Z. Gholston, decd, Sold 25 Dec 1853
Page 104

Purchasers: John Jones, W. D. Gholston, J. C. Roe, I. S. Gholston.
John McAllister and John M. Walker, Admrs

2nd Return of Alexander Johnson, Gdn of Samuel A. Mann, minor of S. D. Mann, decd, for the year 1851
Page 104

Hire of Peter for the year 1851
18 vouchers (not included)
Sworn 2 May 1852

2nd Return of Alexander Johnson, Gdn of John A. Q. Mann, minor of S. D. Mann
Page 105

16 vouchers (not included)
Sworn 2 May 1853

Sale Bill of the Negroes and Real Estate Belonging to the Estate of Paul A. Haralson, decd, Sold on the 1st Jan in Dec 1852 for Cash
Page 105

Matilda, a woman, sold to S. Howard
Julia, a woman, sold to S. Howard
Jordan, a boy, sold to J. F. Alexander
Harriett, a woman, sold to William Nesbit
Fanny, a woman, sold to Caroline R. Scott
Charles, a boy, sold to C. A. Haralson
John, a man, sold to M. Winningham
Narcissus, a child, sold to Uriah Smith

James F. Leonard and C. A. Haralson, Admrs

Sale Bill of the Personal Property Belonging to Estate of Paul A.
Haralson, decd, Sold 10 Mar 1852
Page 107

Provisions on hand sold to George W. Frazier.

James F. Leonard and C. A. Haralson, Admrs

James F. Leonard and C. A. Haralson, Admrs of Estate of Paul A.
Haralsn, decd, in Account Current for the year 1852 and up to the 1st
day of Apr 1853
Page 106-107

48 vouchers (not included). To cash paid - Mrs. Mary B. Haralson, C. A.
Haralson, etc.
Sworn 3 Jul 1853

Sale of the Personal Property of Paul A. Haralson, decd
Page 108-113

James F. Leonard and C. A. Haralson, Admrs
Lemuel Dean, a major purchaser.

Sale Bill of the Perishable Property Belonging to the Estate of James W.
Reeves, decd, at Public Outcry
Page 114-116

John Y. Flowers, Exr
Purchasers: Sarah Reeves, Samuel Eads, R. I. Greer, J. F. Trimble, Stephen
Spruell, Jr., R. F. Williams, Stephen Tilley, Laugli Arnold, A. W. Reeves,
John Isom, J. R. Evins, John M. Ridling, S. F. Johnston, R. M. Wilson, E.
Williams, etc.

Sale of the Land and Negroes of the Estate of James W. Reeves, Sold on
1st Tues in Dec 1852
Page 116-117

Tom, age 26, sold to W. M. McAfee
Milley, age 38, (and child) sold to W. W. Roark
Milley, age 10, sold to W. J. Donalson
Letty, age 7, sold to A. W. Reeves
Lucinda, age 4, sold to John Trimble
Harriet, age 4, sold to John Trimble
Jacob, age 1, sold to A. W. Reeves

177 acres sold to W. McElsey
Lots in 18th Dist. sold to J. F. Trimble
134 acres in Lot No. 375, sold to J. F. Trimble
55 acres, Lot No. 382, sold to J. F. Trimble
Lot No. 11 in 18th Dist. sold to Samuel House

Sworn 8 Dec 1852 by John Y. Flowers
Appraisers: James Elliott, George Humphries and E. Washington

Sale Bill of the Property Belonging to Estate of W. Beauchamp, decd, 2 Dec 1853
Page 117-123

Among purchasers: W. Beauchamp, Martha Beauchamp
Martha Beauchamp, Admx

Distribution of Estate of Christopher Connally
Page 123-124

Georgia, DeKalb County} By virtue of an Order from the Honorable Ordinary of said county on the 1st Mon. in Nov. last past and to us directed authorizing and requiring us to make distribution of the Estate of the late Christopher Connally, decd, amngst the distributees entitled to said estate. We proceed this day to performance of that duty...seven distributees to-wit:

Elizabeth Connally, widow of said Christopher Connally, decd, Thomas A. Kennedy, son of decd Christopher C. Connally of full age, and John Connally, Price Connally, Margaret F. Connally and William Connally children of said Christopher Connally, decd.....numbers were written on a piece of paper...then a number was drawn (by the heirs)...the following is the result.

No. 1 consists of negro man, Washington, to Elizabeth Connally
No. 2 consists of negro boy, Edmond, to Thomas A. Kennedy
No. 3 consists of negro man, Tolbert, to Christopher C. Connally
No. 4 consists of two negro boys, Isham and Jacob, to John Connally
No. 5 consists of negro boy and girl, Parker and Mary, to Price Connally
No. 6 consists of negro man, Keenan, to Margaret F. Connally
No. 7 consists of negro woman, to William Connally

15 Dec 1852.
William C. Chambless, Joseph Willis, Thomas Kennedy and T. W. Connally, Commissioners

Estate of William Annsley, decd, in Account for the year 1852 with
William Ezzard, Admr
Page 124-125

9 vouchers (not included)

Samuel F. A. Mann, minor, in Account with William Ezzard, Gdn, for the
year 1852
Page 126

11 vouchers (not included) To cash paid - P. M. Sheebley (tuition), Mrs.
Mann (board), W. A.Powell, J. A. Reeves, J. E. George.

By cash recd from State R. R. for hiring of man, Peter
By cash recd of Mr. Smith, hire of Peter, 9 months
By cash recd and paid from Dr. Johnson, former Gdn

Sworn 25 Jun 1853

Estate of Hardy Ivy in Account with William Ezzard, Admr de bonis non
for the year 1852
Page 126-128

19 vouchers (not included). To cash paid - Sarah Ivy, one of the
distributees, Michael Ivy, one of the distributees, and William Ivy, Admr
of Samuel Ivy, Henry P. Ivy, a distributee

By rent of land - 18 acres and 10 acres to William Yarborough and 16
acres of Michael Ivy
Brick yard rented to William Yarborough
By sale of 41 lots in City of Atlanta sold on 21 Nov 1852

Lot 118 sold to Michael Ivy
Lot No. 120 sold to Henry Ivy
Lot No. 99 sold to Sarah Ivy

Sworn 25 Jun 1853

William A. Green, minor, in Account with William Ezzard, Gdn, for the
year 1852
Page 128-129

To hire of negroes -

Daniel hired to Clement C. Green
Tom hired to William Baker
Matilda hired to William Center
Jacob, boy, hired to Mrs. Green

Margaret and 3 children hired to Mrs. Green

Sworn 25 Jun 1853

Estate of Alston H. Greene, decd, in Account with William Ezzard, Admr, for the year 1852
Page 129

6 vouchers (not included)

By rent of 34 acres of cotton above the ferry, and 12 acres through the lane

Cordelia E. Greene, minor, in Account with William Ezzard, Gdn, for the year 1852
Page 130

24 vouchers (not included)
By hire of negroes -

Richard hired to Richard Peters
Horace (boy) hired to Allison Nelson
Miles (boy) hired to Mrs. Greene
Eliza (girl) hired to Allison Nelson
Julia Ann (girl) hired to -

Thomas Johnson, John L. Hamilton and William Johnson, Admrs of the Estate of Andrew Johnson, decd, in Account Current for the year 1852
Page 131-135

30 vouchers (not included)
Sworn 4 Jul 1853
Elijah Steward, Admr of Bynum Alford, decd, in Account Current from the cmmencement up to 2nd day of Jul 1853 inclusive
Page 135-136

To cash paid - Nancy Alford, John Nash, E. C. Hardman, Elijah Pittard, E. J. Briley, etc.
Sworn 11 Jul 1853

Sale Bill of the Personal Property of W. Woolsey Sold on 2nd of Mar 1853
Page 137

Purchasers: L. A. Bleckley, John Eminger, George Tomlinson, I. A. Hayden, , John Glen, JohnBailey.

Sale of Notes, Accounts and other Evidences of Debt to Estate of Moses
W. Formwalt, decd, Sold on 1st of Apr 1853
Page 138-139

Purchasers: L. E. Bleckley, A. Cloyd, T. L. Cooper, Aaron Cloud, Henry
Almond, T. A. Thomas, George K. Hamilton, Hiram Embry.

Joseph Thompson, Admr

Sale of Real Estate and one Negro Belonging to M. W. Formwalt, decd,
Sold on 8th day of Apr 1853
Page 139

Purchasers: L. E. Bleckley, M. M. Tidwell, Thomas Asbury, G. E.
Johnson.

Annual Return No. 1. Joseph Thompson, Admr, in Account Current with
the Estate of M. W. Formwalt, decd, from commencement of the
Administration to 31 Dec 1852
Page 140

17 vouchers (not included)

Estate of James Crowley, decd, in Account Current with Seaborn
Crowley, Admr with the Will Annexed for the year 1852
Page 141

9 vouchers. (not included)
Sworn 2 Jul 1853

Annual Return of Martha H. Hilburn, Admr of N. G. Hilburn of said
county, decd
Page 141

6 vouchers (not included)
Sworn 22 Jun 1853
Martha H. Hilburn, Admx

Sale of Personal Property of N. G. Hilburn, decd, made this 14th May
1852
Page 142

Purchasers: John Bird, A. S. Myres, D. J. Gilbert, Willis Corlisle, N. G.
Harville, B. F. Lamb, Joshua Gilbert

Sale Bill of Lands and Negroes Belonging to Estate of William Hulsey, decd, sold on first Tues. in Oct 1852
Page 143

Samuel B. Crawford, Admr

241 1/2 acres of land in DeKalb Co. sold
Negro man, Abraham
Negro woman, Clarissa and her 3 children
Negro girl, Martha, sold to D. Adams
Negro boy, Willis, sold to Eli Hulsey
Negro man, Ephraim, sold to John Williamson

Samuel B. Crawford, Admr with the Estate of W. Hulsey, decd, for the year 1852
Page 143

12 vouchers. (not included)
Sworn 3 Jun 1853

William F. Ivy, Gdn for James A. Ivy, minor of H. Ivy, decd, in Account Current for year 1852
Page 143-144

4 vouchers (not included)
Sworn 28 Apr 1853

Colman Ford, Exr of Estate of William Terrell, in Account Current for the year 1852
Page 144

17 vouchers (not included)
Sworn 16 May 1853

Robert McWilliams, Admr of Estate of William Holdabram, decd, in Account Current for the year 1852
Page 144

3 vouchers (not included)

George Key, Gdn for his two minor children in Account Current for the year 1852
Page 145

1 voucher.
Sworn 7 Jun 1853

John C. Austin, Admr with the Will annexed of Thomas Austin, decd, in Account Current for the year 1852
Page 145

7 vouchers (not included)
Sworn 5 Jul 1853

James F. Leonard, Gdn of S. Jane Haralson, minor of R. A. Haralson, decd, in Account Current for the year 1852 up to 1 Apr 1853
Page 145-146

To cash recd from the Admr of R. A. Haralson Estate
To hire of Susan
3 vouchers.
Sworn 1 Apr 1853

Mary A. Reed, Extrx of John Reed, decd, in Account Current for the year 1852 and up to 9 Jul 1853
Page 146

5 vouchers.
Sworn 11 Apr 1853

Avey Peacock, Gdn of Thomas J. Peacock, minor of Lewis Peacock, decd for the year 1852
Page 146

To hire of Moses
6 vouchers.
Sworn 31 May 1853

A. J. Walraven, Admr of Land Gilbert, decd, in Account Current for the year 1852
Page 147

To cash received from John Bailey, G. G. Smith, Stephen Terry, Reubin Haynes, M. McCullock,
John Kile and Nancy Gan.
Sworn 1 Jul 1853

Annual Return in the year 1853 by Ezekiel Reeves, Admr of Estate of George M. Reeves, late of Alabama, decd
Page 147

5 vouchers.
Sworn 1 Jul 1853

S. P. Wright, Gdn of James M. Joice in Account Current from 1st day of Jan 1852 to 31 Dec inclusive
Page 147-148

7 vouchers. To cash paid - William A. Parks, J. S. Elliott, Joseph A. Reeves, E. N. Calhoun

Sworn 1 May 1853

Return No. 2, Estate of Henry Brickman, decd, in Account Current with Edwin Plaster, Admr and Ruth Ann Brickman, Admx, from 1 Aug 1852 to 31 Dec inclusive
Page 148

6 vouchers.
Includes sale of real estate and negroes. 70 acres and 101 acres. Negroes sold to John Bryce.
Sworn 3 May 1853

C. Murphey's Annual Return as Admr of William Cash, decd, of the Amount Collected
Page 149

8 vouchers. To cash paid - S. P. Cash, Martha Cash (widow of William Cash).

Annual Return of C. Murphy, Gdn for Elizabeth McKey for the year 1852
Page 150

9 vouchers.
To hire of William and Milly
Sworn 1 Jun 1853

C. Murphy, Gdn of J. J. McKey for the year 1852
Page 150

10 vouchers.

The Following is a true Appraisement and Inventory of the Estate of Leonard Winters, late of Mississippi, decd, of the Real and Persnal Property produced to us by Elamander Washington, Admr of said Estate
Page 151

The E half of Land No. 293 in 18th District of DeKalb Co.
various ntes, one fi-fi against M. C. Austin
Appraisers: John Y. Flowers, John McElry, Robert Baxter, and James Elliott
Sworn 30 Aug 1853

C. Murphy, Gdn of William McKey for the year 1852
Page 152

8 vouchers. To the hire of Charles to James Loyd at Atlanta

To the hire of Sally to John Simpson
To the hire of Ritter to W. A. Powell

Inventory and Sale of the Perishable Property of the Estate of Isaiah N. G. Bohannon, decd, Sold on 24th Feb 1853 by C. W. McGinnis, Admr
Page 152-154

Among purchasers: R. Hollingsworth, P. H. Burford, W. W. Mitchell, G. Johnson, R. Cobb, A. Johnson, B. Crowley, J. P. Bradley, J. C. Thurmon, G. Norton, I. M. Bishop, B. I. Ayers, etc.

Appraise Bill of the Goods and Chattels of Land Gilbert, decd
Page 154-156

Appraisers: J. Gilbert, I. Tomlinson, sworn 11 Oct 1853
List of Sales follows. Among purchasers: J. Gilbert.
A. J. Walraven, Admr

Estate of Henry G. Collier, decd, in Account Current with William Ezzard, Exr
Page 156

5 vouchers. To hire of two negroes and rent of house given for board and clothing, widow andchildren

Sworn: 25 Jun 1853

Return No. 1, Estate of James W. Reeves, decd, in Accunt Current with John Y. Flowers, Exr of said decd, from 7th day of Jun 1852 to 21 May 1853 inclusive
Page 156-157

19 vouchers. Sworn 6 Jun 1853
Sale Bill of balance of born and fodder

Return No. 2, Joseph Willis Admr of Estate of William Willis, decd, fr the year 1852 and up to 10 Jun 1853 in Account Current
Page 158

To cash paid James M. Willis, Julian Willis, legatee

James M. Willis, Gdn to H. G. Willis, Orphan of William Willis, decd in Account Current from Dec 1852 to 2 Jul 1853 inclusive
Page 159

By cash paid - Joseph Willis, R. E. Manbum, Susan A. Smith, Gilbert Wilson, etc.
Sworn 2 Jul 1853

James Yancy, Executor of Francis Griffin decd, in Account Current for the year 1852
Page 159

12 vouchers. Sworn 10 Jul 1853.

James Coldwell, Gdn of Mary J. Baley, minor, in Account Current from 7 May 1852 up to May 1853
Page 160

Sworn 4 Jul 1853.

James Coldwell, Gdn of James A. Baley, minor, in Account Current for the year 1852 up to Apr 1853
Page 160

3 vouchers.

James Coldwell, Gdn of Thomas S. Baley in Account Current for the year of 1852
Page 160

3 vouchers.

Estate of Christopher Connally, decd, in Account Current with Thomas A. Kennedy, Admr, From 1 Jan to 31 Dec 1852
Page 161

Sworn 4 Jul 1853

Estate of P. A. Peacock, minor, in Account Current with Thomas A. Kennedy, Gdn, from 1 Jan to 31 Dec 1852
Page 161

Sworn 4 Jul 1853

Elizabeth Connally, Gdn of John M. Connally, Price Connally, Margaret F. Connally and William Connally, minors in Account Current for the year 1852
Page 162

1 voucher. Sworn 2 Jul 1853

Solomon K. Page, Gdn for Louisa Sentell, Caroline Sentell, Almeda Sentell and Martha Sentell in Account Current for the year 1852
Page 162

3 vouchers

William T. Ivey, Admr of Estate of S. W. Ivey, decd, for the year 1852
Page 162-163

13 vouchers. Sworn 31 May 1853

Return No. 3, Estate of Alexander Joice, minor and orphan of Robert Joice, late of DeKalb Co., decd, in Account Current with James S. Elliott, Gdn, from 1day of Jan 1852 to 31 deay of Dec inclusive
Page 163

Sworn 3 May 1853

S. P. Wright, Gdn of Pararode Rainey for the year 1852
Page 163

2 vouchers. Sworn 15 May 1853

John Henry, in an Account with Alexander Cochran, Gdn, for the year 1852
Page 163

To board and clothing
Sworn 15 May 1853

Return No. 3, Estate of Sarah Joice, minor orphan of Robert Joice, late of DeKalb Co., decd, in
Account Current with George M. Humphries, Gdn, from 1st day of Jan 1852 to 31 Dec inclusive
Page 164

Vouchers numbered 17 thrugh 23

James Hambrick, Gdn of William B. Hill, minor, for 1852
Page 164

Sworn 11 Jul 1853

4 Jul 1853. Estate of Philip P. McDaniel in Account Current with I. O. McDaniel from 5th Jul 1852 to 4th Jul 1853
Page 165

3 vouchers. To cash paid - Nancy B. McDaniel
Sworn 4 Jul 1853

William T. Ivy, Gdn of Richard N. Ivy, minor of Hardy Ivy, decd, in Account for the year 1852
Page 165

Sworn 30 May 1853

George R. Frazer, Gdn of Elizabeth E. Frazer
Page 165

Sworn 1 Jul 1853

Alonzo C. Giles, minor in Account Current for 1852, Andrew Wills, Gdn
Page 166

By hire of negro girl, 12 months. Sworn 1 Feb 1853

Estate of P. B. Ellington, Insane Person, in Account Current with Salina Ellington, Gdn, from 1 Jul 1853 to 31 Dec inclusive
Page 166

Sworn 22 Jun 1853

Annual Return of Marcus A. Bell, Admr de bonis non of Estate of Joseph S. Knox
Page 166-167

Sworn 22 Jun 1853

Stone Mountain, 3 Jun 1853, James M. McAlpin, Gdn of Samuel Hill
Page 167

No activity.

Carroll Co., Ga., Inventory of the Estate of A. H. Tomlinson
Page 167-177

Appraisers: James Baskin, John F. Tomlinson, William F. Tomlinson, sworn 15 Sept 1853

Inventory and Appraisement of Estate (Negroes) of Francis Gideon, decd
Page 178-180

Negro man, 25 years old
woman, age 48
Charles, age 22
Samhan (girl), age 21
Lubertha, age 8
Jane, age 34
Eli, age 27
Harriet, age 27
Dennis, age 25

Nancy Jane, age 19
Jane, 8 months old
Washington, age 14
Mary Ann, age 10
America, age 15
Van Buren, age 11
Francis Gideon
Georgeann, age 9
Eiliza, age 8
Thomas H., age 4
John Anderson, age 9
Amanda, age 5
Caroline, age 5
William, age 3
Susan, age 42
William, age 21
Martha, age 31
Elizabeth, age 2
Henry, age 11

A list of the Effects of A. H. Tomlinson, decd, late, taken by Appraisers on Jul 1853
Page 181-183

Appraisers: Thomas Griffin, Edward M. Taliaferro, M. J. Pool

Inventory and Appraisement of the Estate of Thomas James, decd
Page 183-184

Appraisers: H. G. Forsyth, P. B. Salines, A. B. Forsyth, sworn 8 Oct 1853

Estate of Thomas O. Adair, decd, in Account with R. M. Brown, Admr, for the year 1852 through Jun 1853 inclusive
Page 185

17 vouchers. Sworn 24 Jun 1853.

Inventory and Appraisement of Estate of Thomas Thweatt, decd
Page 186-187

Ephraim, negro man
Abby negro woman

Hagor, negro woman
Clara, negro woman
Joshua, negro man
Violet, negro woman

William J. Mann, Admr of Estate of James Robinson, decd in Account for the year 1852
Page 188

5 vouchers.
Sworn 11 O8 1853

A. B. Forsyth, Gdn of E. A. Warner, Return for 1852
Page 188

3 vouchers. Sworn 27 Sept 1853

Thomas Griffin, Gdn of Margaret E. Griffin, minor in Account Current for the year 1851 and 1852
Page 188

1 voucher. Sworn 5 Sept 1853

Thomas Griffin, Gdn of Susan Griffin, minor, in account for the year 1851 and 1852 inclusive
Page 189

1 voucher. Sworn 5 Sept 1853

Thomas Griffin, Gdn of Narcussa G. Griffin, minor, in Account Current for the years 1851 and 1852
Page 189

1 voucher. Sworn 5 Sept 1853

Thomas Griffin, Gdn of David Griffin, minor, for the years 1851 and 1852 inclusive
Page 189

1 voucher. Sworn 5 Sept 1853

Thomas Griffin, Gdn of Alexander Griffin, minor, for the years 1851 and 1852 inclusive
Page 189

Sworn 5 Sept 1853

Thomas Griffin, Gdn of Leroy Griffin, minor, for the years 1851 and 1852 inclusive
Page 190

To cash received 15 Nov 1851 of Isaiah Mobley, Admr of A. Mobley, decd
Sworn 5 Sept 1853

Inventory and Appraisement of the Estate of Ann Ogilley, decd
Page 190-191

Appraisers: I. O. McGinnis, James Hayden, Stephen Horn, T. L. Thomas
Sworn 21 Apr 1853

Inventory and Appraisement of Estate of Jesse Williams, decd
Page 192-194

Appraisers: E. Rosser, Robert Jones, Joseph F. Clain, J. R. McAllister, sworn 12 Nov 1853

Inventory and Appraisement of Estate of John A. Bellinger, decd
Page 195-198

Negroes -
Hutchins, (man), George (man), Irvin (boy), Manerva (woman), Harriet and her 2 children, Mary and her 2 children, Henny and her 2 children

Appraisers: Robert H. Smith, isaac Fleet, Edwin Plaster, sworn 20 Sept 1853
John Y. Flowers, Elemander Washington, John McElroy and Robert M. Wilson, to make a true appraise bill of all goods and chattels of Israel Miller, decd...certified under Gideon Morris and Jasper Miller, Admrs
Page 199-200

Appraisers sworn 7 Jan 1853, John Y. Flowers, E. Washington, John McElroy and Robert Wilson

Inventory and Appraisement of William J. Kilpatrick, decd
Page 201-202

City lots in Atlanta, Lots No. 47 and 115.
Sworn 2 Jan 1854 by appraisers: N. J. Angier, T. V. M. Rhodes, W. H. Stephens

Bill of a Portion of the Real Estate of John Dobson, decd
Page 203

Lot No. 466 in 17h Dist. Cobb Co.
Lot No. 116 in 4th Dist. of Randolph Co.

Josiah Green, Admr

Inventory and Appraisement of Estate of Margaret Davis, decd
Page 203

Appraisers sworn 1 Jan 1854 - John M. Hawkins, Seaborn Crowley, C. W. McGinnis

Inventory and Appraisement of Estate of Joseph S. Huey, decd
Page 204-205

Sworn 21 Dec 1853. Appraisers: W. Powell, R. M. Evins, W. T. Hardman

Inventory and Appraisement of the Estate of William H. Graham, decd, 23 Sept 1853
Page 205-208

Douglas, negro man
Judd, negro woman
Stephen, in the hands of R. Graham in State of South Carolina
Lot No. 379, 2nd Dist., 4th Section, Paulding Co.
Lot No. 280, 8th Dist., 2nd Section, Cherokee Co.
Lot No. 1052, 14th Dist., 1st Section, Cherokee Co.
Lot No. 192, 6th Dist., 1st Section Union Co.
Lot No. 74, DeKalb Co.
Town Lot No. 38 in Atlanta
Town lot in Decatur

Appraisers: M. C. McDonald, B. F. Deal, A. W. Goldsmith, Thomas Johnson, M. B. Henry,
sworn 23 Sept 1853

Sale Bill of the Personal Property. Among purchasers: G. K. Hamilton, Nathan harris, M. J.
Braden, M. L. Crockett, etc.

Inventory and Appraisement of the Estate of Allen Hardman, decd
Page 208-209
Appraisers: S. Powell, W. D. Mason, sworn 13 Nov 1853

Inventory and Appraisement of Estate of Joel Fowler, decd
Page 209-212

H. J. Fowler and A. M. Fowler, Exrs
Appraisers: W. L. Williams, Alfred S. Fowler and Robert M. Cobb, sworn Feb 1854

Account of Sale of Personal Property of Allen Hardman, decd, sold at Public Outcry on 2nd day of Dec 1853, viz.
Page 213-215

Among purchasers: F. V. Hardman, I. M. Dabbs, John J. McMichan, William Roberts, B. Bullock, etc.
R. J. Hardman, Admr

Warrant of Appraisement Directed to P. F. Hoyle, Joseph Pitts, Joseph Clay, Ezekiel Mason and
L. L. Morgan, at late residence of James A. Kirkpatrick, decd....
Page 215-221

Appraisers: P. F. Hoyle, L. L. Morgan,, Joseph Pitts, Joseph Clay, sworn 17 Dec 1853

Sale Bill of the Goods of A. H. Tomlinson, decd, 1 Sept 1853, Carroll Co., Ga., by L. H.
Tomlinson, Admr
Page 222-242

Among purchasers: J. F. Tomlinson, Edward Gresham, etc.

Inventory and Appraisement of Estate of James Russell, decd
Page 242-244

Negroes -
William, a man
Jane, a woman
Mary, a girl
Nibey, a girl

Azariah Mims, Exr.

Azariah Mims, Exr of the Estate of James Russell, decd, in Account
Current for the year 1853 up to 30 Jan 1854 inclusive
Page 244

5 vouchers.
Sworn 7 Jul 1854

Inventory of the Property of Estate of A. L. Dozier
Page 245

Appraisers: Robert T. Kean, James Johnson, James Blackman, sworn 1 Mar 1854

Account of Sale of Personal Property of Estate and Hire of Negroes of Israel Miller, decd, sold at public outcry on 2nd and 4th day of Feb 1854 by Gideon Morris, Admr
Page 246-248

Among purchasers: I. W. Morris, John Jones, I. B. Smith, Reubin Martin, Bennett Rainey, Joel Morris, Newton Miller, W. Miller, etc.

Inventory and Sale of Personal Property of Estate of Ann Ogilby, decd, sold 21st Dec 1853
Page 249-251

Among purchasers: Thurza Ogilby, A. B. Reed, Augustus Haynes, John Clay, Mrs. T. Ogilby, John C. Clay, W. Ogilby, P. Ogilby, etc.

R. M. Brown, Admr

Sale of Negroes on 7 Feb 1854 -

Dick, man, sold to Thomas Mathews
man, John, sold to M. E. Ogilby
Shadrick, man, sold to J. J. Whitaker
woman and 3 children sold to Thomas Kennedy
Caroline and 2 children sold to Philip E. McDonald
Jiney and 2 children sold to Reubin Haynes
Beckey and 2 children sold to Willis Carlisle
Caroline and child sold to B. Z. Martin
Matilda and child sold to B. Z. Martin

Molley sold to Mary A. Edwards
Louisa sold to M. M. Tidwell
James sold to M. M. Tidwell
William sold to Thomas Eaborn
Lucinda sold to M. M. Tidwell
Jane sold to Absalom Baker
Ellie sold to Reubin Haynes
John sold to Thomas Eaborn
Cloah and 3 children (Henry, Bob, Edny) sold to W. Kay

R. M. Brown, Admr

Inventory and Sale of Personal Property of Joseph S. Huey, decd, Sold on 25th Jul 1854
Page 251-252

Among purchasers: Joseph Huey, Mrs. Huey, Charles Huey, etc.

Sale of Personal Property of Estate of Thomas Thweatt, decd, Sold in Atlanta 25 Jan 1854
Page 252-253

Purchasers: C. S. Thweatt, E. Parsons, W. Seago, S. C. Thweatt
Uriah J. Thweatt, Exr

11 Mar 1854, An Inventory of Estate of Arthur Leich, late of said county, decd
Page 253-254

Appraisers: W. L. Wells, John C. Harris, M. B. Henry, sworn 11 Mar 1854

John B. Luckey, Gdn of Virginia E. Emerson, in Account Current for the year 1853
Page 254-255

By cash received of hire of Stephen for 1853, Harriet and child, Linda and child, Leantha (old woman), Ben (boy) ande Donald (boy)

Sworn 21 Feb 1854

Richard Shackelford, Admr of Estate of William Shackelford, decd, in Account Current for the year 1852 and 1853 inclusive
Page 255

7 vouchers. To cash paid - Francis M. Shackelford, J. H. Shackelford, Eliza Ann Shackelford

Sworn 9 Mar 1854

E. J. Bailey, Admr on Estate of John M. Corley
Page 255-256

By amount paid for one years support for family
By amount paid A. Johnson
By amount paid J. M. Born for family
By cash paid Reubin Bishop, auctioneer. Sworn 6 Mar 1854
J. A. Reeves, Gdn, in Account with J. A. O. Mann, ward, 1 Jan 1853
Page 256

By cash paid Mrs. Mann for boarding
Sworn 27 Dec 1853

Estate of James W. Reeves
Page 256

Sale of one 40 acre-lot of land lying in Cherokee Co., and No. 361, 34d Section, Dist. 12 ...sold on first Tues. in Aug 1853, sold to Inman Lay..../s/John B. Flowers, Exr

Sale of a Portion of the Real Estate Belonging to the Estate of Leonard Winters, late of Mississippi, Sold for Cash on 1st Tues in Dec 1853
Page 256

Half of lot of land 10293 it being the E half of said lot in 18th Dist. sold to Robert Baxter ....
/s/E. Warbington, Admr

The Following Negroes were Sold on the first Tues. in May last at the Town of Decatur, the property belonging to the Estate of James W. Reeves, decd, on a credit until the first day of Jan next, this 5th Jun 1854
Page 257

Bet, a woman, and Joe, her child, sold to James W. Crockett
Beckey, a girl sold to James W. Crockett
Jude, a girl, sold to Samuel Potts
Rose, a girl, sold to S. P. Wright
/s/John Y. Flowers, Exr

Miss Elizabeth A. Tholston to G. C. Gholston, Gdn, 1853
Page 257

Cash for hire of three negroes (1853). Sworn 11 Jan 1854

The Estate of Margaret Ann H. Meadow with Samuel B. Hoyt, Gdn
Page 258

Jan 24, expenses per trip to Walker Co. for negroes
To P. E. McDaniel, receipt for four negroes, as per voucher No. 6
Sworn 6 Dec 1853

Jacob Chupp, Gdn of Daniel R. Chupp, in Account Current up to 10th Jan 1854
Page 258

By cash paid ward, Alex Johnson and J. N. Bellinger (3 vouchers)
Sworn 10 Jan 1854

Estate of W. Carroll to William J. Mann
Page 259

3 vouchers. Sworn 3 Jan 1854

Georgia, Walker Co., Estate of Edward Howard, late of South Carolina, in Account Current with
Edward Howard, Admr de bonis non with Will annexed for 1853
Page 259

Expenses from Chattanooga to Decatur, and Decatur to Chattanooga, sitting at court one day
Sworn 4 Jan 1854

James S. Elliott, Gdn of Alexander Joice, minor and orphan of Robert Joice, decd, for 1853
Page 259

Voucher 6 and 7. Sworn 4 Mar 1854

John B. Johns, Exr, Estate of Garland Dabney, decd, frm 1853 up to 25 Feb 1854 inclusive
Page 260

5 vouchers. Vou. #3 paid Elizabeth Dabney. Sworn 22 Feb 1854

Inventory and Appraisement of the Estate of Nancy Camron
Page 260-263

Appraisers: Gardner Adams, J. M. Holley and Joseph Morgan, sworn 16 Feb 1854
Inventory of the property 18 Feb 1854. Purchasers: James Blackstock, Elijah Rosser, E. W. Calhoun, J. M. Holley, W. Ezzard, W. Jackson, etc.

Sale of the Negroes Belonging to the Estate of Thomas Thweatt at Decatur 7 Feb 1854
Page 263

Raymond (boy) sold to John T. Thweatt
Hazor (woman) sold to John T. Thweatt
Abby (woman) sold to John T. Thweatt
Clary (woman) sold to P. M. Hodge
Vilot (woman) sold to J. M. Morris
Joshua (man) sold to D. Beall and B. W. Jackson

Sale of mill and lot 4 Apr 1854 in Fulton Co. to Henry W. McDaniel
/s/ Uriah Thweatt, Exr

Mary Parker, Extrx of Estate of John G. Parker, decd, in Account Current for the year 1853
Page 264

4 vouchers. Sworn 18 Feb 1854. /s/ Mary Parker, Extrx (x, her mark)

James T. Peacock, Admr of Lewis Peacock 1853
Page 264

By cash paid - J. H. Kirkpatrick, Alex Johnson, D. H. Westmoreland, L. H. Connally, D. P. Peacock (distributive share), and paid taxes, etc. Sworn 21 Mar 1854

Colman Ford, Exr of Estate of William Terrell in Account Current for the year 1853
Page 264

4 vouchers. Sworn 1 Mar 1854

Estate of Henry Brockman to Edwin Plaster, Admr, 1853 May 3rd
Page 265

Vouchers No. 19-24. Sworn 27 Apr 1854

Inventory and Appraisement of the Estate, Goods, Chattels, Lands and Tenaments of Ephraim Salmond, late of said county, decd
Page 265

1/4th of lot of land in 16th Dist. of DeKalb Co. adj. lands of Henry Hollingsworth, John Parker, containing 50 acres. Appraisers: John L. Bradley, James Crockett, A. M. Hairsten, sworn 25 Apr 1854

Sale Bill of the Real Estate Belonging to the Estate of A. T. Dozier, late of said county, decd
Page 266

One lot lying in and near City of Atlanta, the same being 10 acres, Lot No. 3 of Johnsons Subdivision of original Land Lot No. 46 in 14th Dist. of originally Henry Co., now Fulton Co., sold on first Tues. in May 1854 in the City f Atlanta....sold to William Ezzard, Allison Nelson and Adison Dulin.../s/R. M. Brown, Admr

S. P. Wright, Gdn of Parasade Rainey, minor of John Rainey, decd, for the year 1853 from the 1st Jan to 31 Dec inclusive
Page 266

To hire of Beverly, Eliza and F. for the year 1853
8 vouchers. By cash paid - Sarah Rainey, Thomas Akin, Levi Willard, A. Johnson, John G. Ramey, etc.
Sworn 18 Jul 1854

S. P. Wright Gdn of James Joice in Account Current for the year 1853, 1st Jan to 31st Dec Page 267

6 vouchers. To cash paid - J. S. Elliott, T. L. D. Medlock, J. A. Reeves, etc.
Sworn 18 Feb 1854

Return of Hiram H. Embry, Admr on Estate of Jesse Childress, decd
Page 267

1854, April, to Hiram H. Embry, one days service attending Superior Court of DeKalb Co.

Sworn 2 May 1854.

R. M. Brown, Admr on Estate of James Daniel, decd, in Account Current fro the year 1853 up to 14th Jun 1854 inclusive
Page 267

5 vouchers. To cash paid - Rosser & Adams, Richard Burdett, F. M. Liddell, etc.

Estate of Thomas Thweatt to Uriah J. Thweatt, Exr
Page 268

To hire of negroes - Ephraim, Ramon, Clara, Hazor and Abby. Sworn 4 May 1854

Jesse Childress, Gdn of James S. Childress, minor child of said Gdn in Account for the year 1853 and up to 30th day of May inclusive
Page 269

By cash recd of John Y. Flowers, Exr of Estate of James W. Reeves, decd. 2 vouchers. Sworn 30 May 1854

Jesse Childress, Gdn of John A. Childress, minor child of said Gdn in Account for the year 1853 and up to 30th day of May 1854 inclusive
Page 269

To amount of cash recd from John Y. Flowers, Exr. of Estate of James W. Reeves, decd, on 20 Jan 1854
2 vouchers. Sworn 31 May 1854

Estate of Zachariah Gholston, decd, in Account Current with James R. McAlister and Joseph Walker, Admrs, from the 31 Dec 1852 to 1st of Jun 1854 inclusive
Page 269-270

Vouchers numbered 21 to 48. To cash paid - S. J. Anderson, Thomas Akin, Joseph Walker, Gdn of W. D. Gholston, Isaac S. Gholston, G. C. Gholston, Gdn of Z. Gholston, Nancy and E. A. Gholston, G. C. Gholston, M. W. Whitlow, Gdn of his minor children, Joseph B. White, G. R. Hamilton, W. A. Powell, C. W. McGinnis, W. D. Gholston, Ebenezer Loveless, G. C. Gholston, Gdn, M. W. Whellon, Gdn, J. S. Gholston and Joseph R. White (on division).

Estate and Return No. 1, sworn 1 Jun 1854.
/s/James R. McAllister, Admr

Return No. 3, Joseph Willis, Admr of William Willis Estate in Account Current from 18 Jun 1853 to 6 Dec 1842 inclusive
Page 270

By cash paid A. Johnson, 1853 tax, R. M. Brown, Aber Johnson. Sworn 12-6-1853
Joseph Willis, Admr

R. M. Brown, Admr, with LWT annexed of Est. of Ann Ogilby, decd, for 1853 and 1854
Page 271-272

To cash paid E. L. Harvey, Dr. Weaver, C. D. Parr, C. R. Hanbeter , R. C. Venable, Rev. Roberts, R. Haynes, J. Norcross, M. Mitchell, R. Haynes, Mrs. Ogilby, W. Calo, W. Markham, B. F. Bonner, L. Robinson, Gilbert & Wilson, S. B. Hoyd, J. O. McDaniel, U. J. Thweat, G. A. Pilgram, J. M. Boring, T. S. Ogilby, R. Haynes, P. E. McDaniel, Guardian of Exa M. Bell, as per vou. No. 19, P. E. McDaniel, Gdn of Ann H. Meadow, as per vou. no. 20., Alex Johnson, Robert Brock, H. W. Brown, M. M. Hill, C. Powell, R. E. Mangum, O. S. Bentley, A. G. Murray, W. Key.

Inventory of Est. of James Crowley, Jr., due Estate of James Crowley, 1/10th part of $3740.80 undivided portion of Estate of James Crowley, Sr., decd, in hands of Seaborn Crowley, Admr.
P. 273

Sworn 6-26-1854

Estate of Christopher Connally, decd, with Thomas A. Kennady, Admr from 1st Jan 1853 to 30 Jun 1854 inclusive
Page 273-274

To cash paid A. T. McCook, T. A. Warwick, A. E. Johnson, R. E. Gardner, Jesse Clark, Mathew Morris, Jacob Hass, Robert Jones, William Johnson, J. T. Drane, C. M. McGinnis, S. A. See, N. Mangum note, John Collier, M. Magee, A. N. Clarida, J. M. Calhoun, J. M. Smith, M. L. Wright, M. McCloud, John Collier note, Chapman Powell, Mary Wells, J. F. Alexander, J. B. Silvey, R. M. Brown. Sworn 6-29-1854 Thomas A Kennedy, Admr.

Elemander Warbington, Admr on Estate of Leonard Winters, decd, for 1853 to 5 Jun 1854 inclusive
Page 274

To cash paid David Irwin, George Baxter, Robert Baster, F. Aviston, Garland Grogan, J. C.Harris,A. Johnson, Ordinary.
Sworn 6-15-1854

John Bryce, Gdn of G. G. Butler minor in account current from 1 Jan 1853 to 3 Dec 1853 inclusive
Page 275

To cash paid 1852-3 taxes. Sworn 7 Jan 1854. John Bryce, Gdn

Sale Bill of Portion of Personal Property of Estate f J. W. D. Bohanan, decd, sold Jan 1854 for cash

C. W. McGuinns , Admr. Sale of cotton, rent.

Marcus A. Bell, Admr de bonis non with LWT annexed Estate of Joseph S. Knox, decd, for 1853
Page 275

To cash paid G. M. T. Perryman, S. L. Rennean. Sworn 6-28-1854
Marcus A. Bell, Admr

J. T. Peacock, Gdn for L. R. Peacock
Page 276

Paid Alex Johnson for return, Calvin Ewen, R. M. Deavers, D. W. Peacock, B. Willaford, City Tax, J. M. Smith, L. P. Peacock. Sworn 3-21-1854. James T. Peacock, Gdn

C. W. McGinnis, Admr Estate of J. W. D. Bohannon, decd for 1853 to 30 June 1854 inclusive
Page 274-277

To cash paid Rosser & Adams, J. W. Kirkpatrick, J. R. McAlister, G. K. Smith, W. Ezzard, J. E. George, P. F. Hoyle, Nat Austin, L. Willard, Andrew Wills, J. B. Wilson, P. F. Hoyle, C. W. McGinnis, W. Jordan, J. A. Reeves, John Fannin, Elisha Webb, Joseph Walker, Alex Johnson, Robert Jones, B. F. Veal, Haden Coe, B. Gregor, Robert Jones, A. C. Tuggle, J. A Reeves, L.Tuggle, Robert Hollinsworth, J. M. Hawkins, E. N. Calhoun.
Sworn 6-30-1854. C. M. McGinnis, Admr.

Annual Return No. 1, Joseph Thompson, Admr of Wilson Wood, decd
Page 277-278

To cash paid J. Thompson, A. J. Wynns, Oliver & Nichols, George Tomlinson, O. Huston & Son, Woodgate & Roome, A. Johnson, J. A. Crayton.

Notes of Isaac Bartlett, Rawley White, W. Lester, George Tomlinson acct, J. A. Hayden, James Ruse accts,Paker on note, J. M. Crayton, J. C. Davis note.

Joseph Thompson, Admr of Estate of Wilson Wood, decd, Annual Return, filed 7-1-1854.

Annual Return No. 2, Joseph Thompson, Admr of M. W. Formwalt, decd., 1863
Page 278 -279

To amount from R. W. Bullard on note, G. C. Rodgers, Mrs Ivy, R. M. Brown note, S. T.Downs, L. B. Breedlove note, B. Plaster, T. J. Perkinson fees, Allen Ester, M. M. Tidwell as 1/spayment, J. W. Rucker per I. McDonald, Willis M. Cash per Holland, John Williamson as 1/2payment, S. B. Right, M. A. Bell on J. Bell's note, M. M. Tiwell as note given for negro woman,Ann, amountfrom A. J. Williams, Admr.

To cash paid R. M. Brown, S. T. Downs, G. W. Grant, commissons, J. L. McGinnis, James Yancy, Exr note, A. S. Rhodes, James Yancy, exr note, Joseph Windship, G. Schoenberger, W. B. Ruggles, E. W. Holland, H. C. Holcomb, Joel A. Guin, Davis Clark, A. Johnson, N. D. Alvegeny, A. J. Williams, Admr, George Gunby a/c. Sworn 7-1-1854. Joseph Thompson, Admr

Estate of P. A. Peacock with Thomas A. Kennedy, Gdn for 1853.

To cash paid P. A. Peacock, Cozard & Pegg, M. J. Peacock, H C. Holcomb, A. P. Peacock, T. A. Warwick, J. M. Smith.

Sworn 6-27-1854. Thomas A. Kennedy, Gdn

Avey Peacock, Gdn of Thomas J. Peacock, minor of L. Peacock, decd, for 1853
Page 280

To cash paid Honeycut & Silvey, D. W. Peacock, G. Fields, W. W. Roark, L. Lawsha, A. Johnson, City tax 1853, F. M. Eddleman, sate tax for 1853, Thomas Hawley.
Sworn 7-3-1854. Avey Peacock, Gdn.

E. Stewart, Admr of Est. of B. Alford, Decd, for 1853
Page 280-281

To cash paid C. H. McCurdy, A. Stoddard, A. Camp, H. H. Dean, W. C. Russean, John L. Veal

To account collected of B. N. Bolton, Thomas H. Jones,W. Mc Kinney. J. F. Leonard, M. H. Jackson, G. W. Holt, A. R. Jordan,F. M. Jordan, W. Wright, W. C. Johnson, T. Camp, G. K. Hamilton, John W.Fowler.

Cash paid G.K. Hamilton, N. Mangum fee, W. C. Russian, R. M. Brown, Clerk, Joseph Fox, G. W. Ferry, G.K. Smith, John W. Fowler, Joseph Wooten, Hickman & Westcot, N. L. Hutchins for Chamberlain & Bancroft, D. G. Barrett.

Sworn 6-28-1884. E. Stewart, Admr of B. Alford Estate

Return No. 2, Estate of James W. Reeves, decd, in account with John Y. Flowers, Exr from first
Jun 1853 to 1st Jul 1854

Page 282-283

To cash paid W. D. Reeves, J. R. McAlister, post office dept, R. F. Daniel, Sheriff, S. Reeves, legatee, Sal Powers, J. G. Martin, A. B. Donalson, legatee, C. Murphy, E. Reeves, S. Reeves, legatee, J. T. Tumble, legatee, S. P. Wright, gdn of J. M. Reeves, J. F. Tumble, gdn of J. C. Reeves, J. Childress, gdn of J. A. D. and J. Childress, Levi Willard, Mrs. F. Champion, J. M. Reding, John Blake, Dr. C. Powell, J. F. Trimble, gdn for W. J. C. Reeves, S. P. Wright, Joseph Morgan, S. P. Wright, gdn for J. M. Reese, J. N. Bellinger, Lewis Thomas, John Houser, W. L. Manning, W. Stewart (for shoes), J. C. Cannon,E. Bogs, A. Gardner, L. Wright, Joseph A. Bales, Thomas V. Eads, David Wade on note, J. M. Riding, James Guess on Fi.Fa., John Reynolds.
Sworn 7-3-1854. John Y. Flowers, Exr.

Sale made by Joseph T. Bellinger Exr on Est. of John N. Bellinger, decd sold 1-1854
Page 283

One negro woman to J. G. Johnson for $800. One mule sold to Mr. Dunahoo for $100. Joseph T. Bellinger, Exr.

Joseph T. Bellinger, Exr of Estate of John N. Bellinger, decd, from 9-5-1853 to 6-16-1854 inclusive
Page 283-284

To cash received of L. Willard on note, R. S. Brown on note, J. C. Comer on note, S. P. Wright on note,, F. N. Hardman on note, A. Lord on note, E. C. Hardman on note, G. W. Humphries on note, J. M. Collier, W. W. Sentill on note, E. Washington on note, J. .S. Elliott on note, James Guess, Thomas Farr, W. Wadsworth, E. Campbel, L. Dean.

To cash paid A. Johnson, ordinary, G. W. Humphries, L. Willard, W. Wardsworth, J. M.

Lord, R. S. Brown, J. M. Smith, James M. Calhoun, W. B. Ruggles, A. Wooddall, L. G. Johnson, S. K. Pace, E. C. Hardman, A. Johnson, James Guess, Thomas Farr, E. Campbell, H. M. Grier.
Sworn 6-29-1854. Joseph T. Bellinger, Exr..

Inventory and Appraisement of Estate of John Blake, decd, with the necessary Certificate annexed to it, to-wit:
Page 285-288

Lot of land No. 265 in 18th District.
Lot of land No. 266 in 18th District
85 acres of land Lot 249
5 acrs of land No. 264
Lot of land, No. 284, 232
100 acres, No. 231
Lot, No. 267
Lot, No. 283
100 acres, No. 383
Negroes: George, age 33, Clarke, age 28, Buck, age 24, Joe, age 16, Bob, age 32, Hiram, age 28,
Andrew, age 3, Newton, age 2, Floyd, 6 months, Ann, age 17, Caroline, age 20, Lane, age 8
mos., Clary, age 29, Tildy, age 20, Jane age 24, Harriet age 10, Mary age 8, Eliza age 5, Texaner
age 6 mos., Fanny age 14, Abe age 57, Crease age 65, little boy known by little boy, age
14(afflicted).

Notes of: R. H. Brazzell, D. B. Anderson, J. F. and William Johnston, Micajah Stone, Thomas D. Johnson, John Jett, D. Waid, S. W. Grisham, Thomas Thompson, James Sprewill, W. G. Jones, Sterling Goodwin, T. T. Langley, R. Pennill

Proven account of Joseph Huey Estate.
Open accounts: Joseph and E. F. McCord, W. McCaw, R. Baxter, W. G. Henderson, G. Morris, John Bagwell, Thomas J. Akins, Jesse W. Dobbs, E. N. Calhoun, L. S. Morgan, Ichabod Williams, James Gunter, James Akins.

Sworn 7-5-1854 by James S. Elliott
/s/ E. Washington, John Y. Flowers, Ezekiel Reeces, Jasmus S. Elliott, appraisers.

Sale Bill of Real Estate of John Bankston, decd, sold in City of Atlanta on 7th day of March 1854 on a credit until 25th of 1854
Page 288

One lot of land No. 245 in 14th Dist. and bid off by J. R. Philips with interest from date of sale this 8th March 1854. /s/R. M. Brown, Admr.

Annual Return of A. J. Walravin, Admr of Land Gilbert, decd, up to this date June 20, 1854
Page 288

Cash received of Hiram Casey
Cash received of Georgia R. R. and Banking Co.
Sworn 6-20-1854
/a/A. J. Walravin, Admr

William Clark, Admr of Thomas Clark, late of said county, decd, in account current for the year 1853
Page 288

Board, clothing for three minor children of Thomas Clark for 1853
By board of Rebecca Clark, widow of decd, year 1853
Sworn 7-13-1854
/s/William Clark, Admr

W. E. Sprewell, Admr in Account Current with Estate of Sarah Wates, decd, for 1853
Page 289

Taxes paid for 1852-3
Sworn 7-3-1854
/s/W. E. Sprewell, Admr

Appraisement of North Half of Lot of Land No. 22 in 15th Dist. originally Henry, now DeKalb Co.valued at $300
Page 289

Appraisers: James F. Stubbs, Y. R. Jones, Laborn Sturgis (x, his mark)
Sworn 9-11-1854

William L. Ivy, Guardian of Richard N. Ivy, minor of Hardy Ivy in account current for 1853
Page 289

Cash received of William Ezzard 1853, 1854, S. W. Ivy Estate.$75.00
ash paid: A. Johnson, Ivy Ward

Sworn 6-29-1854
/s/William T. Ivy, Gdn

W. T. Ivy, Guardian of James L. Ivy, minor of H. Ivy, decd, in account current for year 1853
Page 290

Received of W. Ezzard, S. W. Ivy's Estte 6-29-1854 $75.00 and 4-6-1853 $50.20.
Cash paid - A. Johnson, T. and A. B. Kile, J. L. Ivy, J. J. Cain, tax for 1853.
Sworn 6-29-1854.
/s/W. T. Ivy, Gdn

William T. Ivy, Admr de bonis non on estate of S. W. Ivy, decd, in account current for year 1853
Page 290-291

Cash received of W. Ezzard, J. A. Hayden, Kile & Ivy
Cash paid - A. Johnson, 1853-4 city tax, state tax 1853, Sarah Ivy, H. P. Ivy, Thomas Baker, James M. Ellis, Lucinda Hill, J. J. Cain, M. J. Ivy, M. Self, W. Ezzard
Cash paid myself as Gdn of J. L. Ivy and R. N. Ivy.

Sworn 6-29-1854
/s/William T. Ivy, Admr

C. Murphey, Gdn of Elizabeth McKoy in account current for year 1853 and part of 1854
Page 291

Cash paid - Levi Willard, Simeon Frankford, J. A. Reeves, W. A. Powell, Thomas Akins, Kirkpatrick & Calhoun, B. F. Chamberlain.
Sworn 6-13-1854
/c/C. Murphey, Gdn

C. Murphey's Return for the year 1853 and first part of 1854 as Admr of Estate of William Cash, decd

Page 292

To cash paid - John M. Smith, Stephen D. Cash, Martha Cash, Howard Cash and wife, William Wright and Sarah, A . Logan & Elizabeth, his wife (Wright), A. Logan and Malinda, his wife (Wright) , W. May and his wife Nancy (Wright), Thomas Zimmerman and his wife Martha (Wright).

Sworn 6-27-1854
/s/C. Murphey, Admr

Annual Return of Charles W. Stell, Exr of Estate of Bartholomew Stell for 1852
Page 292

Paid - Mason & Davis, Thomas Whaley, William W. Stell, J. H. Ward, Sheriff, John Glenn, H. N. Byers, David Langshore, Joseph Bryan, Brackston Drake, E. J. Bailey, Martha P. Tell, S. A. Robinson, W. H. Prichard, A. G. Murray, Lewis Eheridge, W. M. Johnson, Henry N. Stell, L. J. Robinson, Abner Johnson, Lewis Etheridge, W. Goldsberry, Thomas Lynch, G. K. and J. L. Hamilton, Vason & Davis, J. M. Born, A. W. Hammond, R. G. Lake, R. G. Byers
Sworn 8-16-1854
/s/Charles W. Stell, Exr.

Annual Return of Charles W. Stell, Exr of Estate of Bartholomew Stell for year 1853
Page 292-293

Paid H. A. Caldwell, Clerk, H. N. Byers, tax receiver for 1853, W. L. Grier for tuition of Elizabeth Stell, orphan J. H. Ragan for medical services for Elizabeth Stell, William Oner, James W. Wear, James H. Born, Jacob Boswell
Sworn 8-16-1854
/s/Charles W. Stell, Exr

Thomas Johnson, Guardian of G. W. Johnson in account current up to this date
Page 293-294

Cash paid Thomas Guess, D. and W. H. Lee, H. Holmes, W. Ezzard, James & Gardner, Tarpley Camp, J. J. Pool , W. Ezzard, James Veal, B. F. Veal, C. W. Johnson, L. Dean, W. L. Yarborough, W. C. Russean, A. Camp, R. D. Pounds, C. M. McGinnis, A. Camp, S. B. Hout, A. Alexander, Sidney Alford, James Gardner, A. Cloud, J. E. Williams, G. E. Elford, W. L. Yarborough, R. D. Pounds, N. L. Hutchins, L. Dean, J. B. Badger, J. C. Maxey, F. D. Fanning, J. M. Smith, A. G. Murray, Abner Johnson
Sworn 8-2-1854
/s/Thomas Johnsn, Admr

Estate of George M. Reeves, decd in acccunt with Ezekiel Reeves, Admr from firs of Jul 1853 to first Jul 1854
Page 294

Cash paid Ruth Reeve, legaee, James A. Reeve, legatee, S. W. Reeves, legatee, N. V. Reeve, legatee, E. Garrett, Gdn of F. M. and Mitty? L. Reeves, Elizabeth Slaten, Stephen Nailor, E. Bowen, R. C. N. Reeve, N. R. eeve, A. Johnson, W. G. Reeve.
Sworn 7-3-1854
/s/Ezekiel Reeve, Admr

S. K. Pace, Gdn of Almeda Sentell, minor of B. Sentell, decd, in account current for the year 1853 and up to 14 June 1854 inclusive
Page 295

Cash paid J. F. Buchanan, A. Johnson, E. Sentell, Tax 1853
Sworn 6-14-1854
/s/S. K. Pace, Gdn

S. K. Pace, Gdn of Caroline Sentell, minor of B. Sentell, decd, for 1853 (as above)
Page 296

Cash paid A. Johnson, Elizabeth Sentell, Tax for 1853, J. R. Swift, J. M. Collier
Sworn 6-14-1854
/s/S. K. Pace, Gdn

S. K. Pace, Gdn for Martha Sentell, minor of B. Sentell, decd (same as above)
Page 296

By cash received of the Admr of Estate of Be. Sentell, decd
Cash paid - J. F. Buchanan, A. Johnson, E. Sentell, 1853 tax.
Sworn 6-16-1854
/s/S. K. Pace, Gdn

S. K. Pace, Gdn of Louisa Sentell, minor, in account current for the year 1853 up to June 14,1854
Page 296

Cash paid J. F. Buchanan, A. Johnson, E. Stentell, 1853 tx, J. R. Swift, J. M. Collier
Sworn 6-14-1854
S. K. Pace, Gdn

Thomas Griffin, Gdn of Leroy Griffin, minor of Leroy Griffin up to 7 Nov 1853
Page 297

Cash paid ordinary, etc.
Sworn 11-7-1853
/s/Thomas Griffin, Gdn

Estate of James Crowley to Seaborn Crowley, Admr
Page 297

Paid - Harris Crowley, Allen Crowley, Z. D. Cross, G. W. Crowley, Benj. Crowley, Allen Crowley, B. S. Jennings, J. M. Smith, tax
Sworn 5-24-1854
/s/Seaborn Crowley, Admr

John C. Austin, Admr withLWT annexed of Estate of Thomas Austin, decd, for 1853
Page 297-298

Cash paid - E. N. Calhoun, 1853 tax, A. Johnson, N. H. Austin, J. A. Reeve, L. Willard, J. Byce,
J. M. Hockens.
Sworn 7-3-1854
/s/John C. Austin, Admr

Thomas F. Austin, Admr of Estate of John Austin, decd, in account with said estate for 1853
Page 298

Paid John R. Humphries, E. Washington, Admr of L. Winters, J. Ball, Alex Johnson
Sworn 7-3-1854

William Hairston, Gdn of his own minor children: Amanda, Clementine, Little Toliver in account for year 1853
Page 298

Cash received from H. D. Williams, Exr of Estate of Isaac Towers, decd
Cash paid Ivy Wards
Sworn 8-2-1854
/s/William Hairston, Gdn

Sale of a portion of Real Estate of N. G. Hitchum, decd, on 1st Tues in Dec 1854 for cash
Page 299

Lot No. 43, 13th Dist., 2d Sec.
Lot No. 114, 13th Dist., 2d Sec.
Lot No. 132, sold to D. J. Davis
Lot No. 131 sold to J. M. Layton
Lot No. 128 sold Wilkerson

Martha H. A. Hilburn, admx of Estate of N. G. Hilburn, decd, in account current for 1853
Page 299

Cash paid John Bird, Russel Rennean
Sworn 6-29-1854
/s/Martha H. A. Hilburn, Admx

John T. Alford, Admr of B. Alford, Sr., in account current for year 1853
Page 299

Cash paid A. Johnson, J. J. Diamond, Nancy Alford, H. H. Bolton, Clem Godddard, William Self
Sworn 6-30-1854
/s/John T. Alford, Admr

James J.Diamond, Admr Estate of W. H. Graham, decd, in Account for 1853 and up tp Jun 1854
Page 300

Received of W.L. Wells, J. R. Smith's note, P. F Hoyle, S. McBryan, S. P. Wright, J. B. McAlister, Cash paid on execution of G. W. T. Goldsmith, received on J. T. Thoms note.

Cash paid J. W. Scruggs, G. W. Lee, J. M. McAlpin, 1853 tax, R. M. Brown, G. K. and J. L. Hamilton, B.M. Smith, S. P. Wright, Sheriff, M. Winningham, A. Johnson, James R. Smith, A. Johnson
Sworn 6-30-1854
/s/James J. Johnsn, Admr

C. H. McCurdy, Admr of Robert McCurdy, decd, in account current up to date this 31st Dec 1853
Page 300

Cash paid J. P. Bufford, L. Tuggle, Lewis Wiggins, J. L. Bradley
Sworn 10-31-1853
/s/C. H. McCurdy, Admr

DeKalb Co., To Judge, Ordinary Court, Andrew Wills, Gdn of Alonzo C. Giles
Page 301

To hire of negro girl for 1854
By boarding, clothing and school of ward
Sworn 6-15-1854
/s/Andrew Wills, Gdn

A. B. Forsyth, Gdn of E. A. Wemer in Account Current for 1853
Page 301

Cash paid Abner Johnson
Sworn : 8-11-1854
/a/A. B. Forsyth, Gdn

James Yancy, Exr of Francis Griffin, decd, in Account Current for 1853
Page 301

Cash paid - Alex Johnson, Robert Yancy, S. A. Cavaness, Killis Brown, 1853 Tax, Z. Griffin, Elizabeth Hargins, Hez. Griffin, A. Johnson
Sworn 7-3-1854
/s/James Yancy, Exr

R. M. Brown, Admr with LWT annexed upon Estate of Ann Ogilby, decd, in Account current
For year 1854 up to 29 Jul 1854

Page 302

Cash paid G. W. Campbell, H. C. Holcomb, Reubin Haynes
Sworn 7-29-1854
/s/R. M. Brown, Admr

John W. Richerson, Gdn of Orphans and Minors of W. Richerson, decd, in account current for 1852
Page 302

Cash paid - Elizabeth Richerson, A. Johnson.
Sworn 10-3-1853
/s/John W. Richerson, Gdn

Thomas Farr, Admr of Estate of Eleanor Fair, decd, in account current for 1853
Page 302

Cash paid A. Johnson, Ordinary, Esther Fair

Sworn 7-3-1854
/s/Thomas Farr, Admr

Robert McWilliams, Admr Estate of W. Hilderbrand decd, in account current for 1854
Page 302

Cash paid A. Johnson
Sworn 7-1-1854
/s/R. McWilliams, Admr

John Glen and B. D. Shumate, Exrs of Estate of Mason Shumate, decd, in Account Current for year 1853 up to 10th Jun 1854
Page 303

By Fi.Fa. Mason Shumate as Allen Hardman proved to be insolvent nd given to Franklin Shumate by consent of all the legatees.

Cash paid - J. A. Hayden, J. Glen, B. D. Shumate, their amount of commission, Abner Johnson.

Sworn: 6-10-1854
/s/John Glen, Exr

E. C. Harris Return as Admr on Estate of James F. Montgomery, decd up to 28th Jun 1854
Page 303

Paid H. G. Dean on note, D. and D.M. Young, J. C. Holmes, A. G. Chovanan (tuition for 1849), A. N. Simpson (services), A. Johncon, ck. Hugh B. T. Montgomery, on notes
Sworn 6-28-1854
/s/E. C. Harris, Admr

Rezin Lyon, Exr of W. Kilpatrick, decd, in Account Current for year 1853
Page 303-304

Cash paid J. C. Davis, Clark & Grubb, W. B. Jones, J. W. Blackwell, H. Pettis, O. H. Jones, N. L. Anger, J. A. Hayden, city tax, L. P. Parr, Mrs. J. Kilpatrick, G. A. Pilgram, E. B. Farmer, A. Johnson, 1853 tax, H. F. Eddleman, A. Johnson.
Sworn 7-3-1854
/s/Rezin Lyon, Exr

Atlanta, Nov. 3, 1853, Reubin Haynes, Admr of Thomas Haynes, sold at auction on a credit until 1 Oct 1854
Page 304-307

Inventory of various items.
H.B. Latimer, Gdn in account with W. E. Wilson
Received for hire of Levi for 1854, Sold Harriett to W. M. McAfee by order of W. E. Wilson, H. B. Latimer, Gdn, in account with W. E. Wilson paid - W. L.Wright, Dr. W. B. Jones, Dr. Ayett,etc.

Sworn 8-7-1854
/s/Henry B. Latimer, Gdn of W. E. Wilson

C. Murphy, Gdn of W. McKoy in Account Current for 1853
Page 308

Cash paid - Joseph A. Reeves, S. E. Scudder, James Blackstock, L. Willard, P. F. Hoyle, F. M. Smith, Benjamin Camp, keeping Mary & children, Miss Sarah Nesbit, W. A. Powell

I purchased of John S. Oliver on 22d Jun 1854 a negro slave by the name of Andrew about 9 years of age, the Bill of Sale says 18 years and 6 months old of dark complexion which purchase was made at Decatur in the County of DeKalb and at a price of $1200 to be paid 25th Dec next as per vou. No. 9

Sworn 6-27-1854

Samuel A. T. Mann, minor in Account with William Ezzard, Gdn for the year 1853
Page 309

To cash paid - Samuel E. Sudder, tuition, W. Kay, Joseph A. Runs, W. A. Powell, Mrs. MalindaMann

By hire of negro man, Peter
Sworn 7-1-1854
/s/William Ezzard, Gdn

Miss Cordelia E. Green, minor in Account with William Ezzard, Gdn for the year 1853
Page 309-310

To cash paid - W. F. Chewning, G. Wean, Sarina Robinson, Sarah Brices, Mrs. Sarah Swanton, C. E. Smith, Sarah Holley, E. M. Edwards, Sarah Wilkerson, Ann E. Groves, A. J. Tinsley, W. D. Luckey, John S. Wilsn, C. D. Pace for tuition, Daniel Stone (freight for piano), J. E. George, Col. Thomas Akins, B. O. Jones, S. Frankford, E. Lawsha, Jacob Haas, Dr. P. F. Hyle, W. A. Powell, Joseph A. Reeves, Levi Willard, William Ezzards By hire of her negro for 1853; negro man, Richard, boy, Horace, Miles, woman Eliza, Juliann, Emeline.

Sworn 7-1-1854
/s/William Ezzard, Guardian

Estate of H. G. Collier, decd, in ccount with W. Ezzard for the year 1853
Page 310

Estate of H. G. Collier, decd, in Account with W. Ezzard, for the year 1853
Page 310-311

To cash paid C. W. McGinnis, Richard T. Burdett, George C. Clark, in right of his wife.

By following articles of property sold to Mrs. Clark, formerly Mrs. Collier, on 17th May 1853, to-wit:

House lot in Atlanta to Merrell Collier
Town Lot on Collier Block No. 1 to W. Markham
Town Lot on Collier Block No. 2 to W. Markham
Town Lot on Collier Block No. 3, George C. Clark
Town Lot on Collier Block No. 4, Stephen Terry
North 1/2 of Lot of Land No. 143 in 14th Dist., originally Henry, now Fulton, L. J. Parr.

Negro man, Andy, sold to Merrill Collier; negro boy, Jcob, sold to Thomas G. W. Coupell, Negro boy, Lem, sold to Thomas G. W. Coupell; negro girl, Louisa, sold to Thomas Moore
Sworn: 7-1-1854
/s/William Ezzard, Exr

Estate of William Annesley, decd, in Account Current with William Ezzard, Admr
Page 311

1853 tax, etc.
Sworn 7-1-1854
/s/William Ezzard, Admr

Estate of Hardy Ivy, decd, in Account Current with William Ezzard, Admr de bonis non for year 1853
Page 312-313

To cash paid - Stephen Terry for surveying, Distributees: Sarah Ivy, Henry P. Ivy, James M. Ellis, W. Yarborough, John G. Terry, Thomas Baker, John J. Cain, John Ivy by his agent, William M. Hill, Richard N. Ivy, Michael J. Ivy, James L. Ivy per his gdn.

By rent of land to W. T. Ivy
Sale of 26 pine trees to Orme & Alexander, sale of 16 lots in City of Atlanta.

Lots sold on 3d day of Nov 1853:

Lot No. 7 sold to William T. Ivy
No. 48 to Lewis J. Parr
No. 138 to Henry A. Vaughn
No. 141 to John J. Cain
No. 139 to Lewis J. Parr
No. 140 to John J. Cain
No. 146 to Lewis J. Parr
No. 147 to H. T. Ivy and M. A. Bell
No. 148 to George Schoenburger
No. 149 to Willis Carlisle
No. 150 to H. T. Ivy and M.A. Bell
No. 151 to Lewis J. Parr
No. 144 to Thomas Baker
No. 143 to Thomas Baker
No. 145 and 142 to Thomas Kile
/s/William Ezzard, Admr

Estate of Alston H. Green, decd, in Account Current for year 1853
Page 313-314

Distributees: C. C. Green, A. Nelson, Mrs. C. Green.
Money collect on note of S. T. W. Miner, C. C. Clay, E. W. McGinnis

Sold lands 7-5-1853:

Lot 16, 14th Dist., Fayette Co. sold to Y. R. Jones
Lot 25, 14th Dist., Fayette Co. sold to Mrs. Cynthiana Green
Lot 49, 14th Dist., Fayette Co. sold to Clement C. Green
Lot 50, 14th Dist., Fayette Co. sold to Clement C. Green
Lot 51, 14th Dist., Fayette Co. sold to Cynthia Green
Lot 208, 14thDist., Henry, now Fulton Co., sold to Daniel Adams
Lot 171, 17th Dist., Henry, now Fulton Co. sold to John N. Swift

Sworn 7-1-1854
/s/William Ezzard, Admr

William A. Green, minor in Account with William Ezzard, Gdn for year 1853
Page 314-315

To cash paid William F. Chewning, Col. Thomas Akins, J. T. Doane, R. E. Mangum, Levi Willard, A. V. Brumby, J. W. Carlton, Thomas A. Lyon, J. T. Sveleton, J. M. Blackstock,

H. Pitts, M. Humphries, P. F. Hoyle, J. F. Northcut, J. N. Higgins, Jacob Haas, W. A. Powell, Joseph A. Reeves, Dr. E. N. Calhoun, Sarah E. Wilkinson, William Ezzard

Hire of negro man, Daniel, to John Oliver and Tom, to J. J. Anderson To negro woman, Matilda, to W. Center; Margaret to John C. Dehforth, Margaret's 3 children to Mrs. Green.
Sworn 7-1-1854
/s/William Ezzard, Gdn

Charles Murphy, Gdn of John McKoy in Account Current for year 1853
Page 315

Cash paid J. A. Reeves, James Blackstock, Rosser and Adams, L. Willard, S. E. Scudder, for keeping Mary H. children, John M. Smith, Berry Camp, W. A. Powell
Sworn: 6-27-1854
/s/C. Murphy, Gdn

Salina Ellington, Gdn of David B. Ellington, in Account Current for 1853
Page 316

To cash paid E. W. Monday, W. P. Johnson, W. B. Smith, John Yates, J. G. Johnson, J. T. Doane, Jacob Haas, J. H. Roberts, H. Irby, Rich Giftens, W. T. Johnston, T. B. McCrary, Silas M. Donalson, E. W. Monday, W. Johnston, M. Collier, Overton Harris, D. C. Spankey, A. W. Halls, W. T. Johnson, J. Norcross,, J. T. Whitaker.

To cash recd for hire of negroes 1853
Sworn 6-24-1854
/s/Salina Ellington, Gdn

1853 Account of Sale of Land Belonging to Estate of William Goldsmith, decd
Page 317

10-4 B. F. Veal to Ice Water Spring and 5 acres of land
10-4 B. F. Veal 40 acres land N of said spring, and one lot, No. 93 in 18th Dist. 202 1/2 acres

To Daniel Adams
To Lot Land 122,18th Dist., 202 1/2 acres
A.J. Goldsmith
To Lot in town No. 49
Lucretia Goldsmith
Dwelling house and 2 acres of land
97 1/2 acres of land part of No. 90
J. W. Whitaker
To Indian Creek place 380 acres, 18th Dist.
To Lot Land in Earley
/s/A. J. Goldsmith, Admr

Andrew J. Goldsmith and B. F. Veal, Admrs of Estate of William Goldsmith, decd, in Account Current for year 1853 and up to 25th Oct. 1854 inclusive
Page 317-318

To cash paid Force Connally, Robert Jones, Turner Goldsmith, John R. Worring, G. K. Smith, Alex Johnson, Lewis Towers, W. L. Norman, W. P. Anderson, C. W. McGinnis, Alex Johnson, B. F. Veal, W. F. Morris, Thomas Goldsmith, W. E. and G. T. Jackson, A. E. Titton, G. W. Webster, D. G. Waldrup, Thomas Johnson, Alfred Williams, G. W. Lee, A. J. Botton, W. B. Ruggles, S. S. Stafford, James Veal, B. M. Smith, G. K. and J. L. Hamilton, L. Dean, John W. Scrugs, L. Towers, M. M. Willis, E. N. Calhoun, John G. Maxey, E. Stewart, Joseph Winship, James G. B. Jones, Lewis Wiggins.

Sworn 10-25-1854
/a/A. J. Goldsmith, Admr

Sale Bill of Personal Property Belonging to Estate of Allen T. Dozier, decd, sold on 12th day of August 1854
Page 319

Only purchaser: Susan Dozier (personal property)
/s/R. M. Brown, Admr

Sale of Real Estate Belonging to Estate of Joseph S. Henry, decd
Page 319

100 acres in 18th Dist. DeKalb Co., being place whereon Joseph S. Henry died, sold 8-1854 to E. Mason

/s/R. M. Brown, Admr

Georgia, DeKalb Co.
Whereas, there having been six negroes relinquished by Sarah Reeve, the widow of James W. Reeve, late of said county, decd,said negroes having been legally advertized first Tues. in Nov. 1854
Page 320

John, a boy,age 21,sold to H. W. Reeves
Tom, a boy, age 46, sold to A. W. Reeve
Mary, a woman, age 27, and Amanda, a girl, age 4 years and Newton, a boy, 17 mos., sold to W. J. Donalson, Titus, a man, age 40 (no bid and returned 11-7-1854)

Sale of lot of land belonging to Estate of James W. Reeves, decd, said lot lying in Paulding Co., No. 863, in 19th Dist., said lot lying in Paulding Co., No. 863, 19th Dist., 3 Sec. sold to Barnett Cooper

/s/John Z. Flowers, Exr

Inventory and Appraisement of Estate of Doct. Richard S. Wright
Page 320

Misc. payments.
Appraisers: P. F. Hoyle, James M. Backstock, Daniel Adams, J. R. McAllister, 1/16/1855

Inventory and Appraisement of Estate of John McDaniel, decd
Page 321-323

Appraisers: Narat Magin, C. G. Green, Claborn Harris

Inventory of notes and accounts: Thomas J. McDonald, Thomas Diggs, John Diggs, W. C. Grisham and Josiah Grisham, A. S. Smith, Parmascus McDaniel, A. J. Pettey, John and James Roberts, John Boyd, Benjamin Englett, Joseph W. McDonald, William Waits and A. B. Waits, M. T. Ivy, C. C. Green, W. C. Alsobrooks, Josiah Higgins, E. C. Cochran.
/s/Parmascus McDonald, Exr

Sale of Personal Property of Estate of James Russell, decd, sold on 13th day of Dec 1854
Page 323-326

Purchasers - James Simpkin, J. G. Mitchell, W. D. Mitchell, J. C. Grand, Aaron Hollinsworth, O. S. Morris, G. W. Parker, Charles Powell, E. W. Sheapherd, Nat Carroll, John T. Huff, Thomas Barns, F. H. Guy, O. S. Morris, Mance Townsend, William Barton, James Simpkins, F. H. Gay, J. B. Dobe, G. W. Parker, B. W. Garr, J. N. George, Mary Ivy, Andrew Johnson, John A. Powell, G. B. Alford, Joseph Simkins, John Morrison, James Rhodes, J. M. Born, G. L. Hamilton, F. H. Gay, Thomas Fee, D. Puckett, A. Scott, James Farmer, Nelson Philips, Lewis Stowers, A. L. Scott,, Z. Bailey, M. L. Warren, Dr. Benj. Overby.
/s/O. S. Morris, Admr

George W. Humphries, Gdn of Sarah Joice for 1853
Page 326

Hire of negro woman, Nerve, negro man, Charles, and George for 1853. Cash paid - Alex Johnson, Nancy McElroy, John R. Humphries, Thomas M. D. Medlock, J. S. Elliott
/s/George W. Humphries, Gdn
Sworn 12-28-1853

Alexr. Vaughn, one of Admrs on Est. of W. B. Anderson, decd, for 1854

To cash paid W. H. Anderson, John N. Bellinger, E. A. Turner
Sworn 10-27-1854
/s/Alexr. Vaughn (x, his mark)

Joseph Walker and J. R. McAllister, Admrs of Est of Zachariah Gholston, decd for 1854
Page 327

Cash paid W. Ezzard, atty fee, J. R. McAllister, legatee, J. R. McAllister, Alexr Johnson,
Ordinary.
Sworn 1-1-1853
/s/Joseph Walker, Admr
/s/J. R. McAlister, Admr

Jinnie L., Serene A. and Seleta E. Hulsey, minors of W. M. Hulsey, decd, to A. G. Hulsey, gdn
Page 327

Paid Alex Johnson, Ordinary
Sworn 5-23-1854
/a/A. G. Hulsey, Gdn

George Key, Gdn of his two minor children in Account Current for 1853
Page 328

To cash paid - A. Johnson
Sworn 6-28-1854
/s/George Key, Gdn

J. F. Trimble, Gdn of W. I. C. Reeves for 1853 to 1855
Page 328

Cash recd of John Z. Flowers, Exr, 3-1-1852
Cash paid -Alex Johnson, W. McElroy, J. A. Reevers
Sworn 1-16-1853
/s/J. F. Trimble, Gdn

Josiah Greer, Admr of Est. of John Dobs, Decd, for 1853 and 1854
Page 328

To cash paid A. Johnson, B. M. Goodwin, M. W. Latimer, Clk, to 12 days attwending court,
Troup Co., etc.
Sworn 12-14-1854
/s/Josiah Greer

John C. Carmon, Gdn of G. W. Cash's minor children for 1853
Page 329

3 days service going to Dallas, cash paid Alexr Johnson
Sworn 2-14-1854
/s/J. C. Connor, Gdn

1853 Rhoda Brown, Admr of Est. of Fannin Brown
Page 329

To cash paid - J. A. Reeves (note), C. J. Adamson (note), Thomas Ragan, S. McWilliams, P. M. Darnall, Alex Johnson, Elijah Turner, M. W. Lord, Allen Wooddall, Thomas M. Darnall, James Brown, Thomas Terry.

Sworn 6-28-1854
/s/Rhoda Brown (x, her mark), Admx

Annual Return of James W. Mappin, Admr of Thomas W. Mappin
Page 330

Paid James Bellons, W. P. Meyefee, Alexr Johnson, James Garvey, N. E. Pruden.
Sworn 9-27-1854
/s/J. W. Maffin, Admr

Schedule of Personal Property Belonging to a Part to Children and a Part to the Estate of Henry G. Collier, decd, Sold on 2nd day of January 1855
Page 330

Purchasers: W. E. Wilson, W. Gilbert, Dr. Boon, George Clark, John Woodruff, William Gilbert, G. C. Clark, Joseph Jones, Augustus Wilson, P. B. Tanner, D. McDuffee, Benj. Little, E. Brown..

J. D. Wells, Gdn for James E. Wells, William A. Wells, Samuel P. Wells and Elizabeth W. Wells, minors of John D. Wells in Account for 1834
Page 331

Sworn 7-4-1835
/s/John D. Wells, Gdn

Martha Beauchamp, Admx of Estate of William Beauchamp, decd, in
Account Current for year 1854
Page 331

Cash paid - W.J. Kelley, J. C. Harris, J. W. Scruggs, Thomas Johnson, G.
H. Hopkins, Joseph Roberts, H. H. Dean, J. J. Diamond, D.and M. H. Lee,
W. L. Wells, C.M. McGinnis, D. W. Waldrup, T. K. and J. L. Hamilton,
Lewis Wiggins, Elizabeth Beauchamp.

Sworn 1-8-1853
/s/Martha Beauchamp, Admx (x, her mark)

Sale of Personal Property Belonging to Estate of J. L. Williams, decd, Sold
onn first Tues. in Nov 1853
Page 332-335

Purchasers: James M. Evins, John Cogswell, Thomas Grogan, Shelton D.
Campbell, B. Z. Martin, James M. Crockett, Elijah Webb, William D.
Wright, John Rainey, J. W. Kirkpatrick, John Hawkins, James F. Akins,
Green B. Clay, James S. Elliott, Randolph Payton, T. R. Hoyle, C. W.
McGinnis, Robert Jones, James M. Blackstock, Mrs. Rebecca Williams,
Robert Jones, Shelton Campbell, John Wiley, Michael Winningham,
James Guess, Joseph Clay, James Farris, Raddie Evins, William Reeves,
W. H. Cash, Robert Baxter, Levi Chewning, William H. Wilson, James
Baxter, David Boring, J. W. Crockett.

Sale Bill of Negroes sold first Tues in Jul 1854

One negro woman, Caroline and two children, sold to Greenville
Henderson

Sale Bill of Land Belonging to Estate of J. L. Williams, decd, sold on first
Tues. in Sept. 1854.

Lot No. 10 and No. 29 in 20th Dist., 22d Section, orig. Cherokee, now
Cobb Co., containing 320 acres sold to S. D. Cowen

Lot No. 50 in 18th Dist. DeKalb Co. sold on first Tues. in Dec 1854 to E.
Mason

Chamer Humphries, former Gdn of Chamer Cornwell in Account Current up to 18th Sept 1852 inclusive

Page 336

Cash paid W. Gilbert, J. C. Pollard, J. A. Reeves, J. F. Wilson, A. Johnson, Robert M. Clark, present Gdn.
Sworn 9-18-1854
/s/Chamer Humphries

Lewis R. Stowers, Gdn of Mary Ann Stowers in Account Current for year 1854 up to 15th Oct 1854
Page 336

To cash received of William Robuck, Admr of Estate of Joseph Rucker
By cash paid Alexr Johnson
Sworn 10-16-1854
/s/L. R. Stowers

James M. Hambrick, Gdn of W. Hill, minor, in Account Current for year 1854 and up to 20 Feb 1855
Page 336

By cash paid my ward, R. M. Brown, Clerk, Alexr Johnson, W. Hill, my ward.
/s/James M. Hambrick

John Bryce, Gdn for William McKoy in Account Current for the year 1854 and up to the 22d Jan 1855 inclusive
Page 337

To cash recd of C. Murphey, former Gdn, in Notes
Recd of C. Murphey, former Gdn, the following negroes to wit:

Charles, a man
Ritter, a woman
Polly, a woman
Andrew, a man
Morse, a boy
Milley, a girl

By cash paid G. Adams, W. A. Powell, E. Rosser, Levi Willard, J. E. George, P. F. Hoyle, A. Johnson, John Bryce, S. E. Scudder, C. Murphey
Sworn 33 Jan 1855
/s/John Bryce, Gdn

John Bryce, Gdn of G. C. Butler in Account for the year 1854
Page 337

Cash paid tax for 1854, Alexr Johnson
Sworn 22 Jan 1855
/s/John Bryce, Gdn

W. E. Sprewell, Admr of Estate of Sarah Waits, decd, in Account Current for year 1854
Page 337

By cash paid tax for 1854, Alexr Johnson
/s/W. E. Sprewell

Georgia, Walker Co., the Estate of Edward Howard, late of South Caroina, decd, in Account Current with Edward Howard, Jr., Admr de bonis non with the Will Annexed for the year 1854
Page 338

To one day from Chattanooga to Decatur, cash paid James M. Calhoun.
Sworn 2-7-1855
/s/Edward Howard, Admr

Mary C. Scarfe, Admx of Estate of William Scarfe, decd, in Account Current for year 1853 and
1854
Page 338

By six years board of Martha V. Scarfe.
One negro girl
paid A. Johnson
Sworn 7-3-1854
/s/Mary C. Scarfe

James M. Willis, Gdn of Harriett G. Wills, minor, in Account Current for year 1853 up to 30th Nov 1853
Page 338-339

By cash paid W. Kay, R. E. Mangum, E. Lawsha, B. F. Bomer, J. N. Davis, A. Johnson, A. H. Gregg, W. M. Hatch, J. M. Willis

Sworn 11-30-1853
/s/James M. Willis, Gdn

C. Murphey, Admr of Estate of James Crowley, Jr., decd, in Account Current for year 1854
Page 339

By cash paid Alexr Johnson, Ordinary
Sworn 2-14-1855
/s/C. Murphey, Admr

C. Murphey, Admr in Account Current with Estate of William Cash, decd, for year 1854
Page 339

By cash paid Alexr Johnson, 1854 tax, J. R. McAlister
Sworn 2-14-1853
/s/C. Murphey, Admr

C. Murphey, Gdn of W. McKoy in Account for the year 1854 up to his final dismission
Page 339

By cash paid to John S. Oliver for a slave by the name of Andrew
By amount paid to John Bruce, Alexr Johnson, Ordinary, 1854 tax, retained for boarding W. McKoy 1854.

6 slaves turned over to John Bruce the present Gdn, to-wit: Charles, Ritta, Polly, Andrew, Moss and Milley
Sworn 1-13-1855
/s/C. Murphey, former Gdn

C. Murphey, Gdn in Account Current for the year 1854
Page 340

Cash paid Levi Willard, W. A. Powell, S. E. Scudder, J. E. George, E. Rosser, Gardner Adams, E. A. Davis, tax, Alexr Johnson, Ordinary, Mrs. Tipton, James M. Blackstock
Sworn 2-14-1855
/s/C. Murphey, Gdn

To hire of Peep for year 1855 to J. L. Downing, Henry to Morgan Kirkpatrick, and Louisa to W. A. Powell.

Inventory and Sale of Personal Property Belonging to Estate of Richard S. Wright, decd, sold on a credit util 25th Dec next, sale Feb 6, 1855
Page 340-342

Purchasers: James J. Winn, J. S. Wilson, John Bryce, P. F. Hoyle, T. R. Ripley, D. Pollard, James Winn, R. M. Brown

/s/R. M. Brown, Admr

Georgia, The following is the Sale Bill of the Negroes and Land belonging to Estate of Jane C. Russell of said county, decd, sold on first Tues in Apr 1855 on a credit until 1st Nov 1855
Page 342

One lot of land sold to William Thealds
Boy, Jacob, sold to John Russell
Boy, Louis, sold to John Russell
Boy, George, sold to Edward Watts
Boy, Lewis, sold to John Russell
Ann and two children sold to John Russell
Boy, Prince, sold to William Russell
Girl, Mariah, sold to William Russell
Boy, King sold to S. C. Waters
Boy, Green, sold to Mary A. Russell
Boy, Jefferson, sold to William Russell
Boy, Jesse, sold to Mary A. Russell

/s/Obadiah S. Morris, Admr.

H. H. Embry, Admr of Estate of Jesse Childress, decd, in Account
Current for year 1854
Page 342

By cash paid Alexr Johnson, H. H. Embry
Sworn 4-24-1855
/s/H. H. Embry, Admr

Mary A. Reed, Extrx of Estate of John Reed, decd, in Acount Current for
year 1854 and up to April 21st 1855 inclusive
Page 343

To cash paid - J. M. Reed, J. M. Robinson, J. R. Glore, Haden Coe, J. H.
Ragan, Drewry M. Mauldin, J. M. Robinson, J. E. Bishop, J. C. Maddox, F.
P. Juhan, R. M. Brown, Charles Latimer, W. G. Staple, A. Johnson
Sworn 4-22-1855
/s/Mary A. Reed, Executrix

A. G. Hulsey, Gdn for Jinnings J. Hulsey, Senna A. Hulsey and Seletia E.
Hulsey, minors of W. M. Hulsey, late of said county of DeKalb
Page 343

Paid McDaniels Mitchell and Hulsey for S. A. Hulsey and J. J. Hulsey,
paid John Swan for tuition, McDaniels Mitchell for Seletia Hulsey.

/s/A. G. Hulsey, Gdn

Sarah Joie, minor of J. S. Elliott for 1854
Page 344

To cash paid Alexr Johnson, E. A. Davis, tax collector, Thomas Akins, J.
S. Elliott for board 1854-6. Cash received on B. M. Johnson note, M. C.
Linly note, W. D. Wright note, D. Wood note, M. N. Bolton note and
Bennett Rainey note.
Sworn 3-5-1855
/s/James S. Elliott, Gdn

Inventory and Appraisement of Estate of Merrell Humphries, decd
Page 344-348

Sale of personal property on 1st May 1855. Purchasers: John Wiley, E. Rosser, Thomas Reynolds, W. R. Brandon, C. Murphey, W. A. Dowell, W. Henderson, Col. Murphey, Westley

Mitchell, Dr. Ryals, T. Reynolds, J. R. McAlister, Westly Mitchell, James Blackstock, Samuel Winn, E. Rosser, W. Henderson, John Rainey, Dr. Bufford, C. Murphey, Daniel McNeill, R. M. Brown, T. R. Hoyle, Alex Vaughn, G. Adams, Walter Wadsworth, W. H. Ryals, W. Henderson, John Durham, John T. Wilsn, L. A. Thornton, W. H. Ryals, Robert Jones, W. J. Thrasher, Samuel Winn, J. C. Roe, Robert Jones.

Lewis R. Stowers, Gdn of Mary Ann Stowers in Account Current for 1854 and up to 14th Feb 1855
Page 348

By cash paid Alex Johnson, paid ward, paid W. C. M. Harper, paid Zachariah Bailey
Sworn 2-14-1855
/s/ Lewis R. Stowers, Gdn

Spencer P. Wright, Gdn of James M. Joice in Account Current for year 1854
Page 349

Hire of boy, Harrison, for 1854
Hire of girl, Darcus, for 1854

By cash paid James S. Elliott, W. McElroy, J. A. Reeves, Thomas Akins, Nancy McElroy, Alex Johnson
Sworn 3-15-1855
/s/S. P. Wright, Gdn

S. P. Wright, Gdn of James M. Reeves in Account Current for year 1854
Page 349

To cash received of John Y. Flowers, exr of James W. Reeves Estate
Cash paid A. Johnson, J. R. Reeves, A. E. Ellis, W. McElroy
Sworn 3-13-1855
/s/S. P. Wright, Gdn

Alexr Joice, minor to James S. Elliott, Gdn
Page 350

To cash paid Joseph T. Bellinger, E. A. Dais, T. C., John Rainey, Exr of Robert Joice, Alexr Johnson
Sworn 3-5-1855
/s/James S. Elliott, Gdn

Sale Bill of a portion of personal property belonging to Estate of John Blacke, decd, sold on 3d day of Oct 1854 on a credit of 6 months
Page 350

one yoke of steers sold to J. W. Kirkpatrick, one sorrel horse sold to Willia Jackson, our Jack sold to C. M. Jones

/s/John Carroll, Exr
/s/H. W. Black, Exr

C. W. McGinnis, Admr on Estate of G. W. D. Bohanan, decd, in Account Current for year 1854 up to 5th Mar 1855 inclusive
Page 350

To cash paid G. K. Hamilton, Benj. Crowley, Joel H. Crawford, Alex Johnson, Thomas Akin, James Gardner
Sworn 3-5-1855
/s/C. W. McGinnis, Admr

Georgia, Fulton Co., Before me, Thomas L. Cooper, a Notary Public in and for said county, personally came Joseph Thompsn, Admr, who being duly sworn, sayeh that the foregoing is a full, just and correct account of Sale of Personal Property belonging to Estate of M. W. Formwalt, decd

Sworn 6-30-1855
/s/Joseph Thompson, Admr

Schedule of Sale of Real Estate Belonging to Estate of M. W. Formwalt, decd, and Joseph Thompson as Tenants in Common being subdivisions of land Lot No. 76 in 14th Dist. of Fulton Co. sold Tues. 12-5-1854.
Page 354-356

Purchasers: T. L. Cooper, John Parsons, J. F. Johnson, B. F. Bomer, A. W. Mitchell, J. I. Whitaker, J. McDaniel, J. L. Doane, N. L. Angier, W. N. Kirkpatrick, B. O. Jones, James McDaniel, Thomas L. Cooper, W. A. Bell, G. B. Hoyt, John T. Wilson, A. R. White, A. M. Bell, E. Andrews, J. T. Doan, M. A. Bell, W. N. Kirkpatrick, N. L. Angier, A. M. Watts, J. C. McDaniel

Sale Bill of Real Estate Belonging to M. W. Formwalt, decd, on Tues, Oct 2d 1854
Page 357

Admr, Joseph Thompson
Land Lot No. 52 in 14th Dist. of Fulton Co.
Mrs. T. S. Ogilsby, Lot No 57
Thomas Kile, Lots No. 53 and 54

/s/Joseph Thompson Admr
Sworn 6-30-1855

Sale Bill of Property of James H. Kirkpatrick, decd, Sold on 1-4-1854
Page 357-359

Puchasers: J. W. Kirkpatrick, W. Wright, A. L. Pitts, J. E. Thurmond, Z. R. Jones, Willis Nesbit, J. S. Wilson, W. H. Dick, J. F. Alexander, P. F. Hoyle, Dr. Hoyle, W. Markham, Warren Davis, James W. Kirkpatrick, William Wright, J. W. Kirkpatrick, John S. Means, W. Thurman, Oliver Jones, M. Humphries, Alex Johnson, C. Harrill, O. Mcfell, J. A. Crain, O. H. Jones, J. S. Means, H. B. Kirkpatrick, F. M. Kirkpatrick, J. W. Kirkpatrick, T. M. Kirkpatrick, W. N. Kirkpatrick, J. W. Kirkpatrick, H. T. Kirkpatrick, H. P. Kirkpatrick.

In Account of the Sale of the Personal Estate of Joel Fowler, decd, sold on 20th day of Feb 1854
Page 360-365

Purchasers: H. J. Fowler, J. M. Fowler, Mrs. Fowler, D. Boring, J. Bonnig, Dr. Avey, Thomas Fowler, John Clark, D. A. Cook, J. B. Badger, S. McWilliams, C. Boils, J. Crockett, J. M. Fowler, H. J. Fowler, N. Lumer, B. Lankford

Account of rents of City of Atlanta lots rented one lot rented to P. E. McDaniel

Account of Sale of Atlanta City Estate of Joel Fowler, decd, property sold first Tues. in Jul 1854.

House and lot sold to J. T. Doane, one lot sold of N. E. Gardner, one house and lot sold to J. M.Boring

Account of Sale of lands and negroes, sold 5 Sept 1854:

Saffold lot, frational lot, Will lot, sold to D. Boring
Adam, a man, sold to H. J. Fowler
Richard, a man, sold to H. J. Fowler
A boy sold to H. J. Fowler
A man sold to J. M. Fowler
Catharine, a woman, sold to A. M. Fowler
John, a boy, died 20th Mar 1854
Harrison, a boy, died 8-20-1855

/s/H. J. Fowler, Exr

Estate of Joel Fowler, decd, in Account Current with Hillard and A. M. Fowler, Exrs, for 1854
Page 364

To cash paid Levi Willard, Dr. Ragan, John Hawkins for coffin, C. W. McGinnis, taxes, advertising, Thomas Fowler, one of the legatees, Joel M. Fowler, one of the legatees, W. F. Connelly, Gdn, Drewry Fowler, W. A. Fowler, W. W. Fowler, Amanda M. Franky

Collected on notes of T. A. Warwick, W. Ragan, Thomas Fowler, G. Johnson, H. T. Peoples

Sarah Ann Leitch, Admx of Estate of Arthur Leitch, decd, in Account
Current for year 1854 up to 1st Jul 1855 inclusive
Page 365

To cash received on note of T. Thompson, Arch. Leitch, James Leitch
Cash paid Alexr Johnson, T. Carter, W. J. Russell, C. Powell, Jesse Lowe,
D. and W. H. Lee, W. M. Hill
Sworn 6-30-1855
/s/Sarah Ann Leitch, Admx

P. F. Hoyle, Admr of Estate of J. L. Williams, decd, in Account for year
1854 and up to 28th June
1855 inclusive
Page 365

Cash paid Rufus Henderson, J. W. Kirkpatrick, T. W. J. Hill, Rufus
Henderson, J. B. Anderson, E. Mason, John W. Jones, Robert Jones, E.
Mason, A. Johnson, T. R. Hoyle, W.S. and T. H. Roberts, S. B. Wright,
Alex Johnson, James F. Akins, H. Gullege, J. S. Elliott, W. H. Hunt,
Robert Jones, Green B. Clay, Rebecca Williams, widow, B. Tollison, J. B.
Anderson, W. J. Thrasher, W. B. Ruggles, J. B. Blackwell, J. B. Anderson,
A. T. Williams, P. M. Selton, J. A. Reeves, Daniel Stone, W. A. Powell,
Rebecca A. Williams, James M. Carrol, John Carroll, C. W. McGinnis, L.
S. Morgan, Joseph F. Clay, Rosser & Adams, E. Rosser, J. and L. S.
Morgan, P. F.Hoyle.

Sworn 6-28-1855
/s/P. F. Hoyle, Admr

Estate of William Annesley, decd, in Account Current with William
Ezzard, Admr with
LWTAnnexed for year 1854
Page 367

Paid ordinary, 1854 taxes
Sworn 6-30-1855
/s/William Ezzard, Admr

Estate of Alston H. Green, decd, in Account Current with William
Ezzard, Admr, for year 1855
Page 367

To cash paid Henry Bullard, sale Campbell Co., Clement C. Green, etc.

Rent of county line place to C. C. Green
Sworn 6-30-1855
/s/William Ezzard, Admr

Estate of Hardy Ivy, decd, in Account Current with William Ezzard,
Admr, for year 1854
Page 367

To cash paid 1854 taxes, Sarah Ivy, legatee, James M. Ellis, legatee,
Thomas Baker, legatee, Henry Ivy legatee, W. F. Ivy, Admr of S. T. Ivy,
John G. Terry in right of his wife as legatee, Michael J. Ivy, legatee, and
gdn of James L. Ivy, legatee.

Estate of Henry G. Collier, decd, in Account Current with William
Ezzard, Exr, for 1854
Page 368

To paid 1854 taxes, S. J. Shackelford, George C. Clark, in right of his wife.
Sworn 6-30-1855
/s/William Ezzard, Admr

Estate of Nancy Camron, decd, in Account Current with William Ezzard,
Exr, for 1854
Page 368

To paid crying sale, C. W. McGinnis, Joseph A. Reeves, E. N. Calhoun, P.
F. Hoyle, Cullin Lindsey, R. Remean, J. L. S. Morgan, Alexr Johnson
Sworn 6-30-1855
/s/William Ezzard, Exr

Samuel T. A. Mann, minor in Account with William Ezzard, Gdn for
year 1854
Page 368-369

Paid W. A. Powell, S E. Scudder, Mrs. Manor for board.
By hire of negro man, Peter
Sworn 6-30-1855
/s/William Ezzard, Gdn

William A. Green, minor in Account with William Ezzard, Gdn, for year 1854
Page 369

To cash paid E. Rosser, W. Herring, J. E. Williams, Lewis Lawshe, J. A. Reeves, R. E. Mangum,
J. Haas, J. E. George, Thomas Akins, E. N. Calhoun, A. Johnson, Ordy, C. H. Strong, city tax on negroes hired in Atlanta.

By hire of negro, Daniel to A. Doolin, Thomas to L. J. Parr, Matilda to W. Center, Margaret to Claborn Haws and Harriett to Clement C. Green

/s/William Grizzard, Gdn

Cordelia E. Green, minor in Account with William Ezzard, Gdn for 1854
Page 370

Cash paid tuition spring term 1854, C. C. Green, G. H. Murell & Sons, Mrs. S. A. Comer, A. J. Tinsley, E. Rosser, C. and J. R. Camp, C. Banks, W. D. Tucker, R. E. Mangum, Jacob Haas, William Herring, Dr. J. Gilbert, Dr. Wilson, Thomas J. Perkinson, tuition fall term 1854.

By hire of negro man, Richmond to Loyd & Pulliam; Horace to Harison Pettis; Miles to William Weaver; Eliza, a woman, to A. Nelson; Julia Ann to Mrs. Green; Emaline to Joseph Ogilby.

Sworn 6-30-1855
/s/William Ezzard, Gdn

Thomas Johnson, William Johnson and J. L. Hamilton, Admrs of Estate of Andrew Johnson, decd, for 1854
Page 371

Cash paid H. H. Chandler, E. A. Davis, Dr. W. Johnson, Alex Johnson, C. Murphey, W. Camp, Thomas L. Cooper, atty, Samuel D. Haslett, W. Matherson, Joel Britt, R. M. Brown, James M. Calhoun, D. and W. H. Lee, Joshua Coggins, J. J. Diamond, James W. Goldsmith, A. E. Jetter, W. and J. Nelson, Thompson Allen, atty, Thomas M. Deam, N. L. Hutchins.

Sworn 6-27-1855
/s/Thomas Johnson, Admr

Georgia, Dekalb Co. In Account Current of O. S. Morris, Admr on Estate of Miss Jane Russell of said county, decd from 12-13-1854 to 6-1-1855 inclusive
Page 372

To cash paid B. F Chapman, R. M. Love, E. Rosser, N. Anderson, R. M. Love, O. W. F. Ivy, James A. Stephenson, J. A. Hayne, A. W. Fossett, H. W. Cuzortt, James Word, Thomas Lynch,W. J. Kelly, W. W. Scott, W. R. Pendley, William Stephenson.

/s/O. S. Morris, Admr

1854. Dr. Joseph Thompson in Account with Estate of W.Woods, decd
Page 373

To cash paid T. R. Ripley, Henry Gorts, S. Frankfort, John A. G. Anderson.
Sworn 6-3-1855
/s/Joseph Thompson, Admr

Joseph Thompson in Account with Estate of Moses W. Formwalt, decd, for year 1854
Page 374-376

Sale real estate from S. B. Love, A. C. Jones, N. L. Angier, J. G. Martin, J. T. Doane, R. E. Gardner, J. F. Johnson, B. O. Jones, G. B. Haygood, F. E. Askins, F. M. and A. M. Eddleman, J. O. McDaniel, E. Andrews, A. R. White, James McDaniel, G. C. Rogers, L. J. Glen, J. I. Whitaker.

/s/Joseph Thompson, Admr

R. M. Brown, Admr of Estate of Joseph S. Huey in Account Current for year 1854 up to 6-27-1855
Page 376

Paid W. A. Powell, Thomas Akins, Alex Johnson, Walter Wardsworth, Joseph A. Reeves, James R. McAlister, Robert Jones, Joseph Huey, James Padier, J. E. George, Dr. E. N. Calhoun, E. Strozin, A. Johnson, Lucy Huey, W. M. Hill, Mrs. Lucy Hucy, C. W. McGinnis, C. M. Huey,

Thomas Huey, Joseph huey, Jr., Merrell Humphries, E. A. Davis, J. C. Steel

Sworn 6-27-1855
/s/R. M. Brown, Admr

Georgia, DeKalb Co., The following is a true inventory and appraisement of Estate of William Johnson, late of said county, decd, with necessary certificates annexed.
Page 377-378

Lot No. 197, 18th Dist., DeKalb Co., 202 1/2 acres
Lot No. 202, " " "
Lot No. 241 " " "
part of Lot 198, 18th Dist., 91 acres
1/2 of lot 237, 18th Dist., 101 1/4 acres
1/2 lot No. 10, 17th Dist., Fulton Co.

Negroes - Sam, age 50, Kitty, woman, and two children, boy and girl; Bluford, age 25, Kier (boy), age 25, Mary, age 15, Thomas age 7, Fincher (girl) age 5, Dice, age 30, George age 12, John age 9, Senn? (boy), age 7, boy age 5, Ursley age 60, Nat age 25, Bob age 23.

Notes: Walter Wadsworth, P. R. Edmons, Hiram J. Kelly, W. M. Carter, James F. Akins, Philip P. Calhoun, Chapman Powell. One supena fifa in case J. Dabbs vs. R. D. Greer.

Appraisers sworn 8-3-1855 /s/J. S. Eliott, J. P.

Sale Bill of Negroes and Land belonging to Estate of Israel Miller, decd, sold by G. Morris, Admr on 1st Tues in Jan last on credit to 1st Jan 1856
Page 379

Gid, age 13 sold to Lauret Corley
Adaline, age 22, sold to James M. Calhoun
Lot No. 319, 18th Dist. DeKalb Co. sold to James S. Elliott

/s/G. Morris, Admr

Sale Bill of Personal Property belonging to Estate of Arthur Leach, decd, sold on 26th Oct 1854
Page 379-380

Purchasers: Andrew Browning, Rober Wood, A. Browning, John Goza, W. J. Kelly, M. L. Braden, W. C. Russean, John Bagwell, Thomas Thompson, Asa Wright, Robert Baxter, Mrs. E. C. H. McCurdy, John Nash, W. W. Wells,E. Ellison, W. D. Dicken

Sale of negroes:

Ann, girl, to R. D. Pounds
Anderson, boy, to H. W. Wells
Martha, woman, to Andrew Browning

/s/Sarah A. Leach, Admx

Georgia, DeKalb Co., Account Current with Exrs on Estate of John Blake, decd, up to 1st Monday in June 1855
Page 381-382

Cash recd from M. Stone note, John Brazell, C. Rainey, J. Henry, S. Prewell, R. Brasell note, G. Morris, R. Baxter, Sterling Goodwin note, W. Grishm, J. W. L. Tilly, M. Steel, J. Steel, John McElroy, J. Wilson note, W. G. Henderson, W. B. Wilson, Dr. E. N. Calhoun, L. Morgan, Richard Pennell, W. Grogan, Ichabod Williams, J. Grisham, Joseph Stewart, Wesley Mitchell, James Sprewell, Esther Richerson, J. . Lord, Thomas Thompson note, John Q. Flowers, T. L.Langley.

Cash paid - W. B. Wilson, J. W. Grisham, E. N. Clahoun, Alex Johnson, David Duncan, Jesse Lacy, W. A. Pool, W. A. Powell, J. A. Reeves, J. and L. S. Morgan, W. S. Grogan, J. M. Gordon, John Abernathy, Ichabod Williams, T. W. J. Hill, Bird Goza, M. W. Hill, John Bryce, M. M. Johnson, W. J. Palmer, E. Rosser, Allen Wooddall, A. Browning, John Y. Flowers, H. A. Dorsey, John McElroy, Thomas T. Langley, W. J. Palmer, W. H. Blake, John Carroll.

Sworn 6-4-1855
/s/John Carroll, Exr

2nd Return 1855, James J. Diamond in Account with Estate of W.H. Graham
Page 383

Received of Mark Miller on note, James R. Henry, S. E. Jordon, F. T. McAlpin, A. A. Jordan, Thomas W. P. Hill.
Cash paid -- M. Winningham, C. W. Johnson, B. M. Smith, H. Holmes, S. T. Cash, M. B. Henry, Permelus Reynolds, J. J. Diamond, E. A. Davis for tax, T. W. J. Hall, C. M. McGinnis, D. and H. W. Lee, A. Johnson.
Sworn 1-18-1855
/s/J. J. Diamond, Admr

Martha Beauchamp, Admx of Estate of W. Beachamp, decd
Page 383

Cash paid W. J. Jackson, W. Nesbit, H. H. Dean, J. W. Goldsmith.

/s/Martha Beauchamp, Admx

Estate of Israel Miller, decd, in Account Current with Gideon Morris, Admr from 1st Feb 1854 to 25 Jun 1855
Page 384

Cash paid J. S. Elliott J. W. Buchanan, J. D. Buchanan, E. S. Buchanan, E. Washington, James S. Elliott, John R. Humphries, Joel E. Morris, Zachariah Eidson, Margaret Miller, E. Washington, W. A. Powell, Nancy M. McElroy, J. R. Humphries, E. A. Davis, J. A. Reeves.

Cash recd of E. Washington and R. Bostick.
Sworn 6-25-1855
/s/G. Morris, Admr

Return No. 3, Estate of James W. R. Reeves, decd, in Account Current with John Y. Flowers from 1st Jan 1854 to 31st Dec inclusive
Page 385-386

To cash paid Solomon Goodwin, J. P. Simmons, atty, John Bruce, W. J. Donalson, S. R. Reeves, J. F. Trimble, A. W. Reeves, Jesse Childress, Thomas W. J. Hill, C. Murphey, John M. Ridling,William Ezzard, Atty.

Cash received of Solomon Goodwin and W. G. Heard
Sworn 6-25-1855
/s/John Y. Flowers

Inventory and Appraisement of Estate of David S. M. Boring, decd
Page 386

Negroes : Mary, woman, Ezekiel, boy, Tom, boy.
Appraisers: W. L. Williams, Alfred S. Fowler

Estate of John Austin in Account Current with T. F. Austin, Admr from 3d Jul 1854 to Jul 2,1855
Page 387

Cash paid - G. Tennant, S. Penn, W. W. Surtell, W. R. Hackett, Walter W. Smith, William M. Johnson, J. T. Bellinger, Alex D. Paden, L. C. Simpson, W. McMurty.

Sworn 7-3-1855
/s/T. F. Austin Admr

E. Warbington, Admr of Estate of Leonard Winters, decd, in Account Current for 1854 up to 2d Jul 1855
Page 387

Cash paid - J. M. Redding, W. B. Ruggles, Robert Baxter, Alex Johnson, John Y. Flowers, James S. Elliott, John McElroy, Samuel W. Winters.
Cash receivd of D. Irwin, Robert Baxter
Sworn 7-2-1855
/s/E. Warbington, Admr

Inventory and Appraisement of Estate of Merrill Collier, decd
Page 388-389

Appraisers: W. L. Williams, D. S. M. Boring, Nathan Lumer

Andy, negro man
Elisha, negro man
Guilford, negro boy
Newman, negro boy
Ples, negro boy

Bill, negro boy
Simeon, negro boy
Nubels, negro boy
Elmira, woman and child, Tom
Vina and her child
Caroline, a girl
Rose, a girl
Emeline, a girl

John C. Austin, Admr with LWT Annexed of Thomas Austin, decd, in Account Current for year 1854 and 1855
Page 390

Cash paid H. P. Almond, N. H. Austin, Alex Johnson, John W. Turner, E. B. and J. F. Reynolds, S. Byrant, J. Bryce, E. Rosser, M. H. Minor, Levi Willard, J. C. Austin.
Sworn 7-2-1855
/s/John C. Austin, Admr

Selina Ellington, Gdn of David Ellington in Account Current for year 1854
Page 390-391

Cash recd from Jabez Lord, W. W. Roark, Ed Monday, Sego & Abbit, hire of negroes
Cash paid - W. F. Goodwin, H. Irby, 1854 tax., W. Johnston, L. J. V. Taylor, Jacob Haas, A. Johnson, Josiah Henderson, W. P. Johnson, Richard B. Stell, J. D. Bohannon, W. F. M. Reeve, S.K. Pace, S. Eders, Samuel Eders, W. Roark, H. A. Dorsey
Sworn 6-7-1855
/s/Selina Ellington, Gdn

R. M. Brown, Admr on Estate of Ann Ogilby in Account Current for year 1854 and up to 26 Jun 1855
Page 391

By cash paid W. Ezzard, Reubin Haynes,S. Frankford, W.B. Ruggles, E. A. Davis, T. C., John Collier, S. B. Culverson, A. M. Mugr, Dr. J. F. Alexander, A. Johnson, Ordy.

/s/R. M. Brown, Admr

R. M. Brown, Admr of Estate of A. T. Dozier, decd, in Account Current for 1854 and up to 26Jun 1855
Page 392

Cash paid C. M. Connally, Susan Dozier, widow, Thomas H. Dozier, W. M. Hill, T.L. Thomas, H. C. Holcomb, S. B. Hout, E. A. Davis, W. Ezzard, Atty, J. H. Johnson, Clark Howell, R. M. Brown, Clk, Dr. Stephen Biggers, Susan Dozier widow, the state being insolvent, W. M. Hill, J. B. Brantley, L. C. Simpson, Clark Howell, J. R. Wallace, S. B. Hout, O. Houston.

Sworn 6-26-1855
/s/R. M. Brown, Admr

R. M. Brown, Admr of Estate of John Bankston, decd, in Account Current with said Estate for 1854 up to 20 Jun 1855
Page 393

By cash paid J. R. Philips, A. Johnson, C. W. McGinnis, Henry Bankstn, John Collier, E. A. Davis, Synthia Bankston.
To cash received of H. Bankston for rent
Sworn 6-26-1855
/s/R. M. Brown, Admr

An Account of Sale of Lot of Land No. 300 in 20th Dist. and 2d Section of Cobb Co. to Property of Cealy Leverett, decd, Sold at public outcry on 5th day of Dec 1854
Page 393-394

To cash paid Anderson, Sheriff, Telithia Leverett, Simeon Smith.

Sworn Simon Smith, Admr 6/25/1855

S. K. Pace, Gdn of Louisa Sentell, minor in Account Current for year 1854 and up to June 4, 1855 inclusive
Page 395

By cash paid Aber Johnson.
Sworn 6-4-1855
/s/S. K. Pace, Gdn

S. K. Pace, Gdn of Martha Sentell, minor, in Account Current for year 1854 and up to 4 June 1855 inclusive
Page 395

Cash paid Alexr Johnson.
Sworn 6-4-1855
/s/S. K. Pace, Gdn

S. K. Pace, Gdn of Caroline Sentell, minor for year 1854 up to June 4, 1855 inclusive
Page 395

To cash paid Alex Johnson
Sworn 6-4-1855
/s/S. K. Pace, Gdn

S. K. Pace, Gdn of Almeda Sentell, minor, in Account Current for year 1854 up to June 4, 1855
Page 396

To cash paid Alexr Johnson
Sworn 6-4-1855
/s/S. K. Pace, Gdn

William Hairston, Gdn of Emanda C. and Lillie T. Hairston, minors, in Account Current for year 1854
Page 396

Cash paid out for wards.
Sworn 7-17-1855
/s/W. Hairston, Gdn

Mrs. Mary C. Scafe, Admx of Estate of William Scafe, decd, in Account for year 1854 and up to 7-2-1855
Page 396

To cash paid for tombstone and bury expenses
Sworn 7-2-1855
/s/Mary . Scafe

Sale of Real Estate Belonging to Estate of Ephraim Salmond, decd, Sold on 1st Tues in May Sold for cash to Berry Perkins for $62

/s/W. Jordan, Admx

William Jordon, Admx of Estate of Ephraim Salmond, decd, in Account Current for year 1854
Page 397

Cash paid Alexr Johnson
Sworn 4-3-1855
/s/William Jordon, Admr

Robert McWilliams, Admr of Estate of William Hilderbrand, decd, in Account Current for year 1854
Page 397

Cash paid Alexr Johnson
Sworn 7-4-1855
/s/Robert McWilliams, Admr

Georgia, DeKalb Co., Ezekiel C. Harris' Return as Admr on Estate of James F. Montgomery of said county, decd, for year 1854
Page 397

To cash paid W. J. Kilby, John G. Campbell, A. Johnson, G. D. Rice, W. P. and D. M. Young.

James W. Kirkpatrick, Exr of Estate of James H. Kirkpatrick, decd, in Account Current for year 1854 and up to 30th June 1855 inclusive
Page 398

To cash paid Allen Wooddall, Jane N. Morgan, Thomas F. Hall, W. M. Williams, E. . Calhoun, Mrs. Ann Kirkpatrick, W. R. Smith on settlement.
Sworn 6-30-1855
/s/J. W. Kirkpatrick, Exr

Andrew Wells, Gdn of A. C. Giles, in Account Current for year 1854
Page 398

Board and schooling of ward for 1855
Sworn 6-13-1855
/s/Andrew Wells, Gdn

E. Washington, Gdn of Andrew Miller in Account Current for year 1854 and up to 2 Jul 1855
Page 398

To cash received of G. Morris, Admr on 6-4-1855
/s/E. Warbington, Gdn
Sworn 7-2-1855

Jesse Childress, Gdn of John A. Childress in Account Current for year 1854 up to and including 7-2-1855
Page 399

To cash received of John Y. Flowers, Exr of Estate of J. W. Reeves
Sworn 7-2-1855
/s/Jesse Childressn, Gdn

Jesse Childress, Gdn of James S. Childress in Acount for year 1854 up to 7-2-1855
Page 399

Sworn 7-3-1855
/s/Jesse Childress, Gdn

A. B. Forsyth, Gdn of E. A. Weiner in Account Current for year 1854
Page 399

To cash paid taxes, Alexr Johnson.
Sworn 7-25-1855
/s/A. B. Forsyth, Gdn

Samuel B. Crawford, Admr on Estate of W. M. Hulsey, decd, in Account Current for 1853 and 1854 up to 6-15-1855 inclusive
Page 400

To cash paid Levi Willard, Haden Coe, W. L. Williams, A. G. Hulsey, Gdn, Alexr Johnson, Charles Latimer, William B. Wiley, S. B. Crawford.

Sworn 6-19-1855
/s/Samuel B. Crawford, Admr

Rufus Henderson, Gdn of Samuel B. Williams, a person of unsound mind, in Account Current for year 1855 up to 5 June 1855
Page 400

To cash paid Alexr Johnson.

/s/Rufus Henderson, Gdn

John T. Alford, Admr of Estate of Byrum Alford, Decd, in Account Current for year 1854 up to 6-22 inclusive
Page 401

By cash paid E. Stoward, Admr, James Alford, Bestus Alford, Alexr Johnson
Sworn 6-22-1855
/s/J. T. Alford, Admr

Martha Todd, Extrx of Estate of Richard Todd, decd, in Account Current for year 1853 and 1854
Page 401

To cash paid Alex Johnson
Sworn 4-2-1855
/s/Martha Todd, Extrx

Sale Bill of a Portion of the Negroes Belonging to Estate of Nancy Buie Sold by Thomas Farr ar Trustee for Orphia Stowers sold on 1st Tues in Jan 1854
Page 401

Caroline and her child sold to James Paden
Catharine, a girl, 14 years old, sold to John Tumlin
Jasper a boy, 11 years old, sold to Henry Irby
Andy, a boy 9 years old, sold to Henry Irby

/s/Thomas Farr, Trustee

T. A. Kennedy, Gdn of P. A. Peacock in Account Current for year 1854 and up to 28th June 1855 inclusive
Page 402

Hire of Caroline and children 1854
Cash paid W. Gilbert, A. Johnson, J. T. Bellinger, Alexr Johnson, H. C. Holcombe, P. A. Peacock.
Sworn 6-28-1855
/s/T. A. Kennedy, Gdn

Inventory of Notes Belonging to Estate of J. L. Williams, decd
Page 402-409

Note of Samuel Anderson.
Accounts of A. Adams, Enos Adams, Alexr Crews, W. Allen, D. Adams, John Adams, Elijah Bird, James Baxter, R. Buchanan, Wiley Browning, John Buchanan, John Baxter, B. Corbin, W. Campbell, John Cook, Wiley Cape, E. Crews, Winston Cash, Ned Calhoun, James Dook, J. Durham, John Dabb, John C. Evins, J. H. Eskew, Craft Evins, David Floyd, Daniel Foans, C. Green, Solomon Goodwin, T. B. George, W. H. Graham, John Hawkins, Major Henderson, T. Hill, A. Hawkins, R. J. Hardman, John Henry, Merrell Humphries, W. G. Henderson, W. F. Hunter, Joseph Huey, Cam Haralson, J. A. Heardman, W. Jackson, Robert Jolley, J. Johnson, Wiley Johnson, B. A. Johnson, W. Jolley, N. Johnson, C. A. Johns, C. Livesey, Jesse Simpkins, Thomas C. Morton, James E. McCord, A. Nelson, B. Right, John Osburn, Erbin Powell, R. Robuck, S. Ray, Thomas Reynolds, Bennett Rainey, Peter Reynolds, James Ray, W. P. Reeve, S. Scott, Young Thompson, J. Thompson, Elijah Turner, G. Thomas, John Wiley, C. Wilkerson, W. Wood, William B. Wilson, Allen Woodall, A. S. Wright, S. Winn, J. A. Williams, J. Winn, Robert Webb.

/s/P. F. Hoyle, Admr

Inventory of Notes and Accounts Belonging to Estate of Merrell Humphries, decd
Page 409

Notes on W. C. Grisham, R. J. Hardman, Berry Mullican, T. B. Rainey, S. P. Morgan, Silas Worsham, J. W. Weaver, J. N. Hadden, Thomas C. Reynolds. Numerous accounts.

Inventory and Appraisement of Estate of James Baxter, decd, appraised 11-19-1855
Page 410-411

Accounts of Silas Grisham, J. W. Level, J. M. Carroll, David Chestnut, Palmer & Johnson. Note of David Chesnut

Appraisers: Greenville Henderson, Ezekiel Reeve Bird Gozer, J. W. Level

Sale Bill of one lot of land lying in Campbell Co. Belonging to Estate of W. M. Hulsey decd, Sold 1855 to B. B. Tuchstone
Page 411

/s/Samuel B. Crawford, Admr

Elijah Steward, Admr of Estate of B. Alford, decd, in Account Current for year 1854 and up to 21 June
Page 411

Cash paid J. M. Calhoun, atty, T. J. Diamond, agt, W. Barnett, James M. Calhoun, W. Ezzard, R.M. Brown, Clk, J. W. Goldsmith, Shff, J. R. Smith, Alexr Johnson.

T. A. Kennedy, Admr of Estate of C. Connally, decd, in Account Current for 1854 and up to 6-28-1855
Page 412-413

Cash paid Alexr Johnson, W. B. Ruggles, J. M. Smith, W. B. Sewell, T. W. and C. W. Connally, Elizabeth Connally, Gdn, John Connally, Elizabeth Connally, Gdn, C. C. Connally.
Sworn 6-28-1855
/s/T. A. Kennedy, Admr

Estate of W. J. Kilpatrick to Rezin Lyon, Exr
Page 413

Cash paid Haden Coe, J. M. Smith, H. R. Delay, J. L. Lyon, S. T. Biggers, T. V. M. Rhodes, H. Parks, Alexr Johnson, A. H. Parks, Meridith Brown.

1853. Daniel J. Mitchell, Exr, in Account with Estate of William Mitchell, decd
Page 414

Cash paid J. M. Smith, taxes
Hire of negro woman for 1853
Sworn 6-19-1853
/s/Daniel J. Mitchell, Exr

Mary Parker, Extrx of Estate of John Parker, decd, in Account Current for year 1854 up to 7-4-1855

Page 414

Cash paid Alexr Johnson, W. McDuffell
Sworn 7-4-1855
/s/Mary Parker, Extrx, (x, her mark)

A. J. Walravin, Admr of Estate of Land Gilbert, decd in Account Current for year 1854 up to 7-1-1855
Page 414

Cash paid W. B. Ruggles
Sworn 7-1-1855
/s/A. J. Walravin, Admr

Daniel J. Mitchell, Exr of Estate of William Mitchell, decd, in Account Current for year 1854
Page 415-417

Cash paid G. W. Mitchell, W. J. Langston, J. E. Mitchell, A. G. W. Mitchell, G. W. Mitchell, A. Johnson, J. L Mitchell.
Sworn 3-5-1855
/s/Daniel J. Mitchell, Exr

Georgia, DeKalb Co., Sale Bill of Personal Property of Davies S. M. Boring, late of said co., decd, sold 11-2-1855
Page 417

Purchasers: Mrs. Boring, H. J. Fowler, B. F. Chamberlain, J. M. Fowler, J. M. Boring, David Waldrup, William Terry, J. B. Badger, Cyrus Clay, John Guess, Leborn Sturgis, J. M. Boring.

/s/Nathan Turner, Admr

Georgia, DeKalb Co., True Statement of Sale of Perishable Property
Belonging to Estate of James Baxter, decd, sold on 30th Nov
Page 417-419

Purchasers: G. Morris, D. Chestnut, S. Harman, H. Shuman, J. W.
Gresham, C. Inge, B. Goza, T. Thompson, G. Morris, J. M. Carroll, S. B.
Mclroy, S. H. Campbell, E. T. Harris, J. Y. Flowers, J. S. Jett, John G.
Rainey, S. B. McElroy, W. H. Cash, John Baxter, P. M. Carroll, J. W. Level,
R. Payton, A Goza, E. J. Fuller, G. T. Turner, W. H. Cash, W. J. Akins, W.
G. Henderson, John G. Rainey, G. A. Dickerson, W. C. Gushanfer.

/s/David Chestnut, Admr

Georgia, Henry Co. The following is a list of goods and chattels of John
C. Bartlett, decd, as was produced by Elizabeth Bartlett, Admx of said
Estate
Page 419-420

Appraisers: R. W. Gaar, J. J. Cowen, Leonard Sims
Sworn 2-24-1854

Sale Bill of Personal Property 3-3-1854. Purchasers: Elizabeth W.
Bartlett,L. Sims, Thomas Cook, E. W. Bartlett, N. C. Adamson, Thomas
Cook, G. W. Fuller, A. L. Huey, R. M. Gaar, R. S. Bartlett,Thomas Moon.

Inventory and Appraisement of Estate of Joseph Wooten decd
Page 421-422

202 1/2 acres, Lot No. 86
202 1/2 acres, Lot no. 87
202 1/2 acres, Lot No. 74

Negroes: Sampson, Joe, Linsey, Alexander, Sarah, Mack.
Appraisers: Mark I. Langston, James B. Robertson, W. P. Mead, James H.
Born, R. N. Morris
12-20-1855

Georgia, DeKalb Co. Appraise Bill of Estate of A. E. Ellis, late of said co., decd, 1-19-1856
Page 422-424

172 1/2 acres, Lot No. 294
11 1/4 acres, Lot No. 293
Negroes: Sampson, Rhoda, Henry, Martha, Jane.
Appraisers: Robert Baxter, Greenville Henderson, Alexr Chestnut
1-19-1856

James F. Leonard, Admr of Estate of Paul A. Haralson, decd, in Account Current for 1855
Page 424

Cash paid Alexr Johnson J. H. Murrell & Bros.
Sworn 1-5-1856
/s/James F. Henderson, Admr

Georgia, DeKalb Co., To Ordinary of said county, Estate of Bartholomew Stell, decd, to Charles W. Stell, Exr.
Page 424

To cash paid - W. W. Stell, Samuel Walker (tuitition of S. E. Stell), W. H. Penden, Wicksbury Mobley, Prichet Stewart, J. R. Wells (tuition), L. J. Robinson, Gdn

Samuel Potts and Avis Wooton, Exrs of Estate of Joseph Wooton, decd, in Account Current for 1855
Page 25

To cash paid E. A. Davis, taxes, Samuel Potts.
Sworn 1-14-1856
/s/Samuel Potts, Exr

Estate of James Crowley to Seaborn Crowley, Admr
Page 425

Cash paid W. S. McClain, Jesse Cantrel, Thomas W. J. Hill, C. Murphy, Harris Crowley, C. W. McGinnis, B. Crowley, B. S. Jennings, Z. D. Cross, Alexr Johnson, G. W. Crowley
Sworn 1-1-1856
/s/Seaborn Crowley, Admr

C. Murphy, Final Return as Admr on Estate of W. Cash, decd
Page 426

By cash paid or deposited in the agency of GA Railroad and Banking Co. at Atlanta
Cash paid Alexr Johnson, Admr, E. A. Davis, taxes
Sworn 10-27-1855
/s/C. Murphey, Admr

Elemander Warbington, Admr of Estate of L. Winters, late of Mississippi, decd, in Account for 1855
Page 426

Cash paid John Thuman, R. N. Thomason, John Thomason, W. W. Isom, S. P. Wright, James M. Calhoun, Alexr Johnson, Thomas Farr

Sworn 6-31-1856
/s/E. Warbington, Admr

Thomas Griffin Gdn of Margaret E. Griffin in Account Current with said ward
Page 427

Cash paid J. H. Lovejoy, R. E. Mangum, Alexr Johnson, Caldwell & Griffin.
Sworn 11-15-1855
/s/Thomas Griffin, Gdn

Thomas Griffin, Gdn of Alexr Griffin in Account Current with said ward
Page 427

Cash paid Caldwell & Griffin, J. C. Lively, Alexr Johnson.
Sworn 11-15-1855
/s/Thomas Griffin, Gdn

Thomas Griffin, Gdn of Narcissa G. Griffin in Account Current with said ward
Page 428

Cash paid J. H. Lovejoy, Caldwell & Griffin, James Caldwell, A. S. Wright, R. E. Mangum, Alexr Johnson.
Sworn 11-15-1855
/s/Thomas Griffin, Gdn

Thomas Griffin, Gdn of Susan M. Griffin in Account Current with said ward
Pag 428

To orig. amount received from Admr of Estate of Mobley.
Cash paid Caldwell and Griffin, J. H. Lovejoyn, Alexr Johnson.
Sworn 11-15-1855
/s/Thomas Griffin, Gdn

Thomas Griffin, Gdn of David Griffin in Account Current with said ward
Page 428

To cash paid Alexr Johnson, Ordinary
Sworn 11-15-1855
/s/Thomas Griffin, Gdn

Josiah Greer, Admr of Estate of John Dobson, decd, in Account Current for 1855
Page 429

12 days attendance at Court Troup Co. and going to Meriwether Co.
Sworn 12-24-1855
/s/Josiah Greer, Admr

Charles Murphy, Admr debonis non on Estate of James Crowley, decd, in Account Current
Page 429

Cash paid Allen Crowley, Alexr Johnson
Sworn 1-5-1856
/s/C. Murphey, Admr

Azariah Mims, Exr of Estate of James Russell, decd, in Account Current for 1855
Page 429

Cash paid A. Johnson, Susanah Russell, 1855 taxes.
Sworn 3-3-1856
/s/Az. Mims, Exr.

T. A. Kennedy, Gdn of P. A. Peacock, minor, in Account Current for 1855
Page 429-430

Cash paid Alexr Johnson.

Cash paid Ward.
Sworn 1-10-1856
/s/Thomas A. Kennedy, Gdn

C. Murphy, Gdn of John J. McKoy in Account Current
Page 430

To cash paid trip to Milledgeille, S. E. Scudder, W. H. Rials, Levi Willard, Gardner Adams, E. Rosser, J. E. George, W. A. Powell, Eliza Nesbit, P. F. Hoyle
Sworn 3-22-1856
/s/C. Murphy, Gdn

Inventory and Appraisement of Estate of Richard Taliaferro (of unsound mind)
Page 431

Hulda and chld, Willis and wife and child (Letta), Jesse, Kirby and Peter, Mingo, wife and two children, Green and Mahaley, Clinton and Molly.

Appraisers: W.L. McMiller, J. J. Hutchins, Meridith Brown, Thomas Brown

William L. Williams, Gdn of Penelope K. Williams, his own minor child in Account Current up
to1-7-1856
Page 431

To amt of cash received from Sarah McCalpin of the Estate of Alex McAlphin.

George Key, Gdn of his own minor children in Account Current for 1855 up to 4-20-1856
Page 432

Cash paid Thomas T. Key, my ward, Alexr Johnson.
Sworn 4-22-1856
/s/George Key, Gdn

William T. Ivey, Gdn of James L. Ivey in Account Current for 1854 up to 6-29-1855
Page 432

Cash paid James L. Ivey, his ward, Honeycut & Silvey, Alexr Johnson.
To cash recd of W. Ezzard, Admr of H. Ivy
Sworn 6-29-1855
/s/William T. Ivy

H. H. Embry, Admr de bonis non on Estate of Jesse Childress, decd, in Account Current for 1856
Page 432

Cash paid Alexr Johnson, H. H. Embry
Sworn 4-28-1856
/s/H. H. Embry, Admr

Washington Johnson, Exr of Estate of W. Johnston, decd, in Account Current for year 1855
Page 433

To cash paid Alexr Johnson, Ordinary, Thomas W. J. Hill, J. G. Johnson, F. N. Hardman, J. S. Elliott, E. A. Davis, tax, Jesse C. Cantrell, H. A. Dorsey, C. Powell, Levi Willard. To cash received of S. Bryant, M. C. Lively, J. B. Wilson, W. Mason, Leander Heflin, C. Powell, Loftin Arnld, Philip House, John M. Ridlin, Philip Colleman, John Fannin
Sworn 5-1-1856
/s/W. P. Johnston,, Admr

John Bryce, Gdn of G. C. Butler in Account Current for year 1855
Page 433

Cash paid for taxes, 1855, and Alexr Johnson.
Sworn 4-23-1856
/s/John Bryce, Gdn

S. P. Wright, Gdn of Paraside Rainey in Account Current for year 1855
Page 434

To hire of boy, Beverly, for 1855, of Joe for 1855 and of girl, Eliza for 1855.
Cash paid - ward, Sarah Rainey, W. A. Powell, A. E. Ellis Estate, Levi Willard, Alexr Johnson
Sworn 3-25-1856
/s/S. P. Wright, Gdn

S. P. Wright, Gdn of James M. Joice in Account Current for 1855
Page 434

To hire of boy, Harrison for 1855, and girl, Darcus, for 1855
To cash paid - P. F. Hoyle James S. Elliott, W. A. Powell, N. D. Roberts, Levi Willard, GeorgeA. Braswell, A. E. Ellis.

Sworn 3-25-1856
/s/S. P. Wright, Gdn

Martha Todd, Extrx of Estate of Richard C. Todd in Account Current for 1855
Page 435

Cash paid Jesse Clay Alex Johnson
Sworn 4-2-1856
/s/Martha Todd, Extra

Return No. 2, Rufus Henderson, Gdn of Samuel Williams, in Account Current for year 1855
Page 435

Cash paid Alexr Johnson
Sworn 2-2-1856
/s/Rufus Handerson, Gdn

S. P. Wright, Gdn of James M. Reeves, in Account Current for 1855
Page 435

Cash paid - James M. Reeves, Thomas Akins, E. N. Calhoun, Alexr Johnson
Sworn 3-25-1856
/s/S. P. Wright, Gdn

C. W. MGinnis' Final Return for Estate of J. W. Bohannon, decd
Page 436

Cash paid John M. Reid, Gdn.
G. K. Hamilton Receipt

Sworn 12-3-1855
/s/C. W. McGinnis, Admr

John C. Cannon, Gdn of Allison, George, Sarah Ann and Bryant Cash in Account Current for 1855
Page 436

Cash received of G. L. Strickland
Sworn 2-2-1856
/s/J. C. Cannon, Gdn

Edwin Plaster, Admr of Estate of Henry Brockman, decd, in Account
Current for year 1855
Page 436

Cash paid Alexr Johnson.
Sworn 4-29-1856
/s/Edwin Plaster, Admr

Mrs. E. W. Bartlett, Admx on Estate of John Bartlett, decd
Page 437

Cash paid Thomas Cook, T. Dean, Thomas Wells, George K. hamilton, D. and W. H. Lee, J. W. Scruggs, C. W. Johnson, T. W. Goldsmith, L. Dean, William Goldsmith, G. K. and J. L. Hamilton, George K. Smith, R. S. Bartlett

Sworn 12-25-1855
/s/Elizabeth Bartletter, Admx (x, her mark)

John C. Harris, Gdn of William N. Leitch in Account Current up to this date
Page 437

Cash paid Alexr Johnson
Sworn 4-1-1856
/s/John C. Harris, Gdn

John C. Harris, Gdn for Andrew B. Letich in Account Current up to this date
Page 437

ash received of Sarah Ann Leeitch, Admx of Arthur Leitch, decd, on 4-1-1856
Sworn 4-1-1856
/s/John C. Harris, Gdn

Rhoda Brown, Admx of Estate of Fannin Brown. decd, in Account
Current for year 1854 and up to 25th June 1855
Page 438

By cash paid 1854 taxes, Alexr Johnson.
To rent of land for 1854
Sworn 6-25-1855
/s/Rhoda Brown, Admx (X, her mark)

Simeon Smith, Admr of Estate of Sealey Leverett, decd, in Account Current for year 1855
Page 438

By cash paid Alex Johnson, Buckner Leverett, Burrell Leverett, John Leverett, Tilethea Leverett, Simeon Smith.
Sworn 4-5-1856
/s/Simon Smith, Admr

John C. Harris, Gdn of Susanah T. Leitch in Account Current up to this date
Page 438

To cash recd of Mrs. Sarah Ann Leitch, Admx of Estate of Arthur Leitch, decd, recd 4-1-1854
$555.24
Cash paid Alexr Johnson
Sworn 4-1-1856
/s/John C. Harris, Gdn

John D. Wells, Gdn of James E. Wells, William H. Wells, Samuel P. Wells and E. W. Wells
Page 439

To rent of house one year
Sworn 4-7-1856
/s/J. D. Wells, Gdn

Sale Bill of a Negro man, Stephen, as the Property of Virginia E. Emerson, said boy sold under arbitration held in Madison as appears upon records of Superior Court of Morgan Co.
Page 439

Said boy sold to Charles Campbell for $1400 cash and $600 in note.
/s/J. B. Luckey, Gdn

Rhoda Brown, Admx of Estate of Fannin Brown, decd, in Account Current for year 1855
Page 439

Cash paid Thomas Moore, J. R. McAlexander, Alexr Johnson.
Sworn 5-28-1856
/s/Rhoda Brown (X, her mark)

James Caldwell, Gdn of Mary J. Batey in Account Current up to 23d May 1856 inclusive
Page 439

To cash paid Alexr Johnson, tax collector, cash paid Mary Jane Batey, my ward.

Return No. 4, Account Current with Estate of James W. Reeves up to May 1856
Page 440

Cash recd on not A. Gardner, received Lewis Wright, Thomas Thompson note, Davis Wade, David B. Anderson, Enos Adams on Execution, A. Gardner on note.

By cash paid out for said estate up to May 1856. Paid J. F. Trimble, Gdn for W. J. T. Reeves, minor, one note on Dr. Hoyle ue 12-25-1855
8-11-1855 paid L. Thomas, Admr of Estate of W. Slay.
12-25-1855 paid S. P. Wright, Gdn of J. M. Reeve, minor heir
1-2-1855 Cash paid Lewis Thomas, Admr of W. Slay
10-20-1855 Cash paid Josiah Greer on note, paid Josiah Greer on Subpoena.
Cash paid J. M. Ridling Subpoene
Cash paid Jesse Childress, Gdn for his minor children
1-1856 Cash paid E. Warbington, Admr of Estate of L. Winters paid as Security for John H. Cone
3-27-1856 paid S. R. Reeve, heir, John M. Ridling on Subpoena.
4-19-1856 paid J. F. Johnston on fifa.
5-1856 paid Jesse Childress, Gn of r W. and J. Childress
3-24-1856 paid S. W. Reeve, W. J. Donalson, James F. Trimble
10-23-1855 cash paid Eli McCray on fifa.
Sworn 6-9-1856
/s/John Y. Flowers, Exr

Annual Return No. 4, Joseph Thompson in Account with the Estate of Moses W. Formwalt, decd
Page 441-442

Amt recd from A. M. Watts
To amount receivdd of J. McDonald, C. C. Rogers land note, L. J. Glen, A. R. White, J. O. McDonald, E. Andrews, N. L. Angier, M. A. Bell, T. L. Cooper, H. L. Currier, A. M. Watts, P. E. McDaniel, B. O. Jones, Mrs. T. S. Ogilby, J. S. Martin, T> Kiles, T. S. Ogilby, J. T. Doane, M. L. Anger, M. A. Bell, T. L. Cooper, H. L. Carrier, H. M. Watts, P. E. McDaniel.

By amount paid H. L. Carner, J. Thompson, W. H. Craft, W. B. Ruggles, C. W. McGinnis, C. Humphries, J. Norcross, F. F. Gibbs, costs on 6 insolvent fifas vs. J. W. Ponts, W. Carlile, Hall vs. Thompson, Admr, J. L. Terry, John Bird, W. B. Ruggles, J. D. Sonte note, A. Johnson fees, C. R. Hanlester, W. Ezzard for bad bill paid him, fifa Bartlett vs. Thompson Admr, J. Haas, W. Key, T.F. Gibbs & Son.

Sworn 7-4-1856
/s/Joseph Thompson, Admr

E. C. Harris Return for year 1855 as Admr on Estate of James F. Montgomery, decd
Page 443

Paid A. Cook, Robert Baber, J. J. Northcut, Dillard Young, Samuel Walker for advertising, A. E. Chowan for tuition, C. P. Harris one of the legatees, Thomas H. Mitchell tuition, L. N. Burge, N. N. Smith, Davis O. Scroggs, Charles H. Montgomery, Z. A. Rice on note for fix grave, Puliam & Cox, J. Campbell, C. Cox, A. Johnson, Ordy, E. C. Harris

Sworn 5-5-1856
/s/E. C. Harris, Admr

Washington Cash, Gdn of Eldridge S. Cash in Account Current for year 1855
Page 443

Cash paid Alexr Johnson, G. Adams, Washington Cash, Alexr Johnson.
Sworn 4-4-1856
/s/Washington Cash, Gdn (X, his mark)

Return No. 6 1855 to James S. Elliott for Alexr Joice, a minor and Ediot, Gdn
Page 444

Cash to Alexr Johnson
Sworn 5-28-1856
/s/James S. Elliott, Gdn

Return No. 2 for 1855, James S. Elliott, Gdn for Sarah Joice for year 1855 up to 28th May 1856 inclusive
Page 444

To amount of cash or good notes recd of George W. Humphries, former Gdn, recd 2 May 1855
To hire of nerve fo 1855, and George and Charles
To cash paid A. Johnson, N. S. Liddell, George A. Braswell, Joseph Martin, John McElroy, Exr, James S. Elliott for board, Allen Wooddall, sheriff cost, W. A. Powell.
Sworn 5-28-1856
/s/James S. Elliott, Gdn

John B. Luckey, Gdn of Virginia E. Emerson in Account Current for the year 1855
Page 445

To hire of Stephen, Ben (a boy), Arnold, Mike, Lucinda (a woman), Harriett and four children, May, a small girl, for 1855.

By cash paid J. B. Luckey, Alexr Johnson, Sarah A. Comer, J. L. Jones, G. K. and P. L. Hamilton, C. W. Johnson, Pace Carr and Cody, J. J. Diamond, J. B. Luckey for 8 mos. board and washing for 1855

Sworn 6-12-1856
/s/J. B. Luckey, Gdn

Sale Bill of Land Belonging Jointly to Estates of A. H. Green and Adam G. Saffold Sold on 4th day of December 1855 upon a Credit of 12 mos. with interest from date Sold at Town of Isabella, Worth Co.
Page 445

Fractions, Nos. 192,193,197 and 198 in 15th Dist. of Dooly Co. originally sold to David S. Johnson, 1/2 No.s 209 and 240, 16th Dist., Dooly, now Worth co., sold to said Johnston. 1/2 Lot No2. 241 and 242 in said 16th Dist. sold to said Johnston. Lot No. 15 in 15th Dist., orig. Dooley now Worth Co. to said Johnson.

John Carroll and Henry W. Blake, Exrs of Estate of John Blake, decd, in Account Current for 1855
Page 446

Received of Dr. P. H. Hugh, Admr, W. S. Grogan, John Love, Thomas Akins, David D. Wade, James Gunter, W. Wright, B. Plaster, James Akins, L. S. Morgan, Jabez Lord, Jiles Humphries, W. C. Austin, Enel Hardman, John Jones, Jo Grisham, J. F. Johnston, D. Anderson, John B. Womack.

To cash paid John R. Humphries, John G. Rainey, Henry Irby, Micajah Stone, Nancy Mcelroy, John B. Womack, Dr. Hoyle, Admr, Allen Wooddall, Alexr Johnson, Chalres Inge, John Carroll.

Sworn 6-24-1856
/s/John Carroll, Exr

Salina Ellington, Gdn of David Ellington, a person of unsound mind.in Account Current for year 1855
Page 447

To hire of Ben, Wash, Burrell, Jacob and Friday for 1855
Cash paid J. M. Collier, Alexr Johnson, J. T. Dvan, S. B. Rea, J. M. Lord, M. D. Muldin, P. Hayden, E. B. and J. F. Reynods, J. Norcross, E. M. Munday, John Howard, J. L. Doane, H. W. McDaniel, W. G. Coller, J. E. Williams, J. R. Wallace, Harris Goodwin, J. Taylor, Alexr Johnson
Sworn 5-31-1856
/s/Salina Ellington, Gdn

The Estate of Joel Fowler, decd, to H. J. and A. M. Fowler, Exrs, for 1855
Page 448

Cash paid J. W. Crockett, Sarah Fowler, Solomon Johnson, Elias S. Fowler, S. W. Franks, C. W.McGinnis, P. F.Hoyle.

Sworn 6-11-1856
/s/H. J. Fowler, Exr

Estate of William Annesley, decd, in Account with W. Ezzard, Admr, with LWT annexe for 1855
Page 448

By amount on note collected of Isaac Moore
Sworn 7-1-1856
/s/William Ezzard, Admr

Estate of Henry G. Collier, decd, in Account with William Ezzard, Exr, for year 1855
Page 448

Paid George C. Clark, H. B. Laimer, Gdn of W. E. J.
/s/William Ezzard, Exr

Estate of Hardy Ivy, decd, in Account Current with William Ezzard, Admr de bonis non for 1855
Page 449

Cash paid Mrs. Sarah Ivy, a distributee, John G. Terry, James M. Ellis, Thomas Baker, M. J. Ivy,
Gdn of Richard N. Ivy, W. T. Ivy, W. L. Ivy, Admr of Samuel Ivy, John L. Ivy, legatee, J. O. Ivy.
Sworn 7-1-1856
/s/William Ezzard, Adm

Estate of Alston H. Green, in Account with William Ezzard, Admr for 1855
Page 449

Cash paid E. Barbour for Selmy land, Joseph Corinty
Sworn 7-10-1856
/s/William Ezzard, Admr

Samuel A. F. Mann, minor, in Account with William Ezzard, Gdn for 1855
Page 450

Paid Mrs. Mann, his board, J. M. Blackstock, N. S. Liddell, S. E. Scudder, John A. O. Mann,
Gardner Adams
Sworn 2-1-1856
/s/William Edward, Gdn

Estate of Merrell Collier, decd, in Account with William Ezzard, Exr, for year 1855
Page 450

Cash paid J. L. Doane Levi Willard, John Tomlinson, David A. Cook, J. G. Trammell.
Sworn 7-1-1856
/s/William Ezzard, Exr

Miss Cordelia E. Green, minor, in Account Current with W. Ezzard, Gdn for year 1855
Page 451

By hire of negro man, Richard to Loyd & Pulliam, Horace, hire of Miles, Loyd & Pulliam, girl,
Emiline, to Terrell Sewell

To cash paid Dr. George Humphries, President C. Fulton, Mrs. Nelson, Levi Willard, R. L.
Pulliam, Dr. Joshua Gilberts, Sarah A. Comers, F. M. Eudlimens, C. C. Green, H. Bruneller, D.
B. Spaulding, W. Hayes, W. Ezzard.
Sworn 7-1-1856
/s/William Ezzard, Gdn

William A. Green, minor, in Account with William Ezzard, Gdn, for year 1855
Page 451-452

City tax for Atlanta
Paid N. E. Gardner, Dr. Haden Cole, D. Joice, J. E. Williams, W. A. Green in notes.
Sworn 7-1-1856
/s/William Ezzard, Gdn

John Bryce, Gdn of William McKoy in Account for year 1855 and up to 30 May 1856
Page 453

To hire of Charles, Andrew, Rhelta and Polley for 1855
Cash paid J. M. Blackstock, Levi Willard, E. Rosser, G. Adams, W. A. Powell, J. E. George, S. E. Scudder, W. H. Rials, John Byce, W. R. Brandon, C. Murphey, Alexr Johnson.
Sworn 5-3-1856
/s/John Bryce, Gdn

O. S. Morris, June 1856

Admr of Estate of Jane Russell, decd, in Account Current for 1855 and up to 30
Page 453-454

Paid Oliver Richey, James T. Russell, Melvira Russell, William Cromley, Robert Richey, John Russell, William Russell, Henry C. Russell, John Russell, Gdn, John Stewart, G. M. Philips, A. L. Scott, Alexr Johnson, B. F. Chapman, O. S. Morris, Alexr Johnson.

Sworn 6-30-1856
/s/Obadiah S. Morris, Admr

John C. Austin, Admr with LWT annexed on Estate of Thomas Austin in Account Current for year 1855 and up to 3rd July 1856 inclusive
Page 454

Cash paid J. C. Austin, J. M. Austin, J. J. Thrasher, W. T. Atkins, W. A. Powell, Alexr Johnson, Thomas H. Austin, J. Norcross, E. Rosser, T. J. Thrasher, N. H. Austin.
Sworn 7-3-1856
/s/John C. Austin, Admr

Joseph T. Bellinger, Exr of Estate of John N. Bellinger, decd, in Account Current for year 1855 and up to 3d Jul 1856 inclusive
Page 455

To cash recd from Formwalt's Estate, Burch Jett on note, S. Sweat, J. Helton, W. W. Anderson, James T. Akin, J. Collier, atty in Gdn cash on fifi

By cash paid James S. Elliott, John Collier, Burch Jett, Thomas B. Daniel, Alexr Johnson, R. M. Brown, Lewis Wright, John N. Page, Starlin Goodwin, E. Warbington, W. J. Comer, John T. Kean.

Sworn 7-3-1856
/s/Joseph T. Bellinger, Exr

James J. Diamond, Admr of Estate of W. H. Graham, decd, in Account Current for year 1855
Page 456

By cash paid G. W. Diamond, R. M. Brown, John Hardman, George W. Diamond, A. G. Hutchins, John N. Swift, Dr. D. E. Ware.

Sworn 6-30-1856
/s/James J. Diamond, Admr

Thompson A. Browning, Admr of Estate of Joseph Fox in Account Current with said Estate from Granting L/A 8-1855 to 6-30-1856
Page 456

To amt collected on notes of J. F. Seevy, collected on note of H. C. Harris, on note vs. W. P. Smith & Patterson, note, H. Holmes, W. C. Russean on note

By amount paid A. Johnson, J. S. and E. Abbot, A. Ford on note, H. H. Dean, T. Allen, S. G. Roberts, T. P. Hudson, E. Puckett, M. A. Thomas, G. K. and J. L. Hamilton, W. Crowell, A. J. Goldsmith, W. S. Ivy, H. Holms.

Thomas Johnson, William Johnson and John L. Hamilton, Admrs of A. Johnson, decd, in Account Current for year 1855
Page 457

To cash paid W. E. Wright, S. B. Hoyt, Thomas M. Dean, W. Ezzard, John Bruce, Aexr Johnson, E. A. Davis. Lewis Wiggins, J. W. Fowler, Ruggles & Howard.
Sworn 7-18-1856
/s/Thomas Johnson, Admr

Sale Bill of a part of Real Estate Belonging to Estate of W. Goldsmith, late of DeKalb Co., decd
Page 457

One lot of and in 2d Dist. of Irwin Co. sold on 2d Feb 1855 to C. M. Cronie for cash and one lot in Dooly sold to C. M. Cronie for cash, both lots sold for $169, one Lot in Forsyth Co. sold to William Harris, sold Oct 2, 1855 for cash.

/s/A. J. Goldsmith, Admr

A. J. Goldsmith and B. L. Veal, Admrs of Estate of William Goldsmith, decd, in Account Current for year 1854 and 1855 and up to 15th Jul 1856
Page 458

To cash recd of John Holmes, W. M. McKee, W. W. Wells, H. Weaver, Dr. R. M. Braden, W. Wade, James Pearce, H. Holmes, J. J. Diamond, Thomas Linch, D. G. Waldrup, John Hambrick, Thomas C. Hendry, W. H. Anderson, M. A. Veal, John Wiggins, B. G. Kelly, Lewis Wiggins, J. Parker, M. Winningham, J. J. Anderson, H. Mead, J. Prichet, J. Parker, J. N. Lalvney, J. Pritchet, W. B. Hill, T. A. Browning, W. Lee, L. Wiggins, F. M. Towers, W. L. Yarborough.

By cash paid E. Murpht, W. E. Jackson, Lawrence Mayor & Co., Chamberlain Miller, H. Holmes, J. J. Diamond, W. B. Parton, M. Winningham, A. Pulliam, N. L. Hutchens, Alexr Johnson, W. Johnson, E. G. Elford, R. M. Brown, M. A. Veal.

Sworn 7-15-1856
/s/A. G. Goldsmith, Admr

Thomas Far, Admr of Estate of Eleanor Farr, decd, in Account Current for year 1855
Page 459

By cash paid M. E. Carpenter, W. Fair J. L. Bellinger
Sworn 7-12-1856
/s/Thomas Farr, Admr

Robert McWilliams, Admr of Estate of William Hilderbran, decd, in Account Current for year 1855
Page 459

Cash paid Alexr Johnson.
Sworn 7-1-1856
/s/Robert McWilliams, Admr

1855, Estate of David S. M. Borgin, decd, to Nathan Turner Admr
Page 460

To cash pd C. R. Hansteter, Alexr Johnson
Cash recd of A. Philips book account, and Malcom McCloud, book account.
Sworn 7-3-1856

/s/Nathan Turner, Admr

James W.Kirkpatrick, Exr of Estate of James H. Kirkpatrick, decd, in
Account Current for year 1855
Page 460

By cash paid C. W. McGinnis, Thomas M. Darnall
Sworn 7-7-1856
/s/James W. Kirkpatrick, Exr

Thomas A. Kennedy, Admr of Estate of Christopher Connally, decd, in
Accunt Current for year 1855
up to 6-27-1856 inclusive
Page 460

Cash recd of T. M. Smith
Cash paid Alexr Johnson, W. Jordan, James Garvey
Sworn 6-27-1856
/s/T. A. Kennedy, Admr

Gideon Morris, Admr of Estate of Israel Miller, decd, in Account Current
for year 1855 and up to 1st day of Jul 1856
Page 461

Cash paid Zachariah Eidson, J. E. Morris, Margaret Miller, Jasper H. Miller, Larret Corley, N. R.Miller, Margaret Miller, John Y. Flowers, Zachariah Eidson, J. E. Morris, Alexr Johnson, G.Morris.

Sworn 7-1-1856
/s/G. Morris, Admr

James F. Trimble, Gdn for William J. C. Reeve 1855
Page 461

Cash paid James M. Reeve, Jacob Haas, W. Palmer
Sworn 6-31-1856
/s/J. F. Trimble, Gdn

G. Hulsey, Gdn of Selete Hulsey, Serena A. and Jennings Hulsey, minors of W. M. Hulsey, decd, in account Current for year 1853
Page 462

To cash recd of S. B. Crawford, Admr of W. M. Hulsey, decd
By cash paid McDonald Mitchel and Hulsey for (S. A. H.) and (S. E. H.), W. L. Williams for S. E. H. and S. A. H., Alexr Johnson.

Sworn 7-1-1856
/s/A. G. Hulsey, Gdn

Sarah Ann Leith, Admx of Estate of Arthur Leitch in Account Current for year 1855 and up to 30th June 1856
Page 462

By cash pad Tarlton Carter, W. B. Ruggles, W. L. Wells, Alexr Johnson, A. Wood on note, John C. Harris, Gdn of minor children of A. Leitch, decd.

Sworn 7-7--1856
/s/Sarah Ann Leitch, Admx

E. Warbington, Admr on Estate of Leonard Wintes, decd, in Account Current for year 1855
Page 463

By cash paid W. W. Isham, John Winters, Admr of Estate of Leonard Winters, decd, of Miss., Thomas Farr, John Isham, James M. Calhoun, E. Warbington, Alexr Johnson
Sworn 7-3-1856
/s/E. Warbington, Admr

Sale Bill of Lot of Land in Cassh Co., 4th Dist. and 3d Section, No. 253, Sold on first Tues. in Feb 1856 for sum $17.00
Page 463

E. Warbington, Admr

William Hairston, Gdn of his dau., Amanda C. Hairston, in Account Current for year 1855
Page 463

Cash paid by ward
Sworn 7-21-1856
/s/William Hairston

Anderson Wills, Gdn for A. C. Giles, minor in Account Current for year 1856
Page 463

To hire of negro girl for 1856
Sworn 5-26-1856
/s/Andrew Wills, Gdn for A. C. Giles

David Chestnut, Admr of Estate of James Baxter, decd, in Account Current for 1855 up to 7th day of Jul 1856
Page 464

By cash paid Louiza Baxter, widow, Thomas Henderson, Alexr Johnson, Lousa Baxter.
Sworn 7-7-1856
/s/David Chestnut, Admr

P. F. Hoyle, Admr of Estate of Merrell Humphries, decd, in Account Current for year 1856 and up to 7th Jul 1856 inclusive
Page 464

To cash paid W. N. Hill, W. F. Chewning, Alexr Johnson, E. A. Davis, W. J. Thrasher, V. M. Hill, N. H. Humphries, Wash Cash, William Jackson, A. M. Moore, J. B. Anderson, H. H. Hombuckel, Samuel Burdett, Alex Johnson, L. Tuggle, R. Jones, Allen Wooddall, J. M. Blackstock, Sarah E. Wilkerson, John G. Rainey, S. B. Morgan, S. E. Scudder, E. Rosser, Benjamin Burditt, J. E. George.

P. F. Hoyle, Admr of Estate of J. L. Williams, decd, in Account Current for year 1855 and up to 7th Jul 1856 inclusive
Page 465

Cash paid Merrell Humphris Estate, J. T. Mason, E. A. Davis, tax, J. W. Weaver, W. H. Cullege, A. Wooddall, Green B. Clay, T. B. George, W. Wadsworth, James F. Clay, Willis Cash, Thomas M. Grogan, Alexr Johnson, W. P. Johnson, Admr.
Sworn 7-7-1856
/s/P. F. Hoyle, Admr

R. M. Brown, Admr, in Account Current with Estate of Ann Ogilby, decd, for year 1855
Page 465

By cash paid B. H. Overby, E. A. Davis, B. F. Comer, Exr, Alexr Johnson.
Sworn 7-7-1856
/s/R. M. Brown, Admr

R. M. Brown, Admr of Estate of Richard S. Wright, decd, in Account Current for year 1855 up to 1st day of July 1856
Page 466

By cash paid W. Wiley, Nancy Morris, James J. Winn, Aber Johnson, J. J. Winn, Alexr Johnson,Thomas S. Denney, T. R. Ripley, S. Frankfort, J. F. Stubbs.

Sworn 7-7-1856
/s/. M. Brown, Admr

Inventory and Appraisement of Estate of Luke Johnson, decd
Page 466-467

Negroes: Sol, Henry, Ann.
100 acres of land lying in Newton Co. with saw mill.
235 acres of land and improvements hereon whereon the widow of the decd now lives.
Two notes of hand given by W. F. Roberts, one note given by Thomas Williams, one note given
by J. B. O. Nix. Two notes given by Mark M. Ragsdale, one note by J. W. Ferrell and Henry
Braswell, one note by J. H. Born.

Appraisers: W. R. Pendley, John M. Boon, John N. Swift, Jacob Chupp.

Sale of a portion of the Real Estate Belonging to the Estate of William Goldsmih, decd
Page 467

One lot of land in Early Co. sold to William Wade on 20th Sept 1854.
/s/A. J. Goldsmith, Admr

Inventory and Appraisement of Estate of Keziah Boyd
Page 468

Negroes: Nancy (woman), Rose (woman), Alford (boy).
Jeff, a negro man not named in the Will.
Land Warrant No. 19916 not named in Will. 160 cres.
Appraisers: John H. Jones, Jarret L. Morris, L. E. Jones

Inventory and Appraisement of the Estate of James Moore, decd, this 19th Aug 1856
Page 468-469

171 acres land No. 110
202 1/2 acres land No. 111
50 acres of land No. 177
75 acres No. 108
5 acres No. 84
One slave, Fanny. One, Mary.
Four town lots in City of Atlanta

Sale Bill of Perishable Property of James Moore, decd, Sold on a Credit until the 1st Dec 1857,
this 10th Sept 1856
Page 470-472

Purchasers: W. T. Cobb, Eli Clay, George Yancy, James Moore, Thomas E. Moore, James Burns, M. J. Wright, J. J. P. White, John L. Clark, John Moore, Jr., John Moore, J. G. Brown, W. P. Hutching, Leroy Brisendine, John McWilliams, George Young, M. B. Berry, Neal McDuffie, Merriman Baxley, A. L. Pitts, Mason Thimony, Berry Brisendine, W. Simpkins, Seaborn Brown, James Burns, W. Ragan, Thomas Turner, Thomas E. Turner, W. T. Stewart, W. Hutchins, Malcomb McDuffie, James P. White, John Patillo, James C. Avery, Oliver Jones, E. B. Reynolds, A. J. Pool, John A. Casey, William Wright, George Key, S. J. Wates, A. R. Almond, J. McWilliams, J. F. Brumlet, J. F. P. White, W. T. Barton, John Collier, Jr., T. M. Tomlin, James Barnes, W. S. McClain, William Thurman, W. R. Owen, W. S. McLane.

Support was set aside for widow and minor children, on 15th Aug 1856. /s/ A. L. Pitts, George Key, James Burns, William Akers.

Sale Bill of Real Estate Belonging to the Estate of James Baxter, decd, Sold on 4th day of Nov 1856
Page 473-474

One lot of land in the 18th District of DeKalb Co., No. 264 sold to Mrs. Louisa axter for cash.

J. Warbington, Guardian of Audrey Millers in Account Current for the year 1854 up to 3d Jul 1856 inclusive
Page 474

By cash paid Alexr Johnson, John McElroy, Andrew Miller, my ward.
Sworn 7-3-1856
/s/E. Warbington, Gdn

Elijah Steward, Admr of Estate of B. Alford, decd, in Account Current for the year 1855
Page 474

To cash collected of W. Turner, James Diamond, L. M. New, Manning Sheppard, M. Winningham, Margaret McCue, W. Sexton for J. J. Diamond, Diamond for Graves boy

By cash paid J. M. Calhoun. Alexr Johnson, 1855 tax.
Sworn 7-5-1856
/s/E. Steward, Admr

Estate of W. Michels, decd, in Acccount with D. J. Mitchel, Exr for 1855 and up to 5th May 1856 inclusive
Page 474

To hire of negro woman by name of Jamma.
Cash paid Alexr Johnson.

John T. Alford, Admr on Estate of Bynum Alford, Sr., decd, in Account Current for year 1856 and up to 12th Jul 1856
Page 475

By cash paid Elijah Steward, Admr of B. Alford, decd, E. Steward, J. T. Comwell, Admr Burton
Alford, James Price, Alexr Johnson

Sworn 7-12-1856
/s/John T. Alford, Admr
John B. Johns, Exr of Estate of Garland Dabney, decd, in Account Current for year 1856 and up to 4th Aug 1856

Page 476

By cash paid Isaac C. Humphries, Alexr Johnson
Sworn 8-4-1856
/s/John B. Johns, Exr

Appraisement of Inventory of Estate of Jackson F. Johnston, late of
DeKalb Co. decd
Page 475-476

101 1/2 acres of land of Lot No. 337
75 acres of Lot No. 202 in the 18th District
A negro boy named Nat.
A negro boy named Lewis.
Appraisers: John M. Ridling, W. P. Johnson, W. H. C. Evins

Sale Bill of Personal Property of Estate of J. F. Johnston, decd, Sold on
14th Nov 1856
Page 477

Purchasers: S. C. Johnston, the widow, John F> Johnston, R. D. Greer, W.
H. C. Evins, James Thurmon, John M. Ridling, W. P. Johnston, A. B.
Donahoo, John Adams.

Inventory of Estate of Joseph Fox, decd
Page 477-478

Negroes: Jane (woman), Elen (girl)
Appraisers: Drewry Lee, B. F. Veal, M. Winningham, Lewis Wiggins, H.
H. Dean

Charles W. Stell, Exr of B. Stell, decd, in Account Current for year 1855
Page 478

By cash paid G. M. Philips, C. F. and J. M. Newton, Wood & Swift, L. J.
Robinson, James H. Born

Sworn 7-7-1856
/s/Charles W. Stell, Exr

Thomas Griffin, Gdn of Susan Griffin, in Account Current for year 1855
Page 478

By cash paid Alexr Johnson
Sworn 7-20-1856
/s/Thomas Griffin

Thomas Griffin, Gdn of David Griffin, in Account Current for year 1856
Page 478

By cash paid Alexr Johnson
Sworn 7-24-1856
/s/Thomas Griffin, Gdn

Thomas Griffin, Gdn of Alexander Griffin, in Account Current for year 1856
Page 479

By cash paid Alexr Johnson.
Sworn 7-24-1856
/s/Thomas Griffin, Gdn

Thomas Griffin, Gdn of Narcissa G. Griffin, in Account Current for year 1855
Page 479

By cash paid A. C. Griffin, Alexr Johnson
Sworn 7-24-1856
/s/Thomas Griffin, Gdn

Thomas Griffin, Gdn of Margaret Griffin, in Account Current for year 1855
Page 479

By cash paid ALexr Johnson
Sworn 7-24-1856
/s/Thomas Griffin, Gdn

Thomas F. Austin, Admr of Estate of John Austin, decd, for 1856
Page 479

Paid J. Norcross, W. Powers, ALexr Johnson
Sworn 7-7-1856
/s/Thomas F. Austin, Admr

William J. Reid, Exr of Estate of John Reid, decd, in Account Current for year 1855
Page 480

By cash paid Joseph Wooton, W. R. Pendley, W. R. Bond, G. M. Philips, Ragan & Bond, John F. Cowen, Wood & Swift, Alexr Johnson

Sworn 8-20-1856
/s/William J. Reid, Exr

Josiah Greer, Admr of Estate of John Dobson, in Account Current for year 1856 up to 15th Dec 1856
Page 480

By 24 days attendance on the court in Troup Co. and getting up evidence for said case.
By cash paid Alexr Johnson
Sworn 12-15-1856
/s/Josiah Greer, Admr

Solomon K. Pace, Gdn of Louisa Sentell, minor, in Account Current for year 1855 and up to 7th Jul 1856 inclusive
Page 480

By cash paid ward.
By cash paid Alexr Johnson
Sworn 7-7-1856
/s/S. K. Pace, Gdn

S. K. Pace, Gdn of Caroline Sentell, minor, in Account Current for year 1855 and up to 7th Jul 1856 inclusive
Page 481

By cash paid John L. Abernathy, A. Johnson.
Sworn 7-7-1856
/s/S. K. Pace, Gdn

S. K. Pace, Gdn of Martha Sentell, minor, in Account Current for year 1855 and up to 7th Jul 1856 inclusive
Page 481

By cash paid ward, Alexr Johnson.
Sworn 7-7-1856
/s/S. K. Pace, Gdn

S. K. Pace, Gdn of Almeda Sentell, minor, in Account Current for year 1855 and up to 7th Jul1856
Page 481

By cash paid ward, Alexr Johnson
Sworn 7-7-1856
/s/S. K. Pace, Gdn

Premascus McDonald, Exr of Estate of John McDonald, decd, in Account Current for year 1855
Page 482

Cash paid James McDonald, C. H. McDonald, John W. McDaniel, W. C. J. McDonald, Russel Renneau, John S. Wilson, N. D. Alvvegnay, Duncan Lisley, Alexr Johnson, G. W. Summers, Harris Hutchins, A. H. Wilson, C. H.McDonald, B. F. Mayer, R. M. Brown, J. L. McGinnis,Premascus McDonald.

Sworn 8-19-1856
/s/P. McDonald, Exr

Edwin Plaster, Admr of Estate of Henry Brockman, decd, in Account Current for the year 1856
Page 482

Cash paid Rutha Brockman, Gdn of her minor children, Alexr Johnson.
/s/Edwin Plaster, Admr

Mary Parker, Extrx of Estate of John Parker in Account Current for the year 1855 and up to Nov 14, 1856 inclusive
Page 483

By cash paid H. B. Jackson, E. W. Monday, W. McDuffee, Alex Johnson.
Sworn 11-14-1856
/s/Mary Parker (x, her mark)

R. I.. Hardman, Admr of Estate of B. F. Hardman, decd, in Account Current up to date
Page 483

By cash paid Martha P. Hardman, Alexr Johnson.
Sworn 10-10-1855
/s/R. I. Hardman

R. I. Hardman, Admr of Estate of Allen Wooddall, decd, in Account Current up to 10th Oct 1856
Page 483-484

By cash paid - Thomas Akins, Alexr Johnson, Thomas J. Akins, James Reeves, James M. Holley, Syntha Hardman, Rosser W. Adams, J. G. Johnson, Joseph Walker,

Joseph T. Bellinger, J. B. Wilson, M. A. Steel, John Hardman, J. C. Steel, John McMichan, W. Kilndger, J. Steel, W. A. Powell, James Paden.

Sworn 10-15-1856

/s/ R. I. Hardman, Admr

Mrs. E. W. Bartlett, Admx of Estate of John C. Bartlett, decd, in Account Current for 1855, and up to 1st Dec 1856
Page 484

By cash paid Ruggles & Duncan, account to H. H. Dean.
Sworn 12-1-1856
/s/Elizabeth Bartlett (x, her mark)

Inventory and Account of the Lumber Account of Estate of William Johnston, decd
Page 484

Lofton Arnold, John Johnson, James Lowry, Leander Heflin, John Adam, Alpheus Adams, Harris Goodwin, John Lanier, J. B. Wilson, W. Mason, Jonathan Pennell, J. M. Ridling, George House, S. Goodwin, Thomas Johnson, Thomas Jones, John Dabbs, Philip House, R. D. Greer.

Samuel Potts, Exr and Avis Wooton, Extrx, of Joseph Wooton, decd, in Account Current for year 1856 up to January 1 1857
Page 485

By cash paid - E. J. Bailey, John W. Miller, A. J. Brady, J. Norcross, J. H. Polk, Alexr Johnson, Samuel Potts, J. H. Born, Thomas Akins, Avis Wooton, E. C. Hardman, E. A. Davis , John Bishop, J. Maddox, Agt, J. H. Ragan, C. C. Hearn, A. Atkinson, Thomas Lynch, Pendley Maddox.
Sworn 6-12-1857
/s/Samuel Potts, Exr

C. Murphy, Gdn of J. J. McKoy, in Account Current for 1854
Page 486

To cash paid W. Herring, W. A. Powell, A. M. Moore, E. Rosser, G. Adams, J. E. George, Levi Willard, Alexr Johnson, board of 2 negro children in 1856, boarding, washing for J. J. McKoy, 2 mos.

Sworn 1-22-1857
/s/C. Murphy, Gdn

Sale Bill of Two Horses Belonging to Estate of James W. Reeves, decd, Sold on 3d day of March 1857, sold on a credit until 25th Dec 1857.
Page 486

One horse named Sealam sold to Levi Wilson
One horse named Arch to Joseph Heney

/s/John Y. Flowers, Exr

Sale Bill of Portion of Property Belonging to Estate of Keziah Boyd sold on 1st Tues. in Mar 1857 in Decatur on a credit until the first day of Nov 1857
Page 486

One negro man, Jeff, sold to J. H. Smith
One land warrant 160 sold to J. H. Smith

Georgia, DeKalb Co.
The following is a true Inventory and Appraisement of all the goods and chattels, lands and tenements of John Adams, late of said county, decd, with the necessary certificate annexed to it
Page 487-489

Includes 100 1/2 acres of lot No. 237, 18th Dist., DeKalb Co.
East half of Lot No. 238 in 18th Dist.
The house Lot No. 201, 202 1/2 acres, 18th Dist.
53 acres, No. 198, 18th Dist.
Note on John H. Wilson and John W. Johnson and R. M. Wilson, etc.

Georgia, DeKalb Co.
We do certify upon oath that as was presented to us by James S. Elliott, the Admr , the above and foregoing contains a true appraisement of the Estate of John Adams, decd, to the best of our judgement and understanding this 15th Nov. 1856. /s/John M. Ridling, W. P. Johnston, JamesGuess, John L. Evins, appraisers.

Sale of Personal Property of Estate of John Adams, decd, sold at public outcry on 29th day of Nov 1856, on a credit until 29th May 1857

Purchasers: Aditha Adams, Enos Adams, Alpheus Adams, Sansers Adams, James S. Jett, John L.Evins, W. W. Carter, John Adams, M. V. Elliott, James F. Trimble, Justus E. Goodwin, W. H. Cash, Thomas Howell, John Dabbs, Asa Braswell, Oliver B. Campbell, Selathiel Adams, RobertCash,W. House, William G. Pool, J. L. Evins.

Real estate rented on 7th Jan 1857, Lot No. 201, 18th Dist. - to Edith Adams
Lot No. 231, 18th Dist. to Asa Morgan
Lot No. 238 to John Adams
Lot No. 198, north part, to Edith Adams and Alpheus Adams

Joseph F. Clay, Gdn of Sarah, Franklin and Hiram Williams, minors of J. L. Williams, decd, in Account Current for the year 1856.
Page 490

To cash received of P. F. Hoyle, Admr of J. L. Williams
By cash paid Mrs. R. S. Williams, Alexr Johnson, W. A. Powell
Sworn 1-8-1857
/s/Joseph F. Clay, Gdn

W. E. Sprewell, Admr of Estate of Sarah Waits, decd, in Account Current for year 1856
Page 490

By cash paid Alexr Johnson
Sworn 1-6-1857
/s/W. E. Sprewell, Admr

Wilson E. Sprewell, Admr of Estate of Sarah Waits, decd , in Account Current for 1855
Page 490

Cash paid Alexr Johnson.

Sworn 1-5-1857
/s/W. E. Sprewell, Admr

John McElroy, Exr of Estate of A. E. Ellis, decd, in Account Current for the year 1856
Page 490

Cash paid Alexr Johnson, Alexr Chesnut, John McElroy, Ichabod Williams, John Y. Flowers, Nancy McElroy.

Joseph T. Bellenger, Exr of Estate of John N. Bellenger in Account Current for year 1856 up to 15th Oct 1856
Page 491

Cash paid C. Murphy, Henry Irby, Solomon Goodwin, J. B. Anderson, T. C., Alexr Johnson

To cash receivd of T. G. Lankford, R. I. Hardman, H. Irby.
Sworn 10-15-1856
/s/Joseph T. Bellinger, Exr

Inventory and Appraisement of Estate of Joseph E. Bishop, decd, of DeKalb Co.
Page 491

299 acres of land near Lithonia, 135 acres in DeKalb Co., No. 67, one lot in Atlanta, No. 16 Notes of J. M. Robinson, Horton Hombrecke, H. P. Bankston, Augustus H. Wallas, John Sporks, Joel C. Higam, Theophilus Simonton, payable to E. S. Braswell, W. F. Ivy, Joel Hisan, James W.Bishop, Zachariah H. Godard, A. H. Aikers, J. G. Brown, W. H. Bradwell, John Walkins, D. A.Sewn, J. M. Hutchins, Seph Morgan and W. H. Rials, A. A. Arnold, J. W. Mitchell, A. J.Whiteford, Jackson Harris.

Sworn 3-9-1857
/s/ William New, Jacob Chupp, Needham Whitley, James Johnson, Appraisers

Return No. for 1856. James S. Elliott, Gdn of Alexr Joice, a minor and Ediot, in Account Current
Page 492

To cash paid Alexr Johnson, Ordinary,.
Sworn 3-3-1857
/s/James S. Elliott, Gdn

Return No. 3 for 1856
James S. Elliott, Gdn for Sarah Joice, a minor, in Account Current for 1856
Page 493

By cash paid Alexr Johnson, William Hadden, Ryan and Myers for equipage to school, J. R. Humphries.
Cash received of Jules Hume, G. Grogan, Joseph Stewart, B. Rainey
Sworn 3-3-1857
/s/James S. Elliott, Gdn

Return No. 1 for 1856
James S. Elliott, Admr of Estate of John Adams, decd, in Account Current for 1856
Page 493

To cash paid Alexr Johnson, G. A. Braswell, J. L. Evins, Admr of J. F. Johnston
To cash received of L. Willan, C. T.
Sworn 3-3-1857
/s/James S. Elliott, Admr

Georgia, DeKalb Co., The following is a true Inventory and Appraisement o Estate, both real and personal , of Charles Raney, late of said county, decd, with necessary certificate annexted to it
Page 494-495

Lot of Land No. 297, 18th Dist., DeKalb Co.

Lot of Land No. 280, 18th Dist., DeKalb Co.
Negroes: Henry, Austin (boys), Esther (girl), Sealy, Jane (12 mos. old).

Sworn by James S. Elliott 4-6-1857

On A Credit until 25 Dec 1857, Sale Bill of Property of Nimrod Argo, decd, sold on 9th day of April 1857

Page 495-496

Purchasers: Jackson Argofor Edward Argo, Lewis Davis, David Argo, Nico Kelly, G. M. Phillips, David Argo, Samuel Davis, Edmund Argo, Brack Drake, Ira Camp, J. H. Born, J. B. Keys, Matilda King, G. M. Philips, W. J. Langston, D. Maulding, Drewry Maulding, W. P. Bond.

Sale Bill of Personal Property of Estate of Joseph E. Bishop, decd, sold on 7th day of April 1857.
Page 496

Buggy sold to Joshua J. Bishop, and horse
/s/James H. Born
/s/W. H. Braswell, Admrs

Inventory and Appraisement of Personal Property i possession of Morning Huey, a person insane mind in which she has a life estate, she being the widow of Henry Huey, decd
Page 497

Idiotic negro woman named Marian.
Negro woman, Hannah, and her child, Ellen
Man, Sampson
Girls, Lucinda and Phillis
Boy, Harrison
Girls, Manerva and Patsey.

Appraisers: C. W. McGinnis, R. M. Brown, W. R. Brandon, R. Hollingsworth, appraisers
Sworn 4-2-1857

James F. Trimble, Gdn of W. J. O. Reese, in Account Current for year 1856 and up to 7th April 1857
Page 498

To cash paid W. J. C. Reeve, Alexr Johnson
Sworn 4-7-1857
/s/J. F. Trimble, Gdn

Martha Todd, Extx of Estate of Richard Todd, decd, in Account Current for year 1856
Page 498

Cash paid Ezzard & Cllier, 1856 tax, Alexr Johnson
Sworn 4-21-1857
/s/Martha Todd

Isaac Haistings, Admr of Estate of William Lakey, decd, in Account Current for year 1856 and up to May 4, 1857 inclusive
Page 498

Recd for sale of land No.. 351, 7th Dist., Clay Co., sold 1st Tues in Feb 857 sold to

Azariah Doss.

By cash paid A. Johnson, A. P. Barr.
Sworn 5-4-1857
/s/Isaac A. Haistings, Admr

John C. Harris, Gdn of W. N. Leitch in Account Current for year 1856
Page 498
Cash paid Sarah Ann Leitch, Alexr Johnson, 1856 tax.
Sworn 5-4-1857
/s/John C. Harris, Gdn

John C. Harris, Gdn of S. T. Leitch in Account Current for year 1856
Page 499

By cash paid S. A. Leitch, Alexr Johnson, 1856 tax
Sworn 5-4-1857
/s/John C. Harris

John C. Harris, Gdn of A. B. Leitch in Account Current for year 1856
Page 499

Cash paid Sarah A. Leitch, Alexr Johnson, 1856 tax
Sworn 5-18-1856
/s/John C. Harris

Azariah Mims, Exr of Estate of James Russell, decd, in Account Current for year 1856
Page 499

Cash paid Susanah Russell, 1856 tax, Alexr Johnson
Sworn 5-5-1857
/s/Az. Mims, Exr

George W. Key, Gdn of W. B. Key, in Account Current for year 1856 and up to 5th May 1857inclusive
Page 499

Includes principal and interest
Sworn 4-20-1857
/s/George W. Key, Gdn

James H. Young, Trustee for Margaret K. White, appointed by the LWT of Lucy Primrose,
decd, in Account Current for year 1856 and up to 1st May 1857

Page 500

One negro man, Stephen, about 50 years of age, from the Exrs of said LWT of Lucy Primrose
To one girl, Nicy, about 12 years old
To one boy, Charles, 7 years old
Said negroes in the service of Margaret K. White for the year 1857
/s/James H. Young, Trustee

John Bryce, Gdn of W. McKoy, in Account Current for 1856
Page 500

To paid - E. Rosser, W. A. Powell, 1856 tax, Levi Willard, G. Adams, A. M. Moore, A. Johnson, P. F. Hoyle J. E. George, C. Murphy, John Bruce, James M. Blackstock

To hire of negroes for 1856.
Charles a man
Andrew, a man
Ritta, a woman
Polly and child

Sworn 6-1-1857
/s/John Bryce, Gdn of W. McKoy

J. E. Wells, Gdn of James E., William A., Samuel P. and Eliza W. Wells, in Account Current for the year 1856
Page 501

Rent of house in City of Atlanta for 1856
Sworn 7-6-1857
/s/J. D. Wells, Gdn

Sale Bill of Negroes belonging to Orphelia Stowers sold by Thomas Farr, Trustee, sold on 2d
Day of Jan 1857
Page 501

Catharine, a girl, age 14 to John Tomlinson

Jasper, a boy about 11 yrs old to Henry Irby
Jasper, a boy about 11 years old to Henry Irby

/s/Thomas Fair, Trustee

Inventory and Appraisement of Estate of Nimrod Argo, decd
Page 501-502

House and lot in Lithonia, etc.

List of Fifas, Notes and Accounts belonging to Estate of Merrell Humphries decd sold by P.
F.Hoyle, Admr
Page 503

Fifas of W. C. Dorsey, T. C. Reynolds, John Simpson, Richard Gay, W. C. Grisham, etc.
Accounts of Daniel Adams, James Brown, W. L. Brown, Radford Crockett, James . Cash,
Crawford Evins,. Joseph A. Foster, etc.

List of Fifas and Accounts belonging to Estate of Jesse L. Williams, decd, considered insolvent
and sold by P. F. Hoyle, Admr
Page 504-505

Fifas on James Cash, Thomas C. Hill, Robert Jolly, Thomas Reynolds, T. J. Stephens, etc.
(includes a number of accounts, fifas.)
/s/P. F. Hoyle, Admr

Annual Return No. 5. Joseph Thompson, Admr in Account with Estate of Moses W. Trimble
Page 505-506

Received on J. Thompson note, N. L. Angier land sale note, S. B. Hout, A. C. Jones, A. Luckies
a/c, J. McDonald's land sale note in part, N. L. Angier, G. C. Rogers, J. I. Glenn, etc.
Georgia, Fulton Co.
Sworn 7-3-1857
/s/Joseph Thompson, Admr

Estate of Hardy Ivy, decd, in Account with William Ezzard, Admr, for 1856
Page 507

To cash paid - Sarah Ivy, John T. Terry, legatee.
Sworn 7-6-1857
/s/William Ezzard, Admr

Samuel A. F. Mann, minor, in Account with W. Ezzard, Gdn, for year 1856
Page 507

Cash paid W. A. Powell, James M. Blackstock, Mrs. Nesbit, J. J. Richards, S. E. Scudder, J. J. Richards & co., W. Herring, paid him cash to go to New York.
Sworn 7-6-1857
/s/William Ezzard, Gdn

Estate of Merrell Collier, decd, in Account Current with William Ezzard, Exr, for 1856
Page 507-508

By cash received rent of store house to Beach
Cash received rent of office to Harris & Ivy
Cash paid Jeremiah Wells.
Sworn 7-6-1857
/s/William Ezzard, Exr

William A. Green, minor, in Account with William Ezzard, Gdn for 1856
Page 507

Cash paid Alexr Johnson, ordinary.
Sworn 7-6-1857
/s/William Ezzard, Gdn

Estate of Alston H. Green, decd, in Account with William Ezzard Admr, for the year 1856
Page 507

Cash paid S. Rose for advertising, F. M. Eddleman & Co., M. R. Morgan A. J. Morgan and M. & R. Morgan; C. C. Green as a legatee.
Sworn 7-6-1856
/s/William Ezzard, Admr

Miss Cordelia E. Green, minor in Account with W. Ezzard, Gdn, for year 1856
Page 507-510

To hire of negro man, Richmond, for 1856

Hire of Miles and Julia Ann with her childen hired to C. C. Green for 1856
Hire of Emeline hired to T. R. Sewell for 1856
Hire of woman, Eliza and two children hired to R. Gardner for 1856

Paid Pres. Fulton for tuition, W. D. Luckie, M. Brewers, Mrs. Borings, T. Burks, T. F. Saltsman, Sarah Wilkerson, C. D. Page, A. W. Hall, Dr. H. T. Henry, Laura Chewning, H. B. Walon, W. P.Lanier, William Ezzard for board.

Sworn 7-6-1857
/s/William Ezzard, Gdn

Nathan Turner 1857 , Admr of Estate of D. S. Boring in Account Current for year 1856 and up to 1 Jul
Page 510

Cash paid James M. Boring, Robert Hollingsworth, W. F. Connally, E. Rosser, T. M. Darnall, Joel M. Fowler, A. Doonan, A. M. Eddleman, George M. Philips, G. B. Haygood, T. L. Cooper, J. W. Crocket, John Goins,, A. M. Orr, Z. R. Jones, B. Ragsdale, W. L. Williams, Nathan Turner.
Sworn 7-1-1857
/s/Nathan Turner, Admr

List of property belonging to Estate of A. H. Green and A. C. Saffold sold at Hawkinsville on 1st Tues in Feb 1856
Page 511

All sold to Bryan W. Brown as follows: No. 240, 241, 242, 243, 12th Dist., originally Houston, now Pulaski Co. Lands belonging to the sam sold at Thomasville, Thomas Co. on 1st Tues in
May 1856 as follows:

No. 46, 18th Early, now Thomas Co.; 160, 243.
/s/William Ezzard, Admr

Gideon Morris, Admr of Estate of Israel Miller, decd, in Account Current for 1856
Page 5111

To cash paid G. Crosby, Alexr Johnson, Andrew P. Miller, N. R. Miller, Margaret Miller, Jasper H. Miller, Z. Eidson, Joel E. Morris, Charles Gardner, Margaret Miller, J. W. Morris.

Sworn 7-6-1857
/s/G. Morris, Admr

State of Georgia, DeKalb Co., John Y. Flowers, in Account Current with Estate of James W. Reeve, late of said county, decd, returned, Jan 1857.
Return No. 5
Page 512

Cash received from A. Gardner on note, H. M. Greer on note, L. Wright fifa., J. L. Evins, Admr of J. F. Johnston
Paid - Alexr Johnson, W. J. C. Reeve, S. P. Wright, A. W. Reeve, A. J. C. Reeve, S. R.
Reeve, W. P. Donalson, Selathiel Adams, James F. Trimble, W. Ezzard, Atty H. Hamby, John Y. Flowers

Sworn 6-29-1857
/s/John Y. Flowers, Exr

State of Georgia, DeKalb Co., Estate of Joel Fowler to J. H. and A. M. Fowler, Exrs
Page 512

Cash paid ordinary, John M. Boring, Gdn, Lorena Boring, Sarah Fowler, Joel M. Fowler, Mary M. Boring, W. Ezzard, prof. services.

Sworn 6-18-1857
/s/H. J. Flowler, Exr

Inventory and Appraisement of Estate of J. J. Wyley
Page 513-514

Note of W. Knight, Wiley & Thrasher, Thomas Reynolds, etc.
Sworn 6-26-1857
J. B. Wilson, J. P.

Georgia, DeKalb Co., By vitue of a comission to us directed by the court of ordinary....to assign and set apart 12 mos. support to the widow and child of John J. Wiley, decd,....one hundred dollars.
/s/J. B. Wilson, T. B. George, W. L. Wood. Sworn 9-7-1857

P. F. Hoyle, Admr of Estate of Morrell Humphries, decd, in Account Current for 1856
Page 514-515

Cash paid - N. H. Humphries, S. G. Winn, J. B. Wilson, P. M. Sittern, John W. Scruggs, B. F. Hoyle, S. B. Hoyt,, John G. Rainey, E. McAlister, J. B. Anderson, Allen Woodall,

L. S. Morgan, A. Jackson, J. B. Anderson, S. P. Reay, A. C. Tuggle, T. R. Hoyle, Levi Willard, P. F. Hoyle, Admr, Robert Webb, D. S. Floyd, W. H. Ryles, J. F. Akins, W. J. Thrasher, W. A. Powell, J. S.Elliott, H. M. Greer.

Sworn 7-6-1857
/s/P. F. Hoyle, Admr

P. F. Hoyle, Admr of Estate of J. L. Williams, decd, in Account Current for year 1856
Page 515-516

Cash paid - D. Stone P. F. Hoyle, Admr, L. S. Morgan, James Case, W. H. Campbell, D. S. Floyd, E. A. Davis, J. B. Anderson, John Hawkins, W. Burrett, W. H. Cash, John Dabb, J. B. Anderson, J. B. Wilson, Levi Willard, Allen Wooddall, James S. Elliott, John T. Wilson, S. B. Hoyt, S. B.Ray, J. W. Scruggs.

Sworn 7-6-1857
/s/P. F. Hoyle Admr

Sale Bill of Real Estate Belonging to Estate of Joseph E. Bishop, decd, sold on 1st Tues in Oct 1857
Page 516

One lot of land, No. 119, 16th Dist.,DeKalb Co. sold to E. J. Bailey
Sold part of Lot No. 67 containing 135 acres, 15th Dist. to Elijah Bishop.

/s/James H. Born, Admr

Thompson A. Browning in Account Current with Estate of J. Fox from 1st Jul 1856 to 1st of Jul 1857
Page 516

Cash paid J. M. Orr, John P. Hutchins, Alford Montgomery, John Mills, J. N. Glen, A. Ford, A.Johnson.

Sworn 7-6-1857
/s/T. A. Browning, Admr

Thomas Moore, Admr of Estate of James Moore, decd, in Account Current for 1856 up to 30th Jun 1857
Page 517-518

Cash received of R. Crawford, James Burnes, George Key, Mr. McCord, George Young, W.
R.Owen on note, E. Watts on note, James Moore, Jr., W. R. Owen.

Cash paid - John A. Casey, John Burns, Alexr Johnson, James Burnes, W. R. Venable, Ann Moore, John Burnes, W. S. Brown, Ann Moore, R. M.Williams, W. B. Ruggles, George Key.

Sworn 6-30-1857
/s/Thomas Moore, Admr

H. H. Embry, Admr de bonis non on Estate of Jesse Childress, decd, in Account Current for 1856 up to 25th Apr 1857
Page 518

Cash paid H. H. Embry, Alexr Johnson
Sworn 4-28-1857
/s/H. H. Embry Admr

Sale Bill of Real Estate Belonging to Estate of D. S. M. Boring, decd, sold on st Tues in Jan 1857
Page 518

To Mary M. Boring for negroes, Mary and Bain, hiring for 1857 Ezekiel, negro.
/s/Nathan Turner, Admr

James J. Diamond, Admr of Estate of William H. Grayham, decd, in Account Current for 1856
Page 518

Cash paid D. B. Juhan, W. W. Diamond, L. C. Simpson.
Sworn 7-1-1857
/s/James J. Diamond, Admr

E. Howard, Admr of Estate of Edward Howard, decd, in Account Current for 1856
Page 519

Cash paid E. Z. Kill, James M. Calhoun, E. Howard, Alex Johnson
Sworn 4-28-1857
/s/Edmond Howard, Admr

1856. A. G. Hulsey, Gdn for S. A. Hulsey
Page 519

Cash paid John H. Lovejoy, Berry Ragsdale (tuition), J. W. Doane, W. L. Williams.
Sworn 5-28-1857
/s/ A. G. Hulsey Gdn

1856 A. G. Hulsey, Gdn for J. J. Hulsey
Page 519

By cash paid H. H. Peek, Daniel Scott, John Bass.
Sworn 5-28-1857
/s/ A. G. Hulsey, Gdn

A. G. Hulsey, Gdn for S. E. Hulsey
Page 519

Amount paid - W. L. Williams (board), J. A. Doane, Berry Ragsdale, John H. Lovejoy, Adair and Job Ezzard.
Sworn 5-28-1857
/s/ A. G. Hulsey, Gdn

S. P. Wright, Gdn of J. M. Joice for the year 1856 and up to April 1857 inclusive
Page 520

To hire of boy, Harrison for 1856, and girl, Darcus, for 1856
By cash paid ward for tuition, S. P. Wright for board, W. A. Powell, William Hadden.

Sworn 4-10-1857
/s/S. P. Wright, Gdn

S. P. Wright, Gdn of Parasade Rayney in Account Current for the year 1856
Page 520

To hire of boy, Beverly, for 1856 and girl, Eliza, for 1856
By cash paid Sarah Raner, William Hadden, W. A. Powell, Alexr Johnson.

Sworn 4-10-1857
/s/S. P. Wright, Gdn

S. P. Wright, Gdn of James M. Reeves in Account Current for the year 1856 and up to 1st of April 1857
Page 520-521

By cash paid James M. Reeve, my ward, 1856 tax, James M. Reeve, Alexr Johnson.

Sworn 4-10-1857
/s/S. P. Wright, Gdn

Sale Bill of a portion of the personal property belonging to Estate of James W. Reeve, decd, sold on 18th April 1857 on a credit until 25th Dec 1857
Page 521

Cows sold to James O. Elliott, J. M. Reeve, W. H. C. Evins and J. M. Reeve.

/s/John T. Flowers, Exr.

Sale Bill of Real Estate belonging to the Estate of James Moore Sold on 6th day of Jan 1857
Page 521

The home place consisting of five lots the place on which deceased lived sold to William
T.Cobb....

75 acres known as the Defer Place sold to A. L. Pitts
Lot DeKalb Co. Sold to James Brown
One negro woman, Fanney, sold for cash to William T. Cobb
One negro woman, Mary, to W. T. Cobb.

John C. Austin, Admr of Estate of Thomas Austin, decd, in Account CUrrent for the year 1856
Page 522

To money borrowed of Avis Wooten 1856.
Cash paid E. Rosser, Alex Johnson, J. F. Henry, J. F. Austin, R. W. Cobb, E. Rosser, J. E. Bromlow, D. E. Jackson, T. M. Darnell, G. B. Haygood, J. T. Cobb, John C. Austin

Sworn 7-4-1857
/s/John C. Austin, Admr

James B. Gunder, Gdn of Marshal E. Gunter, his own minor child, in Account Current for year 1856 and up to 18 Aug 1857
Page 522

To cash recd of R. E. itchcock and Bennett Sims, Admrs of Estate of Wiley and Mary Sims, late decd, reced on 28th Apr 1857.

Sworn 8-18-1857
/s/James B. Gunter, Gdn

Jesse Childress, Gdn of James S. Childress, in Account CUrrent for year 1855 and up to 5th March 1856.
Page 522-523

By cash paid 1855 tax, Alex Johnson

Sworn 5-28-1856
/s/Jesse Childress, Gdn

Jesse Childress, Gdn of John A. D. Childress, in Account Current for year 1855, and up to 5th
Mar 1856 inclusive
Page 523

To cash recd of John Y. Flowers, exr, recd on 25th Jan 1856
By cash paid tax for 1855, and Alexr Johnson

Sworn 5-28-1856
/s/Jesse Childress, Gdn

Return No. 4, Jesse Childress, Gdn of James S. Childress, in Account Current for year 1856 and
up to 5th Mar 1857
Page 523

By cash paid tax for 1856, and Alexr Johnson

Sworn 6-29-1857
/s/Jesse Childress, Gdn

Jesse Childress, Gdn of John A. D. Childress in Account Current for year 1856 and up to the 5th
March 1857
Page 523-524

To cash recd of John Y. Flowers, Exr of Estate of James Y. Reeves, decd, recd 20 May 1856. By cash paid tax for 1856, and Alexr Johnson

Sworn 6-29-1857
/s/Jesse Childress, Gdn

James M. Collier, Gdn of Mary E. Collier, Georgia Ann and Sarah A. Collier, his own minor children, in Account Current up to 10 Nov 1857
Page 524

To 6 shares of Georgia Railroad stock recd of J. D. Martin and James Hargroves, Admrs of the Estate of Gabriel Martin Jan 1, 1857, $200

10-1-1857 recd of Georgia Railroad, interest on stock (and 4-25-1857)
By cash paid Thomas C. Evans expenses, Alexr Johnson

Sworn 11-10-1857
/s/James M. Collier, Gdn

Sarah Ann Leitch, Admx of Estate of Arthur Leitch, decd, in Account Current for year 1856
Page 524

By cash paid Alexr Johnson, Ordinary.
Sworn 6-27-1857
/s/Sarah Ann Leitch, Admx

Thomas Faar, Trustee for Orphia Stowers, in Account Current for year 1856
Page 524

By cash paid W. Kay, Jordan Wilson, Gartrell & Glen, James Rainey, John W. Tomlinson, C. M. Payne, Silas Donaldson, Solomon Goodwin, Jordan Wilson, John Thomason, Alexr Johnson.

D. J. Mitchell, Exr of Estate of William Mitchell, decd, in Account Current for year 1856
Page 524

By cash paid G. K. and J. L. Hamilton, 1856 tax.
To hire of Jemima for 1856

Sworn 3-3-1857
/s/D. J. Mitchell, Exr

Georgia, DeKalb Co., E. C. Harris, Return as Administrator of the Estate of J. F. Montgomery, decd, made Jul 6 1857
Page 524

By amount paid A. Cook, Cary Cox, J. R. Mayson for tuition, John Campbell for books, Ga tax, expenses to Decatur, A. Johnson

Sworn 7-7-1857
/s/Ezekiel C. Harris, Admr

John Carroll and Henry W. Blake, Exrs of Estate of John Blake, decd, in Account Current for year 1856
Page 524-525

By cash paid W. P. Palinex, S. W. Grisham, G. Morris, R. M. Brown, H. W. Blake, John Carroll, Alexr Johnson

To cash recd of David Wade, W. Grogan, W. Austin, James Trimble, Silas Grisham.

Sale Bill of a portion of Real Estate Belonging to the Estate of James Moore, decd, Sold on 4th day of August 1857, 1/2 payable 1st Dec 1857, the balance due 1st Dec 1858, 4 City lots lying in City of Atlanta sold to John Moore for $1020.
Page 526

/s/Thomas Moore, Admr

John C. Cannon, Gdn of Allison, George, Sarah Ann and Bryant Cash, minors of G. W. Cash, decd, in Account Current for year 1856
Page 526

By cash paid Alexr Johnson
Sworn 1-1-1857
/s/J. C. Cannon, Gdn

Salina Ellington, Gdn of David B. Ellington in Account Current for year 1856
Page 526

To hire of Jacob for 1856, also Burrell, Wash and Ben.
By cash paid William Ray & Co., Miller & Andrews, F. Blekley,, West Harris, A. C. Johnson, J. N. Beach, W. B. Johnston, J. Norcross, R. M. Wilson, Thomas Kile, John A. Casey, F. M. Eddleman, Alexr Johnson.

Sworn 6-4-1857
/s/Salina Ellington

O. S. Morris, Admr of Estate of James Russell, decd, in Account Current for 1856
Page 527

By cash paid B. F. Chapman, 1856 tax, Turner H. Warren, James A. Richey, Oliver Richey, George Dusenbury, W. A. Richey, ALexr Johnson, Ordinary.

Sworn 3-25-1857
/s/Obediah S. Morris

P. F. Hoyle, Admr of Estate of J. L. Williams, decd, in Account Current for year 1857 and up to 7 Dec 1857 inclusive
Page 527

To cash recd, collected of Andrew Jackson on notes.
Sworn 12-7-1857
/s/P. F. Hoyle, Admr

George Key, Gdn of W. B. Key, in Account Current for year 1857
Page 527

By cash paid ward as per voucher no. 1
/s/George Key, Gdn

John Byce, Gdn of G. C. Butler, decd, in Account Current for 1856 up to 18 Apr 1857
Page 528

By cash paid 1856 tax, C. Murphy, Ezzard & Collier.
Sworn 4-18-1857
/s/John Byce, Gdn

David Chesnut, Admr of Estate of James Baxter, decd, in Account
Current in year 1856 and up to
6 Jul 1857
Page 528

To cash paid Alexr Johnson, Rufus Hendeson, Richard Pennell, Martha
Inge, P. F. Hoyle, W. J. Palmer, E. Rosser, W. A. Powell, 1855 and 1856
tax, Louisa Baxter, Gdn, Alexr Johnson.

Sworn 7-6-1857
/s/David Chesnut, Admr

Inventory and Appraisement of Estate of William N. Pool, decd
Page 529

One tract of land, and misc items.

Appraiers: F. W. Lilley, M. O. Lively, P. M. Lord, 10-29-1857

Mary A. Reed, Extrx of John Reed, decd, in Account Current for year
1856
Page 529

By cash paid 1856 tax, William McClendon, J. H. Born, N. M. Reed, W>
B. Chapman, H. F. Pitts, Samuel Potts, G. M. Philips, James N. Coe,.

D. D. Anderson, R. C. Anderson and Alexr Vaughn, Admrs of Estate of
W. B. Anderson, decd, in Account Current for 1855 and 1856 inclusive
Page 530

By cash paid J. T. Bellinger, Exr, 1855-6 tax, R. M. Brown, Clerk, John
Ferrell.
Sworn 10-28-1857
/s/R. C. Anderson, D. D. Anderson and Alexr Vaughn (his mark), Exrs.

R. M. Brown, Admr of Estate of Ann Ogleby, decd, in Account Current
for year 1856
Page 530

By cash paid W. E. Ogleby, Alexr Johnson
Sworn 7-6-1857
/s/R. M. Brown, Admr

E. Warbington, Admr of Estate of Leonard Winters, decd, in Account Current for year 1856
Page 530

By cash paid E. Warbington, A. Johnson.
Sworn 7-6-1857
/s/E. Warbington, Admr

C. W. Stell, Exr of Estate of B. Stell, decd, in Account Current for year 1856 and up to 6 Jul 1857
Page 530

By cash paid ALexr Johnson, J. H. Gaar, J. M. Hudson.

Sale Bill, Oct. 24, 1857 of the Property of J. J. P. White, decd, Sold on Credit of one year
Page 531

Purchasers: L. Hudgins, A. L. Pitts, S. C. White, widow, John White, E. McCLain, William Wright, W. C. White, John White, Sr., John Armstrong, Samuel McWilliams, Leroy Hudgins, James Green, J. W. White.

Sale of Real Estate Belonging to Estate of J. J. P. White, decd, sold on first Tues in Jan 1858
Page 532

The grist mill 1/2 lot in 15th Dist. No. 107, sold W. C. White for $1010
Saw mill, lot No. 118, 184 acres, sold to J. W. White for $1528
Lot No. 117 sold to W. N. Ragan

/s/Stephen T. Biggers, Exr

Samuel Potts, Exr of Estate of Joseph Wooten, decd, in Account Current for year 1857
Page 532

By cash paid J. R. and C. H. Walliace, C. D. Parr, L. A. J. Miller, J. M. Philip, J. H. Born, C. Murphey, James Richerson, James A. Roberts, John W. Braswell, Thomas J. Lyon, Thomas L. Robinson, C. D. Parr, S. Potts, J. Norcross, J. H. Park, Alexr Johnson, Avis Wooton.

R. McWilliams, Admr of Estate of William Hildabran, decd, in Account Current for year 1856 and up to 31st Aug 1857 inclusive
Page 533

Cash paid Van Burin L. Hildabran, Malinda C. E. Hildabran, Alexr Johnson.
Sworn 9-1-1857
/s/R. M. Williams, Admr

Washington P. Johnston, Exr of Estate of William Johnston, decd, in Account Current for year 1856 and up to 1st Dec 1857
Page 533

To cash recd of R. D. Grier, Samuel House, Salina Ellington, Harris GOodwin, R. Clark, S. Goodwin, James S. Elliott.
By cash paid P. F. Hoyle, Alexr Johnson
Sworn 12-1-1857
/s/W. P. Johnston, Exr

Georgia, DeKalb Co., Inventory and Appraisement of Estate of James L. B. White, decd
Page 533-534

S. 1/2 of Lot No. 107, 15th Dist., DeKalb.
N. 1/2 of Lot No. 118 with Saw Mill
Lot No. 117 in 14th Dist. DeKalb
Homestead willed to widow
etc.

Rufus Henderson, Gdn of Samuel Williams, in Account CUrrent for 1856
Page 535

By cash paid W. A. Powell, E. Rosser, E. Adams, R. H. Henderson, Alexr Johnson
Sworn 2-3-1857
/s/Rufus Henderson, Gdn

Rufus Henderson, Gdn of S. B. Williams in Account Current for year 1857
Page 535

To cash paid 1857 tax, ALexr Johnson.
Sworn 2-3-1858
/s/Rufus Henderson

State of Georgia, DeKalb Co., We do certify upon oath that as far as was produced bo us by Stephen T. Biggers, Exr, the above and forregoing contains a true appraisement of goods, chattels an credits of Estate of James J. P. White, decd, ...this 28th Sept 1857.
/s/William White, J. G. McWilliams, Y. R. Jones, John H. Jones, Appraisers.
Property assigned to the widow of J. J. P. White, decd -

Sam, a negro boy
homestead and land
mules, etc.

John Bryce, Gdn of W. McKoy, in Account Current for year 1857
Page 536

To hire of Charles for 1857, also, Andrew, Ritta and Moss.
Recd of C. Murphey one note on Smith & Bartlett. 11-25-1857

By cash paid J. R. McAlister, W. A. Powell, B. F. Chamberlain, G. Adams, Alexr Johnson, N. S. Liddell, E. Rosser, Levi Willard, 1857 tax, John Bryce.

Sworn 1-29-1858
/s/John Bryce, Gdn

Georgia, DeKalb Co., Dec. 3, 1857, To: S. House, F. Tilley, Jabez Lord, S. B. Wright and John Z. Flowers, ...you have been appointed by Court of Ordnary for the purpose of setting apart either in money or property 1w months support for widow and children of William Z. Poole, decd...../s/Alex Johnson, Ordinary

Georgia, DeKalb Co. In obedience to the within commission, we have set apart for the support for the next 12 months for the widow and orphans of W. Y. Poole, decd, the following property and money, two feather beds, etc. /s/J. Y. FLowers, S. House, J. M. Lord, J. W. F. Tilley, S. P. Wright.

Asberry W. Reeve, Gdn of minor heirs of Polly M. Wilson, in Account Current for the year 1857
Page 537

To cash recd of John Y. Flowers, Exr of Estate of James W. Reeve, decd, recd 26 Dec 1857 -
$100.00.
Sworn 28 Dec 1857
/s/Asberry W. Reeve, Gdn

Thomas F. Austin, Admr of John Austin, decd, in Account Current with the Estate of John Austin, decd, for year 1856 up to Jul 1857
Page 537

Paid J. S. Smith, Sheriff, Elizabeth Austin, D. C. Venable, 1856 tax, A. Johnson.
Sworn 7-6-1857
/s/John F. Austin, Admr

Elkenneth Powell, Gdn of Howell C. Oliver in Account Current for year 1856 and up to 2 Jun 1857
Page 538

To cash recd for land warrant, cash recd of J. G. Fulton for rent
Cash paid A. Johnson, G. K. Smith
Sworn 6-2-1857
/s/Elkiniah Powell

S. K. Pace, Gdn of Martha Sentell, in Account Current for 1856
Page 538

By cash paid Martin Ball.
Sworn 6-26-1857
/s/S. K. Pace, Gdn

S. K. Pace, Gdn of Almeda Sentell, in Account Current for 1856
Page 538

Cash paid to ward.
Sworn 6-26-1857
/s/S. K. Pace, Gdn

Sale Bill of Real Estate Belonging to Estate of William Y. Poole, decd, sold on 1st Tues in March 1858.
Page 538

70 acres off of Lot No. 204 in 18th Dist. DeKalb Co. sold to Robert D. Grier
100 acres off of Lot No. 235 the South 1/2 of said lot being in 18th DIst. of DeKalb Co. sold to J.
W. F. Tilley

Dec. 3, 1857. The following is a true statement of the Sale of the personal property belonging to the Estate of William Y. Poole, late of DeKalb CO., decd, sold on a credit until 1st March next...
Page 539-540

Purchasers - A. J. H. Pool, R. D. Grier, H. Goodwin, W. Johnston, Thomas Thompson, Josiah Grisham, R. S. Grier, W. R. Rowell, C. M. Jones, A. H. Pere, C. M. Jones, S. Haws, Az. H. Pool, J. M. Ridlin, J. M. Reeve, Sarah Harmon, A. J. H. Pool, Robert Baxter, J. L. Pool, M. A. Candler, Joseph Stewart, J. Chamblee, John Paden, Enos Adams, Thomas Mattocks, J. Y. FLowers, John CHamblee, Allen Thompson, J. L. Pool.

Louisa Baxter, Gdn of John R., Mary J. and Amanda Baxter, minors of James Baxter, decd, in Account Current for year 1856
Page 540

/s/Louisa Baxter, Gdn

Sale Bill of Real Estate Belonging to Estate of Fannin Brown, decd, sold on 1st Tues in Feb 1856
Page 541

Part of Lot No. 148 in 15th Dist., DeKalb CO. sold to James Brown for $350.00

/s/Rhoda Brown, Admx (x, her mark)

Sale Bill of Real Estate Belonging to Estate of Merrell Humphries, late decd, one house and Lot in Town of Decatur sold on 2d day of Nov 1855, sold to J. W. Plunkett.
Page 541

/s/P. F. Hoyle, Admr

Sale Bill of a portion of Real Estate belonging to Estate of Joseph E. Bishop, late decd, sold....25 Dec 1858, one house and lot in City of Atlanta sold to James McDonald for $171, sold 1st Tues.
in Jan 1858
Page 541

/s/James H. Born and W. H. Braswell, Admrs

Georgia, DeKalb Co. Certification of valuation of articles
Page 541

horse, cattle, etc.

State of Georgia, DeKalb Co. Inventory and Appraisement of Estate of John Bond, decd
Page 542

Negro woman, Vina (and child), Lucy, a girl.
15 acres of land, of Lot No. 30, etc.
Appraisers: /s/Andrew Boyd, Martin McKoy, W. J. Clark

James S. Elliott in Account Current with Sarah Joice, a minor for year 1857
Page 543

By cash paid 1857 taxes, Alexr Johnson, W. A. Powell, Miles Mosely, O. G. Kile, W. A. Rogers,
W. A. Rodgers, H. W. Cobb, Dr. N. S. Liddell, G. L. Humphries, James S. Elliott, Gdn.

To hire of George to J. F. Trimble; and Charles.
Swoprn 4-5-1858
/s/James S. Elliott, Gdn

James S. Elliott, Gdn of Alexr Joice, an Idiot, in Account Current for year 1858
Page 543

To cash recd of J. S. Elliott, former Gdn, the following slaves: Daniel, a man, and Rachael, a girl.
Sworn 5-3-1858
/s/James S. Eliott, Gdn for Alexr Joice, Idiot

James S. Eliott, former Gdn of Alexr Joice, minor, in Account Current for 1857 and up to 3d May 1858
Page 544

Cash paid ALexr Johnson, 1857 taxes., J. S. Eliott, Gdn.
Sworn 5-3-1858
/s/James S. Elliott, Gdn

Return No. 2, Account Current with Estate of John Adams, decd, for year 1857 with James S. Elliott, Admr
Page 544

Cash paid 1857 taxes, John R. Humphries, Alexr Johnson, William Rowell, M. S. Donalson, W. D. Johnson, J. J. Robinson, Zachariah Eidson, F. A. and J. S. Williamson, Dr. C. Powell, John M. RIdling, Neoma Johnston, C. P. Fielder and M. Adams, legatees, Nancy Marloro and Sanders Adams, legatee, Nicy Adams, legatee, Enos Adams, legatee, one joint receipt from all the legatees, John Adams, Alpheas Adams, Nicy Adams, Adetha Adams, legatees.

Sale of Real Estate of John Adams, decd, sold first Tues in Oct 1857
Page 545

Lot No. 201 in 18th Dist. to Adetha Adams
1/2 Lot No. 237 to R. D. Greer
1/2 of Lot NO. 238 to Sanders Adams
59 acres of lot to Neoma Johnston
/s/James S. Elliott, Admr

Sale Bill of Estate of Thomas C. Austin, decd, sold on 3d Dec 1857
Page 545-547

Purchasers: Thomas H. Austin, W. Kirkpatrick, Lewis Thornton, R. W. Cobb, J. C. Austin, W. R. Ayers, D. J. Ayers, J. Adkins, T. H. Austin, G. Adams, J. N. Hadden, J. W. McClain, T. H. Austin, John Jones, J. W. Mitchell, Dr. Liddell, John Bryce, E. Rosser, S. Jordan, Jesse Jolley, P. H. Beauford, Joel Adkins.
/s/John C. Austin, Admr

Sale BIll of Land and Negroes Belonging to Estate of Thomas Austin, decd, sold Dec 1, 1857
Page 547

Lot No. 188 in 15th Dist.
2 negroes, Jacob and Mary
2 negroes, Hester and Dorcas.
Negroes, Sarah, Bill and Adaline.
/s/John C. Austin, Admr.
(names of purchasers not given)

Joseph Thompson, Admr Estate of M. W. Formwalt in Account Current for 1859
Page 548

Recd of F. E. Askins on land note, P. J. Emmell, J. J. Whitaker note, F. M. Eddleman, T. A. Kennaday, G. B. Haygood, W. L. Wright, fi.fa. Thompson, Admr, E. Andrews land note, A. K. White, J. S. Knox note, Mrs. Ogilby, fi.fa. J. Thompson, Admr vs. Simpson.

By amount paid - Howell & McAfee, P. J. Immell, Sol Goodall, J. Thompson, T. Kile, W. L. Wright, fi.fa. Bellinger vs Williamson, J. Thompson, A. Johnson, appeal fee in Thompson, Admr vs. W. Kile, M. A. Bell, Admr, O. Houston, Mrs. Asberry.

State of Georgia, Fulton County. Before me, Thomas L. Cooper, a notary public in said county, personally came, Joseph THompson, Admr of Estate of Moses W. Formwalt, decd.....swears that the within is a full and correct account of the receipts, etc. of said Estate, this 1 Jan 1857 to Dec 31 1857.
Page 549

Sworn 7-2-1858
/s/Joseph Thompson, Admr

Samuel F. A. Mann, minor in Account with W. Ezzard, Gdn, for 1857
Page 549

Paid - State tax and city tax for 1857, W. A. Powell, Dr. P. F. Hoyle, Malinda Mann.

By hire of Peter Hire to Mrs. Mann 1857.
Sworn 7-5-1858
/s/Alexr Johnson, Ordinary

Hardy Ivey's Estate in Account with William Ezzard, Admr, for year 1857
Page 549

Paid - 1857 tax city tax, H. P. Ivey, distributee, John J. Jane, Mrs. Sarah Ivy.

Estate of Merrell Collier, decd, in Account with William Ezzard, Exr for 1857
Page 550

Paid 1857 tax, city tax, C. H. Hanteiter, M. J. ivy, J. N. Beach, S. J. Shackelford, W. T. Loftin, F. M. Brantley and Wife, Charlotte Hulsey, N. N. Rawlins, J. N. Beach.

By rent of house for 1857.
Sale of brick storehouse sold first Tues in Apr 1858 to Ryan & Myers.
Sworn 7-5-1858
/s/William Ezzard, Exr

Estate of Alston H. Green, decd, in Account with William Ezzard, Admr for 1857
Page 540-541

Paid State tax for 1857, city tax, W. S. Jones, Hamlin J. Cooks, Ralph Ellison, H. G. Glen, distributee, Clement C. Green, distributee, paid Ordinary for W. A. Green, W. A. Green, a distributee.

By amount recd for sale of fraction No. 386, 18th Dist. oridinally Henry, now DeKalb, sold 1st Tues in Mar 1857 to John B. Sullivan.
By amount collected on note of C. C. Clay.
Sworn 7-5-1858
/s/William Ezzard, Admr

1857. Caroline E. Green, minor in Account with William Ezzard, Gdn, for 1857
Page 551-552

Paid 1857 tax, city tax, J. S. Wilson, G. C. Rodgers, O. G. Kile, H. Brumueller, Mrs. Anna Garrison, A. Johnson, E. S. Swift, G. W. H. Murell, J. D. Lockheart, Mrs. M. A. Swift, J. M. Bonnys, J. Taylor, Theo Harris, D. Mayers, J. N. Beach, William Ezzard, C. H. Strong, A. Johnson, Ordinary.

By hire of negro man, Richard, to J. B. Peck.
Negro, Horace to Harris
Negro, Miles to C. C. Green
Negro, Julia Ann to C. C. Green
Negro, Emiline to Terrell Sewell
Negro, Eliza with children to W> P. Orme

Sworn 7-5-1858
/s/William Ezzard, Gdn

A. J. Goldsmith, Admr of Estate of William Goldsmith, decd, in Account Current for 1858
Page 552

Cash paid - William Johnson, ALexr Johnson, Force Connally, H. H. Williams, Thomas C. Brodders, Lawrence Myers, G. W. Goldsmith, Thomas W. J. Hill, 1856 tax.
Sworn 6-11-1858
/s/A. J. H. Goldsmith, Admr

Nathan Turner, Admr of D. S. Boring, decd, for 1857
Page 552

By cash paid H. P. Flowler, 1857 tax, Robert Boring, John M. Boring.

Thomas Johnson, John L. Hamilton and William Johnson, Admrs of Estate of Andrew Johnson, late decd, for 1857 up to 5th Jul 1858 inclusive
Page 553

Cash paid - Alexr Johnson, W. Ezzard, E. A. Davis, W. Matherson, S. H. Dean, John Bankston, John Ervins, R. M. Brown, M. L. Adair, N. L. Hutchins, J. J. Wood, J. Bryce,

James M. Calhoun, E. A. Davis, Oliver Winningham.
Sworn 6-6-1858
/s/Thomas Johnson and James L. Hamilton, Admrs

James H. Born and William A. Braswell, Admrs of Estate of Joseph E.
Bishop, decd, in Account
Current for 1857 and up to 29th Jul 1858
Page 553-554

By cash received of J. M. Reid for rent, of W. F. Chewning, of Pitts.
Cash paid - John T. Bishop, Nancy Biship, W. P. Bond, John W. Braswell,
Reuben Bishop, Robert A. Johnson, S. E. ordan, Albert Wiggins, John .
Bishop, J. T. Bishop, W. H. Braswell, James McDonald, John M. Ridling, J.
J. Bishop, Reubin Bishop, James N. Coe, James M. Calhoun, C. W.
McGinnis, W. M. Hill.
Sworn 7-30-1858
/s/W. H. Braswell and James H. Born, Admrs

Thomas Moore, Admr of Estate of James Moore, decd, in Account
Current for 1857 and up to 5th Jul 1858 inclusive
Page 554-555

By cash paid Ann Moore, 1857 city tax, S. J. Shackelford, Alexr Johnson,
J. H. Mead, J. W. Duncan, James Moorehead, E. A. Davis, W. T. Cobb,
James Garvey, John Moore, Thomas Moore.
/s/Thomas Moore, Admr
Sworn 7-5-1858

Account Current with Estate of Charles Rainey, decd, with John Jett, Exr
up to 22d Jun 1858
Page 555

Cash recd from C. M. Jones note, B. Rainey, Jonathan Moore.
Cash paid - J. S. Elliott, John Y. Flowers, Alexr Johnson, Joseph Steward,
Rebecca Rainey, J. R. Humphries, B. Rainey, Edward Powell.
Sworn 6-26-1858
/s/John Jett, Exr

S. P. Wright, Gdn of Parasade Rainey in Account Current for 1857 and
up to Apr 10 1858
Page 555-556

Cash paid H. W. Cobb, 1957 tax, L. Upshaw, W. A. Rodgers, Miles
Mosely, Levi Willard, A. Johnson, S. P. Wright.
Sworn 4-23-1858
/s/S. P. Wright, Gdn

Spencer C. Wright, Gdn of J. M. Joice, minor, in Account Current for 1857
Page 556

To hire of Harrison for 1857, and girl, Darcus.
Cash paid H. W. Cobb, W. A. Powell, Moses Richerson, S. B. Wright.

H. H. Embry, Admr de bonis non on Estate of Jesse Childress, decd, for 1857 and up to 29 Apr 1858
Page 557

Recd of John Y. Flowers, Exr of Estate of James W. Reeve, $856 7-25-1858 (and $250)
Paid J. P. M. Calhoun, Atty, Alexr Johnson
Sworn 4-29-1858
/s/H. H. Embry

Return No. 1, Estate of James J. P. White, decd, in Account with S. Biggers, Exr.
Page 557-558

Paid A. Johnson, Ordinary, W. A. Kennedy, A. Rodgers, J. W. White, S. McWilliams, Harris Crowley, R. McWIlliams, Stephen Terry, John Scarboro, James Moore, E. A. Fowler, W. G. Roberson, W. S. Carter, B. L. Hudgins, A. B. Forsyth, Robert Jones, C. H. Strong, Elijah Turner, W. W. McCutchen.

Received of G. B. Almond, H. Crowley, L. Sturgis, J. N. Cravin, J. Wells, Thomas Kenneday, J. Pitts, George Carter, J. C. Avery, S. McWilliams, John W. White, B. M. Sprayberry, A. W. Stone, Whiteford note, Haynes note, J. Amesby note, W. W. McArthuers, A. J. Wills note.
Sworn 7-5-1858
/s/Stephen T. Biggers, Exr

C. Murphey, Gdn of Mourning Huey for year 1857 up to a part of 1858
Page 558

Cash recd of E. P. McDaniel, for Lucinda's hire to Mrs. Swanton, R. Hollingsworth, John Sharp, B. Woodson.
Cash paid John Lamar, George K. Hamilton, E. Rosser, Benjamin Woodson.

Ezekiel C. Harris' Return on Estate of James F. Montgomery made 1st Jul 1858
Page 559

Cash paid N. Young, A Cook, P. D. Wheelan for tuition, J. R> Randle, W. J. Kilbey, Robert Baber for taxes, T. W. Whitehead, W. R. Montgomery, minor.
Sworn 7-1-1858
/s/Ezekiel C. Harris, Gdn

C. Murphey, Gdn of J. J. McKoy for 1857 and a part of 1858
Page 559

Paid T. Burk, C. E. Scudder, G. Adams, J. M. Smith, A. M. Moore, John T. Wilson, Levi Willard, E. Rosser.
Keeping Louisa during her lying in and her child and children for 4 mos.

John C. Austin, Admr with LWT annexed of Thomas Austin, decd, for 1857
Page 560

Cash paid J. G. Austin, B. F. Bomer, 1857 tax, N. S. Liddell, E. Rosser, John Bryce, G. Adams, J. M. Fowler, William A. Austin, ALexr Johnson, C. Murphey, N. H. Austin, M. H. Moore, Levi Willard, P. F. Hoyle.
Sworn 6-26-1858
/s/John C. Austin, Admr

6th Return. An Account Current with Estate of James W. Reeve, decd for 1857 and part of 1858
Page 560-561

Cash recd of Davis Wade on judgment, J. R. Abercrombie, Admr of J. Duglass, Agt, of Ed Collier note, A. Gardner note, Lewis Wright judgment, Ed Collier, A. W. Reeve, Gdn, polly WIlson ch.,
A. W. Reeve according to Will of, Lewis Thomas, R. M. Brown.
Sworn 6-25-1858
/s/John Y. Flowers, Exr

John L. Evins, Admr of Estate of Johnson L. Johnson, decd, for 1857
Page 561-562

Cash recd of James S. Elliott, Admr of John Adams, decd; Salathial Morgan from sale of Negro boy, Mat; hire of Sam, boy, 2 fifas vs. Alpheus and John R. Adams recd on settlement with defendant; J. F. Johnson part of still house.

Cash paid Adams Oliver, P. F. Hoyle, Admr of J. L. W., A. Johnson, Ordinary, Enos Adams, John R. Adams, E. A. Davis, T. C., Norma Johnston, W. P. Johnston, Ichabod Williams, John Dobbs, John R. Wallace, James S. Elliott, J. Y. Flowers, C. W. McGinnis, THomas W. J. Hill, E. S. Lucky, J. F. Trimble, A. J. H. Pore, R. D. Greer, E. B. Reynolds, Henry A. Morgan, J. R. Evins, C. Murphey, W. H. C. Evans, Thomas Akins, E. Rosser, J. Norcross, J. M. Ridling, T. L. Cooper, G. Adams, E. Mason, A. Wooddall, S. C. Johnston, widow, H. M. Greer, J. A. Powel, Thomas Akins.
Sworn 9-16-1858
/s/J. L. Evins, Admr

S. P. Pace, Gdn of Almeda Sentell for year 1857
Page 563

Cash recd of Benjamin Cox for lot of land.
Cash paid J. R. McAlister, Ordinary, Reubin H. Abernathy

Sworn 3-28-1858
/s/S. K. Pace, Gdn

John McElroy, Exr of Estate of A. E. Ellis, decd, for 1857
Page 563

Cash paid Alexr Johnson, 1857 tax, A. E. Ellis, widow.
Sworn 3-16-1858
/s/John McElroy, Exr.

A. G. Hulsey, Gdn of J. J. Hulsey for 1857
Page 563

Cash paid 1857 taxes, T. A. Walker, Alexr Johnson.
Sworn 4-15-1858
/s/A. G. Hulsey

A. G. Hulsey, Gdn of S. A. Hulsey for 1857
Page 563-564

Cash recd of A. G. Hulsey, Exr of Estate of Jennings Hulsey, decd, 4-5-1853
Cash paid 1857 taxes, T. A. Walker, ALexr Johnson
Sworn 4-15-1858
/s/A. G. Hulsey, Gdn

A. G. Hulsey, Gdn of S. E. Hulsey for 1857 up to 15 Apr 1858
Page 564

Cash recd of A. G. Hulsey, Exr of Estate of Jennings Hulsey, decd, 5 Apr 1856
Cash paid W. L. Williams, 1857 taxes, J. M. Fowler, T. A Walker, Alexr Johnson.
Sworn 4-15-1858
/s/A. G. Hulsey, Gdn

Allen Wooddall, Admr of Estate of John Wyley for 1858 up to 22d Sept 1858
Page 564

Cash paid Alexr Johnson, E. Rosser, W. N. Kirkpatrick
Sworn 9-22-1858
/s/Allen Wooddall, Admr

John Bryce, Gdn of William McKoy for 1858
Page 564-565

To hire of Charles, Ritta and Polly (and her two children) foir 1858
Cash paid J. Bryce, L. Willard, Alexr Johnson, 1858 tax.

Sworn 10-1-1858
/s/John Bryce, Gdn of William McKoy

John Chamblee, Admr of Estate of W. Y. Pool, decd, for 1857 and up to 3d Jun 1858
Page 565

Cash paid Alexr Johnson, Lewis A. J. Dorsey, Samuel House, Margaret Maddox, James S. Elliott, S. C. Johnston, Julia L. Poole, John Y. Flowers, Isaac L. Hughs, Naomi Johnston, A. G. H. Pool, John W. F. Tilley, John Chamblee, B. Burdett, S. B. Wright, S. P. H. Poole, James Powell, W. A. Powell.
Sworn 6-3-1858

E. A. Davis, Admr of Estate of Seaborn Jones, decd, for 1856 to 6-2-1857
Page 566

Cash paid James Vaughn, S. H. Smith, Alexr Johnson, E. A. Davis
Sworn 6-2-1857
/s/E. A. Davis, Admr

E. A. Davis, Admr of Estate of Seaborn Jones, late decd, for year 1857
Page 566

Cash paid Albert Jones, Josina Jones, Marion Jones, Sarah Jones ($25 ea.)
Sworn 6-29-1858
/s/E. A. Davis, Admr

Mrs. Salina Ellington, Gdn of David B. Ellington, for 1858
Page 566-567

To hire of Ben, Burrell, Jacob and Wash for 1857
Cash paid Larkin Simpson, 1857 taxes, Samuel McElroy, J. R. and C. H. Wallace, F. A. Wattes, J. R. Pitts, F. R. Ripley, J. J. Rice, J. R. Pitts, F. A. Wates, W. E. Sprewell, T. R. Ripley.
Sworn 6-24-1858
/s/Salina Ellington

Inventory and Appraisement of Estate of William F. Chewning, decd
Page 567-569

Negroes - Sam and wife, Jude, Ned, Charles, George, Jim, Dallas (boy), Henry, Nelms, Ben, Reubin, Louisa (woman), Harriet, Mahaly and child, Adaline, Emiline, Martha, Rose, Thena, Lizza, Ex Ann, Frances, Ann, Carolina, Talula, Kittey.

12-20-1858
/s/J. W. Kirkpatrick, R. M. Brown, John N. Pate, appraisers

Georgia, DeKalb Co., Support set apart for Widow of Lewis L. Cash, decd, for 12 mos.
Page 569-570

/s/W, H, Cash, Watson Kitridge, John Fannin, appraisers.

Appraisement of Estate of James A. reeve, decd, 29 Nov 1858
Page 571

Appraisers: John Cochran, W. J. Palmer, Seaborn Crowley, James A. Miller
/s/John Y. Flowers, Admr

Sale of Personal Property of Estate of James A. Reeve, decd, Dec 9, 1858
Page 571-573

Purchasers: J. B. Henderson, L. W. Mitchell, Greenville Henderson, W. L. Maddox, Thomas Henderson, L. W. Mitchell, James M. Reeve, S. B. McElroy, W. G. Henderson, G. J. West, J. W. Level, J. M. Reeve, Seaborn Crowley, M. H. Jackson, J. W. Grisham, John Cockran, J. Hughs, T. THompson, E. Reeves, Y. Estis, Thomas THompson, M. E. Richerson, B. P. McCurdy, G. W. Moore, J. F. Akins, S. J. Hughs, Robert W. Wood, Joseph Stewart, S. V. Flowers, J. M. Reeve, Thomas Henderson, N. W. Lafoy, D. T. White, T. Camp, J. W. Line, John Jett, J. L. Loveless, Greenville Henderson, A. C. Nesbit, J. B. Henderson, J. M. Carroll, W. H. Cash, Vianna Reese, George Chewning.
/s/John Y. Flowers, Admr

Inventory and Appraisement of Estate of Edward Jones, decd
Page 573-574

Negro woman, Milley. Negro woman, Ranney and child, Martha.
Notes: E. Rosser, R. W. Jones, Eliza Stokes, John Jones, Elizabeth Brown, John W. Jones, Robert Jones, E. Rosser, Elijah Webb.

One account on C. W. McGinnis for negro hire.
Appraisers: J. W. Wilson, E. Rosser, J. E. George. 8-6-1858

Inventory and Appraisement of Estate of William Clark, decd, 8th Oct 1858
Page 574-576

Negroes: Charles, Tempy, Thomas.
Appraisers: Simpsy Perkinson, J. R. Jones, James W. Crockett 10-8-1858

Appointed for purpose of making a Division of Negroes belonging to Estate of William F. Chewning, late of said county, decd, amongst the distributees.
Page 576-577

To Mrs. Lorena W. Chewning, negroes, Sam and Judy, Ann, Emiline, Henry, Talula, Kittey, Ben.

To J. E. George, negroes, Martha, Nelms, Thena, Harriet, Louisa

To Laura S. Chewning, negroes, Charles, Lizza, Exum, Dallas.

To William Ezzard, Gdn of Jesse G. Chewning, negroes, Ned, Rose, Mahaly and child, Caroline

To W. Ezzard, Gdn of John A. Chewning, negroes, George, Jim, Frances, Adaline.

/s/B. F. Chamberlain, Robert Jones, R. M. Brown, J. B. Wilson, C. Murphey

Sale Bill of Estate of Seaborn Jones, decd, one lot of land in Cass Co. sold on 1st Tues in Oct 1856
Page 577

Sold for $580. /s/E. A. Davis, Admr

Sale Bill of Property of Estate of Solomon Hodges, sold 20th Nov 1858
Page 577

Purchasers: Hugh Norman, John S. C. Wilson, John McMecassins, J. S. C. Wilson.

Sale Bill of personal property belonging to Estate of Lewis L. Cash, decd, sold 24th Dec 1858 on 12 mos. credit
Page 578-579

Purchasers: W. Kitridge, W. Whitlock, G. B. Hudson, J. Pennell, David Burdett, W. H. Cash, D. T. White, John Fannin, B. Jones, W. A. Powell, A. P. Campbell, widow, Henry Sheman, Robert Jones, W. A. Powell, L. W. Cash, W. H. Cash, James E. Cash, W. J. Plunkett, J. G. Jones, J. Pennell, R. W. Cash, Jesse Jolley, M. Jones.

Sale Bill of portion of Negroes and personal property belonging to Estate of James Brown, decd, sold at Decatur on 1st Tues in Jan 1859
Page 579

Negro boy, Holland, sold to A. L. Pitts
Negro girl, Frankey, sold to A. L. Pitts
Negro boy, Charles, sold to James W. Brown

/s/William D. Brown, Admr

Inventory and Appraisement of Goods and Chattels of Estate of Lewis L. Cash, decd
Page 579-580

Appraisers: John Fannin, Watson Kitridge, James F. Akins.
11-13-1858

Sale Bill of Estate Real of Josiah Power, late decd sold on 1st Tues in Nov 1858
Page 580

Lot No. 352 in 18th Dist. sold to S. P. Wright
Lot No. 353 in 18th Dist. sold to S. P. Wright
Lot No. 361 in 18th DIst sold to S. P. Wright

/s/A. H. Power, Admr

Inventory and Appraisement of Estate of James Brown, decd
Page 580-581

Holland, a negro boy.
Charles, a boy
Franky, a girl.
Notes of B. C. Brown, Thomas Wilkins, T. M. Wilkins.
Appraisers: Berry Ragsdale, R. W. Garr, W. M. Barton. 10-2-1858

Inventory of Notes, fifas, receipts, etc. of James W. Kirkpatrick, former Exr of Estate of James H. Kirkpatrick, decd
Page 581

Notes of: H. P. Kirkpatrick, A. Nelson, James M. Calhoun, Thomas Terry, Dr. D. Alvigney, W. Carlisle, H. P. Ivey, A. E. Johnson.
/s/Thomas Kirkpatrick, Admr

END OF BOOK B, SALES, INVENTORIES, ESTATES

ABBOT
E. 263
J. S. 263

ABBOTT
M. J. 90

ABERCROMBIE
J. R. 307

ABERNATHY
James 162
John 161,235
John L. 273

ACKERMAN
Charles 81
Lena 81

ACRES
J. L. 145

ADAIR
M. L. 304
Thomas O. 184

ADAMS
Adetha 301,302
Aditha 277
Alpheus 275,277,301
C. T. 105
Cardman 159
D. 176,244
Daniel 215,216,283
E. 297
Edith 277
Elizabeth 8,165
Enos 244,256,277,300,301
G. T. 84
G. 222,226,257,261,276,282,298,302,307
Gardner 193.224,251,261
John 20,244,271,275,276,277,279,301,302,307

John R. 307
John B. 12

M. 301
Nicy 301
O. M. 136
Rosser W. 274
Salathiel 277,286
Sanders 277,301,302
W. D. 84

ADAMSON
C. J. 219
Ethel 133
N. C. 247
Nancy B. 9

ADKINS
Joel 302
J. 302

AIKENS
A. H. 278

AKERS
W. 162
Akers, William 161,269

AKIN
Ann W. 75
James 50
M. C. 114
Martha N. 75
Martha Elizabeth 50
Nancy Dora 75
Thomas T. 1
Thomas 194,195,227

AKINS
Allen R. 41
Donald W. 41
Eliza L. 41
G. 8, 11

Harriet E. 41
Henry M. 41
J. F. 287
J. 165
James F. 29,41,220,230,234,312

James 201,259
Jefferson P. M. 41
John 5
John M. 41
Lewis L. 41
Sarah S. 41
Thomas J. 41,201,203,232,253,274
Thomas 213,226,233,259,274,275
Thomas B. 41
W. J. 247
William G. 41

ALBERT
John J. 63,130
Albert, J. W. 113

ALEXANDER
A. 205
J. R. 197,238
J. F. 170,228
James F. 159
Milton 86
Samuel F. 26,34
Thomas 161

ALFORD
Alford S. 83
B. 245
B. 161,199,245,270
B., Sr. 207
Bestus 243
Burton 270
Bynom, Sr. 157,174,243,270
D. A. 83
Foster 83
G. B. 217
J. T. 66,243

J. O. 66,83
James 243
John T. 48,79,207,243,270
Luther 83
Nancy 157,174,207
Ruth 83
Sidney 205
Syrena 83

ALINSON
H. R. 142

ALLEN
A. S. 122
Beverly 3
Cornelius 56
J. A. 77
Lucy 110
Sally 3
T. M. 27
T. 263
Thompson 232

ALMAND
A. J. 129
A. J. 75
H. C. 53
Z. J. 116

ALMOND
A. R. 269
G. B. 306
H. P. 238
Henry 175

ALSOBROOKS
W. C. 217

ALSTON
Robert C. 80
R. A. 34

ALVEGENY

D. 313
N. D. 199, 274

AMESBY
J. 306

D. 259
D. B. 201
D. D. 295
David B. 256
Edgar M. 39
Harvey 11
J. B. 230,267,278,286,287,
J. J. 214,264
J. Bliss 108
John A. G. 233
Joseph B. 39
Louis 90
Mae 150
Martha C. H. 39
Martha A. 11
Mary F. 108
N. 233
Nelson 10
R. C. 3,295
Rosetta F. 39
S. J. 195
Sallie Harris 108
Samuel 244
Sarah J. 22
Sarah F. 71
Sarah 5
Susan Harper 15
Susan Dora 108
T. E. 113,120
W. W. 262
W. B. 217,295
W. P. 215
W. H. 217,264
William 5,50
William C. 39

ANDERSON
Arminda Armon 50
Benjamin Simons 15
Brownie 108

ANDREWS
E. 228,233,256,302
James W. 77
Rufus W. 147

ANGER
M. L. 256
N. L. 32,210

ANGERS
N. L. 16,187,228,233,256,283

ANNESLEY
Sarah 13
William 13,173,212,230,260

ANSLEY
H. I. 82

APPERSON
J. H. 147, Jr.

ARGO
David 279
Edmund 279
Edward 279
Elizabeth H. 71
Fannie E. 73
Fannie H. 118
Jackson 279
Nimrod 279,283
Robert T. 73,118
Samuel L. 73
Samuel 118

ARGOE
Margaret A. 50
Martha A. 50

Robert S. 50
Samuel L. 50
Sarah F. 50

ARMISTEAD
W. E. 138

ARNOLD
A. A. 278
Laugli 171
Loftin 252,275

ASBERRY
Mrs. 302

ASBURY
Thomas 175

ASHFORD
C. H. 85
W. T. 85

ASKEW
Elbert 150
Ellen Garner 152
James A. 150
Mary A. 150

ATKINS
F. E. 233,302
Mary 13
Thomas 1
W. T. 262

ATKINSON
A. 275
J. S. 76

ATWOOD
Nancy 13

AUCHENACTIE
Jennie 113

ARMSTED
Elizabeth 13

ARMSTRONG
John 12,296
Jonathan 12
John J. 135

AUSLEY
H. J. 98

AUSTIN
A. 162
Adaline (colored) 302
Alex 162
Arch Avery 149
Bill (colored) 302
E. 162
Elizabeth 299
Green 5
H. C. 91, 107,162
Ida May 132
J. F. 290
J. A. 132
J. G. 307
J. C. 238,262,302
J. M. 262
Jacob (colored) 302
James W. 104
John C. 13,166,177,206,238,262,290,302,307
John 161,162,206,237,272,299
John B. 8
Maggie 132
Mary (colored) 302
Mary Melissa 149
N. H. 206,238,262,307
Nat 198
Nathaniel R. 13
S. K. 116
Sarah (colored) 302

Sarah 5,13
T. H. 302
T. F. 162,206,237
T. H. 302
Thomas H. 262,302
Thomas 13,177,206,238,262,290,307
Thomas J. 206
Thomas F. 272
Thomas C. 302
Thomas W. 299
J. C. 37
J. C. 28,34
James C. 30,38
James E. 40

AVERA
Virginia 131

AVERY
James C. 269
J. C. 306

AVEY
Dr. 229

AVISTON
F. 197

AWTERRY
Armenty 2
Isaac 2

AYCOCK
BAGWELL
J. M. 71
John 201,235
R. R. 163

BAILEY
C. J. 160
E. J. 160,191,204,285,287
Edmond J. 13
Edmond T. 129

W. C. 162,259
W. 293
W. M. 116
William A. 307
William C. 7

AVARY
Arch, Jr. 155
Arch 108,155
Eugene Fulton 155
Franklin T. 43
George T. 43
Sarah E. 43

AYERS
B. I. 179
D. J. 302
Daniel J. 13
W. R. 302
William R. 13

AYETT
Dr. 210

BABER
Robert 257,306

BADGER
Badger, J. B. 205,229,246

BAGLEY
George W. 33
Winney 33
J. H. 116,156
John 174,177
John J. 49
Martha J. 153
Nancy 49
Susan C. 53
Thomas S. 181
William P. 129
Z. 217
Zachariah 226

BAKER

Absalom 190
Eliza J. 73
J. S. 165
J. M. 102
Joel C. 73
John D. 53
M. L. 102
M. E. O. 113
Mary 5
R. S. 15
James A. 180

BALINGER
Sarah 4

BALL
Andrew J. 75
Georgia Hendree 55
J. 206
James M. 55,56
Martin 299
Peter 96

BALTAGER
John N. 4

BANKSTON
H. P. 278
H. 239
Henry 239
John 202,239,304
Mattie 51
Synthia 239

BARBOUR
E. 260

BARFIELD
D. R. 140,141
Sarah 105

Robert T. 73
Samuel W. 73
Thomas 173,203,212,213,231,260
William 173

BALENHEIMER
J. Ed 112

BALES
Joseph A. 200

BALEY
Mary J. 180
Frank R. 105
John 105
Malcom 105

BARGE
J. J. 147

BARKEY
W. D. 91

BARNES
Charles O. 89
E. J. 77
Edgar F. 89
James 269
Mary B. 92

BARNETT
W. 245

BARNS
Thomas 217

BARR
A. P. 281
James A. 166
Caroline 10
Elizabeth Rebecca 10
Kizza 10

BARRETT
D. G. 199
Elvira Ann 18

BARROW
Dave 148
David C. 148
Pope 148

BARTLETT
E. W., Mrs. 275
E. W. 247,254
Elizabeth 247,254,275
Elizabeth W. 247
John 254
John C. 247,275
R. S. 247,254

BARTON
W. T. 269
William 217

BASIN
Smith 148

BASKIN
James 183

BASS
John 289

BATES
Charles F. 105
E. E. 66
Edward F. 94
John F. 140
Lenna Conn 105
Lina Conn 101
Mary 105
Mary Jane 256
Mary Linn 101
W. T. 90

BATEY
Mary J. 256

BATTEY
Alfred M. 134

BAUBB
Jesse 66,67
Robert Lucas 66
Sopha 66,57

BAUGG
Robert Lucust 67

BAXLEY
Merriman 269

BAXTER
Amanda 300
Annie 67
Birdie 67
E. S., Mrs. 121
Emeliza S. 58
Fannie 67
George 197
Hubert 67,98
James 220,244,247,267,270,295,300
James H. 67
John 36,244,247
John R. 300
John B. 28
Lois 67
Louisa 267,270,295,300
Mary J. 300
P. E. N., Mrs. 121
R. 201,235
Robert 179,191,220,297,235,237,248,300

BEACH
Beach, J. N. 294,303,304

BEALE
Charles 13

BEALL
D. 193
Exa Maria 15

BEAUCHAMP
Elizabeth 220
J. W. 161
Martha 25,172,220,236
W. 172,236
William 160,162,220

BEAUFORD
P. H. 302

BEAUTY
J. L. 128

BECK
Ann 44
Charles J. 44
Lew H. 54
Marcus W. 133
Roberta 44
W. Gilman 44

BEDDINGFIELD
Charles P. 151

BEGGERS
Stephen T. 21

BELCHER
James M. 126

BELL
A. M. 228
Exa M. 196

BEASLEY
Thomas Weldon 128

BEATTY
Ben Troy 132

BEATY
James W. 53
William H. 53

George F. 115
Hepsey 101
J. 198
M. A. 198,213,256,228,302
Marchus A. 183,197
Mary 105
Piromis N. 130
Thomas 16
W. A. 228

BELLAH
Mary E. 74

BELLENGER
John N. 278
Joseph T.1 278

BELLINGER
George (colored) 186
Harriet (colored) 186
Henny (colored) 186
Hutchins (colored) 186
Irvin (colored) 186
J. T. 237,243,295
J. L. 264,295
J. N. 192,200
John N. 15,164,168,186,200,217,262
Joseph T. 16,200,227,262,275
Laura Jane 15
Manerva (colored) 186
Martha Florence 15
Mary (colored) 186

Nelson Tallulah 15
Sarah Ann 15

BELLINGRATH
H. F., Mrs. 156

BELLONS
James 219

BELSCHIG
Josie 154

Thomas Cobb 99

BENSON
Louisa Francis 93

BENTLEY
O. S. 196

BERMAN
Belle 139

BERNARD
Annie L. 148
Hugh 148

BERRY
M. B. 269
Milly 23

BESSANT
V. G. 81

BESSART
Virginia F. 80

BETTERTON
Levi 7,8

BIDWELL
Caroline Bucher 82
Everett C. 82

BENEFIELD
S. F. A. 43

BENNETT
Fannie May 136

BENNING
A. H. 99,100
Augustus H., Jr. 100
Elizabeth L. 99
Margaret R. 99
Theodore K. 99

BIGGERS
S. 306
S. T. 245
Samuel T. 298
Stephen 239
Stephen T. 296,306

BILLUPS
Alice Farr 111
Lanier R. 111
Robert W. 111

BILLWELL
Carrie B. 95

BIRD
Elijah 244
John 175,207,257

BIRDSONG
Susan F. 15

BISHOP
B. T. 106
Bailey 94
Barters 94
Benjamin 94
Edmond 33
Elijah 33,287
Elizabeth 94

I. M. 179
J. J. 94,305
J. James 33
J. E. 225
J. T. 305
James W. 278
H. W. 227

BITTLE
Leander 31

BLACK
Dameron 131
E. G. 132

BLACKE
Jack (colored) 227
John 227

BLACKMAN
James 189
Ruth 133

BLACKSTOCK
J. M. 213,260,261,267
James M. 216,220,224,282,284
James 193,211,214,226

BLACKWELL
Blackwell, J. W. 210
Blackwell, J. B. 230

BLAKE
Allen 19
Andrew (colored) 201
Ann (colored) 201
Bob (colored) 201
Buck (colored) 201
Caroline (colored) 201
Clarke (colored) 201
Clary (colored) 201
Crease (colored) 201
Dashey 24

John T. 33,305
John 275,305
Joseph E. 280,287,300,305
Joseph 94
Joshua 33
Joshua J. 280
Eliza (colored) 201
Fanny (colored) 201
Floyd (colored) 201
George (colored) 201
H. W. 293
Harriet (colored) 201
Henry M. 19
Henry W. 258,293
Hiram (colored) 201
Jane (colored) 201
Joe (colored) 201
John 18,168,200,201,235,258,293
John B. 201
Lane (colored) 201
Lucy 148
Luke 33
M. W. 89
Margaret 33
Marion 94
Martin 94
Mary (colored) 201
Mary 24,94
Nancy 20,33,305
Newton (colored) 201
Reubin 94,191,305
Sisero 24
Texaner (colored) 201
Thomas 24,94
Tildy (colored) 201
W. H. 235
W. J. 64
William J. 94

BLALOCK
Gibson F. 53

BLECKLEY
F. 294
L. E. 175
L. A. 174

BLOODWORTH
L. E., Mrs. 127
N. R. 18

BOATRIGHT
D. M. 123

M. N. 225
Easom J. 72
Elam J. 37
Daniel E. 63,64
David 37
Esom J. 48

Mary M. 55
Nancy 94
Nannie 136

BOGS
E. 200

BOHANAN
G. W. D. 227
J. W. D. 197

BOHANNON
J. W. 253
J. D. 238
J. W. D. 198

BOMAR
Emma Elford 103
Jarman Elfora 103
Louise Blassingame 103
William A. 101,103

BOMER
Bomer, B. F. 223,228,307

N. G. 179

BOILS
C. 229

BOLTON
B. N. 199
Charles J. 55
David E. 136
H. H. 207

BOND
Atticus Y. 72
George R. 72
George W. 116
Ira A. 72
J. T. 72
James E. 37
John 301
Joseph T. 37
Joseph B. 72
Lucy (colored) 301
Mollie E. 72
Smitha E. 37
Vina (colored) 301
W. P. 272,279,305
William A. D. 72

BONING
David 160

BONNIG
J. 229

BONNER
B. F. 15,196

BONNYS
J. M. 304

BOON
Dr. 219
John N. 268

BOORSTON
Sam A. 148

BOOTH
Robert 85

BORGIN
David S. M. 264

BORING
Addie H. 61
Bain (colored) 288
D. 229
D. S. M. 20,237,288
D. S. 285,304
David 18,220
David, S. M. 237
David S. 35
Davies S. M. 246
Ezekiel (colored) 237
Harriet C. 61
Isaac A. 61
J. M. 196,246
Jesse 61
John M. 286,304
John K. 61
Lorena 286
Mary (colored) 237,288
Mary M. 286,288
Mary A. 18
Robert 304
Sallie J. 61
Tom (colored) 237

BORINGS
Mrs. 285

BORING
James M. 285

BORN
J. L. 70
J. H. 268,275,279,295,296

J. M. 160,191,204,217
James H. 204,247,271,289,287,200305
James L. 108
James T. 108
John M. 13
John M., Jr. 27
John S. 108
Katie E. 108
Martha A. 108
Sarah 27
William L. 32

BOSARD
Annie M. 105

BOSIN
Ellen 53

BOSSO
Louis A. 124

BOSTICK
R. 236

BOSWELL
Jacob 204

BOTHWELL
Nannie Bell Thornton 132
Walter G. 132

BOTTON
A. J. 215

BOULIGUY
Alfred 126,137,140,144

BOWDEN
Amanda C. 45
Walter T. 46

BOWEN
E. 205

BOWER
George W. 130

BOY
Jeff (colored) 268

BOYD
Alford (colored) 268
Andrew 5,301
H. M. 168
Hugh M. 21
Jeff (colored) 276
John 11,217
Kezia 21,268,276
M. A. 156
Margaret 21
Nancy (colored) 268
Nancy 21
Rose (colored) 268
S. B. 196
W. H. 101
J. T. 80

BOYLE
B. F. 286

BRANDON
W. R. 226,261,280
William R. 22

BRANON
J. C. A. 94

BRANTLEY
F. M. 303
J. B. 239
Margaret E. 20

BRASELL
R. 235

BRASSELL
William H. 86

BRADEN
M. J. 187,235
R. M. 264

BRADLEY
G. P. 27
J. P. 179
J. L. 208
John L. 194

BRADWELL
W. H. 278

BRADY
Brady, A. J. 275

BRAND
A. M. 149,156
John T. 75,79
W. H. 27

BRASWELL
Arci 138
Asa 277
Avis 33
Avy 113,114
B . B. 121,123
B. B., Jr. 121
Burrell B. 53
D. C. 123
E. S. 278
E. A. 152
Elijah 45,138
Flonnie 138
George P. 131
George A. 252,258
Georgia A. 131
Henry 268
J. W. 113,160
John W. 113,296,305

Loutie E. 131
Maraway 26
N. A. 121,123
Samuel H. 131
W. H. 280,300,305
Wesley 37,158,160
William A. 305
William H. 33
William B. 77

BRAZELL
John 235

BRAZZELL
R. H. 201

BREEDLOVE
L. B. 198

BREWERS
M. 285

BRICE
H. J. 80

BRITT
Alfred L. 135
C. J. 123
C. N. 135
George W. 135
James 123
Jane M. 61
Joel 232
Minnie 135
W. E. 91

BROADNAX
W. D. 130

BROCK
Robert 196

BROCKMAN

BRICES
Sarah 211

BRICKMAN
Henry 178
Ruth Ann 178

BRIDEWELL
Mary S. 146

BRIDGEWELL
William J. 146

BRILEY
E. J. 174

BRINSON
I. H. 77

BRIREO
Ed 121

BRISENDINE
Brisendine, Berry 269

Brockman, Henry 193,254,274
Brockman, Rutha 274

BROCKSTON
Louvenia C. 76

BRODDERS
Thomas C. 304

BROGDON
Harriet E. 60

BROMLOW
J. E. 290

BROOKS
Eugene 121
Fannie 121

J. T. 138
J. H. 139
Josiah 152
Mary Julia 151
T. J. 152
W. H. 80

BROS
Venable 74

BROWN
B. M. 161
Bryan W. 285
Charles (colored) 312
E. 219
Elizabeth 23,311
Emanuel 162
Fannan 161,219,254,255,300
Fanning 1
Frankey (colored) 312
George P. 71
H. T. 125
H. W. 196
Holland (colored) 312
Isabel Chivers 114
Isham 162
J. G. 99,269,278
Susan 34
Thomas 251
W. S. 288
W. P. 139
W. L. 283
W. T. 104
William D. 22,34

BROWNING
A. 235
Andrew 235
Caroline 63
T. A. 264,287
Thompson A. 63,263,287
Wiley 244

J. R. 109
J. F. 106
Jackson 22,34
James 71,22,219,283,290,312
James W. 22,34,312
James F. 71
Julind 46
Killis 12,208
Linna 127
Lydia 22
M. M. 159
Martha 34
Mary N. 34
Meridith 245,251
N. W. 162
Nancy E. 90
R. M. 25,42,54,58,
168,184,189,190,194,195,196,197,198,199,
200,202,228,209,215,216,221,224,225,226,
232,233,234,238,239,245,262,264,268,274,
280,293,295,304,310
R. S. 200,201
R. W. 37
Rhoda 219,254,255,300
Rhody 162
Seaborn 269

BROYLES
E. N. 99

BRUCE
A. C. 118
John 223,236,263,282
Nancy 164

BRUMBY
A. V. 213

BRUMLET
J. F. 269

BRUMUELLER
H. 304

BRUNELLER
H. 261

BRUNT
Anna M. 39
Bradford B. 39
Carrie D. 39

BRYAN
Ella B. 126
Fred 127
James S. 126
Joseph 204
Mary E. 127

BRYANT
S. 238
William 12

BRYCE
John
76,169,178,197,221,224,235,261,252,282,2
94,298,302,307,309
Bryce, J. 222,238,304,309
George W. 76

BRYSON
BUGG
E. M. 74
Minnie L. 142

BUIE
Andy (colored) 243
Caroline (colored) 243
Catharine (colored) 243
Jasper (colored) 243
Nancy 243

BULLARD
Henry 231
R. W. 198

BULLOCK

F. M. 63

BUCHANAN
E. S. 236
Hattie 99
J. D. 236
J. W. 32,236
J. F. 205,206
John 244
Lucy 99
Nellie 99
R. 244
W. T. 113,141
William F. 141,147

BUCHER
J. C. 82

BUCKER
Annie C. 95
Hannah C. 95
Mary S. 95
Susan 95

BUFFORD
Dr. 226
J. P. 208
B. 188

BUNNES
Jane 24

BURDETT
B. 309
Richard 195
Richard T. 162,212
Samuel 267
Viola 58

Viola 58

BURDITT
Benjamin 267

BURFORD
P. H. 179

BURGE
L. N. 257

BURK
T. 307

BURKS
T. 285

BURNES
James 288
John 288

BURNEY
James Selkirk 139

BURNHAM
A. Z. 57
Bernard 141
E. 31
J. W. 57,92
Roy 141

BURNS
Ina 151

BUTWELL
W. B. 161

BYERS
H. N. 204
R. G. 204

BYRD
Mary Ann 42

BURGESS
B. F.
74,93,96,100,102,106,114,118,125,137,138,
141,144
Ben W. 151
H. H. 67,100,113
Henry H. 94
Mary E. 94
R. F. 147
W. H. 78

BURNSIDE
T. R. 70

BURRETT
W. 287

BURRISS
J. R. 128

BURTON
Lewis William 56

BUTLER
Alfred 149
G. C. 169,222,294
G. G. 197
Mary Lou 70
O. Alfred 149

BUTTERFIELD

Pearl 127

CAGLE
Aley 71
David D. 71
Robert 71

CAIN
Ellen 66

J. 161
J. J. 203
John J. 212,213
Sarah H. 121

CALAWAY
A. M. 64

CALDWELL
H. A. 204
James 249,256

CALE
Lounds 81
M. M. 245
Ned 244
P. H. 110
Philip P. 234
W. L. 110

CALLAWAY
A. M. 69
Alonzo M. 129
Blanche 129
Ernest E. 129
Sarah L. 129
Sarah A. 129
Thomas G. 129

CALO
W. 196

CAMERON
N. W. 144

CAMP
A. 199,205
Andrew 74
Benjamin 211
Berry 214
Ca. 232
Catherine 74
Charles 255

James K. 71

CALHOUN
E. N. 163,166,178,193,198,201,214,231,232,2 235,253
E. W. 193
E. 241
J. P. M. 306
J. M. 197,270
James M. 17,22,201, 222,234,245, 249,266,288,305,313
Charley 65
Dock 65
E. 201
Elias 3
G. W. 209
Hattie 99
Ira 279
J. 257
J. R. 232
John 293
John G. 241
Mattie 65
Oliver B. 277
S. H. 65,247
Sarah J. 65
Shelton 220
Shelton D. 220
T. 199
Tarpley 205
W. 232,244
W. H. 287
William 161

CAMPBELL
Shelton H. 48

CAMPBELL
E. 200

CAMRON

CAMRON
Nancy 18,293,231

CANDLER
C. M. 61,96,207,119
Charles Murphy 96
Claude Mrs. 146
Eliza C. 146
M. A. 300
Mary S. 146
Mary H. 95
Milton A. 46,61,70,87
93,94, 107,108,113,114,146
Nellie B. 95
Rebekah S. 146
Scott 142,146
Wilton A. 44

CANNON
J. C. 200,253,293
John C. 163,253.293
M. E. 163

CANTREL
Jesse 248

CANTRELL
Jesse C. 252
J. H. 89

CANUTH
W. T. 27

CAPE
Wiley 244

CARLISLE
W. 257,313
William 12
Willis 160,168,189,213

CARLTON
Eugene 121,147

J. W. 213
Tom 146

CARMICHAEL
R. H. 168

CARMON
John C. 219

CARNALL
T. M. 285

CARNER
H. L. 257

CARNES
C. A. 165

CARPENTER
George M. 75
John S. 75
M. E. 264
Susannah 75

CARRELL
George W. 133

CARRIER
H. L. 256

CARROL
Charles J. 50
James M. 230

CARROLL
Bessant 80
C. J. 72
C. O. 148
Charles J. 19,21,49
F. M. 247
Ida J. 55
J. M. 36,244,247

James 28
James F. 55
James M. 55
Jessie F. 80
Jessie 80
John 19,227,230,235,258,259,293
Julia A. 55
L. G. 141
Lorenzo F. D 55
M. E., Mrs. 139
M. E. 102
Martha 141
Mary M. 21
Nat 217
R. E. 141
Rhoda 19
Robert T. 55
W. W. 277
William H. 60

CARTER
Amelia 47
Carrie C. 70
Charles B. 60
George 306
Malachi C. 22
Mary Jane 121
S. S. 71
T. 230
Tarlton 266
W. S. 306
S. M. 234

CASH
Allison 253,293
Amanda Jane 52
Bryant 253,293
Eldridge S. 257
G. W. 319,293
George 253,293

George M. 52
George W. 52
Howard 204
James 283
James E. 51
John Moses 52
Lewis L. 310,310
Lucinda 51
Martha 178,204
Mary Frances 52
Nancy Belinda 52
Robert 277
S. T. 236
S. P. 178
Sarah Ann 253,293
Stephen D. 204
W. 249
W. H. 220,247,277,287,310
Wash 267
Washington 163,257
William 178,204
Willis 267
Willis M. 198
Winston 244
William H. 60

CARTER
Amelia 47
Carrie C. 70
Charles B. 60
George 306
Malachi S. 22
Mary Jane 121

CASSELLS
Louie J. 93,104

CASSELS
Clara M. 95

CASTLEBERRY
James 18

CATHMAN
James M. 161

CATHRON
Ernest 155

CAVANESS
S. A. 208

CAVINS
Stella 12

CENTER
Nathan 6,10
W. 214
William 173

CHAMBERLAIN
H. H. 232
Milton A. 100
Permelia C. 67
W. B. 30
William J. 8

CHAPIN
Adna 101

CHAPMAN
B. F. 233,262,294
Benjamin F. 5
Benjamin 5
Eli T. 5,32
James H. 5
Narcissa 32
Theba 5
W. B. 168,295
William F. 32

CHARTERS
William A. 88

CHASE
B. F. 246,298

CHAMBLEE
J. 300
John 300,309

CHAMBLESS
William C. 172

CHAMPION
W. L. 151
W. L., Mrs. 155

CHAMPION
F., Mrs. 200

CHANDLER
David P. 67
Elizabeth 30
Albon 16

CHEEK
Martha J. 9

CHESHIRE
Catharine 9
H. 13
Hezekiah 9
R. P. 144

CHESNUT
Alexander 21
Alexr 248,278
C. S. 36
D. A. 75
D. 247
David 36,59,244,247,267,295
Sallie E. 143

CHEWNING
Adaline (colored) 310
Ann (colored) 310
Ben (colored) 310

Carolina (colored) 310
Charles (colored) 310
Dallas (colored) 310
Emiline (colored) 310
Ex Ann (colored) 310
Frances (colored) 310
George (colored) 310
Harriet (colored) 310
Henry (colored) 310
Jim (colored) 310
Jude (colored) 310
Kittey (colored) 310
Laura 285
Levi 220
Lizza (colored) 310
Lorena W. 311
Louisa (colored) 310
Mahaly (colored) 310
Martha (colored) 310
Ned (colored) 310
Nelms (colored) 310
John A. D. 291,292
W. 256

CHIPLEY
E. S. 118

CHIVERS
Bernice 114
Emma 23
Fannie Isabella 23
Frances E. 23
Harriet 23
Isodore 23
Joel R. 23
Miller 114
Thomas H. 23,24

CHOVANAN
A. G. 210

CHOWAN
A. E. 257

R. A. 36
Reubin (colored) 310
Rose (colored) 310
Sam (colored) 310
T. E. 52
Talula (colored) 310
Thena (colored) 310
W. F. 211,267,305
William F. 213,310,311

CHILDRESS
C. C. 140
Henrietta 14
J. 200,356
J. M. 256
J. A. D. 200
James S. 195,242.291
Jesse 169,194,195,225,236,242,252,256,288,2
292,306
John A. 195,242

CHRISTIAN
Emma C. 94
Katie 93
Nancy C. 93
T. J. 59

CHUPP
Blanche 129
Daniel R. 21,45,192
David B. 45
David 21
Edward 152
Elizabeth 45
Emer S. 45
J. E. 129
J. 160
J. L. 138
J. C. 71,129
Jacob 21,45,158,192,268,278
James C. 45
John H. 106

Josiah L. 45
Mary Lucinda 106
Mary M. 45

CHURCH
Melvin 88

CLAIBORNE
Christopher James 117
Thomas 117
William 117

CLAIN
Joseph F. 186

CLARIDA
A. N. 197

CLARK
  Albert A. 40
  Alberta A. 39
  Alice E. 39,40
  Alice Eugenia 40
  Sarah A. 78
  Tempy (colored) 311
  Thomas 170,202
  Thomas (colored) 311
  W. A. 101
  W. J. 69,85,301
  W. H. 120
  Warren J. 107
  William 311
  William H. 39,40,84,85,86,170,202

CLARKE
Mary E. 15

CLARKSTON
E. R. 127

CLAY
C. C. 213,304

Martha A. 152
Charles (colored) 311
Davis 199
Elijah H. 39,40
Fannie P. 67
Frances 167
G. C. 219
George C. 212,219,231,260
J. W. 78
James Edward 78
Jesse 197
John L. 269
John W. 78
John 30,229
Julia A. 39
Kate 126
Mary S. 157
Mary Jane 61
Mary Ann 107
R. 297
Rebecca 202
Robert M. 67,68
Robert 221
S. M. 142
Cyrus 246
Eli 269
Green B. 220,230,267
J. W. 50,116
James F. 267
James 37
Jesse 253
John 189
John C. 189
Joseph 188,220
Joseph F. 230
R. L. 87
Zipporah Lanora 71

CLAYTON
J. B. 15
Laura 107

CLEBORNE

Alan 117
Arthur 117
Christopher C. 117
Christopher Clifford 117
Cornelia Du Val 117
Cuthbert 117

CLEGHORN
Col. 98

CLEMENCE
Harriet A. 53

CLINE
R. A. 154
W. L. 154

CLINTON
William 15

CLOTFELTER
David A. 51

CLOUD
A. 205
Aaron 175
Mary E. 90
Robert B. 90

CLOYD
A. 175

COAKLEY
A. J. 94

COATES
Sue V. 149

COBB
Cordelia E. 89
H. W. 301,305,306
J. T. 67,290
J. F. Cobb

Edith 117
Edward Bryce Du Val 117
Jane E. 117

COBB

J. C. 63
James R. 89
James T. 89
M. V. 91
R. 179
R. W. 290,302
Robert M. 188
Robert W. 35
Samuel H. 89
Susan A. 89
W. T. 269,290,305
William T. 29,290

COBBS
Robert W. 24

COCHRAN
Alex 16
Alexander 182
E. C. 217
Hilda M. 12
John 24,48,49,310
Julia A. 58
Julia 58
S. W. 121
Samuel W. 59
Sarah B. 58
Seaborn 161
William 12

COE
James N. 295,305
Haden 198,225,242,245
Hayden 166

COFER
Minnie L. 147

COFFEE
T. E. 93

COGGINS
Joshua 232

COGSWELL
John 220

George W. 20
Georgia Ann 292
Guilford (colored) 237
H. G. 212
Henry G. 9,20,179,219,231,260
J. 262
J. M. 205,200,206,259
J. E. J. 30
Jacob (colored) 212
James M. 292
James J. W. 30
John, Jr. 269
John W. 138
John 9,20,32,162,197,238,262,239
Joseph H. 30
Joseph M. 30
Lem (colored) 212
Louise (colored) 212
Lucinda Caroline 30
M. 214
Malinda 20
Mary E. 292
Merrell 20,212,237,261,303
Mrs. 212
Nancy 30
Newman (colored) 237
Nubels (colored) 238
Parthenia A. 76
Ples (colored) 237
Rose (colored) 238

COLDWELL
Francis 155
James 180,181
Mary 155

COLE
Haden 261

COLEMAN
Dossey 94

COLLEMAN
Philip 252
Sarah A. 292
Simeon (colored) 238
Tom (colored) 238
Vina (colored) 238
W. G. 259
W. 162
William F. 30
William C. 20

COLLIER
Andy (colored) 212,237
B. F. 30
Bill (colored) 238
Carolina (colored) 238
Charles 141
D. 307
Ed 307
Elisha (colored) 237
Elizabeth 20
Ella 141
Elmira (colored) 238
Emeline (colored) 238
G. W. 30

COLLINGS
R. E. 144

COLLUM
John 161

COMAN
J. K. 143

COMER
B. F. 268
J. C. 200
S. A., Mrs. 232
W. J. 262

COMERS
Sarah A. 261

COMPTON
Martha A. L. 147

COMWELL
J. T. 270

CONE
Betsey (colored) 158
Emiline (colored) 158
Felix (colored) 158
Isham (colored) 172
Jacob (colored) 172
John 172,245
John M. 181
Keenan (colored) 172
L. H. 193
Margaret F. 172,181
Mary (colored) 172
Parker (colored) 172
Patrick 14
Price 172,181
T. W. 172,245
Tolbert (colored) 172
W. F. 285
Washington (colored) 172
William 172,281

CONNELLY
Lorena S. 18
Sarah A. 18

Francis H. 5
Gabriel 14
Jack (colored) 158
John H. 14
Lucinda 8,165
Lucy (colored) 158
Mary (colored) 158
Peter (colored) 158
Reuben 9,158

CONN
Adna C. 94
Charles Francis 101
Milly M. 94

CONNALLY
C. 245
C. M. 239
C. W. 245
Christopher 172,181,197
Edmond (colored) 172
Elizabeth 172,281,245
Force 215,304
Sarah M. 18
W. F. 229
William F. 18

CONNER
W. T. 100

CONNOR
R. H. 48

CONSTANTINE
J. E. 119

COOK
A. 257,293,306
Anderson 9
Anna E. 93
D. A. 229
David A. 261
J. R. 68

James M. 165
John 244
Mary E. 132,133
Nancy W. 20
Thomas 247,254
Willie 93

COOKS
Hamlin J. 303

COOPER
Annie Irvin 95
Barnett 216
T. L. 175,228,256,285
Thomas L. 96,227,228,232.303

COPLELAND
G. W. 96

CORBIN
B. 244
CORINTY
Joseph 260
Harriet 8

CORN
Harriet 165

CORNETT
Hardy 7

CORNWELL
Chamer 221
Charles 169

CORLEY
Anna Elizabeth 76
Cardin 160
Eliza Jane 60
H. H. 76
John M. 158,160,191
Larret 265
Lauret 234

Lucy 160
Sarah Elizabeth 60

CORRY
Harriet 165

CORY
Harriet 8

COTTON
Lizzie 90

COUCH
M. G. 132

COUEY
William 3

COULMAN
Cana 42

COUPELL
Thomas G. W. 212

COVINGTON
Bell S. 115
Belle S. 114
Ellen Levnona C. 145
Henry Clay 115
M. L. 115,118
Mary A. 145
Varina Adolph 114

COWAN
J. J. 82
John L. 66
Mary O. 82

COWEN
J. J. 247
John F. 272
S. D. 220

COWERS
Cowers, C. A. 107

COX
A. T. 98
Albert Troup 93
Albert H. 98
Benjamin 308
C. 257
Cary 293
Martha F. 30
William M. 33

CRABILL
C. C. 131

CRAFT
Craft, W. H. 167,257

CRAIG
Isalinda C. 61

CRAIGG
Burtin 149
Collin 149

CRAIN
CRESTHURST
Lillian C. 131

CREWS
Alexr 244
E. 244

CRITTENDEN
F. E., Mrs. 127

CROCKET
J. W. 285

CROCKETT
Andrew J. 29
George 29

J. A. 228

CRANE
B. J. 96

CRAVILL
C. C. 125

CRAVIN
J. N. 306

CRAWFORD
Abraham (colored) 176
Clarissa (colored) 176
Ephraim (colored) 176
Joel H. 227
Leroy 12
Martha (colored) 176
Mary M. 71
R. 288
S. B. 242,266
Samuel B. 176,242,245
Willis (colored) 176

CRAYTON
J. M. 198

J. P. 30
J. 165,229
J. W. 220,259
James 194
James W. 29,30.191
James M. 220
Joel J. 29,30
John W. 30
Lucinda 29
M. L. 187
Lucinda 29
Mary 30
Mary Ann 29
Radford 283
Robert P. 29
Sarah Ann 29

Sarah Ann Caroline 86

CROFT
George N. 115

CROMLEY
William 262

CRONIE
C. M. 263

CROSBY
G. 285

CROSS
Z. D. 206,248

CROSSLEY
W. L. B. 53

CROUHEIM
E. C. 154

CROWELL
W. 263
William 34

CROWEY
Harris 57
Mary Jane 57

CRUMBY
Mrs. 125

CULLEGE
W H. 267

CULVERSON
S. B. 238

CUMMINGS
W. L. 47

CUNNINGHAM
Isalinda 38

CROWLEY
Allen 14,206.250
B. 159,179,248
Benj. 206,227
Benjamin 14,23,161
Cynthia (colored) 159
Darcus 14
Edna (colored) 159
Ezekiel (colored) 160
Fannie E. 63
G. W. 159,160,206,248
George W. 160
Green (colored) 160
H. 159,306
Harris 14,206,248,306
Isaac (colored) 160
James 14,159,175,196,206,248,250
James, Jr. 196,223
Josiah 14
Nancy 14
S. 159
Seaborn 14,63,161,168,175,187,206,248,310
Sealey 14
Simon (colored) 160
Susan 14
W. V. 143
Washington 14
John 98
Shelvy John 98
Susy E. 105
T. G. 114
Thomas Gould 98

CUREINGTON
Joe 101

CURIER
Catherine 8

CURRIER
C. E. 88

H. L. 256

DABB
John 244,287

DABBS,
I. M. 188
John 275, 277

DABNEY
  Anderson B. 12
  Elizabeth 192
  Garland 11,12,163,192,270
  J. H. 77
  W. T. 163
  William G. 12
  William 8
DABO
  Sarah Ann 38

DABY
  W. R. 105

DADE
  T. M. 32

DAHLGREN
  J. A. 67

DAILEY
  T. B. 100
  J. B. 142
  John B. 43
  Leonard B. 142
  Pearl M. 142
  W. H. 113
  William H. 142

DAVIES
  Daisy 108
  M. M. 108

DAVIS

DANIEL
  B. L. 157
  Daniel Adams 213
  Dorey 4
  James 159,161,195
  James 195
  R. F. 200
  Thomas B. 262

DARNALL
  P. M. 219
  Thomas M. 219,265
  T. M. 290

DAUGHERTY
  Mary Ann 14

DAVES
  Joel T. 110
  Sophie W. 110,111

DAVICE
  Huldah J. 43

DAVID
  John L. 145

DAVIDSON
  Adeline 142
  J. K. 121,123
  Arminda 84
  D. J. 207
  J. N. 223
  E. A.
  25,46,47,224,225,227,232,234,236,238,
  248,249,252,263,267,268,275,287,304,
  309
  Eli 25
  J. E. A. 166
  J. C. 198,210
  J. J. 125
  James 21

Jane 4
Josephine 127
Lewis 158,279
Margaret 17,287
Mattie Walker 125
Meriam 29
Milton A. 104
Oscar 152
R. F. 166
Samuel 160,279
Susan 25
W. T. 39

DEAKEN
W. 162

DEAL
51,65
B. F. 187
S. E. A. 51

DEAM
Thomas M. 232

DEAMAN
James J. 157

DEAN
Elizabeth 47
H. G. 165,210,220,236,263,271,275
H. H. 199
L. 160,162,200,205,215
L. C. 151
Lemuel 171
S. H. 304
T. 254
T. J. 105
Thomas J. 25,26
Thomas M. 263

DEAVERS
R. M. 198

Thomas J. 29
W. W. 23
Warren 228

DAVISON
James 82

DAWS
Amanda 94

DAWSON
DEBELLE
Robert F. 98

DEERING
Gertrude P. 124
John R. 124

DEFOOR
Martha 12

DEGRAFF
Mayme Mourny 150
DEGRAFFENRIED
Eugene 153

DELAY
H. R. 245

DELOACH
Oveana 56
W. B. 90

DEMARAS
Sarah Ann 22

DEMPSEY
Georgia Hunnicutt 156

DENFORTH
John C. 214

DENHAM
Jack 121

DENK
Anna 154
August 154
Christian 154

DENNEY
Thomas S. 268

DENSON
Ella 130
Walker 133

DILLARD
Toliver 70

DIAMOND
G. W. 262
George W. 262
J. J. 207,220,232,264,270
James 270
James J. 207,236,262,263,288
T. J. 245
W. W. 23,288

DICK
W. H. 228

DICKEN
W. D. 235

DICKERSON
G. A. 247
J. W. 123
M. H. 123

DIGGS
Thomas 217

DILL
Kate Tichenor 92

DOAN
J. T. 228

DOANE
J. W. 289
J. A. 289
J. L. 228,259,261
J. T. 213,214,229,233,256
Jesse W. 201
Lucinda 1

DOBBS
J. 234

DILDA
Noah 36

DOBE
J. B. 217

DOBS
John 218

DOBSON
John 259,187,250,273
N. S., Mrs. 153

DOLLOR
Sarah A. 92

DONAHOO
A. B. 271
Abner B. 35
David H. 35
Virginia Jane Elizabeth 35

DONALSON
A. H. 91
Amanda A. 92

Cordelia 91
Donald 115,122
J. G. 91
Milla A. 91,92
Sadie J. 115,116,122
Silas 292
Thomas W. 91
William A. 91
William J. 91,92

DONALSON
A. B. 200
M. S. 301
Nuty L. 14
Silas M. 214
Geneva 14

DORKES
Anna Lizar 85

DORSEY
C. A. C. 39
H. A. 235,238,252
John M. 39
Lewis A. J. 309
Mary K. 39
Peyton S. 39
W. C. 283

DOSS
Asa M. 6
Azariah 281
George W. 6
J. A. 6
James M. 6
William Jasper 6

DOUGHERTY
Catherine 99

DOUGLAS
Marcella 41
Peyton 111

W. P. 286
W. J. 41,171,216,236,256
William J. 14

DONNELL
E. O. 48

DOOK
James 244

DOOLIN
A. 160,285

DOONAN
Virginia A. 111

DOWELL
W. A. 226

DOWMAN
Anna W. 102
Charles 102
Charles E. 102
Ellen 89

DOWNING
J. L. 224

DOWNS
S. T. 198,199

DOYAL
Mary 163

DOZIER
A. L. 189
A. T. 194,239
Allen T. 215
Susan 215,239
Thomas H. 239

DRAKE
Aney 79
B. 79,160
Bankston 79
Brack 279
Brackston 204
I. R. 79
Lula Hunnicutt 156

DRANE
J. T. 197

DUBOSE
Jesse B., Mrs. 61

DUGLASS
DUNESS
Mollie Lula 155

DUNLAP
J. V. 133

DUNWODY
C. A. 100
Cornelia Robson 135
Cornelia 135
Corrie Robson 135
Elizabeth 135
Ellen C. 96,100
George H. 96,100
Jefferson Davis 100,135
Julia 135
Kate Hester 135
Kate 135
Lessie 100
Mabel 135
Norwood 135
Roberta 135
W. G. 100

DURHAM
J. 244

J. 307

DULIN
Adison 194

DUNAHOO
Mrs. 200

DUNBAR
D. H. 49
James 50
John H. 50
Joseph 50

DUNCAN
David 235
J. W. 305
John 226
W. W. 37

DUSENBURY
George 294

EADS
Samuel 171
Thomas V. 200

EAKES
Grace 121

EARL
J. A. 84

ECHOLS
Samuel A. 54
Sarah E. 59
EDDLEMAN
A. M. 233,285
F. M. 199,210,214,233,302
H. F. 210
P. A. 145

EDERS

S. 238
Samuel 238

EDMONS
P. R. 234

EDWARDS
Andrew 56
Barnard 56
E. M. 211
Eliza P. 56
Eva 55
George M. 56
Jackson 56
Mary P. 56
Mary A. 190
Milton 56
Samuel 56
Sarah C. 55,56
Lena Stadel 112

ELFORD
E. G. 264
G. E. 205

ELLINGTON
Ben (colored) 259,294,310
Burrell (colored) 259,294,310
David 238,259,294
David B. 214,310
Friday (colored) 259
Jacob (colored) 259,294,310
P. B. 183
Salina 183,214,238,259,294,297,310
Wash (colored) 259,310

ELLIOTT
Andrew Adell 26
B. M. E., Jr. 131
Charles S. 74
Cicero C. 26
Franklin Pierce 26
George P. 75

Theodore 56

EIDSON
Boyce 41,42
Catharine 41
J. G. 41,42
Jane 41
Julia Almeda 41
Margaret C. 41
Mary Jane 41
Newton E. 41
Robert 41
Robert W. 41
Sarah Ann 41
William 41
Z. 285
Zachariah 41,236,265,301

ELBERTA
George Pressley 74
H. M. 59
J. M. 95
James 21,172,179
James O. 290
James Monroe 26
James S. 19,20,26,182,
192,201,226,227,230,234,236,237,252,257,
258,262,277,278,279,287,301,302,305,307,
309
Jesse Mercer 74
John C. 26
Joseph E. 26
J. S. 178,194,200,217,225,230,236,287,301
Levi Septimus 74
M. V. 277
Nancy C. 74
Nancy 26
Nancy V. 74
Toder Jane 74
William P. 26
ELLIS
A. E. 226,248,252,278
Augustus E. 20

E. P. 69
Ebenezer P. 55
Elizabeth 20
Henry (colored) 248
J. N. 145
James Lucian 20
James M. 203,212,231,260
Jane (colored) 248
John Calvin 20
Lula 145
M. T. 131
Mahala 20
Martha (colored) 248
Minnie L. 86
Paratine 20
Permelia 20
Polly Ann 20
R. M. 20
Rhoda (colored) 248
Sampson (colored) 248
W. D. 73
V.. E. 167
Virginia E. 255,258

EMINGER
John 174

EMMELL
P. J. 302

ENGLAND
G. M. 63
William 24

ENGLETT
Benjamin 217

ERVINS
John 304

ERWIN
Frank 142
Howell C. 142

W. P. 20
William H. 86

ELLISON
E. 235
Ralph 303

EMBRY
H. H. 169,225,252,288,303,306
Hiram 175
Hiram H. 194

EMERSON
Arnold (colored) 258
Ben (colored) 258
E. 190
Harriett (colored) 258
Lucinda (colored) 258
May (colored) 258
Mike (colored) 258
Stephen (colored) 258
Howell C., Jr. 142
Hugh Milton 142
Ophelia T. 142
Runa Patterson 142

ESCHEW
James 5

ESKEW
J. H. 244
Jincy 22

ESKINS
Richard H. 22
Thomas J. 22

ESTER
Allen 198

ESTES
Ira A. 92
J. C. 139

ETHERIDGE
Lewis 204
Paul S. 127

ETHRIDGE
Annie 96

EUDLIMENS
F. M. 261

EUGENE
M. T. 145

EVAN
J. T. 259

EVANS
 Dicy 27
 Florine 60
 Adelaid Louise 145
 Adelaide 66
 C. A. 145
 Cornelia Adelaide 66
 Edgar 66,145
 Elfrida 145
 George M. 66
 Henry 145
 Laurena 66
 Laurence 145
 Laurence, Jr. 145
 Lay 145
 Loy Hampton 66
 Mary Sue 66
 Susy 145

EVINS
 Craft 244
 Crawford 283
 J. R. 171
 J. L. 277,286,307
 James M. 220
 John L. 277
 John C. 12,163,244

J. M. 161
James 27
James F. 27
John L. 8,14
John 161
John F. 27
L. G. 129
Martha 94
N. P. 121
R. W. 130
R. D. 69
Reuben D. 27
Thomas C. 292
W. P. 121,123
William A. 27

EVERHART
Addia 145
Adelaid 145
Nancy Elliott 19
R. M. 187
Raddie 220
W. H. C. 271,290
William H. C. 19

EWEN
Calvin 198

EWING
F. M. 119
Nancy H. 119

EZZARD
Job 289
W. 193,196,203,205,212,218,239,245,251,257, 260,261,263,284,286,303
 William 9,12,25,31,173,174,179,194,203,211,212,213,214,230,231,232,236,260,261,283,224, 85,303

EZZARDS
William 211

FAIR
Eleanor 209
Thomas 283
W. 264

FANIN
Elizabeth Lucinda 38
Isalinda 38
John 38

FANLEY
Ella Kimbro 111

FANNIN
Jane 58
John 198,252,310,312

FANNING
M. C. 153
Nancy P. 26
Sarah 8,165

FARRER
Sarah 165

FARRIS
Ezekiel 162
James 220

FEE
Samuel 6
Thomas 217

FENDALL
Sarah Ann W. 26

FENN
Russell A. 162

F. D. 205

FARMER
E. B. 210
James 217
Joel A. 79
S. 1
Thomas W. 5
Waverly 115

FARR
Eleanor 264
Thomas 164,200,201,209,243,249,264,266,282,29

FARRAR
A. M. 165
Abner 8,165
Essie Tamora 77
John M. 77
Laura 8

FERBEY
Katie Sue 130

FERGUSON
Daniel 3
Elizabeth 3
Flora Jane 3
Nancy 3
William 3

FERRELL
J. W. 268

FERRY
G. W. 199

FIELD
Alonzo 148

FIELDER
C. P. 301

FIELDS
G. 199
FINCHER
Allison M. 131
Alonzo 131
Edgar F. 131
J. S. 40
Thomas H. 131
Thomas N. J. 131

FITZPATRICK
W. E., Mrs. 104

FLAKE
T. J.55, 95

FLANDERS
Elizabeth 106
Laura G. 106,107,137

FLEET
Isaac 186

John E. 152
John B. 191
Lamar 152
Lula B. 152
John F. 26
James A. 28
G. N. 26
W. J. 50
G. N. 42
George N. 152

FLOYD
D. S. 287
David 244
J. M. 120
L. E. 110
Mary Butler 110
Mary Butler 110
T. A. 66

FLEMING
J. M. 51
John A. W. 40,133
Mary N. 133
William A. 135

FLEMMING
A. F. 78

FLODING
W. E. 150

FLOWERS
A. P. 42
Arthur P. 152
Daisy 152
F. Y. 58
J. Y. 247,298,300
J. E. 131
John Y. 14,19,21,28,29,33,35,
171,172,179,180,186,191.195,200,201,
216,218,226,235,236,237,242,265,278,286,
290,291,292,298,305,306,307,309,310
John Z. 298

FOANS
Daniel 244

Fowler, J. W. 263

FONTAINE
Belle 149

FOOT
W. O. 80

FOOTE
Benjamin 162
Elizabeth 1

FOOTMAN
Isabel C. 145

FORD
A. 263,287
Charlie 114
Claud P. 114
Colman 176,193
Jesse Fernando 114
Mary 12
O. P. 114
Sarah 23
Virginia M. 114,137
William Terrell 12
William 12

FORMWALT
M. W. 175,198,228,302
Moses W. 11,175,233,256,303

FORSYTH
A. B. 165,168,184,185,208,242,306
H. G. 184

FORTRESS
R. B. 142

FOSSETT
A. W. 233
Elizabeth Emma 18
Frances E. 109
Gaspen 18
H. J. 188,229,246,259,304
Harriett 46
Harrison (colored) 229
Hilliard J. 18,35
Hilliard 67
J. M. 246,263,307,308
J. S. 67
J. H. 286
Joel 18,188,229,259,286
Joel M. 18,35,285
John W. 22,46,199
John L. 109
John F. 46
John W., Jr. 74

FOSTER
Joseph A. 283
Mary Jeffie 119
S. A. 56

FOWLER
A. S. 67
A. M. 188,259,286
A. C. 46,47
Adam (colored) 229
Alexander C. 109
Alfred S. 17,188
Alfred M. 18,35
Alfred S. 7,30,31,237
Amanda M. 35
Amanda 67
Catharine (colored) 229
D. Elener 47
D. Elmer 109
Drewry 229
Drury 18
E. A. 306
Elias S. 259
Elias 35
Eliza 18
John (colored) 229
John 18
John S. 122
Juliett 109
Juliette 109
Labonah A. 109
Maletos A. 109
Marcellus R. 109
Mary M. 35
Nancy 122
Reany 65
Richard (colored) 229
Royal J. 46
Sarah 18,35,259,286
Thomas A. 109
Thomas 18,229
W. W. 229

Thomas 18,229
W. W. 229
W. A. 229
William J. 18
William A. 109
William N. 35

FOX
Elen (colored) 271
J. 287
Jane (colored) 271
Joseph 199,263,271

FRANKLIN
David 8
James Samuel 3
Tabitha 8

FRANKS
Amanda M. 18
George 18,35
S. W. 259

FRANKY
Amanda M. 229

FRASER
Daniel 66
Mary Parks 87
Mary H. 156

FRAZER
E. H. 101
Elizabeth E. 183
George R. 183
George W. 171

FRECH
Rosa 154

FREEMAN
J. S. 107
Thomas T. 134

FRANCIS
Mary F. 67
William M. 67

FRANK
S. 238
Simeon 203

FRANKFORT
S. 233,268

FRONT
B. 162

FULBRIGHT
Mary 127

FULLER
E. J. 247
G. W. 247

FULTON
Pres. 285
President C. 261

FURLOW
C. W. 123
George E. 123
Georgia Ella 123

FUTRAL
L. E. 119

GAAR
J. H. 296
R. M. 247
R. W. 247

GALLOWAY
T. L. 82
V. A. 119

GALVESTON
John 41

GAN
Nancy 177

GANEY
James 167

GARBER
William 9

GARDNER
GARNER
A. A. 152
Irene 152
Said A. 152

GARR
B. W. 217
R. W. 312

GARRETT
E. 205
Margaret M. 80

GARRISON
Anna 304

GARTREE
Louisiana O. 16

GARVEY
Garvey, James 219,265,305

GASTON
J. M. T. 104

GATENS
Joseph 14

GAY
 Caroline Larendon 75

A. 41,200,256,286,307
Charles 285
James 33,205,227
Martha 41
N. E. 229,261
R. E. 233
R. 284

GARMAN
Calvin 162

GARMANY
Mrs. 22
 Charles A. 75
 F. H. 217
 H. C. 80
 Hayden C. 79
 John F. 79
 Rebecca E. 79
 W. F. 50
 Walter S. 75

GAZAWAY
Mary 122

GENN
Jeff 94

GENTRY
Henry 22

GEORGE
Ann 27
Benjamin F.35, 64,87,116
Gracia 141
Homer F. 102
J. E. 34,44,168,173,211,217,222,224,232,233 1.261,267,276,282,311
James R. 5,27,91,106,107,108,109
John H. 116
John 35
John R. 27,116

M. H. 102
Marshal H. 106
Mary 116
Mary A. 35
Mercer M. 27
T. P. 129
T. B. 25,244,267,286
Thomas T. 27
Tunstall B. 35
U. F. 44
Vashti P. 27
W. N. 129
William R. 116
William H. 27

GHOLSTON
E. A. 195
Elizabeth 164
G. C. 164,192,195
Gilbert C. 164
I. S. 170
Isaac S. 195
J. S. 195
Nancy J. 164
Nancy 195
W. D. 170,195,195
Z. 164,170,195
Zachariah 164,165,195,218

GIBBS
Charles E. 122,126
F. F. 257
H. W. 60
Henry (colored) 184
Jane (colored) 183,184
John Anderson (colored) 184
Laura Leila 111
Lubertha (colored) 183
Martha (colored) 184
Mary Ann (colored) 184
Nancy Jane (colored) 184
Samhan (colored) 183
Susan (colored) 184

Thomas H. (colored) 184
Van Buren (colored) 184
Washington (colored) 184
William (colored) 184

GIBSON
Alma Bayne 151
John 136
Joseph 89
Mary 151
Thomas H. 151,152
W. Bayne 152
William 31

GIDEON
Amanda (colored) 184
America (colored) 184
Caroline (colored) 184
Charles (colored) 183
Dennis (colored) 183
Eli (colored) 183
Eliza (colored) 184
Elizabeth (colored) 184
Francis 16,183
Francis (colored) 184
Georgeann (colored) 184
Harriet (colored) 183

GIFFENS
Rich 214

GILBERT
D. J. 175
J. 179,232
Joshua 175
Land 177,202,246
W. 219,221,243
William 219

GILBERTS
Joshua 261

GILDER

GILDER
Henry 167

GILES
A. C. 241,267
Alonzo C. 183,208

GILFILLAN
John 113

GILL
Ida M. 120
William C. 120

GILLESPIE
David 113
Ida A. 112,113
Henry 47
J. N. 287
J. 209
John 165,174,209,210
L. J. 233,256

GLENN
Charley 121
J. I. 283
John 204
Joshua N. 79

GLORE
J. R. 225

GLOVER
Henry W. B. 117
Lucy Cleborne 117

GLYNN
L., Mrs. 99

GOBER
Elizabeth 4
George W. 5

GILLIAM
R. T. 134

GILMER
Shastley 18

GIRARDEAU
William P. 70

GITTENS
Richard 31

GLEN
Eliza 165
Elizabeth 8
H. G. 303

J. H. 5
Milly G. 1
Thomas C. 1,5

GODARD
Zachariah H. 278

GODDARD
Clem 207
E. W. 106
Harriett Eliza 119
J. D. 152

GOFF
Robert C. 7

GOINS
John 285

GOLDBERRY
W. 204
William 12

GOLDSBERG
William 10

GOLDSMITH
A. J. 90,263,264,304
A. W. 187
A. J. 163,215
A. J. H. 304
Andrew J. 215
Charlotte (colored) 160
G. W. 304
G. W. T. 163,207
J. W. 162,236,245
James W. 232
Lewis (colored) 160
Lucretia 23,215
Mary J. 60
Sarah (colored) 160
Thomas 215
Turner 215
W. L. 35
W. 263
B. M. 218
Harris 28,259,275,297
Justus E. 277
Martha 109
Mary 28
S. 275,297
Sarah E. 9
Solomon 28,236,237,278,292
Solomon, Jr. 9
Solomon, Sr. 9
Starlin 262
Sterling 201,235
W. F. 238
William 28

GOODY
Narcissa J. 12
William G. 12

GOOGER
Googer, M. D. 106,125
Marcus D. 151

GOOLSLEY

William 160,162,214,215,264,268,304

GOLITLE
Sara Ann 136

GOODALL
Sol 302

GOODE
C. C. 126

GOODEWIN
H. 300

GOODMAN
S. C. 110

GOODWIN
A. H., Mrs. 109
Sarah E. 123

GOOSE
J. T. 110

GORDON
Andrew 33
Eleanor 19
Fannie H. 98
Fanny 98
Frank 98
Hugh H. 98
J. D. 63
J. M. 235
John 19,85
John B. 98

Martha 33

GORTS
Henry 233
GOSS
J. H. 112

GOWER
Annie Lee 130
Harry 130
Luther J. 130
Mary Bell 130
Robert Lee 130
Sarah Frances 130

GOZA
A. 247
Aaron 35,36
B. 247
Bird 235
Elizabeth 35
John 36,235
Leannah 35
M. E. 35
R. D. Ferdeinand 36

GOZER
Ezekiel Reeve Bird 245

GRAHAM
Amanda 36
Douglas (colored) 187
E. A. 130
F. A. 155
James 36
John Austin 36
Josiah 36
Josiah Thomas 36
Judd (colored) 187
R. (colored) 187
Rebecca 36
Stephen (colored) 187
W. H. 207,236,244,262
William 36
William H. 187

GRAND
J. C. 217

GRANT

Ed L. 68
Edgar 68
Ella G. 68
G. W. 199
Irby H. 68
Irby 68
John 68
Martha Eliza 68
Susan Eliza 68
Thomas P. 55
Walter 68

GRAY
J. R. 73
Richard 283

GRAYHAM
William H. 288

GRAVES
Mary C. 26
Parthenia 26

GREEN
A. H. 258,285
Alston H. 213,231,260,284,303
C. C. 213,217,231,232,261,304
C., Mrs. 213
C. 244
C. G. 216
Caroline E. 304
Clement C. 173,213,231,303
Cordelia E. 211,232,261,284
Cynthiana 213
D. 162
Daniel (colored) 173,214,232
Elijah W. 70
Eliza (colored) 284
Eliza (colored) 211,232,304
Emeline (colored) 211,261,284,304
H. 32
Horace (colored) 211,232,261,304

J. W. 125
J. Howell 125,142
Jacob (colored) 173
James T. W. Sr. 73
James 296
Julia Ann (colored) 232,284,304
Juliann (colored) 211
Marietta 30,174,214
Matilda (colored) 173,214
Miles (colored) 211,261,284,304
Mrs. 173
Richard (colored) 211,261
Richmond (colored) 232,284
Sarah Frances 124
Tom (colored) 173,214
W. A. 261,303
William A. 173,213,232,261,284
William Henry 124

GREENE
Alston H. 174
Cordelia E. 174
Eliza (colored) 174
GRIER
H. M. 201
R. D. 297,300
Robert D. 299
W. S. 300
W. L. 204

GRIFFIN
Alexander 186,272
Alexr 249
David 185,250,272
Elizabeth 60,78
Francis 12,180,208
Hez. 208
Hezekiah 12
James M. 82
Leroy 186,206
Margaret 272
Margaret E. 185,249
Narcissa G. 185,249,272

Horace (colored) 174
Julia Ann (colored) 174
Miles (colored) 174
Richard (colored) 174

GREER
H. M. 286,287
Josiah 159,218,250,256,273
R. D. 234,271,275,302
R. I. 171

GREGG
A. H. 223

GREGORY
B. 198
Nancy S. 96
Rebecca S. 96

GRESHAM
Edward 188
Elizabeth 34
W. 247
Susan 185,250,271
Suzana 12
Thomas 184,185,186,206,249,250,271,272
William 85
WilliamW. 47
Z. 208
Zepeniah 12

GRISHAM
Davis E. 8
J. 235
J. W. 235
Jo 259
Josiah 217,300
S. W. 201
S. W. 293
Silas 244,293
W. C. 217,244,283
W. 235

GRIVER
Lilly 56

GROGAN
Garland 197
Henry 5
Lucy 5
Nelly 5
Richard 5
Thomas 220
Thomas 5, 6
W. S. 235,259
W. 235.293
William 5

GROVES
Ann E. 211

GUDE
Valdeman 126

GUESS
Andrew White 119
Carl N. 155
E. H. 119,120
Parthena E. 58

GUSHANFER
W. C. 247

GUY
F. H. 217

HAAS
Aaron 81
J. 232,257
Jacob 214,232,238,265

HACKETT
James S. 6
W. R. 237

HADAWAY

Green 246
James 200,201,220,277
Robert E. Lee 119
Thomas R. 71
Thomas 205

GUIN
Joel A. 199

GULLEGE
H. 230

GUMER
E. A. 157

GUNBY
George 199

GUNTER
Helen M. 58
James B. 291
James 201,259
M. A., Mrs. 121
Marshal E. 291
P. E., Mrs. 121
Milledge Lee 110
W. P. 110

HADDEN
Elizabeth 69
J. N. 244,302
William 279,289

HAFLEY
Mr. 126

HAID
Herbert 124

HAIRSTEN
A. M. 194

HAIRSTON

HAIRSTON
A. M. 62
Albert M. 11,31,50
Amanda C. 266
Amanda 207
Amanda C. 11
Arminda A. 11
Clementine 207
Emanda C. 240
Lavinia F. 11
Lillie T. 240
Lucinda 11
Martha A. E. 11
Matilda C. 11
Miles 50
Toliver 207
Toliver Little 11
W. R. 165
W. M. 63
William R. 11
William 50,102,165,207,240,266

HAISTINGS
Isaac A. 281
Isaac 280

HALL
James 182
John 264
Joseph 161

HAMBY
A. C. 34
Atty H. 286

HAMILTON
Ada I. 90
Adelaide 153
C. K. 160
E. P. 140
G. R. 195
G. K. 167,

A. W. 285
Eugenia Herbert 66
Frank W. 87,88
Jake 131
L. C., Mrs. 87
Martha 118
Mary Cornelia 66
Orville H. 88
T. W. J. 236
Thomas F. 25,241

HALLMAN
Addie F. 73
John C. 73
John F. 73
Marcellus B. 73

HALLS
A. W. 214

HAMBRICK
Caroline E. 63
Elizabeth 10,166
I. W. 74
Isaac F. 63
Isaac E. 70
J. M. 31,161
James M. 221
187,199,204,215,217,227,253,263,293
George K. 23,26,34,175,254,306
Ida 153
J. W. 254
J. L. 34,294,208,215,220,232,254,263,293
J. C. 93
J. T. 90
James L. 305
Jane 153
John L. 23,26,48,174,263,304
John C. 103
Martha 4
Mary C. 48
T. K. 220
W. H. 44

HAMMOND
A. W. 204
Florida Floyd 110
George H. 66, 108

HAMPTON
Loy 66
Mary J. 107

HANBETER
C. R. 196

HANCOCK
Sarah 1

HANDSMAN
Pauline J. 133

HANES
Mary E. 62

HANEY
Elizabeth 22
Gertrude Elizabeth 22

HANKS
William 149

HARALSON
C. A. 170, 171
Cam 244
Charles (colored) 170
Fanny (colored) 170
Harriett (colored) 170
Hugh A. 98
John (colored) 170
Jordan (colored) 170
Julia (colored) 170
Mary B. 171
Matilda (colored) 170
Narcissus (colored) 170
Paul A. 170, 121, 177, 248

HANLEN
Joanna 48

HANLESTER
C. R. 257

HANLEY
Cornelus 48

HANLON
Cornelius 48
Hanorah 48
Johannah M. 48
John Jeremiah 48
Julia 48
Mary Ann 48
Owen 48

HANNADA
Hannada, Nancy A. 29
Hannada, N. A. 29

HANNAH
P. Pearl 131

HANSLETER
C. R. 264
C. H. 303

R. A. 177
S. Jane 177
Susan (colored) 177

HARBERT
High 77
Ida 77

HARDAGE
D. C. 77

HARDAMAN
Eugene, Sr. 126

HARDIN
J. R. 113
N. J. 145

HARDMAN
Allen 187,188,209
B. F. 158,274
E. C. 174,200,201,275
Enel 259
F. V. 188
F. N. 200,252
H. L. 128,152
John 262,275
Martha P. 158,168,274

R. I. 168,188,244,274, 275,278
Remick I. 168
Rena I. 158
Syntha 274
W. T. 187

HARGERS
Elizabeth 12

HARGINS
Elizabeth 208

HARGROVES
James 292

HARMAN
H. C. 263
H. G. 76
Hazel 151
Henry R. 150
J. C. 197,220
J. F. 137
J. C. Evins 163
John C. 190,254,255,266,281,476
L. W. 137
Lucins L. 150
Lula N. 150
Mary F. 137

Bessie N. 95
Charles E. 96
S. M. 32
S. 247
Sarah 300

HARPER
Clary Ann 83
J. F. 156
J. J. 83
John J. 30
Lula 86
Mary J. 123
W. C. M. 226

HARRELL
L. B. 167

HARRILL
C. 228

HARRIS
A. C. 294
Benton Neal 150
C. P. 257
Claborn 216
E. C. 165,210,257,293
E. T. 247

Edmund T. 28
Ezekiel C. 293,306
Mary 2
Nathan 187
Oliver M. 53
Overton 214
R. C. 127
Robert H. 150
Robert 1
Theo 304
W. E. 149
West 294
William 263
Willis B. 39

HARRISON
D. 56
Jackson 278
John T. 97
Maria C. 89
Z. D. 56

HART
Jesse Burtz 51
Laura 56
Nancy 51
Robert H. 51
Williai Riley 51

HARTLEY
J. M. 135

HARTSFIELD
Lucinda 30

HARTSON
Betty 3
Levin 3

HARVEY
E. L. 196

HARVILLE
N. G. 175

HASKETT
Jewell W. 142
Thomas 199

HAWS
Littleton 11
S. 300

HAYDEN
I. A. 174
J. A. 159,198,203,209,210
James 186

HASLETT
Samuel D. 232

HASSEL
Mary Ann 31

HATCH
W. M. 223

HATCHER
Harvey 124
J. F. 141,142
L. E. 68
Leo E. 141

HATCHESON
Texie Ann 131

HAULEY
W. L. 145

HAWKINS
A. 244
Elizabeth 125
J. M. 70,198
John M. 161
John 23, 220,229,244,287
John M. 166,187
Valera Ann 38

HAWLEY

P. 259

HAYES
Charles 132
Loretta J. 91
W. 261

HAYGOOD
J. G. B. 233,285,290,302
William B. 84

J. G. B. 233,285,290,302
William B. 84

HAYNE
J. A. 233

HAYNES
Andrew 59,147
Augustus 189
Harriett (colored) 210
J. N. 147
Judith Ann 15
Levi (colored) 210
R. 196
Reubin 177,189,190,209,210,238
Thomas 210

HAYNIE
John F. 71
Sarah 71

HAYS
Ann H. 11
John 11

HAZDEN
J. A. 16

HEAD
James 12
R. G. 142
William G. 162

HEARD
John 162

HENDREE
C. P. 56

HENDRICK
O. 167

HENDRIX

W. G. 237

HEARDMAN
J. A. 244

HEARN
C. C. 275

HEFLIN
Leander 275

HELMS
J. 262
R. F. 146

HENDERSON
Agatha S. 71
George B. 47
Greenville 29,36,214,245,248
John F. 126
Josiah 238
M. A. 29
Major 244
Nancy 36
R. H. 297
Rufus 230,242,243,253,295,297
Sarah A. 80
Thomas 267
W. G. 201,235,244,247
W. N. 47,139
W. 226

HENDON
G. M. 31

Clarence 112
Emma 112

HENDRY
Thomas C. 264

HENEY
Joseph 276

HENKINS
H. B. 138

HENRY
Eleanor 108
Gertrude T. 108
H. T. 285
Harriet G. 152
Henry Clara D. 108
Henry 6,7
Hugh T. 108
J. 235
J. F. 290
James R. 236
John T. 157
John 7,162,182,244
Joseph S. 216
M. B. 187,190,236
Mary Lacy 108
W. T. 154

HERONTON
W. S. 39

HERRING
Joel 166,167
W. 232,276,284
William 232

HERRINTON
W. S. 44

HERRONTON
William S. 48

HESS
Daniel 104
Paschal H. 30
Stephen 60,61
T. J. 143
Thomas J. 143
Thomas Jefferson 143

Kate 104
Philemon 104

HESTER
R. O. 105

HICKEY
E. T. 97

HICKS
D. Y. 45
Mary 136
R. B. 33

HIGAN
Joel C. 278

HIGGINS
Josiah 217
J. N. 214
Reuben 3

HIGHT
Emmett 112
James L. 112

HIGHTOWER
Albert Sidney 143
Allen R. 143
Debby 60
Georgia H. 143
Harrison H. 143
J. B. 143
John Bedney 143
Margaret P. 30
Mary 143
Milton H. 143

HILBURN
Martha H. A. 207
Martha H. 175
N. G. 175

HILDABRAN

Malinda C. E.1 297
Van Burin L. 297
William 297

HILDERBRAND
W. 209
William 241, 264

HILL
  Benjamin B. 3
  C. 283
  H. M. 104
  Lucinda 203
  M. M. 196
  Samuel B. 3
  Samuel 183
  T. 244
  T. W. 167, 230, 235
  Thomas W. J. 236, 248, 252, 304
  Thomas W. P. 236
  V. M. 267
  W. 221
  W. M. 230, 233, 239, 305
  W. B. 264
  W. N. 267
  William B. 182
  William M. 212

HILLARD
  Levi 229

HINESLY
  A. H. 156
HINSON
  Seleta 12

HISAN
  Joel 278

  Mary Jane 4
  Robert W. 4
  Samuel 78
  Sarah Caroline

HITCHCOCK
  R. E. 291
  S. C. 93
  Samuel C. 93

HITCHUM
  N. G. 207

HITMELBURGER
  John 99
  Minnie 99

HOCKENS
  J. M. 206

HODGE
  P. M. 193

HODGES
  Solomon 311

HODGSON
  Fred G. 115

HOLBROOK
  H. C. 128
  J. A. 59
  Nathan 16

HOLCOMB
  Alder 148

HOLCOMBE
  Elizabeth Ann 4
  Eva 78
  H. C. 243
  James Richison 4
  John, Sr. 5
  Mary J. 78
  Susan 4
  William H. 79

HOLDABRAM

William 176

HOLDER
Ed, Mrs. 151
HOLES
E. L. 99

HOLLAND
E. W. 199
E. M. 138
Margaret Ann 15

HOLLEY
H. H. 147
J. M. 18,165,193
James M. 274
Sarah 211

HOLLINGSWORTH
Alisey 46
Berry 34
Charlotte 46
Emily 46
Henry 194
J. T. 73
Thomas 23

HOLMES
H. 205,236,263,264
J. C. 210
John 264
Lora Ella 101,103
Mary E. 121
Sam 121

HOLMS
H. 263
HOLSTON
Elizabeth A. 192

HOLT
G. W. 199
J. H. 79

J. H. 46
James M. 46
John N. 46
John 46
John A. 46
Lee 140
Mary E. 47
R. 179,280,306
Rebecca J. 46
Robert 29,285
Robert H. 53
Sally 46
Sarah Ann Caroline 86
Sarah A. C. 29
Sarah 46
Thomas 46
W. H. 60
Williamson 54

HOLLINSWORTH
Aaron 217
Robert 198

HOLLY
R. J. 141

HOLTCLAW
Eutoka 98
Ida Bell 98
Margaret Caroline 98

HOMBRECKE
Horton 278

HOMBUCKEL
H. H. 267

HONOUR
Ida T. 85

HOOPER
M. H. 59

HOPKINS
G. H. 220
G. F. 63
T. T. 119

HORN
Stephen 186

HORNE
Charles 4
Mary A. 62
Nelly 5
Paschal 163
Philip 43,252,275
S. 298
Samuel 43,172,297,309
T. J. 58
Thomas J. 43
W. 277
W. P. 78,140
William 5

HOUSER
John 200

HOUSTON
Amanda K. 111
Anna 111
Anna Louisa E. 111
Appolonius Bahon 111
Appolonius 111
Charles W. 111
John Chapman 111
John C. 111
O. 239,302
Tyler Peeples 111
W. J. 61,87,102,111,114,160
Washington J. 111

Dr. 228,259
Eli W. 27
George S. 27

HORTON
W. C. 132

HOUSE
C. H. 135
Elizabeth 43
Gazel 43
George 275
Jacob G. 43

HOUT
Hout, S. B. 205,239,283

HOWARD
A. W. 51
A. W., Jr. 69
A. H. 34
Asa W. 20,40
E. 288
Edmond 288
Edward 169,192,222,288
Edward, Jr. 222
John 259
Moses 166
S. 170
W. H. 144

HOWELL
Clark 239
G. A. 81
G. M. 89
George M. 89
James 89
Oby 89
Thomas 277

HOYLE
A. H. 27

Margaret Ann 17
P. F. 24,198
P. R.

P. F. 24,198
P. R. 188,198,207,211,214,216,220,222,223,224, 226,228, 230,231,244,251.252,267,277,282,283,286, 287,294,295,297,300.307
T. R. 24,27

HOYT
G. B. 228,263,286,287
Samuel B. 192

HUBBARD
Elisha 2
Oliver 2

HUDGINS
B. L. 306
J. H. 115
L. 296
Leroy 36,296
Mattie M. 142
W. T. 115

HUDSON
Charles M. 59
Forrest P. 59
George B. 47,59
George G. 59
J. M. 296
J. J. 130
James D. 59
John L. 59
Margaret 27
Pliny E. 59
S. P. 167
Sarah Evaline 59
Sarah E. 59
T. P. 263
W. G. 126
William T. 59

HUEY
A. L. 247
C. M. 233
Charles 190
E. B. 50
Ellen (colored) 280
Hannah (colored) 280
Harrison (colored) 280
James M. 30
John 161
Joseph M. 53
Joseph, Jr. 234
Joseph 201,244
Joseph S. 187,190,233
Lucinda (colored) 280,306
Lucy 233
Manervy (colored) 280
Marian (colored) 280
Morning 280
Mourning 306
Mrs. 190
Patsey(colored) 280
Phillips (colored) 280
Sampson (colored) 280
Sarah G. 53
Thomas 234

HUFF
John T. 217

HUGH
P. H. 259
P. F. 165

HUGHES
L. J. 54
Nuttey 2
W. E. 135

HUGHS
Isaac L. 309

HULSER
Charlotte 20

Aaron G. 10
Addie S. 45
Charlotte 303
Dicey 166
Dicy 10
E. J. 166
Eli 10,176
Eli J. 10
J. J. 90,225,289,308
Jennings 10,266,308
Jennings J. 45
Jimmers 166
Jinnie L. 218
Jinnings J. 225
M. C. 10.
S. A. 225,289,308
Sarah E. 10,218
Seleta E. 218,266
Seletia E. 225
Senna A. 225
Serene A. 218,266
Susan A. 10
W. M. 218,242,245,266
William M. 10
William 176

HUMPHREYS
Laura Ann 136
Nat 136

HUMPHRIES
C. 257,271
Chamer 221
Charles 258
Charles 169
David 130
G. W. 200
G. L. 301
George W. 14,217,258
George M. 182
George 172,258,261
Harriett 130
Isaac 11

J. R. 236,259,279,305
Jiles 259
John R. 42,156,206,236,269,301
John D. 156
M. 214,228
Mary M. 11
Merrell 226,234,244,267,283,286,300
Mr. 1
N. H. 267
N. H. 286

HUNEY
C. Q. 99

HUNNICUTT
George F. 156
Lydia J. 156
Martha Emily 156
Thomas P. 156
Wilbur L. 156

HUNT
W. H. 230
William H. 165

HUNTER
Hunter, W. F. 244
Hunter, James 44,58,99

HUSE
W. P. 116

HUSON
M. A. 32

HUSTON
W. J. 94
Washington J. 111

HUTCHENS
N. L. 264

HUTCHING

HUTCHIN
N. L. 199,205,232,251,304

HUTCHINS
A. G. 262
Harris 274
J. M. 278
John P. 287
W. 269

HUTCHISON
Leander 93
Leroy A. 93

HUTSON
G. B. 161

IMMELL
P. J. 302

INGE
C. 247
Charles 259
Martha 295

IRBY
Fernando S. 144
H. 214,238,278
Henry 243,259,278,283
James 123
Laura G. 144

IRELAND
James 16

IRWIN
D. 237
David 197
J. R. 119

ISHAM
John 266
W. W. 266

ISOM
John 171
W. W. 249

IVEY
H. P. 303,313
Hardy 303
James L. 251
Jane 303
John J. 303
S. W. 181
Sarah 303
William T. 181,251

IVY
H. T. 213
H. 176,251
H. P. 203
Hardy 173,182,203,212,231,260,283
Henry 173,212,231
J. L. 203
J. O. 260
J. N. 203
J. Morgan 235
James A. 176
James L. 212
John L. 260
John 212
M. T. 217
M. J. 203,260,303
Mary 217
Michael 173
Michael J. 212,231
Mrs. 198
O. W. F. 233
Richard N. 182,203,212,260
S. W. 203
S. T. 231
Samuel 173,260

S. T. 231
Samuel 173,260
Sarah 173,203,212,231,260,283
W. F. 231,278
William L. 168,203
William 173
William F. 176

JACKSON
A. 287
Amanda 86
Andrew 294
Ann 36
B. W. 193
Carl Sherwood 150
D. E. 290
D. C. 12
Daniel E. 36
Dicy 41
Efford 141
G. T. 215
H. B. 274
Helen Ruth 150
Hiram 113
J. R. 70
John 86
Lee H. 141
Littleton G. 25
M. H. 199
Queen Terrell 141
R. M. 85
Sarah Ann 118
Stewart 141
T. J. 67
Thomas J. 36,87
Thomas C. 87,140
Thomas 86
W. J. 236
W. 193,244
W. E. 215,264
William 139,267
William A. 141
William J. 25

W. T. 203,212,260
W. L. 260
W. S. 263
William T. 182,203,213,251
Willis 227

JAMES
Josiah 49
Thomas 184

JARDINE
Gordon F. 154
Lillie 154
Ruth 154

JARRELL
Kate 150

JEFFARES
Bennett Wiley 121
John N. W. 121

JEFFERIES
John E. 4

JENKINS
George W. 124
J. A. 139

JENNINGS
B. S. 206,248
Jenning M. C. 10

JERDINE
Gordon 154
William 154

JETT
Burch 9,262
J. S. 247
James S. 277
James S. 28
John 21,201,305

JETTER
A. F. 232
I. M. 143

JOHNSON
A. 167,168,179,191,194,196,197,199,200,201, 203,205,206,207,208,209,210,218,221,222, 223,225,230,232,233,236,238,239,241,243, 246,250,257,258,263,273,281,282,287,296, 299,302,304,305,3 306
A. S. 79
A. E. 313
Aber 268
Abner 204,205,208,209,239
Alex 192,193,196,198,206,208,215,217,226,228, 231,232,233,235,237,238,243,253.255
Alexander 163,165.166.167,169,170
Alexr 218,219,221,222,223,224,227,230, 240,241,242,243,245,246,248,249,250, 251,252,254,255,256,257,259,261,262,263, 264,266,267,268, 270,271,272,273,274,275,276,278,279,280, 281,284,286,288,290, 291,293,294,295,296,297,298,301,303,304, 307,308,309,
Alpheus (colored) 307
Andrew 174,217,232,304
Ann (colored) 268
Anna Elizabeth 76
Annie L. 111
Archibald 19
Archibald G. 90
Ava Ann 21
B. A. 244
B. M. 225
Bluford (colored) 234
Bob (colored) 234
C. W. 205,236
Charlotte 18

J. I. 98
John B. 12,192,271

JOHNS
C. A. 244
Daniel 19,42
David J. 26
David S. 258
Dice (colored) 234
Dority Andrews 19
Dr. 173
E. E. 82
Edward 111
Elizabeth 19
F. L. 130
Fincher (colored) 234
Florence 113
G. W. 205
G. E. 175
G. L. 106,116,147
G. 17,179,229
George W. 21,23,113
George (colored) 234
Henry (colored) 268
I. A. 80
I. J. 90
J. L. 45,113,143
J. H. 60
J. J., Rev. 90
J. H. 93,239
J. F. 228,233
J. G. 200,214,252,274
J. N. 113
J. 244
James 189,278
James A. W. 26
Jane 23
John (colored) 234
John C. 85

John B. 270
John 4,19,275
John W. 85,276
Johnson L. 307
Julius C. 155,156
Kier (colored) 234
Kitty (colored) 234
Martha A. 155
Martha Jane 129
Mary (colored) 234
Mary 19,148
Mat (colored) 307
N. 244
Nancy Ann Permeathea 76
Nannie 151
Nat (colored) 234
Paul E. 109,156
Peter (colored) 170
R. E. 197
Robert A. 305
Robert W. 139
Ruth 19
S. A. H. 266
S. E. H. 266
Sam (colored) 234
Sam (colored) 307
Sarah E. 139
Sarry J. 76
Senn (colored) 234
Shelton 162
Sol (colored) 268
Solomon 18,259
Thomas 23,158,160,162,174,205,215,220,232,233,263,27,304,305
Thomas (colored) 234
Thomas D. 201
Ursley (colored) 234
Vashtin P. 113
Very 39
W. 232,264
W. D. 301
W. W. 90

L. G. 201
L. A. 148
Lachlin 18,26
Ludocia 59
Luke 21,268
Luke 268
M. M. 235
W. M. 204
W. C. 199
W. T. 214
W. P. 214,238,271
W. S. 139
Washington 252
Wiley 244
William M. 237
William S. 27,55
William 23,174,197,232,234,263,304

JOHNSTON
J. F. 201,256,259,271,286
Jackson F. 19,271
John F. 271
Lewis (colored) 271
Nancy 22
Naomi 19,309
Nat (colored) 271
Neoma 301,302
S. C. 271,309
S. F. 171
W. P. 252,271,277,297
W. 214,238,252,300
W. T. 214
W. B. 294
Washington P. 19,297
William 19,201,275,297

JOHNSTONE
Mary F. 108

JOICE
Alexander 182,192
Alexr 227,278

Charles (colored) 217,301
D. 261
Darcus (colored) 226,252
George (colored) 217,301
Harrison (colored) 226,252,289,306
J. M. 289,306
James 194
James M. 178,226,252
Nerve (colored) 217
Betsey Ann 51
Clem 150
Robert 283

JONES
A. C. 233,283
A. K. 102,109
Albert 309
Ann B. 52
Arthur 153
B. O. 228,233,256
C. M. 227,300,305
Catherine E. 102
Clara M. 124
D. W. 83
E. L. 123
Edward G. 153
Edward 7,23.24.311
Edward G., Jr. 153
F. M. 102
F. W. 83
Francis Andrew 151
Frank L. 153
H. C. 44,102,114,118
Henry C. 52
High 123
J. J. 159
J. A. 102
J. F. 102
J. Q. 102
J. C. 102
J. R. 102
James G. B. 215
John 23,189,259,302,311
Robert 182,192,226
Sarah 182,217,225,258,279,301

JOLLEY
Jesse 302
Robert 244
W. 244

JOLLY
John W. 230,311
John W., Dr. 52
John B. 52
John H. 2,268,298
Joseph 219
Josina 309
Julia A. 144
L. E. 268
L. M. 137
L. H. 39,55
Liser A. 43
M. T. 102
Marion 309
Martha (colored) 311
Martin 23
Mary Taylor 137
Mary Caroline 38
Mary 52
Mary Ann 43
Milley (colored) 311
N. C. 58
Nancy 1
Nancy E. 92
O. H. 228,228
Oliver 228,269
P. E. 102
R. 267
R. W. 311
Ranney (colored) 311
Richard W. 23
Robert 12,23,186,197,198,215,220,226,230,2336,311
S. L. 102

12,23,186,197,198,215,220,226,230,233,306,311
S. L. 102
Sarah 309
Seaborn 309,311
Stewart D. 120
T. T. 69
Thomas H. 199
Thomas 275
Virginia Stuart 137
W. S. 303
E. D. 147
Elijah B. 29
F. M. 199
H. C. 115
Jesse 29,30
S. E. 236,302.305
Solomon E 29
W. 198,240,265
William I. 29
William 241

JOYCE
James M. 4
Nancy 4
Robert 4
Sarah 4
Thomas A. 4

JUHAN
D. B. 288
F. P. 225

JUNCKEL
Frances 127

JUSTIN
W. T. 107

KACH
Fred 144
Marguerite 144
KAMISEY

W. C. 126
W. H. 15
W. B. 210
W. G. 201
Y. R. 202,213,298
Z. R. 228,285

JORDAN
A. A. 236
A. R. 199

Charles J. 98

KAY
A. E. 136
W. 190,211,223,292

KEAN
John T. 262
Robert T. 189

KEEN
Mrs. 125

KEES
F. P. H. A. 57

KEHELEY
J. W. 49

KELLEY
Jennins, Mrs. 86
W. J. 220

KELLY
B. G. 264
Hiram J. 234
James 132,133
Janette 132
Nico 279
R. A. 87
R. J. 103
W. J. 233,235

KEMP
M. M. 165

KENDRICK
C. A., Mrs. 153
Clara 153

KENNADAY
T. A. 302
Thomas 306

KENNEDY
Julia Pratt 126
T. A. 243,250,265
Thomas A. 172,181,197,199,251
Thomas 189
W. A. 306

KENT
Alexander Sr. 134
Alexander Jr. 134
Clement F. 134
Edgar Ross 134
Harry W. 134
Thomas S. 134

KERFROT
F. A. 92

KERS
Caroline 54

KEY
George W. 281
George 56,57,176,218,251,269,288,294
James L. 151
Mary J. J. 56
Sarah J. 9
Thomas T. 251
W. 196,257
W. B. 281,294
William B. 57

James Maud George F. 153
John F. 153
Louise 58
W. S. 153

KEYER
Louise 58

KEYS
C. G. 51
J. B. 279
Lewis A. 124
Margaret C. 124

KIDDOO
Elizabeth Ann 26\

KILBEY
W. J. 306

KILBY
W. J. 241

KILE
A. B. 203
John 19,177
O. G. 301,304
T. 203,302
Thomas 168,213,294
W. 302

KILES
T. 256

KILGORE
Daniel C. 78
James L. 78
John 59
P. A., Mrs. 78
Savannah 78

KILL
E. Z. 288

KILLEY
Sanford 161

KILPATRICK
J., Mrs. 210
J. D. 122
Mary Jane 16
W. 210
W. J. 245
William J. 16,186

KIRKPATRICK
Ann 17,241
Elizabeth Anna 87
F. M. 228
H. B. 228
H. T. 228
H. P. 228,313
Hugh P. 17
J. H. 193
J. W. 61,76,98,99,168,198,220,227,228,230
James H. 17,168,228,241,265,313
James W. 12,17,87,228,265,313,241,
James M. 87
James A. 188
John C. 87,100
John L. 17
Lizzie A. 156
Mary A. 100
Mattie Flowers 87
Morgan 224
T. M. 228
Thomas 313
Thomas S. 87
Thomas M. 17
Thomas Parks 87
W. 302
W. N. 228,309
Wallace M. 87

KIMBRO
B. F. 57,58
John R. 57
Joseph M. 57
Mary F. 57
Virginia A. 111

KING
J. T. 129
James D. 114
L. A., Mrs. 81
M. P. 81
Mary Jane 114
Matilda 279
Rebecca Ann 114
Wallace 156
William N. 17

KITTREDGE
Edward M. 142,143
Eliza 142
Emma 142

KITTRIDGE
Amos A. 128
Ed M. 38
Em. M. 105
Watson 38,152

KNAPP
Beulah G. 140

KNIGHT
A. B. 8
W. 286

KNOW
Carlos 84

KNOX
Allen 11
Frances J. 11
J. S. 302

Joseph S. 10,183,197
Sam 151

KURTZ
Ernest C. 104

LAC
J. B. 255

LACUENT
Ann 34

LACY
Jesse 235

LAKE
R. G. 204

LAMBERT
J. T. 31

LANCASTER
C. M. 128

LANDRUM
John W. 105
Mary P. 105
Will T. 105

LANE
Clifton E., Mrs. 150
Joseph 144
Joseph W. 112
Maria Louisa 118
O. R. 118
Owen Randolf 118
Sarah Emiline 35
W. G. 69,74

LANG
David C. 119
Francis 9
J. W. 167
Mary 151

LALLERSTEDT
Martha 72
T. L. 72

LALVNEY
J. N. 264

LAMAR
John 306
Nathan 20

LAMB
Albert 136
B. F. 175
Fannie R. 136
Pat 136
S. B. 50

LANGLEY
T. L. 235
T. T. 201
Thomas T. 235
W. J. 150

LANGSHORE
David 204

LANGSTON
Mark I. 247
W. J. 246,279

LANIER
John 275
W. P. 285

LANK
A. 162
Abe 101
B. 229
Howe P. 77
Savanah 101
T. G. 278

W. P. 115,151
Will 101

LARENDON
Charles A. 75
G. 75
Josh 75
Mary Elizabeth 137
W. M. 75
Walter S. 75,137,138

LATHER
Jonathan 19

LATIMER
Charles 225,242

H. B. 163,210,260
Harriet (colored) 163
LEAVELL
J. A. 143

LEDBETTER
Bular 123
Buhlar 123

LEE
  D. 205,220,232,236,254
  Drewry 163,271
  Fitzhugh 122
  G. W. 208,215
  H. W. 236
  H. 122
  H. R. 109
  James J. 43
  John 17
  M. H. 220
  Milton Brown 163
  Samuel T. 17
  W. H. 205,230,232,254
  W. 264
  William 153

Henry B. 210
Levi (colored) 163

LAW
Anney G. 98
Fred B. 151

LAWSHA
E. 223
L. 199
Lewis 232

LAYTON
J. M. 207

LEACH
Leach, Ann (colored) 235
Leach, Anderson (colored) 235

LEETSON
Daniel E. 37

LEFTWICH
J. M. 46,47
James M. 47
M. P. 47
R. S. 47
R. M. 47
Sarah J. 47
Sarah Jane 47

LEICH
  Arthur 190
  Ben (colored) 190
  Donald (colored) 190
  Harriet (colored) 190
  Leantha (colored) 190
  Linda (colored) 190
  Stephen (colored) 190

LEITCH
A. 266
A. B. 281

Andrew B. 254
Arthur 230,254,255,266,292
James 230
Lemmond, D. 100
S. A. 281
Sarah A. 281
Sarah Ann 230,254,255,266,281,292
Susanah T. 255
W. N. 281
William N. 254

LEMON
James 4
John 4
Mary 4,9
Robert 4

LENARD
Mrs. 86

LEONARD
J. F. 199
James F. 171,248

LESLIE
William 154

LETSON
L. H. 139

LEVEL
J. W. 244,245,247

LEVERETT
Buckner 255
Burrell 255
Cealy 239
John 255
Marthy Frances 134
Mary Elizabeth 134

LICHINSTADT
W. L. 26
Margaret M. P. 26

LIDDELL
Dr. 302
F. M. 195
Freeman Hardy 22
Harriet Susan 22
John C. 77
Laura Amanda 22
Mary 22
Mary Isabella Jane 22
Moses 22,23
Moses Franklin 22
N. S. 258,260,298,301,307
Newton Stiles, 22, 23
Sealey 255
Simeon E. 134
Telithia 239
Tilethea 255
W. F. 166

LEWIS
Carrie 98
G. E. 136
George E. 136
Lee F., Mrs. 151
Mollie 121
Ulysses 108

LIDE
B. A. 96
David R. 96
J. W. 96
Maggie A. 96
Mary Allston 96
Mary A. 96
Samuel W. 96
Sarah Jane 96

LIETCH
J. G. 125

LILLEY
F. W. 295

LIN
R. M. 168

LINCH
Thomas 264

LINDSEY
Addie L. 127
Cullin 231
Francis 18
G. C. 146

LINLY
M. C. 225

LISLEY
Duncan 274

LITTLE
Benj. 219
Harvey 6
Lucinda 6
Mary Ann 6

LIVELY
Charles 1
Elizabeth Ann 1
J. C. 249
Judith Matilda 1
M. C. 27
M. O. 295
Mary 1
W. W. 70,114

LIVESAY
James M. 59
R. T. 59

LIVESEY
C. 244

LOCK
Talitha 69

LOCKHEART
J. D. 304

LODER
G. L. 141

LOFTIN
W. T. 303

LOFTON
Hannah R. 37
J. B. 160
James B. 37

LONG
C. D. 128
D. L. 128
F. C. 128
J. R. 115
Lora Jane 115
M. B. 128
Mollie 128
P. M. 128
Paul F. 128
W. B. 128

LONGFELLOW
J. L. 149

LORD
A. 200
J. M. 201,235,298
Jabez 238,259,298
Jabez M. 5
M. W. 219
P. M. 295

LOVE
John 259
R. M. 233
S. B. 233
LOVEJOY
J. H. 249,250
John H. 289

LOVELESS
Ebenezer 195
William 163

LOVELY
Polly M.

LOWE
Jesse 230

LOWERS
L. 160

LOWERY
J. H. 135

Ben (colored) 167
Harriet (colored) 167
John B. 167
Lacie L. 115
Leantha (colored) 167
Sidney (colored) 167
Stephen (colored) 167
W. D. 285

LUMER
Lumer, N. 229
Lumer, Nathan 18,237

LYNCH
John 14
Patrick 14
Thomas 204,233,275

LOWRY
James 275

LOYD
Charles M. 62
J. B. 140
J. M. 28
J. M. C. 62
Jabez M. 62
James 179
James E. B. 62
John M. 85
Samuel P. 62
Susan A. 62
James 167

LUCK
A. M., Mrs. 109
J. B. 157,258
John B. 167,190,258
W. D. 211

LUCKIE
A. 283
Arnold (colored) 167
LYON
J. L. 245
James 7
Rezin 16,210,245
Thomas A. 213
Thomas J. 7,296

LYONS
Martha A. 49

MABLE
Elizabeth 126
M. I. 126

MADDOX
George W. 65
J. 275
J. P. 65

J. C. 225
John R. 57
M. D. 155
M. C. 24
Margaret 309
Pendley 275
W. D. 86
W. N. 136

MADISON
Indiana M., Mrs. 61

MAGEE
M. 197
Marat 11,16

MAGIN
Narat 216

MAHAFFEE
J. R. 161

MAHAFFEY
Carter 3

MALLETT
John O. 260
Malinda 211,303
Miles M. 48
Mrs. 173,303
Peter (colored) 173,211,231,303
S. D. 170
Samuel A. F. 260,284
Samuel A. 170
Samuel F. A. 173,303
Samuel A. T. 211
Samuel.T. A. 231
William J. 185,192

MANNING
Jethro W. 33
W. L. 200

Lula 153

MALONEY
George 72
Joseph 72

MANCELEY
Mattie 136
Raymond 136

MANEY
Thomas A. 135

MANGUM
Mary 7
N. 197,199
R. F. 232
R. E. 180,196,213,223,249
William S. 8
William 7

MANN
B. B. 152
J. A. O. 191
John A. O. 169,170

MANRY
W. F. 103

MAPPIN
J. W. 167
James W. 161,219
Thomas W. 161,167,219

MARBUT
J. K. 114
Job J. 53
John P. 53
Mary I. 53
Michael 21
Susan 53

MARKHAM
Markham, W. 196,212,228

MARLORO
Nancy 301

MARTIN
Abraham 27,37
Algernon 148
Ambrey 75
Aubrey 6
B. Z. 189,220
Benjamin S. 33
Gabriel 292
J. G. 200,233
J. S. 256
J. D. 292
James D. 167
John 167
Joseph 258
Margaret 33
Martha 33
Mary J. 33
Nancy 74
Nancy T. 33
Neomy 33
Parthenia J. 71
Reubin 189
Mary Jane 84,85
Samuel C. 46,55,84
Samuel 85
Samuel W. 84
Washington 85
William G. 84

MATHERSON
W. 232,304

MATHEWS
Francis C. 77
George W. 95
George 24
Louisiana 19

S. C. 54
Samuel C. 42
Sarah 33
Semanthey 33
Sopha C. 33
Stephen 33
William S. 33

MASON
E. 165,168,220
E. H. 74,86,99,109,114,122,125,134,138,147,1
E. N. 108
Ezekiel 188
Frank 145
J. C. 109,112
J. T. 267
J. A. 62
Mary Amanda 21
Miles 48
W. D. 187
W. 275
William 161

MASTERS
Amanda Ellen 85
Henry T. 85
John G. 84
Suzaney 24
Thomas 189

MATTHEWS
Julia Jane 95
Annie 95
George W. 55,69
Henry 77
Henry J. 77
Johnny 69
T. J. 85
Virgil C. 95

MATTOX
H. J. 72

MAULDIN
Drewry M. 225
Drewry 40

MAULDIN
Will 103

MAULDING
Drewry 279
Hudie 89
D. 279

MAXEY
John G. 215
J. C. 205

MAY
Edith K. 133
Ethel 133
F. W. 204
Marion 133
N. Florence 133

MAYER
B. F. 274
M D. 304

MAYES
MCALPIN
Alex 251
F. T. 163,168,236
F. L. 167
Floyd T. 167
J. M. 208
James M. 183

MCARTHURS
W. W. 306

MCAULEY

John 46

MAYHEW
Cecilia A. 132

MAYFIELD
A. J. 78

MAYSON
F. J., Mrs. 80
J. W. 86
J. R. 293

MCAFEE
W. M. 171,210
William M. 158,159

MCALEXANDER
J. R. 255

MCALISTER
E. 286
J. R. 198
J. R. 61,159,165,198,200,207,226,298,308
James R. 195,122

MCALLISTER
J. R. 166,186,216,218
James R. 166,198
John 170

W. A. 49

MCBRYAN
S. 207

MCCALLA
W. E. 91,107

MCCALPIN
Sarah 251

MCCAW

W. 201

MCCLAIN
E. 296
J. W. 302
W. S. 248,269
William S. 38

MCCLELLAN
Marianne 105

MCCLELLAND
L. F. 112

MCCLENDON
William 295

MCCLINTOCK
Martin 133

MCMALCOM
Malcom 264

MCCLOYD
M. 197

MCCOMMONS
H. 82

MCCOOK
A. T. 197

MCCORD
J. D. 147
J. A. 138
J. Steve 123
J. W. 110
J. S. 81,120
J. DeWit 130
J. Augustus 151
James 19
John W. 57,86,89,106
Marie P. 106

E. F. 201
James F. 244
Mark J. 103
Mr. 288

MCCRARY
Andrew 31
T. B. 163,214

MCCRAY
Eli 256

MCCUE
Margaret 270

MCCULLOCK
David H. 25
James W. 25
John 25
M. 177
Margaret 25
Solphiah 25

MCCURDY
Angus Alexander 19
Archibald 19
C. H. 208
C. H., Mrs. 163
D. H. 199
Delia A. 156
Douglas Nash 129
E. C. H., Mrs. 235
J. A. 137
Marietta 129
Rachel 19
Robert 208
W. R. 128
W. T. 120
W. S. 110,154

MCCUTCHEN
W. W. 306

MCDANIEL
Ira O. 9,10

MCDONALD
C. H. 274
Henry J. 16
I. 198
J. O. 256
J. 256,283
James 300,305
John 16,274
Joseph W. 217
M. C. 187
Martha Jane 16
Nancy Elsnetta 16
Parmascus 217,274
Philip E. 189
Sary Elizabeth 16
Thomas J. 217
W. C. J. 274
William Jackson 16

MCDOWELL
L. T. 131

MCDUFFEE
D. 219
W. 274

MCDUFFELL
W. 246

MCDUFFIE
Malcomb 269
Neal 269
C. M. 220
C. W. 7,17,23,159,165,167,168,179,186,187,195,197,198,205,212,219,220,227,229,230,231,233,236,239,248,253,257,259,265,280,305,311

MCELREATH
Walter 127

MCELROY
A. J. 54
Archibald 54
I. N. 54
J. N. 86,102
John 29,35,179,237,238,258,270,278,308
Nancy 217,226,259,278
Nancy M. 236
S. B. 247
Samuel 310
W. 172,226

MCEVER
Joseph D. 2
J. D. 8
William 2

MCFAIL
V. E. 80

MCFELL
O. 228

MCGAHEE
A. J. 110

MCGAHEE
John W. 106

MCGINNIS
C. B. 106

E. W. 213
I. O. 186
J. L. 199,274

MCGIRTH
John J. 105

MCGRADY
Jane T. 1
Sarah M. 27

MCGRANN
Joe Julin 127

MCGUINNS
C. W. 197

MCGUIRE
J. E. 48

MCKEE
A. A. 28
Charles (colored) 179
D. M. 142
Elizabeth Jane 71
Elizabeth 178
George M. 84
J. J. 178
John Ross 86
M. C. 69
Madison C. 54,84
Martin C. 54,55
Mary R. 54
Mary Ann 54
Samuel 84
Sarah E. 84
W. W. 95
W. M. 264
Wilkan 42
William W. 84
William 179
Z. T. 54

MCKOY
Andrew (colored) 223,261,282,298
Charles (colored) 223,261,282,298,309
Elizabeth 203
Henry (colored) 224
J. J. 276,307
John J. 251

John 214
Louisa 224
Martin 301
Milley (colored) 223
Moss (colored) 223,298
Peep (colored) 224
Polley (colored) 261
Polly (colored) 223,282,309
Rhelta (colored) 261
Ritta (colored) 223,282,298,309

MCLAIN
James 25

MCLENDON
James S. 93
Martha E. 93

MCLEOD
Angus M. 43

MCKINNEY
Charles D. 119,154,156
Charles S. 149
Delila 97
M. M. 146
W. 199
W. 210,223,282,298
William 221,261,309
W. C. 142

MCLINDON
Clark 29
Judah 29

MCMANORS
Carrie 123

MCMASTER
Martha 85
Martin 85
Margaret Elizabeth 85

MCCESSINS
John 311

MCMICHAN
John 275
John J. 188

MCMILLAN
R. L. 90

MCMILLER
W. L. 251

MCMULLEN
Charles Young 151

MCMURTY
W. 237

MCNAIR
Harriet E. 29

MCNEAL
Fleta Annie 146
Mary Lizzie 146
Mollie May 146

MCNEIL
Leanna 58

MCNEILL
Daniel 25,38,226
Nancy B. 25

MCNIGHT
Aid 58
Nancy 58

W. P. 247

MEADOR
Casander 106

MCREYNOLDS
Fred A. 117

MCSHAFFENY
Daniel 14

MCVEY
Bruce 149
Gladys 149
Juanita Lucile 149

MCWILLIAM
Robert 57

MCWILLIAMS
A. 24
Alexander 22,34
David 34
Harriet 22
J. 269
J. O. 89
J. G. 57,298
John 34,269
John G. 34
Josephine Margaret 71
Polly 68
R. 297,306
R. M. 57
R. 29,30
Robert 34,42,176,209,241,264
S. 219,229,306
Samuel 22,28,34,296

MEACHAM
J. H. 77

MEAD
H. 264
J. H. 305
Polly 23
W. T. 10

MEADOW

Ann H. 196
Margaret Ann H. 192

MEADOWS
Margaret Ann H. 15

MEANS
Means, J. S. 228
Means, John S. 228

MEDLOCK
John W. 13
Robert 45
T. L. D. 194
Thomas M. D. 217

MELL
B. J. 80

MERRITT
Maggie E. 146

METLOCK
Susan 128

MEYEFEE
W. P. 219

MICHELS
Jamma (colored) 270
W. 270

MIDDLE
Grover C. 144

MIDDLEBROOKS
W. M. 85
MIDDLETON
Ida B. Haig 126
William Green 126

James A. 28,115,310
Jasper H. 76,186,265,285

MILAM
H. M. 88

MILES
John E. 82

MILL
M. W. 235

MILLER
A. B. 76
Aaron B. 76
Andrew 241
Andrew P. 285
Andrew J. 53
Andrew 270
Annie C. 52
Aubrey 270
Burt O. 52
Chamberlain 264
D. G. 75
David G. 131
E. Payson 56
Ebenezer 76\
Edner L. 97
Elizabeth 97
Ella C. 115
Frank H. 52
G. E. 152
G. S. F. 97
George H. 115
George E. 97
H. G. 97
H. G. M. 97
H. G. H. 97
Israel 189,234,236,265,285
J. D. 115
J. D., Mrs. 115
J. L. 97
J. W. 97
J. M. 97
John W. 28,51,80,275
Katie 136

L. A. J. 296
Luther D. 76
Mabel C. 115
Malissa 56
Margaret 236,265,285
Mark 236
Martha Irene 147
Martha B. 53
Missouri 94
N. R. 76,265,285
Nancy Jane 97
Nancy A. 115
Nancy E. 51,115
Newton 189
Rebecca A. 76
Robert 51
Roxie D. 76
Sarah Veda 147
T. W. 29
T. C. 145
W. G. 123
W. 189
W. A. 97
William W. 136
William 6,136
William A. 115

MILLS
John 287

MILNER
R. W. 79,95

MILNETT
R. W. 149

MIMS
Az. 281
Azariah 17,188,189,250,281

MINER
G. W. 31
S. T. W. 213

MINOR
Lavonia 110
M. H. 238

MIRANDON
Elizabeth 31

MISBET
William 24

MITCHEL
D. J. 270
J. W. 55
John W. 162
Mary A. 9
McDonald 266

MITCHELL
A. D. 106
A. M. 65
A. G. W. 246
A. W. 228
Ava Marian 6
B. G. 65
D. J. 293
Daniel 79
Daniel J. 245,246
Daniel Jackson 6
Dolly Ann 6
E. G. 106
Elizabeth 6
Eugene 150
Eugene M. 107,124
G. W. 246
George Washington 6
George T. F. 37
Gordon F. 107,124
Green Cleveland 6
Henry 106
Irene 6
J. G. 217
J. B. 102

J. L. 246
J. W. 132,278,302
J. E. 246
James Wesley 6
Jane 2
John Allison 6
John W. 7
Joseph 79
L. M. 72
Larkin W. 24
Leangle Hershel 6
Louisa E. 24
Louisa 6
Lucy 2
Lugenia A. 79
M. 196
Margaret Jane 79
Mary 66
McDaniels 225
Nancy 79
Norman Parker 79
Rebecca 6,65
Sarah W. 15
Susie 113
Synthia 6
Thomas H. 257
W. W. 179
W. D. 217
Wesley 45,235
Westley 226
William H. 76
William J. 65
William Jasper 6
William W. 27
William 6,245,293
Winaford 6

MOBLEY
A. 186
Harry 156
Isaiah 186
Ruby 156
Wicksbury 248

MONDAY
E. W. 274
Ed 238
E. W. 214,274

MONDY
E. W. 168

MONROE
Joseph Fennel 3

MONTGOMERY
Alford 287
Charles H. 257
Harriet M. 3
Hugh B. T. 210
J. F. 293
James Floyd 3
James F. 160,165,210,241,257,306
James M. 3
Rhadamanthus 3
Sarah A. 26
Tarleman Farlow 3
W. R. 306

MOON
Thomas 247

MOONEY
J. J. 152

MOORE
A. M. 267,276,282,307
Ann 288,305
Arthur E. 124
Fanny (colored) 269
H. D. 83,92
Isaac 260
J. D. 83,92
J. W. 122
J. T. 133
James 269,288,293,306

James J. 128
John 269,305
John W. 103
Jonathan 305
Louise Harris 150
M. H. 307
Martha C. 43
Mary (colored) 269
Nancy Ann S. E. 43
O. R. 139
Octave V. 92
Sarah Ann 124
Thomas E. 269
Thomas 212,255,288,305
W. C. 64

MOOREHEAD
James 305

MORGAN
A. J. 58,284
Ann 2
Asa 277
Asa 162
Benjamin F. 92
Benjamin 2,92
C. A. 137
Caroline 137
Elijah 2
Eliza Catharine 80
F. B. 80
G. 201,234,235,236,265,285,293
Garet L. 92
Garrett T. 2
George A. 69
George Washington 2
Gideon 32,186,189,236,2865,285
Henry B. 60
I. W. 189
J. L. S. 166
J. H. 111
J. A. 95
J. L. S. 231

John, Jr. 269
John D. 124
J. 230
J. W. 285
J. M. 193
J. E. 265
James R. 69
James D. 83
James B. 2
James 7
Jane 17
Jane N. 241
Jarret L. 268
Joel E. 32,236,285
Joel 189
John A. 92
John F. 80
John W. 2
John 2
John B. 2,46
John M. 7
Joseph 2,17,193,200
Joseph G. 32
Kendley N. 20
Kenley S. 6
L. 235
L. S. 11,165,201,230,235,259,287
L. L. 188
Laura A. 32
M. R. 284
Mary J. 32
Mary 32
Mathew 197

MORRIS
Nancy 7
Nancy 268
Nancy E. 92
Newton S. 32
O. S. 217,133,262,294
Obadiah S. 224,262,294
Phillis Margaret 137
Polly 2

R. N. 247
S. P. 244
S. 230
S. B. 267
W. F. 215
William L.
William F. 2

MORRISON
D. 76
J. J. 98
John 217

MORROW
H. 76

MORTON
Thomas C. 244

MOSELEY
Emma 46
Lou A. 46
W. 22

MOSELY
Miles 301, 305

MOSS
Nicholas A. 33
P. S. 112

MOTTOCKS
Thomas 300

MOURY
David 149
Leiota M. 149

MOZLEY
H. 76

MOUNCH
Augusta 154

Salathial 307
Sarah H. 92
Seph 278
V. S. 141

MUGR
A. M. 238

MULDIN
M. D. 259

MULLICAN
Berry 244

MUNDAY
E. M. 259
J. W. 152
Joseph E. 128

MURELL
G. W. H. 304

MURPHEY
Andrew 221
C. 1,20,25,34,178,203,204,221,222,223,226,232,236,261,296,306,307
Charles (colored) 221
Col. 226
Milley 221
Morse 221
Polly 221
Ritter (colored) 221

MURPHY
C. 11,34,179,200,210,248,249,251,264,276-8,282
Charles 250
Charles 214
William (colored) 178
Milly (colored) 178
Ritter (colored) 179
Sally (colored) 179

M. W. 83

MURRAY
A. G. 196,204,205
Archie G. 124
Cecil R. 124
MYERS
Lawrence 304

MYRES
A. S. 175

NAILOR
Nailor, Stephen 205

NAPIER
George 148
George M. 148

NASH
Arabella M. 26
Arthur 235
Bertha Ellen 120
Elizabeth Frances 132
Emmer L. 115
I. N. 81,100,129.130
Indiana 129
J. P. 96
J. I. 120
John 174,235
L. T. Y. 79
Lois 110
Mary K. 110
Reuben 26
T. T. 134
T. J. 116
T. Y. 97,129
Tandy Y. 110
W. R. 112
William R. 32

NASWOOD
Elizabeth 2

George C. 124
George F. W. 124
Imogene 124
Mabel Davis 124
Marjorie M. 124

NEEL
W. S. 49

NELMS
Lillie Lee 146

NELSON
A. 162,213,232,244,313
Allison 174,194
J. 232
Mrs. 261
W. 232

NESBIT
Eli Hoyle 27
Eliza 251
Elizabeth H. 27
John W. 27
Louisa 66
Lula L. 115
Mary 135
Mrs. 284
Sarah 211
W. 236
Willis 228

NESBITT
William 170

NEW
L. M. 270
William 278

NEWMAN
Mattie t. 94

NEWTON
C. F. 271
J. M. 271

NICHOLS
James 161

NICKELS
James 1

NINSON
Martha A. 157

NIX
B. O. 268

NORCROSS
J. 168,196,214,257,259,262,272,275,294,296

NORMAN
Alvea P. 81
Gideon T. 81
Hugh 311
James M. 81,82
John G. 81
Louise 81
Mary P. 81,82
W. L. 215

NORTHCUT
J. J. 257
J. F. 214

NORTHEN
E. A. 114

NORTON
S. B. 133
G. 179
L. B. 110,114,121,123
L. J. 59

NUCHELS
Nannie 156

NUSOM
Nancy 2

NUTTING
James R. 133

OGILBY
Ann 196,209,238,268
Beckey (colored) 189
Caroline (colored) 189
Cloah (colored) 190
Dick (colored) 189
Ellie (colored) 190
James (colored) 190
Jane (colored) 190
Jiney (colored) 189
John (colored) 189,190
Joseph 232
Louisa (colored) 190
Lucinda (colored) 190
M. E. 189
Matilda (colored) 189
Molley (colored) 190
P. 189
Shadrick (colored) 189
T., Mrs. 189,192,302
T. S. 196,256
Thurza 189
W. 189
William (colored) 190

OGILLEY
Ann 186

OGILLY
Asa 15
Frank 15
Martha 15
William E. 15

OGILSBY
Ann 295
T. S., Mrs. 228

OGLEBY
W. E. 295
Young B., Dr. 52,53

OLIVE
Young B., Dr., 52,53

OLIVER
Andrew (colored) 211
Howell C. 299
John 214
John S. 211,223

OLOFTON
Jane B. 20

ONER
William 204

ORME
W. P. 304

ORR
A. M. 285
J. M. 287

OSBURN
John 244

OUSLEY
N. B. 91

OVERBY
B. H. 16,268
Benj. 217
B. H. 16

OVERSTREET
J. C. 143

OWEN
W. R. 288

OWENS
Benjamin 55
Fannie 56
Joseph S. 147
Lillie F. 111
M. T., Mrs. 147
Mrs. 125
S. L. 146
S. C. 100
W. B. 103,147,269
William D. 104
William Jr. 37

OZMER
Elizabeth 65
J. W. 50
R. C. 79

OZUIER
J. W. 140
John N. 140
R. C. 140
William A. 140

O'BRIEN
L. A. 118

O'SHIELDS
Adaline 72
Catharine 72
Charles 72

PACE
C. D. 211
J. M. 126
S. K.
201,205,206,238,239,240,273,299,308
Solomon K. 273

PADEN
Alex D. 237
James 30,31,233,243,275
Jane 30
John 30,300
Lettice 30
Thomas M. 31
Thomas N. 30,31

PAGE
C. D. 285
John N. 262
Solomon K. 181

PAGETT
Anna 81

PAINE
C. H. 127

PALINEX
W. P. 293

PALMER
Thomas I. 54
Violia 54
W. J. 235,295,310
W. 265
William J. 24
William 18

PANEL
Thomas A. 35

PARK
Frances R. 51
J. H. 296
J. W. 97
John G. 143
Russell 51,65

PARKER
A. C. 103

Anna Eliza 37
Billings Washington 37
Celia 26
D. M. 46
David 1
Elizabeth Gresham 1
G. W. 103,217
H. C. 103
Isaiah P. 25,26
J. 264
James 1,163
John 30,38,194,246,274
John W. 170
John G. 193
John H. 38
John C. 1
Joseph Gresham 1
Kesiah 150
Lizzie 141
Lucy 117
Margaret Ann
Mary 170,193,246,274
Mary Jane 34,143,144
Mary Jane Graham 1
Mrs. 125
Nancy A. 25
R. S. 50
Robert 1
Robert L. 37
Robert G. 34
Sarah Graham 1
Sarah F. 38
W. F. 103

PARKS
A. H. 245
H. 245
Lloyd B., Mrs. 145
W. R. 89
William A. 178

PARR
C. D. 196,296
L. J. 212
Lewis J. 213
P. 210

PARRAMORE
Martha Kipp 119

PARRY
Harvey L. 116,122
Jessie Grinnell 116

PARSONS

PATEY
Miles 164

PATILLO
John 269
John I. 47
W. F. 56
Weyman 137

PATTERSON
B. B. 140
D. C. 111
J. H. 154
Roy E. 143

PATILLO
J. W. 72
Ruth 105
W. F. 46,108
Wayne 125

PAXON
Angeline 81

PAYNE
C. M. 292
Edwin 9,158,159

E. 190
John 228

PARTON
W. B. 264

PASCHAL
Harry M. 149

PATE
John N. 310
J. T. 116,129
J. T. 106
Lila 110
John N. 24,37
H. V. 87
W. H. 83

PAYTON
Leonard C. 76
Martn N. 76
Melvin C. 76
R. 247
Randolph 76,220
Serena E. 76
Thomas C. 76
William P. 76

PEACOCK
Avey 177,199
Avy 168
D. W. 199
D. P. 193
D. M. 168
DE. W. 198
J. G. 169
J. T. 168,198
James T. 168,193
L. P. 168,169,198
L. 199
Lewis 177,193
M. J. 199
Moses (colored) 177

Ophelia 56
P. A. 181,199,243,250
Thomas J. 177,199

PEARCE
Eliza Ann 46
G. J. 46
James 264
John W. 46
Lena 152
W. D. 152

PEAT
Irwin L. 72

PEAVY
W. R. 45
Emma F. 107
P. 49

PENCE
Ada 122
Josephine 122
Nellie Lee 122

PENDEN
Penden, W. H. 248

PENDLEY
W. R. 233,268,272

PENN
S. 237

PENNELL
Jonathan 275
Richard 235,295

PENNILL
Pennill, R. 201

PEOPLES
H. T. 229

PECK
J. B. 304

PEED
Eugenia 155
M. T., Mrs. 155
Virginia 155

PEEK
H. H. 289

PEEPLES
Henry C. 133

PELHAM
E. F. 49

PERE
A. H. 300

PERKERSON
Dempsey 45
Thomas J. 45

PERKINS
Berry 240
Berry C. 38
Eva Allen 113
James A. 38
Martha Ann 38
Martha Elizabeth 38
Reuben B. 5,38,168
William Eugene 113
William T. 38

PERKINSON
T. J. 198
Thomas J. 232

PERRY
A. C. 81
Alice W. 132

Alice Patrick 132
Charles Henry Mayhew 132
G. O. 81
Grace E. 120
H. L. 98
Helen Frances 132
John James P. 132
William G. 120

PERRYMAN
G. L. M. 167
G. M. T. 197

PETAWAY
Darcus Jane 57

PETERS
Richard 174

James L. 64
Nelson 217
Paschal C. 64
Pierce R. 64

PHILLIPS
C. W. 115
D. P. 151,154
D. T. 133
Edwin L. 48
Frank P. 106
G. M. 279
James 40
James J. 48
Joseph J. 116
Mary S. 106
Rebecca M. 21
Rebecca J. 116
Sarah 40
Susan B. 95
Thomas J. 106,107

PHINEGER
Benjamin 149

PETTEY
A. J. 217

PETTIS
H. 210
Harison 232

PHILIP
J. M. 296

PHILIPS
A. 264
Crawford 64,66
D. P. 114,149
G. M. 262,271,272,279,295
George M. 285
J. M. 10,166
J. R. 202,239

PHINIZY
Hamilton 155

PIERCE
Elizabeth 66
John W. 153,154
John W. Jr. 153
Marie Elizabeth 153
William 153

PILGRAM
G. A. 196,210

PINNELL
G. W. 111

PITTARD
Elijah 174
J. T. 131
Myrick B. 130
Sarah E. 130

PITTMAN

D. N. 163
N. 131

PITTS
A. L. 57,103,228,269,290,295,312
Ann A. 42
Anna 4
Augustus L. 24,42,102
Frances M. 42
H. 214
H. F. 295
J. R. 310
J. 306
John R. 42
Joseph 42,188
Mary 102

PLASTER
B. 198,259
Benjamin 3,4
Edwin 4,186,178,254,274
Piety 4
Sally 3

PLUNKET
W. M. 73

PLUNKETT
J. W. 300
W. 257

POLK
J. H. 275
James Knox 15
James H. 33
James 43,45,49

POLLARD
D. 224
J. C. 221

PONTS
W. A. C. 28

Wesley H. 27
William G. 277
William N. 295

POOL
A. G. H. 309
A. J. 269
A. J. H. 27,300
Az. H. 300
J. L. 300
J. H. 28
J. M. 27
J. J. 205
W. A. 235
W. Y. 309

POOLE
Julia L. 309
S. P. H. 309
W. Y. 298
William Z. 298
William Y. 299,300

POPE
Ruth Candler 146

PORTER
Patrick 4

POSS
Emeline 54

POSSEY
Camote 95
G. W. 95
George W. 95
Mildred 95
S. D., Mrs. 95

POTTS
Alexander 47
Avia 34

Avis 33
John Hl. 51
Martin E. 51
Mary A. 51
S. 296
Samuel J. 51
Samuel 20,33,51,248,275,295,296

POUND
J. W. 88
John 55
Sylvester 55

POUNDS
D. I. 115
J. C. 81
James C. 86
R. D. 205,235
Sylvester 152
W. M. 163

POWELL
C. 168,196,200,230,252,252
Samuel 162
W. S. 84,112
William S. 75

POWERS
James C. 31
Sal 200
Sylvester 48

PRATER
Fannie E. 116
Guy S. 146
Lula 146
Martha E. 146

PRATHER
S. M. 72

PRATT
Fannie L. 126,127

Chapman 197,234
Charles 217
Edward 305
Eliniah 299
Elkenneth 299
Erban 168
Ervin 244
J. L. 74,94,118
James 309
John A. 217
S. 187
W. A.
159,166,168,163,179,187,195,203,211,214,
222,224,230,231,233,235,236,251,252,261,
262,275,276,282,284,289,295,297,298,301,
303,306,309,
Wilbur S. 133

POWER
A. H. 312
James 162
John 162
Joseph S. 96
Nathaniel P. 126

PREWELL
S. 235

PRICE
James 270

PRICARD
W. H. 204

PRICHET
J. 264

PRIMROSE
Primrose, Lucy 282

PRITCHARD
Mary Ann E. 29
Silas 29

PRITCHETT
L. A., Mrs. 78
Moses 127
Nancy 69
PROSSER
Douglas 111
Roberta Douglas 111
Robert O. 111

PRUDEN
N. E. 219

PRUITT
Julia E. 129
N. P. 129
Palmer 129

PUCKETT
D. 217
E. 263
J. W. 96

PULLIAM
A. 264
RAGAN
C. J. 40
Dr. 229
J. H. 204,225,275
James H. 24
James J. 40
James 161
Jane 24
Josiah H. 24
Talitha C. 40
Thomas 219
W. N. 296
W. 229,269

RAGSDALE
B. 285
Bartow D. 48
Berry 289,312

R. L. 261
Thomas 61

PURCELL
C. W. 59
C. 59
E. S. 59
J. C. 59
James 48
Jarrett C., Sr. 59
Laura M. 59
Mary 59
R. R. 59

QUILLIAN
Fletcher A. 63
George R. 63,64
Harwell P. 63,64
James R. 68
Samuel 138
William F. 63,64

QUINN
James M. 105

Bertie C. 90
Eugenia 48
J. B. 125
J. T. 125
John C. 37,45,48
L. A. 72
Louise 90
M. C. 125
Minerva 49
Nancy 48
O. L. 125
Oscar 150
W. M. 62
William 105

RAILEY
Charles 19

RAINEY
B. 305
Bennett 2,26,189,225,244
Beverly (colored) 194,252
Burdine 28
C. 235
Charles 21,305liza (colored) 252
Eliza (colored) 194,252
F. (colored) 194
James 292
Joe (colored) 252
John 5,194,226,227
John G. 247,259,267,286
Mary E. 61
Pararode 182
Paraside 252
Prasade 305
Rebecca 21,305
Sarah 194,252
T. B. 244

RAIRDON
Thomas 149\

RAMEY
John G. 194

RANKIN
Charles A. 75
John C. 104

RANSON
Annie 146

RANSPESS
R. W. 112

RAWLINS
N. N. 303

RAY
James 244
John P. 46

RAMSPECK
G. A. 102
George A. 61,100
Ida 62
Margaret M. 100
R. W. 114,118
R. C. W. 134
Robert W. 122
Theodore R. 62

RANDALL
R. H. 71

RANDLE
J. R. 306

RANER
Sarah 289

RANEY
Austin (colored) 279
Charles 279
Esther (colored) 279
Henry (colored) 279
Jane (colored) 279
Sealy (colored) 279

S. 244
S. B. 287

RAYNEY
Beverly (colored) 289
Eliza (colored) 289
Parasade 289

REA
Andrew J. 16
Richard 16,28
S. B. 259
Sarah Elizabeth S. 28

READ
Ruban 123

REAGAN
Susan Isabel 155

REAGEN
W. J. 139

REAGIN

E. H. 139
E. O. 108,147
E. W. 121,123
T. H. 139
REAY
S.. P. 287

REDDING
J. M. 237

REDENSLEN
F. F. 144

REDING
J. M. 200

REED
A. B. 189
John 295
Lenorah M. 123
Newton (colored) 216
Noan R. 2
Nuttey 2
S. R. 256,286
S. W. 256
Sarah 216
Thomas W. 2
Titus (colored) 216
Tom (colored) 216
W. F. M. 238
W. P. 244
W. J. C. 280,286
William 2

Mary A. 177,225,295
N. M. 295

REELLY
Father 48

REESE
J. M. 200
John R. 76
Lucy 60
W. J. O. 280

REEVE
A. W. 216,286,307
A. J. C. 286
Amanda (colored) 216
Asberry W. 298
Ezekiel 36
George W. 2
J. A. 206
J. C. 265
J. M. 256,390,300
James M. 265,290
James A. 310
James W. 216,286,306,307
John (colored) 216
Joshua S. 2
Mary (colored) 216
N. V. 205
REEVES
A. W. 171,236
Arch (colored) 276
Beckey (colored) 191
Bet (colored) 191
E. 200
Ezekiel 24,178,201,205
F. M. 205
George M. 178,205
H. W. 216
Harriet (colored) 171
I. A. 168
J. A. 173,191,194,198,203,214,219,221226,2:

J. A.
173,191,194,198,203,214,219,221226,230,2
32,235,236
J. R. 226
J. M. 200
J. W. 242
J. C. 200
Jacob (colored) 171
James A. 8,163,205
James W.
14,171,180,191,195,200,216,226,256,257
James 274
James W. R. 236
James M. 253
James Y. 292
Joseph A. 165,178,169,211,214,231,233
Joseph A., Col. 211
Jude (colored) 191
Katharine 144
Letty (colored) 171
Lucinda (colored) 171
Mahala J. 14
Milley (colored) 171
Mitty L. 205
N. 205
R. C. N. 205
Rose (colored) 191
Ruth 205
S. 200
S. W. 205
S. R, 236
Sally 14
Sarah 14,171
Sealam (colored) 276
Tom (colored) 171
W. J. T. 256
W. D. 200
W. G. 205
W. J. C. 200
W. I. C. 218
William 220

REFORCEY

John 13

REID
Bella 136
C. S. 138
Emily 138
Ethel 138
Florence 138
Grave 138
Ira 136
J. M. 305
John M. 253
John 10,272
Katherine 138
Laura 138
N. M. 34,66
Nettie Handley 138
Newton M. 37,83
William J. 272

REMEAN
R. 231

RENNEAN
Russel 207,274
S. L. 197

REYNOLDS
E. B. 238,259,269
J. F. 238,259
John 200
Permelus 236
Peter 244
T. C. 283
T. 226
Thomas 226,244,283,286
Thomas C. 244

RHODES
A. S. 199
Elizabeth 111
James 217
T. V. M. 187,245

RIALS
W. H. 251,261,278

RICE
Charley P. 57
G. A. 57
G. C. 241
George D. 9
J. J. 310
Mary Jane 57
Minnie Lee 57
Sarah Elizabeth 57
William H. 145
Z. A. 257

RICHARDS
Alain T. 115
J. J. 284

RICHARDSON
Alan 144
Alexander 169
Elton 89
Gertrude Ely 144
Grace 144 (colored)
Isaac 169
John 169
John W. 169
Joseph Lane 144
Louise Bradsley 144
Mary 144
Moses 25
Thomas J. 40
John M. 5,171,236,252,271,277,301,305
John U. 72
Omie 72

RIDLING
Sarah 72

RIGHT
B. 244
S. B. 198

Thomas 169
W. R. 169

RICHERSON
Elizabeth 209
Esther 235
James 296
John W. 209
Moses 306
W. 209

RICHEY
James A. 294
Oliver 262,294
Robert 262
W. A. 294

RICHIE
Mary 26

RICKEL
Eliza Jane 42

RIDING
J. M. 200

RIDLEY
Cobbie Hoad 125
R. B., Jr. 125

RIDLIN
Adaline 72
J. M. 256,275,300

RIGNEY
James A. 48
Thomas 48
Washington 48

RIPHERN
Charles M. 111

RIPLEY

F. R. 310
Sarah Amanda 111
T. R. 224,233,268,310

ROACH
W. H. 139

ROARK
W. W. 171,199,238

ROBBINS
William J. 70

ROBERSON
Lee 121
M. J., Mrs. 97
W. G. 306

ROBERTS
G. C. 143
J. H. 41,214
James A. 296
John 4,41,217
Joseph 161,220
N. D. 252
Nancy 41
Rev. 196
S. G. 263
Stewart R. 155
T. H. 230
Ursula 56
W. F. 268
W. S. 230
W. H. 15
William 188
Elizabeth 4
R. 244
Robert 4
William 221
Willis 4

RODGERS
A. 306

ROBERTSON
A. P. 49
Bennett 49
Harriett 32
James A. 32,49
James B. 20,32,49,247
James D. 49
Thomas L. 49

ROBERSON
Martha G. 35

ROBINSON
C. H. 81
J. J. 301
J. M. 225,278
James 26,185
Jane E. L. 26
Jesse I. 69
L. 196
L. J. 160,204
L. P. 160
S. J. 160
S. A. 204
Sarina 211
Thomas L. 296
W. D. 49

ROBSON
Henry 135
Kate 135
Paul 135

ROBUCK
Andrew 31
G. C. 198
G. C. 304
J. W. 101
W. M., Mrs. 121,123
W. A. 301,305

ROE

J. C. 170,226

ROGERS
C. C. 256
Charles 101
Edna 101
Edward 101
G. C. 233,283
H. S. 120
Jennie N. 101,103
M. T. 47
Rollin 101
W. A. 301

ROMAN
P. 88

ROPER
David 2

ROSE
Mary 97
Pauline 132
R. C. 144
S. 284

ROSS
Bessie A. 131
F. G. 159
Robert 161

ROSSER
E. 159,186,222,224,226,230,232,233,238,251, 261,262,267276,,285,290,295,297,298,302, 306,307,311
W. B. 166,167,169,199,201,215,230,237,238,245, 246,257,266,288

RUNS
Joseph A. 211

E. B. 85
Elijah 193

ROWDEN
Martha A. 116
W. M. 116

ROWDUP
W. M. 58

ROWELL
William 301
W. R. 300

ROWLAND
Alice Cleborne 117
Johnanna E. 74
William H. 74

ROWLIN
Edward R. 134

ROYAL
Marcellus 109
William A. 109

RUCKER
J. W. 198

RUDICILE
A. J. 72

RUDISAIL
Mary 153

RUGGLES
RUSE
James 198

RUSH
George B. 104

RUSH
George B. 104

RUSK
Thomas 168

RUSSEAN
W. C. 199,205,235,263

RUSSELL
A. B. 81
Ann (colored) 224
Annie Kent 134
George (colored) 224
Green (colored) 224
Harring 119
Henry C. 262
J. R. 62,76
Jacob (colored) 224
James T. 262
James 17,188,189,217,250,281,294
Jane 233,262
Jane (colored) 188
Jane C. 224
Jefferson (colored) 224
Jesse (colored) 224
John 224,262
King (colored) 224
Lewis (colored) 224
Louis (colored) 224
Mariah (colored) 224
Mary A. 224
Mary (colored) 188
Melvira 262
Nibey (colored) 188
Prince (colored) 224
Susanah 250,281
Susannah 17
W. J. 230
William (colored) 188

SARGENT
J. B. 146

William 262

RUSSIAN
W. C. 199

RUTHER
Andrew 22

RUTLEDGE
Amanda Clementine 50
Joseph 50

RYALS
Dr. 226
W. H. 226

RYLES
W. H. 287

SAFFOLD
A. C. 285
Adam G. 258

SALINES
P. B. 184

SALMOND
Ephraim 194,240,241

SALTSMAN
T. F. 285

SAMS
Eliza Katherine 111

SANSSUE
John M. D. 147

SAPPINGTON
M. E. 151

SAUNDERS
Hazel 136

SCAFE
Mary C. 240
William 240

SCARBORO
John 306

SCARFE
Elizabeth 1
Jemerson 1
Jesse 1
Joel F. 1
Martha V. 222
Mary C. 222
W. 1
William Jr. 1
William 1,222

SCHOENBERGER
G. 199
George 213

SCHUMLER
S. 118

SCOTT
A. L. 217
A. 217
Alfred W. 95
Allen G. 95
Caroline R. 170
Carrie Irvin 95
Daniel 289
G. B. 153
George B. 96,102
George W. 95
George C. 82
J. W. 140
Joseph M. 15
Julius Augustus 70
M. P. 140
Nancy Ellen 95
M. 203

S. 244
W. W. 233

SCREVELL
John E. 6

SCROGGINS
Henry 153

SCRUGGS
Davis O. 257
J. W. 208,229,287
John W. 26,27,215,286
Martha Jackson 141

SCUDDER
Scudder, S. E.
207,211,214,222,231,251,260,261,284

SCULLY
Thomas F. 57

SEAGO
W. 190

SEAVY
James H. 117,118
N. R., Mrs. 117

SEAY
Mahala 70

SEE
S. A. 197

SEEVY
J. F. 263

SEGAR
Daisy Wesst 113

SELF
William 207

SELKIRK
James Melrose 139

SELTON
P. M. 230

SENTELL
 Almeda 181,205,240,273,299,308
 B. 205,206
 Caroline 181,205,240.273
 E. 205,206
 Elizabeth 205
 Louisa 181,206,239,273
 Martha 181,206,240,273,299
 W. W. 161

SENTILL
 W. W. 200

SEWELL
 T. R. 284
 Terrell 261,304
 W. B. 245

SEXTON
 W. 270

SHACKEL
 Eliza Ann 190
 Francis M. 190
 J. H. 190
 Richard 190
 S. J. 231,303,305
 William 190

SHAPARD
 R. P. 132

SHARP
 John 306
 W. B. 107

SHAW
 Mary Ann 17

SHED
 R. C. 51

SHEEBLEY
 P. M. 173

SHEEHAN
 C. J. 78,115,118

SHELTON
 Charles B. 155

SHELVERTON
 Addie 104
 C. J. 104
 George Barron 104
 Minnie May 104
 W. E. 104
 William 104

SHEPHERD
 E. W. 217

SHEPPARD
 A. J. 149
 Andrew J. 43
 David C. 42,43
 David M. 42
 David U. 25
 George W. 43
 Henry J. 43
 Huldah F. 42
 J. A. 57
 James A. 42,43
 John 66
 Manning 270
 Nattie 136
 Sam S. 136
 Samuel 136
 Sarah A. 68

SHEVE
T. C. 156

SHIR
John 13

SHOTWELL
Mrs. 22

SHUMAN
H. 247

SHUMATE
B. D. 165,209
B. F. 165
Benjamin Franklin 8
Charles F. 102
D. F. 102
E. G., Mrs. 102
Etta C. 59
Francis F. 38
Franklin 209
Henry C. 125
J. D. 165
Joseph D. 8
Mason 8,209
R. C. 125,126

SHUTER
Ladonia Texas 119

SILVEY
J. B. 197

SIMKINS
Joseph 217

SIMMEY
Charles L. 65

SIMMONS
C. J. 71
J. P. 236

Mrs. 125

SIMMS
Harriett 93

SIMONTON
Theophilus 278

SIMPKIN
James 217

SIMPKINS
Benjamin J. 111,118
James 217
Jesse 244
W. 269

SIMPSON
A. N. 210
Amanda M. 54
I. M. 99
James A. 157
Joe P. 157
John 179,283
L. C. 237,239,288
Larkin 310
Levi 42
Lizzie E. 131
Louise E. 157
Thomas L. 157
William R. 54

SIMS
Alice 31
Bennett 291
John Lawrence 31
Joseph 31
Julius Fayette 31
L. 247
Leonard 31,247
Marietta 31

Mary 291
Orpha Jane 31
Sallie 31
SINGLETON
Frank P. 70

SISSON
Caroline 147
Charles Amows 147
Gustave Beauregard 147
Ida Ruth 143
Leila L. 75,109
Louise 147
Lula Larendon 147
V. P. 109
Vardy Pritchard 147

SISSONS
Charles A. 137
Leila L. 137

SITTERN
P. M. 286

SLATERN
Elizabeth 205

SLATER
M. F., Mrs. 77

SLAY
W. 256

SMITH
A. S. 217
A. R. 167
Amandy 135,136
Andrew J. 53
B. M. 208,215,236
Beulah Josephine 118
Beulah Richardson 118
C. E. 95,211
Charles W. 89,121,147

Thomas L. 84
Trull Marth 31
Wiley 291
Charles Whitefoord 111
Cicily 152
D. T. 40
Donald F. 152
E. Dan 148
E. M. 116
Edward P. 152
Elizabeth 44
F. M. 211
Fannie W. 111
G. K. 161,177,215,197,199,215,299
George K. 254
George W. 148
George F. 24
Gladys 118
Harvey J. 46
I. B. 189
I. M. 53
J. Henley 73
J. M. 6,12,16,43,197,198,201,205,206,245,307
J. T. 157
J. S. 299
J. R. 207
J. H. 276
J. D. 118
James R. 134,152,208
James M. 31,50,54
Jane 24
John 13
John A. 136
John T. 17
John Meredith 15
John M. 3,204,214
Mary 41
Mattie Lumpkin 147
Mr. 173
N. N. 257
Rebecca 118
Robert H. 9,44,45,186

Rebecca 118
Robert H. 9,44,45,186
Rosalie 118
S. H. 309
Sarah H. 24
Sarah V. L. E. 46
Uriah 170
W. B. 214
W. R. 241
W. H. 157
Walter W. 237
William 135

SNEAD
Syrena E. 128

SNIDER
John 13

SNOW
Nelson 141
Zelma 148

SONTE
J. D. 257

SOUTH
Francis C. 46

SPAIN
Sarah Elizabeth 30

SPAN
D. C. 214

SPARKS
Drury 169

SPAULDING
D. B. 261

SPEER
W. W. 104

Seaford 41
Simeon 239,255
Stephen S. 24
Susan A. 180
T. M. 265
Thomas F. 108

SPINKS
John 33
Loula 72
Susan 33

SPIVEY
B. S. 46
SPORKS
John 278

SPRUILL
C. A. 100

SPRAYBERRY
Adella 120
Amy 7
B. M. 84,107,120,306
Benjamin 7
Brice M. 45
Harvey J. 45
J. E. 120
J. G. 120
John G. 46
Lula V. 157
Permelia Elizabeth 45
Sarah V. L. E. 46
W. W. 46
W. H. 84
W. H. E. 101,120
William H. 45

SPREWELL
James 201,235
W. E. 162,202,222,277,278,310
William E. 7

SPRINKS
J. W. 72

SPRUELL
James 41
Jane 162
Stephen, Jr. 171
STAF
S.S. 215

STALLINGS
Anna Lou Ella 131
Luther Kennedy 131

STANLEY
E. T. 120
Frank M. 78
Jesse W. 77

STAPLE
W. G. 225
William G. 47

STARLING
Harris 9

STARR
F. M. 151

STEAVINS
William H. 16

STEEL
J. 275
J. C. 234,275
J. 235
M. 235
M. A. 275
Michael A. 45

STEELS
L. J. 93,141
M. A. 38

SPRUILL
S. H. 100

STADEL
Louis O. 112

T. J. 154
W. O. 98

STELL
B. 271,296
Bartholomew 204,248
C. W. 296
Charles W. 204,248,271
Elizabeth 204
Henry N. 204
John D. 18
Martha P. 204
Richard B. 238
S. E. 248
W. W. 248
William W. 204

STELLE
L. J. 106

STEPHENS
W. H. 187
W. 168

STEPHENSON
A. F. 10
Alice Eugenia 80
C. 139
James A. 233
John 5,10
Mary 129
Moses R. 129
R. S. 80
William 233

STEVENS

H. D. 119
Lucy 85
Mary Ann 85
William 85

STEWARD
E. 270
Elijah 161,174,245,270
John B. 62,57,76
James W. 2
John 262
John B. 62
Joseph 49,235,300
Mary 18
Prichet 248
W. 200
W. T. 128

STILL
Bartholomew 13

STODDARD
A. 199
Absalom 161

STOKER
Missouri N. 119

STOKES
C. A. 147
Eliza 23,311

STONE
A. W. 306
Amherst W. 22
Cynthia 8,165
D. 287
Daniel 211,230
Emma G. 87
Flora 6
Joseph 6
M. 235
Micajah 201,259

Joseph 14,305

STEWART
A. P. 110
Arthur H. 153
E. 199,215,243
Elizabeth 49
Ella C. 61
Georgia V. 74

STOWERS
Catherine (colored) 282
E. L. 125
Elizabeth Frances 93,94
Jasper (colored) 283
John 46
Lewis R. 221,226
Mary Ann 221,226
Orphelia 282
Orphia 243,292
T. J. 93

STRANGE
James 30
Lettice Caroline 30

STRAWBERRY

Ausbery W. 14
James M. 14
William J. C. 14

STRAYER
Charles 149
Evy 149

STRICKLAND
G. L. 253
Riff 122
S. C., Mrs. 99

STRONG
C. H. 232,304,306

STROZIN
E. 233

STUBBS
J. F. 268
James F. 202

STURGIS
L. 306
Leborn 246
T. N. 96

SUMMERS
D. King 132
G. W. 274

SUMMEY
Charles L. 103,104
Harry H. 103
Hattie E. 104
Lula G. 104

SURTELL
W. W. 237

SUTTLES
Alfred G. 12
Wiley 6

SVELETON
J. T. 213

SWAN
Anna K. 10
John 10,166
Sarah E. 10
Susan A. 10

SWANSON
Samuel A. 143

SWANTON
Laborn 202

SUBER
H. H. 120

SUDDER
Samuel E. 211

SULLIVAN
D. B. 71
John B. 304
B. F. 61
Eleanor Miles 82
Joe Wallace 82
John B. 82
Josephine F. 82
Mrs. 306
Sarah 211
Scott K. 82

SWEAT
Nathaniel 3
S. 262

SWEN
A. 278

SWIFT
Annie Ray 60
Dean T. 60
E. S. 304
J. R. 205,206
John N. 27,32,35,60,159,213,262,268
John N., Jr. 60
M. A., Mrs. 304
N. 161
Thomas Latimer 60
Thomas F. 60
Thomas L. 32,78

TAEGE
Mari 133
Marie 133

TALIAFERRO
Edward M. 184
Hulda 251
Letta 251
Richard 251
Willis 251

TALLEY
C. H. 86
J. W. 120

TALLY
J. W. F. 59

TALTON
H. F. 76
L. W. 64

TANNER
E. W. 83
P. B. 219

TAPP
N. Dora 131
William 17
W. P. T. 96

TATE
Ann 91
Frances 91,107
Jeff 91
John N. 26

TAYLOR
Florence Williamson 44
Florinda 44
Georgia W. 44
Grant 23
J. 259,304
John Ross 137
Katie G. 44
L. J. V. 238
M. 85

R. G. 44
Richard Gregory 44
Toulinin 44

TEARING
Edgar D. 112
Nura M. 112

TEAT
Irwin L. 106

TEDDER
William 17

TEETWILER
James 106

TERRELL
William 193
Thomas 128
William 12,17
William 176

TERRY
J. L. 257
John T. 283
John G. 212,231,260
Stephen 158,159,177,212,306
Thomas 219,313
William 246

THEALS
William 224

THIMONY
Mason 269

THOMAS
G. 244
George A. 69
H. M. 89
James M. 65

John 249,292
L. 21,256
Lewis 200,256
M. A. 263
R. N. 249
S. M., Mrs. 89
T. A. 175
T. L. 186,239
William 2

THOMPSON
Allen 300
D. C. 65,112,137
H. T. 140
Ida 56
Young 244

THOMS
J. T. 207

THOMSON
William S. 46,93

THORNTON
Lewis 302,303
L. A. 226
E. H. 103
Austell 145

THRASHER
J. J. 262
T. J. 262
W. J. 226,230,267,287

THROWER
James G. 88
Annie 88,89

THURMAN
J. C. 179
J. E. 228
James 271
John 249

J. 198,244,257,283,302
J. N. T. 99
James C. 22
James H. 23
Jane 56
Joann F. 56
Joseph 256,257,302,303
R. M. 44
T. 230,247
Thomas 160,175,198,199,201,227,228,233,235,256,399
W. E. 97
William S. 100
William S. 61
W. 228
William 269

THWEATT
Abby (colored) 184,193,195
Catharine A. 15
Clara (colored) 185,193,195
Ephraim (colored) 184,195
FC. S. 190
Hagor (colored) 185,193,195
John T. 15,193
Joshua (colored) 185,193
Ramon (colored) 195
Raymond (colored) 193
S. C. 190
Thomas 15,184,190,193,195
U. J. 196
Uriah 193
Uriah J. 190,195
Vilot (colored) 193
Violet (colored) 185

TICHENOR
Isaac T. 92
W. R. 92

TIDWELL
M. M. 175,190,198

TILLEY
F. 298
J. W. F. 298
J. W. 45
John W. F. 309
Stephen 171
W. F. 299

TILLY
J. W. L. 235
H. P. 115
E. 33
H. N. 142

TILSON
V. V. 117
Martha 13,168,243,253,280
R. C. 168
Richard F. 13
Richard C. 13,253
Richard 243

TOLLISON
B. 230

TOMLIN
T. M. 269

TOMLINSON
A. H. 183,184,188
George 174,198
I. 179
J. F. 188
John F. 183
John 261,282
John W. 292
L. H. 188
William F. 183

TOMMEY
Carrie 54
Elizabeth 54

W. J. 117,154

TIMLEY
L. C. 59

TINSLEY
A. J. 211,232

TIPTON
Mrs. 224

TITTON
A. E. 215

TODD
James 13
John C. 13
Lizzie 54
Sarah Mary 54
V. R. 54
Vincent R. 54

TOON
S. J., Mrs. 118

TORBEY
Ethel 130

TORREY
Torrey, Annie R. 90

TOWERS
Elizabeth 11
F. M. 264
Frances N. 11
Isaac 207
Isaac 11,165
L. 215
Lewis 215

TOWNSEND
Mance 217

TRAMMELL
J. G. 261

TRAVIS
Fleta 146
Harry S. 149

TREADWELL
Lottie 93

TREVOR
Edith Pearl 105

TRIMBLE
J. F.
171,172,200,218,236,256,265,280,293,301
James F. 256,277,280,286
John 171
M. J. 33
Joseph F. S. 49
Joseph F. A. 49
Lou 49
Mary P. 49
Orry 49

TUGGLE
A. C. 198,287
Alexander C. 63
H. C. 106
John L. 47
John P. 106
L. 165,198,208,267
Lodawick 7
Mamie 150
Mary E. 106
W. E. 106

TUMBLE
J. T. 200
J. F. 200

TUMLIN
John 243

Moses W. 283

TROTTER
R. W. 114

TROUP
Hugh Brown 3

TUCHSTONE
B. B. 245

TUCKER
A. H. 47
W. D. 232

TUFFLE
L. 166

TUFTS

TURK
Milton 165

TURLEY
N. L. 91

TURNER
Areminda 28
E. A. 59,217
Elijah 219,244,305
Elisabeth Ann 2
G. T. 247
John W. 238
Mary Ann 30
Nathan 28,35,38,246,264,265,288,304
Thomas 2,269
Thomas E. 269
W. J. 37
W. 270
Edward 47
TURPIN
J. J. 116
O. B. 116

Ruth E. 116
William H. 116

TWILLEY
Cyrus 55

TYLER
H. 125

UNDERWOOD
J. C. 103
M. L. 71
M. E. 103

UPSHAW
Iida P. 123
L. 305
Mary C. 123

VAN VALKENBERG
J. E. 124
James 309
W. P. 154

VAWTERS
Annie 70

VEAL
A. B. F. 81,136
Allen B. F. 81
Allen J. 48,81
Asa 31
B. F. 90,161,198,205,214,271
B. L. 264
Benjamin H. 90
Benjamin F. 23
Cynthia 81
Elizabeth J. 90
Francis 31
H. H. 34
James 23,160,161,205,215
John L. 199
John 5

VAN VORST
Christian E. 119
Garnett Henry 119
Julian P. 119
Sarah H. 119
William O. 119

VARNER
W. A. 71
W. D. 64

VAUGHAN
Ira 23
James C. 64
Kate E. 130
Rebecca T. 130,131

VAUGHN
Alex 217, 226,295
Henry A. 213
John W. 81
Larrice Ann 31
M. A. 264
Mary 110
Millard 31
Minnie 81,136
P. 110
Sarah O. 31
W. W. 23
William W. 110
William J. 31,81,134

VENABLE
D. C. 299
R. C. 196
Roan 81
Sarah C. 145
W. R. 288

VENABLES
W. R. 33

VIRGIN
Frederick B. 91
Jonathan A. 91
Judiah S. 91
Mary Green 91
William H. 91

VISBY
Betty Marie 126
Emma Eliza 126

WADE
David 200,293
David D. 259
Davis 256,307
Flora L. 91
J. D. 120
John 13
S. H. 84
Stephen H. 91
W. 264
William 268

WALES
C. H. 110

WALKER
Beulah Parlee 125
E. S. 41
Elizabeth L. 61
G. B. 132
Henry H. 43,50
J. 165
Jabez B. 60
James W. 60
John M. 170
Joseph 13,38,41,60,162,165,166,168,
195,198,218,274
Joseph H. 60
Julia Howard 154,155
Juliann 60
Lillie 125
Lizzie 136

WADSWORTH
W. 200,267
Walter 226,234

WAID
D. 201

WAITS
A. B. 217
Absalom 162
Charles E. 153
Madison 162
Sarah 7,222,277
William 217

WALDROP
O. C. 157

WALDRUP
David 246
D. G. 215,264
D. W. 220
Gracy 169
Loudon 125
Nancy 30
Rachel (colored) 162
Samuel 4,9,248,257
T. A. 308
Thomas I. London 125
Thomas Edward 155
Thomas 163

WALL
Ora 122

WALLACE
C. H. 296,310
Clifford 152
J. R. 239,259,296
J. C. 145
Minnie 152
W. D. 128

WALLAS
Augustus H. 278

WALLCOTT
William W. 46
WALLIS
C. W. 28
James W. 17
Thomas S. 17

WALON
H. B. 285

WALRAVEN
A. J. 177,179,202,246

WALTHOUR
Mary Irene 109

WANNAMAKER
Mary Stewart 146

WARBINGTON
E. 127,256,262,266,296
Elemander 197,249
E. A. 185

WARNOCK
Martha Arminda 112
W. R. 84,92,112

WARREN
Ann Hollingsworth 140
George W. 140
M. L. 217
Turner H. 294

WARWICK
A. A. 104,130
C. A. 104
E. A. 130,150
E. A., Jr. 104
Lou M. 104

J. 270

WARD
Anderson 133
H. W. 148
Ivy 203
J. H. 204
Margaret E. 133
W. J. 154

WARDS
Ivy 207

WARDSWORTH
W. 200
Walter 233

WARE
D. E. 262

WARICK
Elizabeth 31
Patrick 31,32

WARNER
T. A. 197,199,229

WASHINGTON
E. 172, 200,201,206,236,241
Elamander 179,186

WATERS
Franklin 162
S. C. 224

WATES
F. A. 310
S. J. 269
Sarah 202

WATSON
John 278
J. W. 73

John 278
J. W. 73

WATTES
F. A. 310

WATTS
A. M. 228,256
Amey W. 29
E. E. 83
Edward 30,224
H. M. 256

WAYNE
C. D. 144

WEAN
G. 211

WEAR
James W. 204

WEAVE
Dr. 196

WEAVER
Edward T. 89
H. 264
J. W. 244,267
L. A. 156
W. B. 99
William 232

WEBB
E. 63
Elijah 220,311
Elisha 198
George W. 93,140
Guy 140
M. A., Mrs. 87
Mary 140,141
Robert 244,287
William H. 37

Mary A. 36
W. N. 36

WEBSTER
G. W. 215

WEED
James H. 34

WEEKES
John W. 40
P. L. 74

WEEKS
C. L. 74
John W. 44
Mary Leona 74

WEEMS
George W. 60

WEINER
E. A. 242

WEIR
A. M. 101

WEITNAUER
Annie 154

WELCH
M. M. 92

WELD
Charles H. 124

WELDON
Jennie 146

WELL
F. M. 53
M. A. 83

WELLS
Abner 161
Andrew 241
Bonnie Jackson 120
Carl T. 105,120
E. W. 255
Eliza W. 282
Elizabeth W. 219
Emily Winfred 120
G. R. 105
George R. 90
H. W. 235
J. D. 15,219, 282
J. E. 282
J. 306
James E. 255,282
James R. 136
James F. 219
Jeremiah 284
John D. 219,255
John Dean 120
Lucy G. 90
M. P. H. 167
M. M. M. 166

WEMER
E. A. 208

WESLEY
Thomas J. 68

WESTMORELAND
D. H. 193

WHEAT
J. B. 124

WHEELAN
P. D. 306

WHELLON
M. W. 195

Maggie E. 105
Margaret M. E. 166
Mary Elizabeth 120
Mary 197
Myrtie Ida Lou 120
Robert Fletcher 120
Samuel P. 219,255,282
Stephen (colored) 255
Steve Acres 120
Talmon 105
Thomas 166,167,254
Thomas B. 105
Thomas P. 48
W. L. 166,190,207,220,266
W. W. 235,264
William W. 25
William H. 255
Williams A. 219
Willie 105

WHATLEY
James B. 79
Thomas 80,204

WHITAKER
J. J. 189,228,233,302
J. T. 214
J. W. 215
J. B. 124
W. R. 157

WHITE
A. J. 278
A. K. 302
A. R. 228,233,256
Byron 139
Charles (colored) 282
Charles 13,168
Clara G. 122
D. T. 32
Daisy 122
E. P. 154
J. F. P. 269

E. P. 154
J. F. P. 269
J. J. P. 22,269,296
J. W. 38,53,120,157,296,306
J. M. 157
James J. P. 298,306
James L. B. 297
James P. 269
John J. 28
John, Sr. 296
John I. 68
John W. 306
John 21,38,296
Joseph B. 195
L. E. 165
Laura E. 165
M. W. 195
Margaret K. 282
Nancy M. 38
Needham 278
Nicy (colored) 282
Ruth W. 110
S. C. 296
Sam (colored) 298
Sarah 21,42
Stephen (colored) 282
T. A. 90,103,130,140
T. W. 306
Thomas 42
W. C. 44,296
Wesley C. 44
Ada 127

WILEY
John J. 286
John 220,226,244
W. 268
William B. 242

WILKERSON
C. 244
Mr. 207
Sarah 211,285

WHITLOW
William Howard 133
William C. 42
William C. 22
William 298

WHITNER
Emma Lou 92

WICKHAM
Susan 98

WICKS
Susie R. 127

WIGGINS
Albert 305
J. H. 29
John 264
Joseph E. 69
L. 166,264
Lewis 161,208,215,220,263,264.271
M. W. 69
M. D. 72
M. O. 78,83

WIGHT
Martha 46

WILCOX
Sarah E. 267

WILKES
C. J. 99
Clara 99
John W. 99
L. Potter 99
P. L. 99
W. H. 99,112

WILKIE
F. C. 74

WILKINS
Jane 22
Mary E. 127
T. M. 312
Thomas 22

WILKINSON
John R. 90
Sarah E. 214

WILLAFORD
B. 198

WILLAN
L. 279

WILLARD
L. 198,200,206,211,214,261,309
Levi
17,194,200,203,211,213,214,222,224,238,2
42,251,252,261,276,282,287,298,305,307

WILLIAMS
A. J. 198,199
A. T. 230
Alfred 215
Annie Rhea 157
C. C. 134
Caroline (colored) 220
Copeland R. 157
E. 171
Franklin 277

WILLIAMSON
F. A. 301
J. S. 301
John 176,198
John 3
Parthenia A. 11
Sally 4

WILLINGHAM
Ansel 27

H. H. 304
H. D. 165,207
Hiram J. 44,54,153
Hiram M. J. 96
Hiram D. 11
Hiram 277
Ichabod 201,235,278
J. L. 166,220,230,244,261,267,277,287,2
J. A. 244
J. E. 205,232,259
Jesse L. 283
Jesse 186
Joseph F. 277
L. 166
O. O. 124
Penelope K. 251
R. S., Mrs. 277
R. M. 288
R. F. 171
Rebecca 220,230
S. B. 297
Samuel 253,297
Samuel B. 242
Sarah 277
Susan A. 89
Thomas Humes 157
Thomas 268
W. L. 18,25,35,45,
188,237,241,242,266,285,289,
W. M. 241
William C. 2
William L. 251

WILLIS
H. G. 180
J. M. 223
James M. 180,223
Joseph 172,180,196
Julian 180
M. M. 215
William 180,196

WILLS
A. J. 306
Anderson 267
Andrew 183,198,208
Harriett G. 223
John D. 37

WILSON
A. H. 274
Augustus 219
Dr. 232
G. E. 24
Gilbert 180
H. 145
I. N. 40,67,108
Isaac N. 61
J. B. 198,275,286,287,
J. S. 224,304
J. W. 311
J. H. 99
J. 235
J. F. 221
Jane E. 49
John S. 16,211,274
John W. 39
John S. C. 311
John H. 276
John T. 226, 228,287,307
Jordan 292
Joseph F. 39
L. S. 14
Levi 276
Polly 307
Polly M. 14,298
R. M. 171,276,294
Lachlin J. 26
S. 244
S. G. 286
Samuel 226

WINNINGHAM
Frank R. 136
M. 161,170,208,236,264,270,271

Rebecca M. 42
Richard M. 26
Robert M. 186
Sarah V. 39
W. E. 210,219
W. B. 235
Wharton O. 133
William H. 220
William B. 244
William C. 14
William E. 163

WIMPEY
John A. 75

WIMPY
John A. 79

WINDSHIP
Joseph 199

WINFREY
Birt 103
Isaac Henry 103
John W. 103

WINN
Catharine M. 26
Harriet B. 44
J. J. 268
J. 244
James J. 268
James J. 224
James 224
L. J. 44
Michael 220
Oliver 136,305

WINSHIP
Joseph 215

WINTERS
John 266

L. 206, 249,256
Leonard 179,191,197,237,266,296
Samuel W. 237

WISNER
C. E. 153

WOMACK
John B. 259

WOOD
A. 266
D. 225
J. J. 304
Jesse M. 148
Mary Jane 44
Robert 235
W. 244
W. L. 286
Wilson 198

WOODALL
Allen 166,244,286
Elizabeth 41
James 41

WOODALL
A. 201,267
Allen 219,235,241,259,267,274,287,309
C. N. 165

WOODIN
A. W. 168

WOODRUFF
John 219

J. P. 62
James 233
R. C. 62

WORLEY
J. G. 163

WOODS
W. 233
Wilson 160
W. O. 136

WOODSON
B. 306
Benjamin 25,306
Mary 25
William 25

WOODWARD
E. S. 167

WOOLSEY
W. 174

WOOTEN
Alexander (colored) 247
Avia 20
Avis 290
Daniel B. 3
Joe (colored) 247
Joseph 20,33,100,296
Linsey (colored) 247
M. T. 145
Mack (colored) 247
Sampson (colored) 247
Sarah (colored) 247

WOOTON
Avis 275,296
Joseph 248,272,275

WORD
A. M. 62
Frank H. 62

WORRING
John R. 215

WORSHAM
Silas 244

WORSHAM
Silas 244

WORTHERN
M. 127

WORTHINGTON
E. 14

WORTHORP
Sol 127

WRIGHT
A. S. 244,249
Asa 235
Ava A. 61
Elizabeth 204
Elizabeth L. 28
Francis L. 34
Harriet E. 47
Henry S. 118
J. L. 36
J. A. 68,107
James M. 28
L. 200,286
L. T. 114
Lewis 256,262,307
Logan 204
Lucy 47
M. L. 197,269
Martha V. V. 47
Martha C. 47
Martha Jones 153
Zaceny T. 28

YANCY
George 269
James 12,180,199,208
Robert 12,208

YARBOROUGH
W. L. 205,264
W. 212

Mary J. 28
Mary Jane 47
Nancy 34,204
Octavia M. 59
Richard S. 216,224,268
S. P. 19,163,178,182,191,194,200
207,208,226,230,249,252,253,
256,286,289,290,298,305,306,,309,312
Sarah 204
Spencer C. 306
Spencer P. 1,21,24,28,29,226
Susan 57
T. 14
Thomas T. 48
W. 199,228,259
W. D. 225
W. L. 210,302
W. E. 263
William D. 220
William 47,204,228,269,296

WYATT
J. T., Sr. 103

WYLEY
J. J. 286
John 309

WYNN
Robert S. Jr. 135

WYNNS
A. J. 198
William 173

YATES
C. M. 156
Charles Richardson 144
John 214
Julia Richardson 144
Presley D. 144

W. D. 225
W. L. 210,302
W. E. 263
William D. 220
William 47,204,228,269,296

WYATT
J. T., Sr. 103

Zaceny T. 28

YANCY
George 269
James 12,180,199,208
Robert 12,208

YARBOROUGH
W. L. 205,264
W. 212
William 173

YATES
C. M. 156
George 269,288
Ida A. 108
James H. 29,282
L. Q., Mrs. 148
Leonidas Theodore 110
Margaret S. 29
Mary 56
N. 306
W. P. 241

ZACHNER
Robert 93,100

ZETTLER
B. M. 104

ZIMMERMAN
Thomas 204

WYLEY
J. J. 286
John 309

WYNN
Robert S. Jr. 135

WYNNS
A. J. 198
Charles Richardson 144
John 214
Julia Richardson 144
Presley D. 144

YOUNG
D. M. 210,241
D. 210
Dillard 257

www.ingramcontent.com/pod-product-compliance
Lightning Source LLC
Chambersburg PA
CBHW050426240426
43661CB00055B/2284